Premodern ruling sexualities

Manchester University Press

Premodern ruling sexualities

Representation, identity, and power

Edited by

Gabrielle Storey and Zita Eva Rohr

MANCHESTER UNIVERSITY PRESS

Copyright © Manchester University Press 2024

While copyright in the volume as a whole is vested in Manchester University Press, copyright in individual chapters belongs to their respective authors, and no chapter may be reproduced wholly or in part without the express permission in writing of both author and publisher.

Published by Manchester University Press
Oxford Road, Manchester M13 9PL

www.manchesteruniversitypress.co.uk

British Library Cataloguing-in-Publication Data
A catalogue record for this book is available from the British Library

ISBN   978 1 5261 7584 7   hardback
ISBN   978 1 5261 9580 7   paperback

First published 2024
Paperback published 2026

The publisher has no responsibility for the persistence or accuracy of URLs for any external or third-party internet websites referred to in this book, and does not guarantee that any content on such websites is, or will remain, accurate or appropriate.

EU authorised representative for GPSR:
Easy Access System Europe – Mustamäe tee 50,
10621 Tallinn, Estonia
gpsr.requests@easproject.com

Typeset
by New Best-set Typesetters Ltd

For those who have been lost, forgotten, or erased from our collective memory. Your histories and stories are being reclaimed and told.

Contents

List of figures	ix
Note on the cover image	xi
Notes on contributors	xii
Acknowledgements	xv

Introduction: Premodern ruling sexualities: representation, identity, and power – Gabrielle Storey and Zita Eva Rohr — 1

Part I: Scandal, perception, and representation

1 'And though she made use of three openings ...': how and why to sexualise a Late-Antique empress – Alexander Thies — 29
2 Eadwig's coronation scandal: sexuality, rhetoric and the vulnerability of reputation – Matthew Firth — 49
3 Scandal, romance, political affairs: Walter Map's 'Portuguese king' and Anglo-Flemish relations in the twelfth century – Fabrizio De Falco — 71
4 Isabella of France and Roger Mortimer: lovers or allies? – Michael Evans — 89
5 Isabel of Castile and her images: viewing sex, scandal, and sanctity in fifteenth-century Spain – Jessica Weiss — 105

Part II Gender, morality, and desire

6 Gender, moral, and sexual warfare in the *Roman de Silence* – Kathleen M. Blumreich — 153
7 Muslim caliphs and homosexuality: al-Amin (787–813) and al-Hakam II (915–976). Two men in pursuit of *hubb al-walad* – Fatima Rhorchi — 173

8 The Tour de Nesle Affair: succession and sexuality in fourteenth-century France – Emily Lalande   194
 9 Chaste kings and unsuitable women: sex, interfaith relations, and sovereignty in the *Castigos* of Sancho IV of Castile – David Cantor-Echols   214
10 *Sine communi favore*: the intersection of power, perception, and sexual morality in the careers of Piers Gaveston and the 'royal favourites' of fourteenth-century England – Audrey Covert   232

Index   252

List of figures

5.1	Armorial, Hours of Queen Isabel, Cleveland Museum of Art 1963.256., fol. 1v (Image in the public domain, CC0)	108
5.2	Armorial, Breviary of Queen Isabel, British Library Additional MS 18851, fol. 436v (© Alamy Stock Photo)	109
5.3	St Elizabeth of Hungary, Breviary of Queen Isabel, British Library Additional MS 18851, fol. 488v (© Alamy Stock Photo)	111
5.4	St Elizabeth of Hungary, Hours of Queen Isabel, Cleveland Museum of Art 1963.256, fol. 197v (Image in the public domain, CC0).	112
5.5	St Catharine of Alexandria, Hours of Queen Isabel, Cleveland Museum of Art, 1963.256, fol. 189v (Image in the public domain, CC0).	113
5.6	St Catharine of Alexandria, Breviary of Queen Isabel, British Library Additional MS 18851, fol. 495v (©Alamy Stock Photo)	114
5.7	The Coronation of the Virgin, Breviary of Queen Isabel, British Library Additional MS 18851, fol. 437r (©Alamy Stock Photo)	117
5.8	The Coronation of the Virgin, Hours of Queen Isabel, Cleveland Museum of Art 1963.256, fol. 159v (Image in the public domain, CC0)	119
5.9	The Feast of All Saints, Breviary of Queen Isabel, British Library Additional MS 18851, fol. 477v (©Alamy Stock Photo)	121
5.10	O Intemerata prayer, Hours of Queen Isabel, Cleveland Museum of Art 1963.256, fol. 262r (Image in the public domain, CC0)	122

5.11 The Mirror of Conscience, Hours of Joanna of Castile, British Library Additional MS 18852, fol. 14v–15r (© Alamy Stock Photo)   123

5.12 Expulsion from Paradise and Pentecost, Breviary of Queen Isabel, British Library Additional MS 18851, fol. 177v (© British Library Board)   124

5.13 Lamentation, Hours of Queen Isabel, Cleveland Museum of Art 1963.256, fol. 261v (Image in the public domain, CC0)   126

5.14 Title woodcut with Melusine and her descendants, Thüring von Ringoltingen, *Melusine* (Augsburg: Bämler, 1480, fol. A1v (© Alamy Stock Photo)   127

5.15 Raymond spies on Melusine in the bath, Thüring von Ringoltingen, *Melusine* (Augsburg: Bämer, 1480), fol. 51r reused in *La historia de la Linda Melosina* (Toulouse: Juan Parix and Estevan Cleblat, 1489), fol. 119v (©Alamy Stock Photo)   129

5.16 Prayer to St James the Greater, Spinola Hours, Getty Museum MS Ludwig IX 18 (83.ML.114), fol. 253r (Image courtesy of the Getty's Open Content Program)   131

Note on the cover image

Unknown (École de Fontainebleau), *Portrait présumé de Gabrielle d'Estrées et de sa sœur la duchesse de Villars* (Presumed portrait of Gabrielle d'Estrées and her sister the duchess of Villars), last quarter of the sixteenth century, Musée du Louvre, Paris.

> Despite what it might look like to the contemporary viewer, a purely queer reading of the work would be misguided. Rather than a depiction of lesbian foreplay, most art historians interpret the painting as an announcement that Gabrielle is pregnant with the King's illegitimate son. It's her sister who is signalling this to the audience, not her lover. The fingers wrapped around Gabrielle's nipple symbolizes the latter's fertility, an allusion emphasized by the presence of the figure sewing baby's clothes in the back of the painting .... *Gabrielle d'Estrées and One of Her Sisters* is simultaneously a sexualized queer scene, a coded announcement of a royal pregnancy, and an erotic fantasy meant to entice straight audiences. To prioritize one reading over the others would be an injustice, a smoothing over of the very complexities that both enrich and frustrate queer histories.

(Dr Hannah Williams, Queen Mary University of London: "The meaning behind one of the most oddly erotic paintings in Western art", *Artsy*, 11 June 2019, www.artsy.net/article/artsy-editorial-meaning-one-oddly-erotic-paintings-western-art – last accessed 29 November 2023.)

Notes on contributors

Kathleen M. Blumreich earned her PhD from Michigan State University. For thirty-five years, she taught medieval literature at Grand Valley State University, where she was Professor of English. Publications include essays on the *Mystère d'Adam*, the *Roman de Silence*, an edition of Robert de Gretham's Middle English *Mirror*, book reviews, and articles on issues of concern to Student Affairs professionals. Her most recent contribution, co-authored with Corinna McLeod, is 'From Capes to Tuffskin Jeans: Stephen King's Vampires and 1980s Angst' (*Horror Studies* 12.2, 2021).

David Cantor-Echols is Visiting Assistant Professor of History at Wofford College. His research examines the political culture of medieval Iberia, with a focus on royal institutions and the influence of interfaith relations on elite cultural production.

Audrey Covert is a final year PhD student at Trinity College Dublin. Her current work examines the intersection of gender, power, and the politics of access in fourteenth century Anglo-French relations. Her interests include gender, sexuality, identity, foreignness, and power in late medieval Europe.

Fabrizio De Falco is Adjunct Professor of Medieval History at the Università di Bologna, Italy. He is a medievalist with a strong interest in cultural studies and their interconnection with politics. His work focuses on the use of literary themes and texts to promote personal ambitions and political aims, more specifically the literary production at the Plantagenet court.

Michael Evans is an assistant professor in History in the Social Sciences Division at Delta College, Michigan. His research interests include medieval king/queenship, the crusades, the Robin Hood legend, race and medievalism, and medievalism in social media. He is the author of *The Death of Kings:*

Representations of Royal Death in Medieval England and *Inventing Eleanor: The Medieval and Post-Medieval Image of Eleanor of Aquitaine* as well as many published articles on medieval history and medievalism. He is an associate editor for the International Society for the Study of Medievalism's online review *Medievally Speaking*. His current research focusses on the queenship of Isabella of France.

Matthew Firth is Associate Lecturer in medieval studies at Flinders University, South Australia. His research focuses on cultural memory and the reception and adaptation of England's pre-Norman past in the history writing of societies in later times and distant places.

Emily Lalande is a doctoral researcher at the University of Sussex. Her work compares two Franco-Navarrese queen consorts, Marguerite de Valois and Marguerite d'Angouleme, during the sixteenth century. She completed both her BA and MA in History at the University of Toronto. Her research interests include women's history, conflict studies, and life-writing.

Fatima Rhorchi is a retired Associate Professor from the Moulay Ismail University, Morocco. She has presented and participated in several international conferences including Kings and Queens and the International Medieval Congress, UK. Her most recent publication is 'The Role of Court Jews as *Dhimmis* and as Influential Agents of Moroccan Sultans', in Zita Eva Rohr and Jonathan Spangler, eds, *Significant Others. Aspects of Deviance and Difference in Premodern Court Cultures* (Routledge, 2022).

Zita Eva Rohr is an historian of the late medieval and early modern periods. She is a Fellow of the Royal Historical Society, a Chevalier in the *Ordre des Palmes Académiques*, and an Honorary Research Fellow at Macquarie University in the Department of History and Archaeology. Her monograph, *Yolande of Aragon, Family and Power 1381–1442: The Reverse of the Tapestry* was published in 2016 (Palgrave Macmillan). Her most recent book is an edited collection with Jonathan Spangler, *Significant Others: Aspects of Deviance and Difference in Premodern Court Cultures* (Routledge, 2022). Her second monograph, *Anne of France and her Family, 1325–1522: A Genealogy of Premodern Female Power and Influence* is expected in 2024.

Gabrielle Storey is a historian of queenship, gender, and sexuality with a specialism in twelfth- and thirteenth-century England, France, and Navarre. Her research interests include co-rulership, familial relationships, and royal studies more broadly on a global scale. She has a forthcoming biography entitled *Berengaria of Navarre. Queen of England and Lord of Le Mans* (Routledge) and has previously published on Berengaria of Navarre, Angevin queenship, and sexuality.

Alexander Thies is a PhD researcher in Ancient history at the University of Bern in Switzerland, working on a dissertation about 'The Body of Imperial Women in Late Antiquity'. His research includes questions of body, gender and sexuality history, monarchical representation, rituals, and patristics in the 'long Late Antiquity' (200–800 CE).

Jessica Weiss is Professor of Art History, Theory, and Criticism at Metropolitan State University of Denver (United States). Her research focuses on the artistic connections between Iberia and the Low Countries, including the reception of Netherlandish art and Hispano-Flemish painting. The collection practices and patronage projects associated with Queen Isabel of Castile have been a major focus of this research. Her publications on this topic include chapters in *A Companion to the Queenship of Isabel la Católica* (Brill, 2023), *Copies of Flemish Masters in the Hispanic World: Flandes by Substitution* (Brepols, 2021), and *Imagery and Ingenuity in Early Modern Europe: Essays in Honor of Jeffrey Chipps Smith* (Brepols, 2019).

Acknowledgements

This collection of essays had its genesis in a series of sessions sponsored by the Royal Studies Network organised by the present editors for the International Medieval Congress held at the University of Leeds in 2019. The Leeds sessions aimed to unearth diverse ideas of royal sexualities and their representations in the medieval world and have since provided a starting point to expand our collective thinking outwards to the greater premodern world. Questions such as what it meant to be a premodern ruler with a sexual identity, as well as what it meant to be ruled by a particular and sometimes non-conformist and or/diverse sexuality, have been the points of departure for subsequent discussions across time and space. We therefore acknowledge the research and diverse reflections of those who presented at the original Leeds sessions as well as our ten talented scholarly contributors who have expanded the boundaries of what in the past were accepted and received as finite templates for understanding premodern sexualities. As one, they have accepted our combined editorial exactitude with good humour and dedication. This collection's existence is a testament to their hard work and scholarly perseverance, and we are delighted and honoured to have guided it along the path to its publication.

By the same token, we would like to thank and acknowledge the editorial and production staff at Manchester University Press, particularly Senior Commissioning Editor Meredith Carroll who has been unwavering in her support of the project from start to finish. We are also very grateful to the anonymous reviewer who gave significant time and feedback on the draft manuscript, offering essential and insightful appreciations enabling the progress of the collection to its final polished form.

On a more personal level, we would like to thank the co-founder of the Royal Studies Network, Dr Elena Woodacre, as well as its many members who have consistently encouraged and enriched our thinking. Zita would specifically like to thank her hard-working and meticulous co-editor Gabrielle whose good humour, friendship, and scholarly generosity were essential to the realisation of this volume. She thanks her Australian and international research colleagues, mentors, collaborators, and scholarly friends Professor Emerita Theresa Earenfight; Professor Núria Silleras-Fernández; Associate Provost and Professor Dawn Bratsch-Prince; Dr Jonathan Spangler; Professor Tracy Adams; Professor Susan Broomhall; Associate Professor Saliha Belmessous; Dr Claire Ponsich; and Dr Hélène Sirantoine who have nourished, challenged, and encouraged her in significant and durable ways. She would also like to acknowledge and thank Macquarie University, especially Professor Clare Monagle for her consistent support in ensuring the continuation of her status as an Honorary Research Fellow in the Department of History and Archaeology. Gabrielle thanks her co-editor Zita for her camaraderie and friendship, and fortitude in the period of this volume's completion. She would also like to thank her friends, research colleagues, and mentors for their ongoing support: Dr Estelle Paranque, Dr Gordon McKelvie, Dr Christina Welch, and Holly Marsden. She also thanks the University of Winchester, UK, for their support of her status as Visiting Research Fellow in the School of History. Archaeology, and Philosophy.

Introduction
Premodern ruling sexualities: representation, identity, and power

Gabrielle Storey and Zita Eva Rohr

Premodern ruling sexualities

The study of sexualities in the premodern world is a continually evolving and proliferating field. In his four-volume *L'Histoire de la sexualité* published between 1976 and 1984, Michel Foucault shed light upon the emergence of 'sexuality' as a discursive object and separate sphere of life, concluding that the belief that every individual has a sexuality is a relatively recent development in Western societies.[1] Foucault asserted moreover that in his view sexuality has never been truly repressed:

> We must ... abandon the hypothesis that modern industrial societies ushered in an age of increased sexual repression. We have not only witnessed a visible explosion of unorthodox sexualities; but – and this is the important point – a deployment quite different from the law, even if it is locally dependent on procedures of prohibition, has ensured, through a network of interconnecting mechanisms, the proliferation of specific pleasures and the multiplication of disparate sexualities.[2]

While admiring of Foucault the man but frustrated by some of his theories and conclusions regarding sexuality, John E. Boswell's own foundational work in the 1980s has led likewise to the steady emergence of collections and monographs dedicated to studying sexualities in the ancient, medieval, and early modern periods across geographical locations.[3] Jeffery Cisneros explains the source of contention and difference between social constructivists and structural theorists such as Foucault on the one hand and essentialist theorists such as Boswell on the other:

> Queer theory builds upon the work of Michel Foucault and structural theorists who attempted to destabilize simple conceptions of gay or lesbian identity, departing from the essentialist theory of historians who maintain that certain phenomena are natural, inevitable, universal, and biologically determined.

Boswell and essentialists maintain that homosexuality is genetically determined, an argument that is still prominent today. Structuralists argue that biology is only one of a number of factors that determine sexual orientation. Structuralism does not deny that biology is a significant factor, but it allows for the elements of nurture and choice in its arguments.[4]

Despite their theoretical divergences, Foucault and Boswell never considered their research to be anything but complementary. For many since, the social construction versus the essentialist model is out of date, given that extremes and a too literal interpretation of theoretical models rarely hold in the long term. We should therefore take account of a far more nuanced understanding of sexuality, informed as it is by essential biological attributes such as genes and uterine hormones, for example. By the same token, most would not claim that such biological matters do not play out according to specific social and historical contexts.[5]

As a consequence of the increased focus and enthusiasm generated by accumulating work on premodern sexualities, royal and monarchical, and indeed court studies, have been tackling many of the same issues and conundrums. Royal studies can involve court studies, family, political history and so forth, whereas monarchical studies tend to focus explicitly on monarchs and their institutions and instruments of rulership. Bound up in debates and questions about terminology (and its associated anachronisms), like royal and monarchical studies, sexuality studies in English language publications have remained largely Eurocentric with studies of cases outside the Western world often missing from the larger historical narrative. This historiographical weakness in our global understanding in sexuality studies is being transformed as more and more comparative and collaborative work has emerged. We are shifting our collective gaze.[6]

With respect to royal or ruling sexualities, much of the previous work on the topic has focused on either scandal or moral judgements surrounding the ruler, and how this might have impacted upon their legacy and our understanding of their rule. The special issue of the *Royal Studies Journal*, 'Ruling Sexualities', foregrounded work focusing on representations and reputations across a variety of sources including fiction, film, and television series.[7] It serves as a useful foundation for this volume, which considers not only ruling sexualities – the sexualities of those who ruled – but also how those monarchs were ruled by their sexualities. The present collection builds upon this initial foundation by interrogating two essential subjects: firstly, by the editors in the present introduction, issues of anachronism and terminology, and how these can be addressed in premodern royal studies, and secondly, by the work offered by our contributors, representations of monarchical sexualities and how sexualities ruled rulers, with case studies from Christian Europe and Muslim al-Andalus.

There is an undoubted imperative to continue to push analyses of sexuality in royal studies in a variety of directions, particularly with a view to challenging the lingering misconception that royal and elite premodern women inevitably fall into a saint or sinner trope. We must take account instead of depictions of premodern royal women in a range of literatures and images and their recourse to other influential literary and historical figures aside from Eve, ones such as those highlighted by Jessica Weiss in her chapter for this collection.

By the same token, to become an inclusive field, royal studies must address itself to more than just royal women and their depictions. To that end, this volume takes account of European kings, al-Andalusian caliphs and other royal and elite individuals, and courtiers of all genders, to challenge binaries in a number of ways, whether through an examination of terminology, and/ or by examining sexual and gender boundaries. The collection aims to pivot our attention beyond the king and queen partnership – the *consortium coniugali*[8] – to better understand royal sexualities in all their diverse manifestations. By acknowledging premodern sexual and gender fluidity in their diverse forms and multiple manifestations, and by widening the scope of their investigations, our contributors explore representations of their research protagonists and their sexualities in greater detail, advancing possibilities as to how we might redefine, understand, and visualise them. An enhanced reconsideration of royal sexualities, and their expression by rulers and their contemporaries, facilitates our understanding that premodern sexuality was not solely concerned with the fact that royals had sex with their marital partners and others – significant or otherwise. Sexual activity (or in some cases, inactivity) enabled monarchs to express and fashion themselves for an often critical and sometimes dangerous external gaze. With that in mind, it is worth recalling Machiavelli's pragmatic political advice for a successful prince:

> Everyone sees how you appear, few touch what you are; and these few dare not oppose the opinion of many, who have the majesty of the state to defend them; and in the actions of all men, and especially of princes, where there is no court to appeal to, one looks to the end.[9]

The end to which Machiavelli's aspiring prince must look is to gain and maintain power and sovereignty.

Clearly, the sexualities of premodern royals and elites extended well beyond their actions, and from this distance we can only infer a monarch's sexual preferences from their documented actions in the surviving written record. As a result, their true understanding and feelings are otherwise unknown to us. As argued elsewhere by one of the present editors, there is an evident reality in not being able to reproduce the past in all its undisputed entirety and complexity because it is 'inaccessible simply by virtue of no longer existing'.[10] In an attempt to address such frustrating lacunae, the chapters and conclusions woven together in this volume aim to offer interpretations from literary and archival evidence as well as suggestions for further analyses, thereby continuing the discussion of premodern sexualities from a global perspective.

To some extent, the study of sexualities has always been associated with gender studies and this correlation is more relevant than ever because understanding platonic, romantic, and sexual relationships, and delineating them where needed, grants us a deeper and more accurate understanding of the diversity and richness of historical identities. Work on homosociality, for example, has demonstrated the different characteristics of male friendships and the diverse types of masculinities that existed at any one time in premodern society.[11] Where such detail can be found in historical and literary sources, analyses of these have helped to develop our knowledge as to how people of the same sex interacted with one another as well as their own interpretations of platonic and romantic feelings towards each other. In this way, we can further evaluate political and personal relationships to deepen our own understanding of power, agency, gender, and sexuality. In a recent study targeting religious scepticism and sexuality embedded within premodern 'refined literary products' that circulated amongst the 'wider culture of common people, middle rank professionals, and members of the cultivated elite' of the early modern Mediterranean, Umberto Grassi concludes that:

> the extent to which sexual themes, rather than being mere 'divertissements' or manifestations of folk attitudes, were important theoretical tools in a wider critique of religious and political authority and authoritarianism.[12]

Of course, not all sexualities were illicit in the sense of being same-sex. Grassi draws attention to the heterodox opinion circulating to some extent around the early modern Mediterranean that Adam and Eve had committed sodomy in the Garden of Eden and that it was this that constituted their original sin leading to the Fall of humankind.[13] This idea arose from a creative rereading of the myth of the Fall from Grace, which posited that the forbidden fruit plucked from the Tree of Knowledge was a symbolic representation of Eve's buttocks and that their original sin was anal sex rather than insubordination to their Creator.[14] While this rereading did not constitute mainstream belief, it is worth mentioning because of its prominence in Inquisition trials and because it seems to have originated from within ecclesiastical circles themselves and 'subsequently appropriated by networks of lay nonconformists that cultivated a common interest in questioning the established religious beliefs and moral codes of their times'.[15]

Some sexualities were considered transgressive because they operated outside of marital, moral or religious boundaries, whether through infidelity or consanguinity. With the heavy expectation that women bore children for their husbands and/or were otherwise chaste, any sexual activity outside this boundary was usually rendered scandalous, even if transgressive sexual activity might not have occurred. Such is the case of Eleanor of Aquitaine, successively queen of France and England, whose reputation suffered greatly from the sharp wounds inflicted by chroniclers' pens. Accused of incest not once but twice, first with her paternal uncle Raymond of Antioch on the Second Crusade, and later with her eventual father-in-law Geoffrey of Anjou upon her return from the Crusade, Eleanor's legacy has been much tarred by contemporary criticism and in subsequent historical fiction.[16] Such strategic criticism was not grounded in the truth of her sexual misdeeds but was instead triggered by her supposed breaking of hierarchical and social boundaries (and existential anxieties relating to her vast territorial patrimony as *suo jure* duchess of Aquitaine) when it came to the exercise of (geo) political power and dynastic influence. There is also the persistent white noise and gossip surrounding the alleged (now largely discounted) wanton behaviour of Isabeau of Bavaria, queen of France.[17] Powerful and well-placed women who transgressed political and societal boundaries, particularly when it came to gender expectations, were often rebuked by way of sexual scandal to neutralise their authority and to harm *ex post facto* future understandings of their genuine power and influence. That said, political censure could be directed at a king and queen partnership such as that of Magnus Eriksson (1316–1374), king of Sweden, and his consort Blanche of Namur, with the sources demonstrating that contemporary critics could and did believe that deviant sexual behaviour could justify a dethronement. Interested contemporary chroniclers pointed their febrile, ink-stained fingers at an unruly queen who was 'vain and licentious', capable of poisoning her own son, and her 'weak effeminate husband', as justification for Magnus Eriksson's eventual dethronement.[18]

Denunciation of excessive or unusual kingly sexualities were also linked to questioning of authority by some of their contemporary and subsequent chroniclers. Again, as Henric Bagerius and Christine Ekholst have argued elsewhere, criticism of medieval kings by homing in on their sex life and sexuality could be used to undermine their authority and sovereignty. Using several case studies of late medieval European kings, Bagerius and Ekholst note that 'A king's inability to be sexually active indicated a lack of masculine authority... [and] his failure to control his wife represented a serious fault in the rulership'.[19] Thus, while a queen could manage being chaste, embodying the Virgin Mary as a role model, a king could not.[20] A king was expected to produce a legitimate heir, and even though a king's sexual frivolity outside the marital bed was sometimes frowned upon, particularly if it bordered on excess, this was far preferable to a chaste and 'unproductive' king. Whether abstention was enacted through extreme piety, asexuality, homosexuality, physical incapacity, or another unknown reason, kings faced rebuke from councillors and advisors, the murmurings of the wider public, and the feverish scribblings of partisan chroniclers for not attending diligently enough to produce an heir to the throne. Such disregard for the future of their dynasty and the security of their kingdom was often met with pleas and chastisement from contemporaries, whether through the form of a hermit's rebuke (in the case of Richard I of England) or clerical disparagement (directed at Louis VII of France).[21] This was not only the case for Western monarchs, as Fatima Rhorchi demonstrates in chapter 7 of this volume. Rhorchi sheds light upon the example of al-Hakam II, the second Umayyad Caliph of Córdoba (r. 961–976), who did not manage to produce an heir or indeed any progeny before the age of forty-six either as a result of his pederasty or because he was too absorbed in his precious library to waste time on shallow and fleeting sexual gratification.[22]

What's in a name?

Addressing the histories of individuals and communities who might now find themselves corralled together in the LGBTQIA+ tent with regard to categorisation and terminology is inevitably complex and not infrequently perilous. Although many historians who work regularly on the history of sexualities acknowledge the potential for anachronism in their work, for others modern categorisation and terminology seem to provide a useful shorthand to categorise a historical figure, labelling them for example 'homosexual' without too much further thought for what being 'homosexual' in the context of their time and place might have meant. For some, categorising anything non-heterosexual under the umbrella of 'queer' history has been the default solution – the term queer accounting for anything alternative, anything different, and one that encompasses time and space. Understandably, however, those who come from a generation where queer was deployed as an insult have not yet reclaimed the term and continue to find it problematic. The arguments posited by Valerie Traub in her article 'Queer Unhistoricism' put forward a compelling case as to why we can and should employ queer as a historical category, proposing that queer has its uses because it deconstructs sexual identity and highlights the indeterminacy of erotic desire and gender.[23] Yet, we are not so readily convinced. While queer history is a valid and undeniable category of modern identity that takes account of some parts of LGBTQIA+ history, it does not cover the full range of history (and specific historical contexts) and is no more a valid qualifier for premodern gender or sexuality than heterosexual or homosexual. By using anachronistic qualifiers and terminology, we run the risk of misidentifying and mislabelling historical figures who had a very different experience of what it was like to feel and act upon same-sex attraction (or anything else for that matter) when they did not regard themselves as being 'queer'.[24] However, if we can demonstrate context and a justification for our perceived anachronisms, then perhaps the application of contemporary terminology might be sufficiently justified. Unless there is a radical shift in thinking, or a new terminology is established that better accommodates the needs of the historian and the sociologist, this is the framework that perhaps best accords with our present aims and objectives.

So, where do we now find ourselves? This volume will undoubtedly be seen by some as being guilty of perpetuating the use of risky anachronism – no new terminology yet forthcoming. However, we would argue for a degree of justifiable flexibility in terms of categorisation as opposed to the quest to place all historical figures and diverse peoples into our right-thinking modern boxes combined with a commitment to acknowledging the sometimes hazardous issues in utilising contemporary terminology for historical figures. This should not be read as a call to arms to remove queer as a category of historical analysis, nor indeed to remove it entirely from our historiographical vocabulary. However, applying rigid categories can limit potentially our analyses and understanding. On the other hand, by expanding our definitions and exploring the many different ways that premodern people – in this case, the royal and the ruling (and their historians) – conceived of and defined sexual orientation and gender identity, we are better able to express a wide-ranging and more accurate picture of premodern plural sexualities in general and, for our particular purposes here, in a royal context. While the practice of historical research is engineered ultimately towards reaching a point of knowledge to aid understanding and to offer an evidence-based conclusion, it might be more productive to accept that, in the vast majority of cases, we are unlikely to know the actual sexual orientation of any historical figure and what this might have implied. Bed-sharing with women and the begetting of heirs do not necessarily make a man straight. Likewise, uncovering premodern female sexuality beyond alleged infidelity and scandal requires further investigation if we are to understand the deployment of scandal as a tool for undermining the power of ruling women (and indeed their men). This collection adopts the position of recent queer studies in that sexualities need to be viewed by us (and were probably viewed by those on the past, if they vocalised the idea at all) as multi-faceted and fluid – as non-binary. By better focusing on historical and contextualised diversity, we can avoid the risk of concluding that their actions defined their identities.

As we suggest below, the risk of paring everything down to binaries is also unhelpful. There will always be figures or activities that fall outside a binary, and to force them into a binary risks further stigmatisation or problematising. Kathleen Blumreich's chapter in this collection raises the issue of gender fluidity, societal norms, desire, marriage, and morality in literary sources such as the thirteenth-century *Roman de Silence*. New work demonstrating greater nuance in the interpretation of other twelfth- and thirteenth-century literary works, ones focusing upon adventuring male and female couples such as *Eric et Enide*, *Tristan et Iseult*, *Aucassin et Nicolete*, and *Guillaume de Palerne*, raise interesting questions regarding premodern strategies of gender navigation and the exploration of hybrid gender identities.[25] Until very recently, heteronormative, or indeed non-heteronormative, appeared a useful way of distinguishing between a multitude of diverse behaviours. However, such categorisations only serve to reinforce the binary by assuming heterosexual and gender rigidity (a strong adherence to gender-stereotypical behaviour) as default settings. Such assumptions are not infrequently accompanied by other anachronistic terminologies. Using language that only has one flipside also reduces our discussion to that of the 'other',[26] raising further complications and reducing discussions of sexuality to a potential right and wrong, good and bad, acceptable and unacceptable. As Storey notes elsewhere, approaching historical subjects as fluid in both gender and attraction can be a useful starting point for discussing sexualities, removing the immediate need to categorise and apply labels.[27] Nuance and an awareness that one size does not fit all is of paramount importance to historiographical undertaking.[28] Moreover, an awareness of time and place is essential when discussing sexualities, in particular, because the language used to describe them in Tang China would have been far different from the language used in early modern France.[29]

Some might argue that categorisation is a necessary evil – without categorisation, the past would lose any sense of meaning. They may be right. But does fixing the past into categories offer a better path? Well-intentioned categorisations have often fallen into dichotomies or binaries, even as some have looked to move beyond the heterosexual and homosexual binary favouring instead licit versus illicit or reproductive versus non-reproductive sex.[30] Yet this too perpetuates a binary and offers no real solution to meaningful descriptions of premodern sexualities. Past categorisations and discussion of sexualities and their representations were sometimes deliberately misleading and deployed or 'weaponised' for political, dynastic, and financial advantage.

It is with this top-of-mind that we open our collection with an exploration of such weaponised sexualities in 'Part I: Scandal, Perception, and Representation'. The chapters in this section focus on the various ways in which sexualities have been represented and how this can affect reputation, both in the past and in the present. Depictions of sexual scandal, or sexual activities that fell outside societal boundaries, were often portrayed in such a way that they did further harm to a ruler's legacy and reputation, with scandal carrying down through successive generations of scholars and commentators. Royal figures associated with sexual scandal remain some of the most durable in modern memory. For too many, Elagabalus, Edward II, Isabeau of Bavaria, and Empress Theodora are familiar only for their lively and supposed scandalous actions and tenures.[31] While titillating scandal might serve as an initial drawcard and fascination, the perpetuation of largely discredited scandal in current media and popular culture, whether in fiction, in film, or in blockbuster television series, remains a finely balanced challenge for historians and writers to overcome as they seek to redress historical imbalances and cultural memory to work towards more accurate depictions of past (and indeed present) monarchs.[32]

However, we must not too readily assume that all expressions and/or representations of premodern sexuality were uniformly harmful. Those who were chaste, both inside and outside marriage, were praised by contemporaries for their exemplary behaviour, continence, and closeness to God. Louise Tingle reminds us that:

> Queens assumed almost a fictional state of virginity during their coronations as they underwent anointing, even those who had already borne children, through their appearance and emulation of the Virgin Mary, such as wearing her hair unbound.[33]

Like her role model, the Virgin Mary, a chaste or childless queen such as Anne of Bohemia could be viewed as an intercessory asset even though she was expected to bear an heir for the English throne.[34] By the same token, a childless king such as Anne's husband Richard II could play the 'chastity card' where no issue was forthcoming – legitimate or otherwise.[35] This might also have been the case for Edward the Confessor, the last Anglo-Saxon king of England, whose queen Edith of Wessex did not produce an heir, thereby removing the burden of childlessness from her[36] as indeed it did for Anne in Richard II's case. Bringing oneself closer to salvation rather than being tempted into carnal sin attracted the adulation of medieval clerics in particular. In the case of Edward the Confessor, his widow Edith commissioned the *Vita Ædwardi Regis qui apud Westmonasterium Requiescit* (or more simply, the *Vita Ædwardi Regis*).[37] In it, Osbert of Clare, the prior of Westminster, transforms Edward into a saint with all the usual trappings of virtue and chastity.[38] Yet clerics close to a king could also be pragmatic, alive to the imperative for a monarch to produce a legitimate heir. Perceived to be somewhat slow out of the starting blocks, the devout Louis VII of France was regularly prodded by his closest advisor, Abbot Suger, to ensure that he produced an heir to succeed him.[39]

By way of contrast to chaste ideals, perceived or actual infidelity in male monarchs, though outwardly disapproved of, allowed men a 'healthy' outlet for their desires and, provided no noble daughters were besmirched in the process, such indecorous sexuality was largely overlooked. This can be seen quite clearly in the case of Emperor Charles VI, whose sexuality Charlotte Backerra has examined in some detail.[40] His is an interesting case to consider due to his establishment of intimate emotional relationships alongside sexual ones, indicating how he might have valued affection and intimacy on a romantic, rather than merely sexual level. As long as it did not cause disruption to the succession, male infidelity was tolerated, with any illegitimate offspring frequently added to the royal household as was the case for Henry II of England and his natural sons Geoffrey, archbishop of York; William Longespée, 3rd Earl of Salisbury; and Morgan, bishop-elect of Durham; and later for Henry VIII and Henry FitzRoy, 1st duke of Richmond and Somerset, born of his liaison with Elizabeth Blount. That to one side, both excessive and chaste sexuality heralded problems for the monarchy regardless of their acceptance (or not) by wider society and the church. Issues of dynasticism and legitimacy held strong sway in the minds of the king and his kingdom, with an heir – preferably male, born of his queen, typically the only acceptable candidate for the orderly transmission of sovereign authority.[41]

Questions regarding lineage concerned those surrounding the throne, due to the imperative to preserve the royal line and produce legitimate rulers. Property and inheritance needed to be passed to legitimate heirs to preserve dynastic power, wealth, and resources. Concerns over legitimacy and loss of power often led to factions and disputes. The fifteenth-century Wars of the Roses in England underscored the controversy regarding Elizabeth Woodville's second marriage as the new wife of Edward IV. A *cause célèbre* arose due to her large family's potential for seizing power from the Crown with the assent of royal favourites, which inevitably resulted in the dominance of one faction over another at court. Where one faction gained power and the upper hand at court in hostile circumstances, others inevitably suffered their loss. Accordingly, issues around sexuality – both excessive and non-heteronormative – were intrinsically linked to power and its preservation. The necessity to preserve power and invest it in the Crown, and not let it trickle and dissipate downwards and outwards, preserved both the hierarchy and the dominant patriarchy. By ensuring that a legitimate heir was produced by the reigning couple, the succession could continue relatively smoothly, allowing the status quo of power and sovereignty to be maintained, whereas producing strings of illegitimate heirs ran the risk of upending the balance of power at court and raised the existential risk of supplanting a legitimate heir.[42]

All this considered, premodern sexualities, whether operating within a marriage between a man and a woman, or outside it, whether chaste or excessive, held major implications for the preservation of dynastic power and sovereignty. Not only were royals who acted outside received societal norms viewed as transgressive, they also ran the risk of stigmatisation, chastisement, and sometimes dethronement. While excessive sexuality and chastity could be remedied, or tolerated, sexual behaviour that threatened the throne, either by breaking legal or religious codes or by disrupting the dynasty and succession, was a serious cause for concern. Royal authority could be undermined by transgressive behaviour and for kings, in particular, embodying a type of masculinity perceived as compromised also weakened their power, and opened the door for political and societal upheaval, as with the forced abdication and subsequent murder of Edward II by his wife Isabella of France, Roger Mortimer, and other allies.[43]

Queens also faced repercussions for alleged or merely rumoured sexual transgression, though most were able to hold onto their power. Queens tended to endure more damage to their reputations and legacies shortly after becoming widowed and thereafter, with chroniclers and later historians utilising the 'Madonna and whore' stereotypes to a greater extent and to considerable durable effect. Sometimes such destabilising campaigns were deployed to shore up the legitimacy of an incoming queen by the new queen at the expense of her predecessor. This was certainly the case for Violant de Bar (r. 1387–1396), successor to the post of queen-consort of Aragon, and her step-mother-in-law Sibil·la de Fortià (r. 1377–1387) and later still in the case of Violant's successor, María de Luna (1396–1406).[44] At the heart of all these critiques, however, was the *sine qua non* to maintain societal order and royal authority. If the ruler was not able to adhere to accepted norms, they could be castigated and undermined. Yet, as the studies in this volume demonstrate, not all transgressive behaviour resulted in deposition, but it certainly gave opponents considerable ammunition to criticise a transgressive and/or weakened and unpopular monarch.

Dangerous sexualities

Given there is much to be said and explored in terms of the memory and legacy of sexuality, this collection is divided into two discrete yet interlocking parts. Part I 'Scandal, Perception, and Representation' sheds light upon on the deployment of sexualities to inflict harm and/or gain personal or political advantage. As such it is primarily concerned with reputation and scandal. Of course, scandal, especially of a sexual nature, is still being exploited as a weapon against the powerful, the (in)famous, and the aspirational today.[45] It has a long history and has been used from the ancient to the modern world as demonstrated by the Alexander Thies's opening chapter. Thies favours us with a comparative analysis of Byzantine empresses from late antiquity, considering the ways in which sexual slander was used against them to serve the elite and maintain group identity. His chapter highlights the importance of a comparative methodology to understand reputation and legacy in late antiquity, as well how the creation of sexual slander enabled certain members of the ruling elite to maintain its power and authority. In chapter 2, Matthew Firth interrogates the coronation scandal of Eadwig of Wessex, king of England, continuing a comparative approach to place the coronation scandal within wider sexual affairs and highlighting the ways in which the reputations of Eadwig, his sometime consort, Queen Ælfgifu, and her mother Æthelgifu, were subject to such criticism. Both Firth and Thies demonstrate how women could be more susceptible and vulnerable to sexual criticism and how such slander has adhered to their reputations – in some cases enduring to the present day. Even when work has been undertaken to restore their reputations, scandal remains a defining aspect of their legacies and serves as a bait to hook the unsuspecting reader or viewer.

Chapter 3 sees Fabrizio de Falco explore the work of the Angevin chronicler Walter Map and Map's depiction of a king of Portugal who engaged in irregular sexual behaviour. De Falco's analysis again demonstrates the risk to reputation in conducting illicit activities, with Map concealing identifying information to preserve to some extent his protagonist-king's reputation. As De Falco argues, such texts hold political value for informing modern historians of the activities of the courts and their central figures, and what they might reveal about a particular society and its sexual attitudes, which is essential if we are to succeed in unravelling premodern royal sexualities. In chapter 4, Michael Evans returns to the infamous figure of Isabella of France, queen of England, unpicking further her allegedly 'scandalous' liaison with Roger Mortimer. Evans questions the assumed adultery between the pair and posits the need to question why cases of sexual scandal, including adultery, appear at times of political crisis and what this means for our understanding of power and authority in the premodern world. De Falco and Evans's examinations highlight issues of memory and the constructions of legacies, with both royal figures analysed having suffered from the sharp and restless pens of their chroniclers.

In the final chapter of Part I, Jessica Weiss considers notions of sex and sexuality in an Iberian setting. Examining the reign of Isabel of Castile, Weiss dissects Isabel's construction of her complicated identity as a woman and a ruler in her own right through artwork and design, proposing that Isabel's responses to contemporary artwork were not only multi-faceted but moreover reinforced her vision of herself as a legitimate and authoritative female ruler on the Iberian Peninsula. Included in Weiss's study is a discussion of Melusine, the mythological shape-shifting builder and dynastic founder of the noble house of Lusignan, providing us with much to think about

Introduction

concerning Isabel's determined and careful fashioning of herself as a virtuous 'Catholic King' of Castile and dynastic progenitor.[46]

At its core, Part I of our collection demonstrates the ways in which sexualities were created, weaponised, deconstructed and used by contemporaries as well as later historians to not only harm but also challenge perceptions of rulers generally, but more particularly their authority and identity as sexual beings.

Part II, 'Gender, Morality, and Desire'[47] explores purportedly dangerous sexualities in a socio-political context, predominantly within the frameworks of identity, morality, and marriage. It opens with a chapter from Kathleen Blumreich, who deftly explores the gender performativity and fluidity of the heroine Silence in the verse romance *Roman de Silence*. As Blumreich concludes, Silence is not afraid of being a transgressor. Acting outside society's gender and biological sex boundaries was a transgressive act, and something that many of the historical figures in this volume faced to their peril. Transgression against societal, legal, and even conflicted personal boundaries and beliefs was potentially the path of any European in the medieval world whose sexual identity fell outside the heterosexual ideal and society's gender expectations.

Offered by Fatima Rhorchi, the seventh chapter in this volume transports us to medieval al-Andalus, where an examination of the sexual behaviour of caliphs, in particular the preference of some caliphs for young boys, highlights what has been a somewhat veiled history of male love in the Islamic world. Rhorchi's conclusion that contemporary writers attempted to discredit al-Amin's authority by labelling him as 'queer' or 'deviant' draws parallels with many of the northern and western European contemporaries discussed in this volume – and indeed beyond it.[48] Rhorchi's chapter gathers together many of the threads woven through this volume, not least that sexual critique remained one of the most potent and regularly utilised weapons with which to undermine and discredit royal authority.

The discussion by Emily Lalande in chapter 8 shifts our attention northwards to the infamous *Tour de Nesle* affair at the French court of Philip IV. Lalande focuses on the implications of dangerous sexuality for the women involved in the affair, and how it heralded the exclusion of female heirs from the Capetian succession. As noted earlier in this introduction, dynasty and legitimacy were pivotal points for monarchs across time and space, and any concerns regarding the security of the succession could result in disbarment. The *Tour de Nesle* affair held significant implications for female power and sovereignty, not only for those directly involved but also for their successors and the rulers of their successors as well.

In chapter 9, David Cantor-Echols continues our analyses of moral misgivings and the politics of gender and sex in in the Castilian *castigos* (punishments). Cantor-Echols's journey through the *castigos* of Sancho IV is a fascinating exploration of interfaith relations and the attitude of this Christian monarch towards such sexual activities. By means of a narrative featuring lustful kings and interfaith relationships, Cantor-Echols argues that Sancho's *castigos* sought to reconfigure royal authority in himself, through royal abstention from interfaith sex and declarations condemning such behaviour. Undeniably, stepping outside societal boundaries and drawing attention to moral misbehaviour was not unfamiliar territory to Piers Gaveston and other royal favourites, the subjects of our concluding chapter, contributed by Audrey Covert. Covert discusses the pathways to power that English royal favourites chose to navigate in the fourteenth century, highlighting the gender and sexual traits that these late-medieval favourites embodied.

The chapters in this volume intersect in a variety of ways as do both parts of the collection. Evans's chapter in Part I has an impact upon a deeper understanding of Lalande's in Part II. Weiss's study in Part I and Cantor-Echols's contribution in Part II lean into the kingdom of Castile and its rulers, prompting reflections as to whether there was something unique about the Castilian context and the mindset of its rulers and subjects. Both contributions provide considerable food for thought regarding Castilian sovereignty, its phenomenon of regnant queenship, its distinct, almost anxious, emphasis upon chastity and piety as well as interfaith relations more generally in the medieval Mediterranean. Thies's chapter and Firth's study in Part I and Rhorchi and Covert's contributions in Part II examine the power of sexual rumour and innuendo to destabilise rulers and political situations. Finally, Evans, Covert, and Blumreich's offerings dovetail in the ways in which they challenge assumptions of gender expectations, morality, and sexual activity amongst royalty and members of its entourages.

None of the chapters here gathered suggest that there was no toleration or acceptance for sexualities that did not fit what was expected socially in the premodern world. Indeed, while premodern sexualities in a non-royal sense are frequently difficult to uncover, the cases that do survive indicate that societies were willing to sometimes ignore what they might categorise as 'deviant' or irregular sexual behaviour. However, such crafted ignorance did not always extend to the monarchy, which was not only expected to lead by example but also had far higher stakes to consider than members of the middling and lower classes, with issues of dynasticism and legitimacy to rule occupying a space front and centre in its institutional concerns. Transgression against religious codes also risked wider religious and societal discontent and the triggering of further criticism, if regularly and openly flouted. Consequently, the stakes remained high for a monarch of any sexual persuasion or activity because even close, platonic relationships could expect to be analysed and interrogated ad nauseam for fear of deviance and potentially providing opportunities for a monarch's enemies to attack and destabilise sovereignty and power.[49]

Taken as a whole, this collection aims to demonstrate the various ways in which historians of royalty, gender, sexuality, culture, and politics might investigate premodern sexualities. It aims to lay down some durable foundations, particularly on a terminological basis, for wider studies into the ways that sexualities of the past have been represented, criticised, and memorialised. At its heart, it marries literary analysis and historiography, admittedly largely based in Western European case studies (with the notable exception of Rhorchi's Muslim al-Andalusian case study), highlighting the important idea of 'paradoxical reality' – one of the threads binding together this book. It is hoped that our contributions encourage and stimulate further discussion and research into premodern sexualities by taking account of a more diverse and indeed global theatre waiting to be explored. The editors and contributors of this volume eagerly anticipate continued investigations into gender and sexualities from a wider source base, with legal records and further literary and socio-cultural studies offering opportunities for us to investigate and consider. Ultimately, this collection seeks to shed light into persistent darkened corners to reveal how integral and important sexualities were to identity formation and the construction of power in the premodern world.

Notes

1 Michel Foucault, *L'Histoire de la sexualité*, 4 vols. (Paris: Gallimard, 1976–1984). For the English version consult Robert Hurley's translations: Vol. 1 *An Introduction – The Will to Knowledge*; Vol. 2: *The Uses of Pleasure*; Vol. 3 *The Care of the Self*; and Vol. 4 *Confessions of the Flesh* (reprint: London: Vintage, 1990–2022).

2 Foucault, *An Introduction*, 49. For a recent insight into aspects of the history of sexuality and religious scepticism consult Umberto Grassi, 'The Fall from Grace: Religious Skepticism and Sexuality in the Early Modern Mediterranean World', *Journal of Early Modern History* 26.6 (2021): 471–491, available at https://doi.org/10.1163/15700658-bja10040 (accessed 27 November 2023).

3 John E. Boswell, *Christianity, Social Tolerance and Homosexuality: Gay People in Western Europe from the Beginning of the Christian Era to the Fourteenth Century* (Chicago: University of Chicago Press, 1980). For some core works, see Jacqueline Murray and Konrad Eisenbichler, eds, *Desire and Discipline: Sex and Sexuality in the Premodern West* (Toronto: University of Toronto Press, 1996); Ruth Mazo Karras, *Sexuality in Medieval Europe. Doing Unto Others*, 2nd edn (Abingdon: Routledge, 2012); Eve Kosofsky Sedgwick, *Between Men: English Literature and Male Homosocial Desire* (New York: Columbia University Press, 1985); Eve Kosofsky Sedgwick, *Epistemology of the Closet* (Los Angeles:

University of California Press, 1990); Kim Philips and Barry Reay, *Sex Before Sexuality. A Premodern History* (Cambridge: Polity Press, 2011).

4 Jeffery Cisneros, 'John Boswell: Posting Historical Landmarks at the Leading Edge of the Culture Wars', *Journal of the National Collegiate Honors Council* 14.1 (2013): 53–79, available at https://digitalcommons.unl.edu/nchcjournal/381 (accessed 27 November 2023).

5 We acknowledge and thank our anonymous reader for this generous clarification. See Matthew Kuefler, 'The Boswell Thesis', in *The Boswell Thesis: Essays on Christianity, Social Tolerance, and Homosexuality*, ed. Matthew Kuefler (Chicago: Chicago University Press, 2006) 1–31, at 9–11; and Carolyn Dinshaw, 'Touching on the Past', in *The Boswell Thesis*, 57–73. See also the recent and thought-provoking study that concerns itself with the relations between the seasons and sexual differences, conceptualising the seasons as gendered and the climatically ordered procession of the seasons as transgender change as having a direct effect on the bodies of people; François•e Charmaille, 'Trans Climates of the European Middle Ages, 500–1300', *Speculum. A Journal of Medieval Studies* 98.3 (2023): 695–726.

6 See for example, Louise Fradenburg and Carla Freccero, eds, *Premodern Sexualities* (New York & London: Routledge, 1996); Bruce R. Smith, 'Premodern Sexualities', *PMLA* 115.3 (2000): 318–329; Satu Lidman, Meri Heinonen, Tom Linkinem, and Marjo Kaartinen, eds, *Framing Premodern Desires: Sexual Ideas, Attitudes, and Practices in Europe* (Amsterdam: Amsterdam University Press, 2017); Megan Moore, ed., *Gender in the Premodern Mediterranean* (Chicago: ACMRS Press, 2019); Felipe Rojas and Peter E. Thompson, eds, *Queering the Medieval Mediterranean: Transcultural Sea of Sex, Gender, Identity, and Culture* (Leiden: Brill 2021); Justine Howe, ed., *The Routledge Handbook of Islam and Gender* (London: Routledge, 2020); Suad Joseph, Marilyn L. Booth, Bahar Davary, Hoda El Sadda, Sarah Gualtieri, Virginia Hooker, Therese Saliba, and Elora Shehabuddin, eds, *Women in Islamic Cultures: Disciplinary Paradigms and Approaches: 2003–2013* (Leiden: Brill, 2013); Zahra Ayubi, 'De-Universalising Male Normativity: Feminist Methodologies for Studying Masculinity in Premodern Islamic Ethics Texts', *Journal of Islamic Ethics* 4 (2020): 66–97; and Josiah Blackmore and Gregory S. Hutcheson, eds, *Queer Iberia: Sexualities, Cultures, and Crossings from the Middle Ages to the Renaissance* (Durham, NC: Duke University Press, 1999). For other works focusing on cases apart from western Europe and the Iberian Peninsula consider, for example, Nwando Achebe, *Female Monarchs and Merchant Queens in Africa* (Athens, OH: University of Ohio Press, 2020); Stephen Murray and Will Roscoe, *Boy Wives and Female Husbands: Studies of African Sexualities* (New York: St Martin's Press, 1998); Bret Hinsch, *Passions of the Cut Sleeve: The Male Homosexual Tradition in China* (Oakland, CA: University of California Press, 1992); Ndubueze L. Mbah, 'African Masculinities', *Oxford Research Encyclopedia of African History* (Oxford: Oxford University Press, 2019), available at https://doi.org/10.1093/acrefore/9780190277734.013.270 (accessed 27 November 2023); Gary P. Leupp, *Male Colors: The Construction of Homosexuality in Tokugawa Japan* (Oakland,

CA: University of California Press, 1995); R. B. Parkinson, 'Homosexual Desire and Middle Kingdom Literature', *Journal of Egyptian Archaeology* 81 (1995): 57–76; Marc David Baer, *The Ottomans: Khans, Caesars, and Caliphs* (New York: Basic Books, 2021); and Ruth Morgan and Saskia Wieringa, eds, *Tommy Boys, Lesbian Men and Ancestral Wives: Female Sex Practices in Africa* (Johannesburg, SA: Jacara Media, 2005).

7 Katia Wright, Edward Legon, and Matthew Storey, eds, *Royal Studies Journal*, Special Issue: 'Ruling Sexualities', 6.2 (2019).

8 See Marion Chaigne-Legouy, 'Le 'Dossier Agnès Sorel'. État de la question et perspectives de recherche', in *Maîtresses et favorites dans les coulisses du pouvoir du Moyen Âge à l'Époque moderne*, ed. Juliette Dor, Marie-Elisabeth Henneau, and Alain Marchandisse (Saint-Étienne: Presses de l'Université de Saint-Étienne, 2019), 171–184, esp. 178, 181–183. See also Zita Eva Rohr, 'From *Mignonnes* to *Mesdames*: The Rise of the Female Royal Favourite in Late Medieval and Early Modern France', *Parergon* 39.1 (2022): 155–189.

9 Niccolò Machiavelli, 'In What Mode Faith Should Be Kept by Princes', in *The Prince*, trans. with an Introduction by Harvey C. Mansfield, 2nd edn (Chicago: University of Chicago Press, 1998), 68–71.

10 Zita Eva Rohr and Jonathan Spangler quoting Kevin Jenkins, *On 'What is History?': From Carr and Elton to Rorty and White* (London and New York: Routledge, 1995), 16, in Zita Eva Rohr and Jonathan W. Spangler, 'Introduction: Significant Others: Aspects of Deviance and Difference in Premodern Court Cultures. Tales of the Unexpected?' in Zita Eva Rohr and Jonathan W. Spangler, eds, *Significant Others: Aspects of Deviance and Difference in Premodern Court Cultures* (Abingdon: Routledge, 2022), 1–26, at 7.

11 Rachel E. Moss, '"And much more I am soryat for my good knyghts": Fainting, Homosociality, and Elite Male Culture in Middle English Romance', *Historical Reflections/Réflexions Historiques* 42.1 (2016): 101–113; Rachel E. Moss, 'Ready to Disport with You: Homosocial Culture amongst the Wool Merchants of Fifteenth-century Calais', *History Workshop Journal* 86 (2018): 1–21; Gabrielle Storey, 'Questioning Terminologies: Homosocial and "Homosexual" Bonds in the Royal Bedchamber and Kingship in Medieval England and France', *Royal Studies Journal* 9.1 (2022): 33–45.

12 Grassi, 'The Fall from Grace', 491.

13 Grassi, 'The Fall from Grace', 491.

14 Grassi, 'The Fall from Grace', 473.

15 Grassi, 'The Fall from Grace', 473.

16 See Michael R. Evans, *Inventing Eleanor. The Medieval and Post-Medieval Image of Eleanor of Aquitaine* (London: Bloomsbury, 2014); Gabrielle Storey, 'Co-Rulership, Co-operation and Competition: Queenship in the Emerging Angevin Domains, 1135–1230' (PhD diss., University of Winchester, 2020), chapter 3. For further exploration of Eleanor's depiction in historical fiction, see Gabrielle Storey, 'Oh to be a Queen: Representations of Eleanor of Aquitaine and Isabella of Angoulême, Two Scandalous Queens, in Popular Fiction', in *Memorialising Premodern Monarchs: Medias of Commemoration and Remembrance*, ed.

Gabrielle Storey (Cham, Switzerland: Palgrave Macmillan, 2021), 265–290; and Gabrielle Storey, '(Mis)Representing Queens: The Untold Lives of the Empress Matilda and Eleanor of Aquitaine', *Parergon* 39.1 (2022): 191–207.

17 Rumour and gossip could be used by women against other women as well as by male critics and political competitors. See Zita Eva Rohr, 'True Lies and Strange Mirrors: The Uses and Abuses of Rumor, Propaganda, and Innuendo During the Closing Stages of the Hundred Years War', in *Queenship, Gender, and Reputation in the Medieval and Early Modern West, 1060–1600*, ed. Zita Eva Rohr and Lisa Benz (Cham, Switzerland: Palgrave Macmillan, 2016), 51–76.

18 Henric Bagerius and Christine Ekholst, 'The Unruly Queen: Blanche of Namur and Dysfunctional Rulership in Medieval Sweden', in *Queenship, Gender, and Reputation in the Medieval and Early Modern West, 1060–1600*, 99–118, at 99–100.

19 Henric Bagerius and Christine Ekholst, 'For Better or For Worse. Royal marital sexuality as political critique in late medieval Europe', in *The Routledge History of Monarchy*, ed. Elena Woodacre, Lucinda H. S. Dean, Chris Jones, Russell E. Martin, and Zita Eva Rohr (Abingdon: Routledge, 2019), at 648. See also Henric Bagerius and Christine Ekholst, 'Kings and Favourites: Politics and Sexuality in Late Medieval Europe', *Journal of Medieval History* 43.3 (2017): 298–319.

20 See Theresa Earenfight and Kristin Geaman, 'Neither heir nor spare: childless queens and the practice of monarchy in pre-modern Europe', in *Routledge History of Monarchy*, 518–533.

21 For Richard I, see John Gillingham, *Richard the Lionheart*, 2nd edn (London: Weidenfeld & Nicolson, 1989), for Louis VII see Ivan Gobry, *Louis VII, 1137–1180: Père de Philippe II Auguste* (Paris: Pygmalion, 2010).

22 See Fatima Rhorchi, 'Muslim Caliphs and Homosexuality: al-Amin (r. 787–813) and al-Hakam II (r. 915–976), Two men in pursuit of *hub al-walad*', chapter 7 in this volume.

23 Valerie Traub, 'The New Unhistoricism in Queer Studies', *PMLA* 128.1 (2013): 21–39, at 23.

24 See Rohr and Spangler, 'Introduction', 1–26, at 4–10.

25 See for example, Meriem Pagès, 'Navigating Gender in the Mediterranean: Exploring Hybrid Identities in *Aucassin et Nicolete*', in *Gender in the Premodern Mediterranean*, ed. Megan Moore (Chicago: ACMRS Press, 2019), 119–36; and Jacqueline Grace Victor, 'Female Fictions: Gender and Adventure in Twelfth and Thirteenth Century Old French Romance' (PhD diss., University of Chicago, 2020). See also Rosalind Brown-Grant, *French Romance of the Later Middle Ages: Gender, Morality, and Desire* (Oxford: Oxford University Press, 2008).

26 Rohr and Spangler, 'Introduction', 4.

27 Storey, 'Questioning Terminologies', 37.

28 See the recent essay by François•e Charmaille, 'Trans Climates of the European Middle Ages, 500–1300', *Speculum. A Journal of Medieval Studies* 98.3 (2023): 695–726, which discusses the relations between the seasons and sexual differences in humans.

29 See, for example, Ping Yao, 'Changing Views on Sexuality in Early and Medieval China', *Journal of Daoist Studies* 8 (2015): 52–68, available at https://doi.org/10.1353/dao.2015.0002, accessed 27 November 2023; and Katherine Crawford, 'Privilege, Possibility, and Perversion: Rethinking the Study of Early Modern Sexuality', *Journal of Modern History* 78.2 (2006): 412–433, available at www.journals.uchicago.edu/doi/abs/10.1086/505802 (accessed 27 November 2023).

30 Katherine Harvey, *The Fires of Lust: Sex in the Middle Ages* (London: Reaktion Books, 2021), 25.

31 For recent work on Elagabalus and others see Domitilla Campanile, Filippo Carlà-Uhink, and Margherita Facella, eds, *TransAntiquity: Cross-Dressing and Transgender Dynamics in the Ancient World* (Abingdon: Routledge, 2017) and Martijn Icks, *The Crimes of Elagabalus: The Life and Legacy of Rome's Decadent Boy Emperor* (London: I.B. Taurus, 2011). For Edward II, see Gwilym Dodd and Anthony Musson, eds, *The Reign of Edward II: New Perspectives* (York: York Medieval Press, 2006). For Isabeau of Bavaria see the many publications of Tracy Adams and Rachel Gibbons, and for Empress Theodora see David Potter, *Theodora. Actress, Empress, Saint* (Oxford: Oxford University Press, 2015).

32 We need only to look to recent (over)heated and partisan discussions concerning the Netflix series, *The Crown*. See the recent article by Rampazzo Gambarato and Heuman, 'Beyond fact and fiction: Cultural memory and transmedia ethics in Netflix's The Crown', *European Journal of Cultural Studies* (2022) at https://doi.org/10.1177/13675494221128332 (accessed 27 November 2023). Even more recently, consider the emergence of the Netflix series, *Harry & Meghan*, which seeks to lay bare the truth of the 'love story' of the current Duke and Duchess of Sussex as well as the duke's personal memoir and exploration of his life as the second son of the then heir to the throne (now King Charles III) and his ambiguous position as a spare heir within the royal family. *Harry & Meghan. A Royal Love Story*, docuseries directed by Liz Garbus for Netflix, first aired 8 and 15 December 2022; and Prince Harry, Duke of Sussex, *Spare* (New York: Penguin Random House, 2023).

33 Louise Tingle, 'Royal Women, Intercession, and Patronage in England, 1328–1394' (Cardiff University: unpublished PhD thesis, 2019), 78, quoting Katherine J. Lewis, 'Becoming a Virgin King: Richard II and Edward the Confessor', in *Gender and Holiness: Men, Women and Saints in Late Medieval Europe*, ed. Samantha J. Riches and Sarah Salih (London: Routledge, 2002), 86–100.

34 See John M. Bowers, 'Chaste Marriage: Fashion and Texts at the Court of Richard II', *Pacific Coast Philology* 30.1 (1995): 15–26; and Louise Tingle, 'Royal Women, Intercession, and Patronage', 51–63.

35 See Lewis, 'Becoming a Virgin King'.

36 Stephen Baxter, 'Edward the Confessor and the Succession Question', in *Edward the Confessor: The Man and the Legend*, ed. Richard Mortimer (Woodbridge: Boydell Press, 2009), 77–118, at 84–85.

37 For Henry Richards Luard's translation see H. R. Luard, ed., *The Lives of Edward the Confessor* (London: Longman, Brown, Green, Longmans, and Roberts, 1858; Reprint Cambridge: Cambridge University Press, 2012).

38 Luard, *Edward the Confessor*.
39 See Gobry, *Louis VII*; Lindy Grant, *Abbot Suger of St-Denis: Church and State in Early Twelfth-Century France* (London: Routledge, 1998), 37, 50; and Peggy McCracken, 'Scandalizing Desire: Eleanor of Aquitaine and the Chroniclers', in *Eleanor of Aquitaine: Lord and Lady*, ed. Bonnie Wheeler and John Carmi Parsons (New York: Palgrave Macmillan, 2003), 247–263.
40 Charlotte Backerra, 'Disregarding Norms: Emperor Charles VI and His Intimate Relationships', *Royal Studies Journal* 6.2 (2019): 74–88.
41 This does vary by time and place. The Empress Matilda was accepted as heir to her father Henry I in England and Normandy in the early twelfth century. Iberia provides a strong precedent for female rule from the medieval period onwards, and by the early modern period it is evident that women could succeed to the throne, if not always with ease. For more on royal dynasticism, see Ana Maria S.A. Rodrigues, Manuela Santos Silva, and Jonathan W. Spangler, eds, *Dynastic Change. Legitimacy and Gender in Medieval and Early Modern Monarchy* (Abingdon: Routledge, 2020).
42 See Rohr, 'From *Mignonnes* to *Mesdames*', 160.
43 The reputation and legacy of Isabella in France has fascinated many historians. See for example, Sophie Menache, 'Isabella of France, Queen of England – a Reconsideration', *Journal of Medieval History* 10.2 (1984): 107–124; Sophie Menache, 'Isabella of France, Queen of England. A Postscript', *Revue belge de philologie et d'histoire* 90.2 (2012): 493–512; and Kathryn Warner, *Isabella of France: The Rebel Queen* (Stroud: Amberley Publishing, 2016).
44 See Núria Silleras-Fernández, *Power, Piety, and Patronage in Late Medieval Queenship: Maria de Luna* (New York: Palgrave Macmillan, 2008); and Núria Silleras-Fernández, *Chariots of Ladies: Francesc Eiximenis and the Court of Culture of Medieval and Early Modern Iberia* (Ithaca, NY: Cornell University Press, 2015).
45 See for example the case of Malaysian opposition leader Anwar Ibrahim whose trials for sodomy and abuse of power ran from 1998 to 2015. Mark Trowell, *The Prosecution of Anwar Ibrahim: The Final Play* (Singapore: Marshall Cavendish International (Asia), 2015).
46 See Jean d'Arras, trans. and ed. Donald Maddox and Sara Sturm Maddox, *Melusine; or, the Noble History of Lusignan* (University Park, PA: Pennsylvania State University Press, 2012); Donald Maddox and Sara Sturm-Maddox, eds, *Melusine of Lusignan: Founding Fiction in Late Medieval France* (Athens, GA: University of Georgia Press, 1996); and Lydia Zeldenrust, *The Mélusine Romance in Medieval Europe: Translation, Circulation, and Material Contexts* (Woodbridge: D.S. Brewer, 2020).
47 With a nod to the subtitle of Rosalind Brown-Grant's foundational study on these themes: Rosalind Brown-Grant, *French Romance of the Later Middle Ages: Gender, Morality, and Desire.* (Oxford: Oxford University Press, 2008).
48 For comparative work see, for example, Rojas and Thompson, *Queering the Medieval Mediterranean*; Khaled El-Rouayheb, *Before Homosexuality in the Arab-Islamic World, 1500–1800* (Chicago: University of Chicago Press, 2005);

Everett K. Rowson and J.W. Wright, eds, *Homoeroticism in Classical Arabic Literature* (New York: Columbia University Press, 1997); Stephen O. Murray and Will Roscoe, eds, *Islamic Homosexualities: Culture, History, and Literature* (New York: New York University Press, 1997); Robert Mills, *Seeing Sodomy in the Middle Ages* (Chicago: University of Chicago Press, 2015); Robert Aldrich, ed., *Gay Life and Culture: A World History* (London: Thames & Hudson, 2006); and Frederik Roden, ed., *Jewish/Christian/Queer: Crossroads and Identities* (Farnham: Ashgate Publishing, 2009).

49 See Rohr and Spangler, *Significant Others*, and Rohr and Benz, *Queenship, Gender, and Reputation*.

Bibliography

Primary sources

Arras, Jean d'. *Melusine; or, the Noble History of Lusignan*. Trans. and ed. Donald Maddox and Sara Sturm-Maddox. University Park, PA: Pennsylvania State University Press, 2012.

Foucault, Michel. *L'Histoire de la sexualité*. 4 volumes. Paris: Gallimard, 1976–1984.

Foucault, Michel. *The History of Sexuality*. Volume 1 *An Introduction*. Volume 2 *The Uses of Pleasure*. Volume 3 *The Care of the Self*. and Volume 4 *Confessions of the Flesh*. Trans. Robert Hurley. London: Vintage, 1990–2022.

Harry & Megan. Six-episode docuseries directed by Liz Garbus for Netflix. 2022.

Luard, Henry Richards, ed. *The Lives of Edward the Confessor*. London: Longman, Brown, Green, Longmans, and Roberts, 1858. Reprinted Cambridge: Cambridge University Press, 2012.

Machiavelli, Niccolò. 'In What Mode Faith Should Be Kept by Princes'. In *The Prince*. Translated and with an Introduction by Harvey C. Mansfield. 2nd edn, 68–71. Chicago: University of Chicago Press, 1998.

Prince Harry. Duke of Sussex, *Spare*. New York: Penguin Random House, 2023.

Secondary sources

Achebe, Nwando. *Female Monarchs and Merchant Queens in Africa*. Athens, OH: University of Ohio Press, 2020.

Adams, Tracy, *The Life and Afterlife of Isabeau of Bavaria*. Baltimore, MD: Johns Hopkins University Press, 2010.

Aldrich, Robert, ed. *Gay Life and Culture: A World History*. London: Thames & Hudson, 2006.

Ayubi, Zahra. 'De-Universalising Male Normativity: Feminist Methodologies for Studying Masculinity in Premodern Islamic Ethics Texts'. *Journal of Islamic Ethics* 4 (2020): 66–97.

Backerra, Charlotte. 'Disregarding Norms: Emperor Charles VI and His Intimate Relationships'. *Royal Studies Journal* 6.2 (2019): 74–88.

Baer, Marc David. *The Ottomans: Khans, Caesars, and Caliphs*. New York: Basic Books, 2021.

Bagerius, Henric, and Ekholst, Christine. 'The Unruly Queen: Blanche of Namur and Dysfunctional Rulership in Medieval Sweden'. In *Queenship, Gender, and Reputation in the Medieval and Early Modern West, 1060–1600*, ed. Zita Eva Rohr and Lisa Benz, 99–118. Cham, Switzerland: Palgrave Macmillan, 2016.

Bagerius, Henric, and Ekholst, Christine. 'Kings and Favourites: Politics and Sexuality in Late Medieval Europe'. *Journal of Medieval History* 43.3 (2017): 298–319.

Bagerius, Henric, and Ekholst, Christine. 'For Better or For Worse. Royal marital sexuality as political critique in late medieval Europe'. In *The Routledge History of Monarchy*, ed. Elena Woodacre, Lucinda H.S. Dean, Chris Jones, Russell E. Martin, and Zita Eva Rohr, 636–654. Abingdon: Routledge, 2019.

Baxter, Stephen. 'Edward the Confessor and the Succession Question'. In *Edward the Confessor: The Man and the Legend*, ed. Richard Mortimer, 77–118. Woodbridge: Boydell Press, 2009.

Blackmore, Josiah and Gregory S. Hutcheson, eds. *Queer Iberia: Sexualities, Cultures, and Crossings from the Middle Ages to the Renaissance*. Durham, NC: Duke University Press, 1999.

Boswell, John E. *Christianity, Social Tolerance and Homosexuality: Gay People in Western Europe from the Beginning of the Christian Era to the Fourteenth Century*. Chicago: University of Chicago Press, 1980.

Bowers, John M. 'Chaste Marriage: Fashion and Texts at the Court of Richard II'. *Pacific Coast Philology* 30.1 (1995): 15–26.

Brown-Grant, Rosalind. *French Romance of the Later Middle Ages: Gender, Morality, and Desire*. Oxford: Oxford University Press, 2008.

Campanile, Domitilla, Filippo Carlà-Uhink, and Margherita Facella, eds. *TransAntiquity: Cross-Dressing and Transgender Dynamics in the Ancient World*. Abingdon: Routledge, 2017.

Chaigne-Legouy, Marion. 'Le 'Dossier Agnès Sorel'. État de la question et perspectives de recherche'. In *Maîtresses et favorites dans les coulisses du pouvoir du Moyen Âge à l'Époque moderne*, ed. Juliette Dor, Marie-Elisabeth Henneau, and Alain Marchandisse, 171–184. Saint-Étienne: Presses de l'Université de Saint-Étienne, 2019.

Charmaille, François•e. 'Trans Climates of the European Middle Ages, 500–1300'. *Speculum. A Journal of Medieval Studies* 98.3 (2023): 695–726.

Cisneros, Jeffery. 'John Boswell: Posting Historical Landmarks at the Leading Edge of the Culture Wars'. *Journal of the National Collegiate Honors Council* 14.1 (2013): 53–79, available at https://digitalcommons.unl.edu/nchcjournal/381 (accessed 27 November 2023).

Crawford, Katherine. 'Privilege, Possibility, and Perversion: Rethinking the Study of Early Modern Sexuality'. *Journal of Modern History* 78.2 (2006): 412–433.

Dinshaw, Carolyn. 'Touching on the Past'. In *The Boswell Thesis: Essays on Christianity, Social Tolerance, and Homosexuality*, ed. Matthew Kuefler. Chicago: University of Chicago Press, 2006. 57–73.

Dodd, Gwilym, and Anthony Musson, eds. *The Reign of Edward II: New Perspectives*. York: York Medieval Press, 2006.

Earenfight, Theresa, and Kristin Geaman. 'Neither heir nor spare: childless queens and the practice of monarchy in pre-modern Europe'. In *The Routledge History of Monarchy*, ed. Elena Woodacre, Lucinda H. S. Dean, Chris Jones, Russell E. Martin, and Zita Eva Rohr, 518–533. Abingdon: Routledge, 2019.

El-Rouayheb, Khaled. *Before Homosexuality in the Arab-Islamic World, 1500–1800*. Chicago: University of Chicago Press, 2005.

Evans, Michael R. *Inventing Eleanor. The Medieval and Post-Medieval Image of Eleanor of Aquitaine*. London: Bloomsbury, 2014.

Fradenburg, Louise, and Carla Freccero, eds. *Premodern Sexualities*. London: Routledge, 1996.

Gibbons, Rachel C., 'The Active Queenship of Isabeau of Bavaria, 1392–1417', doctoral thesis, University of Reading, 1992.

Gibbons, Rachel C., 'Isabeau of Bavaria, Queen of France: Queenship and political authority as "Lieutenante-Générale" of the Realm', in *Queenship, Gender, and Reputation in the Medieval and Early Modern West, 1060–1600*, ed. Zita Eva Rohr and Lisa Benz, Cham CH: Palgrave Macmillan, 2016, 143–160.

Gillingham, John. *Richard the Lionheart*. 2nd edn. London: Weidenfeld & Nicolson, 1989.

Gobry, Ivan. *Louis VII, 1137–1180: Père de Philippe II Auguste*. Paris: Pygmalion, 2010.

Grant, Lindy. *Abbot Suger of St-Denis: Church and State in Early Twelfth-Century France*. London: Routledge, 1998.

Grassi, Umberto. 'The Fall From Grace: Religious Skepticism and Sexuality in the Early Modern Mediterranean World'. *Journal of Early Modern History* 26.6 (2021): 471–491. At https://doi.org/10.1163/15700658-bja10040 (accessed 27 November 2023).

Harty, Kevin J., ed. *Medieval Women on Film, Essays on Gender, Cinema and History*. Jefferson, NC: McFarland, 2020.

Harvey, Katherine. *The Fires of Lust: Sex in the Middle Ages*. London: Reaktion Books: 2021.

Hinsch, Bret. *Passions of the Cut Sleeve: The Male Homosexual Tradition in China*. Oakland, CA: University of California Press, 1992.

Howe, Justine ed. *The Routledge Handbook of Islam and Gender*. Abingdon: Routledge, 2020.

Icks, Martijn. *The Crimes of Elagabalus: The Life and Legacy of Rome's Decadent Boy Emperor*. London: I.B. Taurus, 2011.

Jenkins, Kevin. *On What is History: From Carr and Elton to Rorty and White*. New York: Routledge, 1995.

Joseph, Suad, Marilyn L. Booth, Bahar Davary, Hoda El Sadda, Sarah Gualtieri, Virginia Hooker, Therese Saliba, and Elora Shehabuddin, eds. *Women in Islamic Cultures: Disciplinary Paradigms and Approaches: 2003–2013*. Leiden: Brill, 2013.

Karras, Ruth Mazo. *Sexuality in Medieval Europe. Doing Unto Others*. 2nd edn. Abingdon: Routledge, 2012.

Kuefler, Matthew 'The Boswell Thesis'. In *The Boswell Thesis: Essays on Christianity, Social Tolerance, and Homosexuality*, ed. Matthew Kuefler, 1–31. Chicago: University of Chicago Press, 2006.

Leupp, Gary P. *Male Colors: The Construction of Homosexuality in Tokugawa Japan*. Oakland, CA: University of California Press, 1995.

Lewis, Katherine J. 'Becoming a Virgin King: Richard II and Edward the Confessor'. In *Gender and Holiness: Men, Women and Saints in Late Medieval Europe*, ed. Samantha J. Riches and Sarah Salih, 86–100. London: Routledge, 2002.

Lidman, Satu, Meri Heinonen, Tom Linkinen, and Marjo Kaartinen, eds. *Framing Premodern Desires: Sexual Ideas, Attitudes, and Practices in Europe*. Amsterdam: Amsterdam University Press, 2017.

Maddox, Donald and Sara Sturm-Maddox, eds. *Melusine of Lusignan: Founding Fiction in Medieval France*. Athens, GA: University of Georgia Press, 1996.

Mbah, Ndubueze L. 'African Masculinities'. *Oxford Research Encyclopedia of African History*. Oxford: Oxford University Press, 2019, available at https://doi.org/10.1093/acrefore/9780190277734.013.270 (accessed 27 November 2023).

McCracken, Peggy. 'Scandalizing Desire: Eleanor of Aquitaine and the Chroniclers'. *Eleanor of Aquitaine: Lord and Lady*, ed. Bonnie Wheeler and John Carmi Parsons, 247–263. New York: Palgrave Macmillan, 2003.

Menache, Sophie. 'Isabella of France, Queen of England – a Reconsideration'. *Journal of Medieval History* 10.2 (1984): 107–124.

Menache, Sophie. 'Isabella of France, Queen of England. A Postscript'. *Revue belge de philologie et d'histoire* 90.2 (2012): 493–512.

Mills, Robert. *Seeing Sodomy in the Middle Ages*. Chicago: University of Chicago Press, 2015.

Moore, Megan, ed. *Gender in the Premodern Mediterranean*. Chicago: ACMRS Press, 2019.

Morgan, Ruth and Saskia Wieringa, eds. *Tommy Boys, Lesbian Men and Ancestral Wives: Female Sex Practices in Africa*. Johannesburg, SA: Jacara Media, 2005.

Moss, Rachel E. '"And much more I am soryat for my good knyghts": Fainting, homosociality, and elite male culture in Middle English romance'. *Historical Reflections/Réflexions Historiques* 42.1 (2016): 101–113.

Moss, Rachel E. 'Ready to Disport with You: Homosocial culture amongst the wool merchants of fifteenth-century Calais'. *History Workshop Journal* 86 (2018): 1–21.

Murray, Jacqueline, and Konrad Eisenbichler, eds. *Desire and Discipline: Sex and sexuality in the premodern West*. Toronto: University of Toronto Press, 1996.

Murray, Stephen O. and Will Roscoe, eds. *Islamic Homosexualities: Culture, history, and literature*. New York: New York University Press, 1997.

Murray, Stephen O. and Will Roscoe, eds. *Boy Wives and Female Husbands: Studies of African sexualities*. New York: St Martins Press, 1998.

North, Janice, Karl C. Alvestad, and Elena Woodacre, eds. *Premodern Rulers and Postmodern Viewers. Gender, sex, and power in popular culture*. Basingstoke: Palgrave Macmillan, 2018.

Pagès, Meriem. 'Navigating Gender in the Mediterranean: Exploring hybrid identities in *Aucassin et Nicolete*'. In *Gender in the Premodern Mediterranean*, ed. Megan Moore, 119–136. Chicago: ACMRS Press, 2019.

Parkinson, R.B. 'Homosexual Desire and Middle Kingdom Literature'. *Journal of Egyptian Archaeology* 81 (1995): 57–76.

Philips, Kim, and Barry Reay. *Sex Before Sexuality. A premodern history*. Cambridge: Polity Press, 2011.

Potter, David. *Theodora. Actress, empress, saint*. Oxford: Oxford University Press, 2015.

Rampazzo Gambarato, Renira, and Johannes Heuman. 'Beyond fact and fiction: Cultural memory and transmedia ethics in Netflix's The Crown'. *European Journal of Cultural Studies* (2022), available at https://doi.org/10.1177/13675494221128332 (accessed 27 November 2023).

Roden, Frederick, ed. *Jewish/Christian/Queer: Crossroads and identities*. Farnham: Ashgate Publishing, 2009.

Rodrigues, Ana Maria S.A., Manuela Santos Silva, and Jonathan W. Spangler, eds. *Dynastic Change. Legitimacy and gender in medieval and early modern monarchy*. Abingdon: Routledge, 2020.

Rohr, Zita Eva. 'True Lies and Strange Mirrors: The uses and abuses of rumor, propaganda, and innuendo during the closing stages of the Hundred Years War'. In *Queenship, Gender, and Reputation in the Medieval and Early Modern West, 1060–1600*, ed. Zita Eva Rohr and Lisa Benz, 51–76. Cham, Switzerland: Palgrave Macmillan, 2016.

Rohr, Zita Eva. 'From *Mignonnes* to *Mesdames*: The rise of the female royal favourite in late medieval and early modern France'. *Parergon* 39.1 (2022): 155–189.

Rohr, Zita Eva and Lisa Benz, eds. *Queenship and the Women of Westeros: Female agency and advice in Game of Thrones and A Song of Ice and Fire*. Cham, Switzerland: Palgrave Macmillan, 2020.

Rohr, Zita Eva, and Jonathan W. Spangler. 'Introduction. Significant Others: Aspects of deviance and difference in premodern court cultures – tales of the unexpected?' In *Significant Others: Aspects of deviance and difference in premodern court cultures*, ed. Zita Eva Rohr and Jonathan W. Spangler, 1–26. Abingdon: Routledge, 2022.

Rojas, Felipe and Peter E. Thompson, eds. *Queering the Medieval Mediterranean: Transcultural sea of sex, gender, identity, and culture*. Leiden: Brill 2021.

Rowson, Everett K., and J.W. Wright, eds. *Homoeroticism in Classical Arabic Literature*. New York: Columbia University Press, 1997.

Russo, Stephanie. *The Afterlife of Anne Boleyn. Representations of Anne Boleyn in Fiction and on the Screen*. Cham: Switzerland: Palgrave Macmillan, 2020.

Sedgwick, Eve Kosofsky. *Between Men: English literature and male homosocial desire*. New York: Columbia University Press, 1985.

Sedgwick, Eve Kosofsky. *Epistemology of the Closet*. Los Angeles: University of California Press, 1990.

Silleras-Fernández, Núria. *Power, Piety, and Patronage in Late Medieval Queenship: Maria de Luna*. New York: Palgrave Macmillan, 2008.

Silleras-Fernández, Núria. *Chariots of Ladies: Francesc Eiximenis and the court of culture of medieval and early modern Iberia*. Ithaca, NY: Cornell University Press. 2015.

Smith, Bruce R. 'Premodern Sexualities'. *PMLA* 115.3 (2000): 318–329.

Storey, Gabrielle. 'Co-Rulership, Co-operation and Competition: Queenship in the emerging Angevin domains, 1135–1230'. University of Winchester, unpublished PhD thesis, 2020.

Storey, Gabrielle. 'Oh to be a Queen: Representations of Eleanor of Aquitaine and Isabella of Angoulême, two scandalous queens, in popular fiction'. In *Memorialising Premodern Monarchs: Medias of commemoration and remembrance*, ed. Gabrielle Storey, 265–290. Cham, Switzerland: Palgrave Macmillan, 2021.

Storey, Gabrielle. 'Questioning Terminologies: Homosocial and "homosexual" bonds in the royal bedchamber and kingship in medieval England and France'. *Royal Studies Journal* 9.1 (2022): 33–45.

Storey, Gabrielle. '(Mis)Representing Queens: The untold lives of the Empress Matilda and Eleanor of Aquitaine'. *Parergon* 39.1 (2022): 191–207.

Tingle, Louise. 'Royal Women, Intercession, and Patronage in England, 1328–1394'. Cardiff University, unpublished PhD thesis, 2019.

Traub, Valerie. 'The New Unhistoricism in Queer Studies'. *PMLA* 128.1 (2013): 21–39.

Trowell, Mark. *The Prosecution of Anwar Ibrahim: The Final Play*. Singapore: Marshall Cavendish International (Asia), 2015.

Victor, Jacqueline Grace. 'Female Fictions: Gender and Adventure in Twelfth and Thirteenth Century Old French Romance'. University of Chicago: unpublished PhD thesis, 2020.

Warner, Kathryn. *Isabella of France: The Rebel Queen*. Stroud: Amberley Publishing, 2016.

Wingard, Tess. 'The Trans Middle Ages: Incorporating Transgender and Intersex Studies into the History of Medieval Sexuality'. *English Historical Review* 138.593 (2023): 933–951.

Woodacre, Elena. 'Saints or Sinners? Sexuality, Reputation and Representation of Queens from Contemporary Sources to Modern Media'. *De Medio Aevo* 10.2 (2022): 371–385.

Wright, Katia, Edward Legon, and Matthew Storey, eds. *Royal Studies Journal*. 'Ruling Sexualities' [special issue], 6.2 (2019).

Yao, Ping. 'Changing Views on Sexuality in Early and Medieval China'. *Journal of Daoist Studies* 8 (2015): 52–68.

Zeldenrust, Lydia. *The Mélusine Romance in Medieval Europe: Translation, Circulation, and Material Contexts*. Woodbridge: D.S. Brewer, 2020.

Part I

Scandal, perception, and representation

1

'And though she made use of three openings ...': how and why to sexualise a Late-Antique empress

Alexander Thies

The period frequently defined as Late Antiquity saw not only the decline of Roman imperial power in the Western Roman Empire, but also its parallel transformation into the Greek-dominated Byzantine Empire of the Middle Ages.[1] A characteristic feature of the Late-Antique period was the increasing relevance of empresses.[2] Imperial women such as Zenobia, Helena, Pulcheria, Galla Placidia and, above all, Theodora, were not only considered exceptional by their contemporaries; they also acquired even greater recognition in posthumous art, literature, and historiography.[3]

Unsurprisingly, these empresses gained high prominence in their contemporary literary traditions. The 'classicising historiography' of Late Antiquity (so defined because of its use of artificial and conservative 'classical' language aimed at imitating the Greek historians Thucydides and Herodot, though these historians wrote in various languages) criticised these empresses often through sexual slander.[4] Scholars of Late Antiquity have put forward several considerations as to why classicising authors portrayed these female rulers as sexually deprived, nymphomaniacs, and/or incestuous.[5] However, a comparative study of this practice of sexual slander has yet to be written and remains a desideratum. Such an examination would provide new insights into the reasons why classicising historians resorted to sexual slander and what led them to target some empresses and not others. The aim of this chapter, therefore, is to explore Late Antique sexual slander deployed against certain empresses in classicising historiography and to investigate their authors' possible motives.

The argument put forward by this chapter is twofold. Firstly, it introduces these classicising authors and their writings on Late Antique empresses, and surveys current research. Secondly, it suggests how theories on misogyny put forward by modern scholars of gender can help historians of Late Antiquity make sense of classicising sexual slander. This chapter demonstrates how misogynist speech enabled classicising authors to articulate and confirm their own group identity as a conservative imperial elite composed of the 'old' Roman senatorial nobility and a 'new' learned elite of bureaucrats and military men from the provinces. Despite the heterogeneous nature of this group, they all shared (or, at least, claimed to share) traditional premises on female sexual morality and the role of imperial women. Further, it will be noted how this misogynist speech served this elite to question past and present practices of imperial rule, and the crucial role that empresses had fulfilled in imperial representation.

Sexualising an empress: ancient notions and modern responses

In the year 360/61, the learned North African parvenu, Aurelius Victor, wrote the *Historiae abbreviatae* (also known as *De Caesaribus*), a *breviarium* (short historiographical piece) on the history of the Roman Empire. The *Historiae abbreviatae* included short but crucial commentaries on the reigns of Roman emperors since Augustus. In 361, as a reward for his outstanding services to Roman historiography, Emperor Julian elevated Victor to the rank of senator. Victor held several influential positions throughout his career and was even appointed *praefectus urbi* of Rome by Theodosius the Great, one of the most prestigious secular offices of Late Antiquity.[6] In his commentary on Caracalla's rule (r. 212–217), Aurelius Victor mentions the following episode targeting his imperial mother, Julia Domna:

> He [Caracalla] had the same fortune and wife as his father. For, captivated by her beauty, he made every effort to marry his stepmother Julia, whose crimes I have recorded above, since she, in her great eagerness for power, had showed herself unclothed to the gaze of the young man as if unaware of his presence. When he passionately declared, 'I should like, if I may, to (...) [make use of it] (though she actually said something much ruder: my modification)', she replied even more shamelessly, for she had stripped off her modesty with her clothes, 'You want to? Certainly you may.'[7]

Victor's account is remarkable in several respects. Firstly, an obvious error occurs when he refers to Julia Domna as Caracalla's stepmother (*noverca*). In fact, Julia Domna was Caracalla's biological mother; a factual misstep reflected in several other pieces of Roman imperial historiography (among others, the so-called *Historia Augusta*, discussed later in this chapter). The error probably first appeared in the so-called 'Enmann's Kaisergeschichte', a lost piece of Roman historiography that seems to have originated from within the senatorial milieu around 300. In the further course of Late Antiquity, this picture of the 'incestuous imperial couple' became very popular in later pagan and Christian historiography.[8] Secondly, in Victor's episodes, it appears as if Julia Domna sought to seduce her son (and succeeded) out of an unmitigated lust for power.[9] Thirdly, and moreover, in a short *breviarium* like Victor's, where the reader would expect accounts of military deeds and political life, this scandalous rumour was highlighted as key in characterising Caracalla's rule.

Scholars have paid little attention to what this sexual invective was meant to achieve other than to depict Julia Domna's alleged hunger for power (resulting from her allegedly 'oriental mentality')[10] or to expose Caracalla as a tyrant.[11] However, Victor's motives for inserting this episode into his *Historiae abbreviatae* can only be fully grasped if we compare it to similar misogynist invectives found in other examples of classicising historiography.

Writing approximately 200 years after Victor, around 550–560, another learned parvenu and one of the last classicising historians, Procopius of Caesarea, created an even more colourful and lascivious portrayal of an imperial woman, the late empress Theodora (d. 548), wife of the then-reigning emperor Justinian.[12] Procopius recounts several episodes from her life, beginning with the fact that, before meeting Justinian and becoming his mistress, later wife and empress, she was born the daughter of a bear keeper in the hippodrome of Constantinople. Allegedly, as a child, her mother had her trained as a stage dancer in the hippodrome.[13] As an adult, Theodora is said to have worked as a 'straightforward prostitute' (ἑταίρα εὐθὺς), offering herself to anyone who wanted her. Reportedly, she frequently undressed in public and engaged in sadomasochistic practices.[14] During intercourse, she always found new ways to pleasure men, which made her one of the most sought-after prostitutes in the capital. Procopius describes how, at a banquet, Theodora slept with ten young men in the first instance, to which she then added thirty more.[15] At another banquet featuring many noblemen, she leapt up and undressed before their eyes.[16] Procopius then states that 'and though she made use of three openings' of her body, she had wished nature had gifted her even larger breasts to provide men with additional sexual pleasure.[17] According to Procopius, she was often pregnant; however, she could always find a way to induce an abortion.[18] His invective then describes how, performing in the theatre, she stripped down to her loincloth and lay down. She then sprinkled crumbs on her loincloth and let geese peck at them in front of everyone.[19] Eventually, she became the courtesan of a provincial governor named Hekebolos of Tyros, who briefly took her on his travels. However, he dismissed her shortly afterwards, and she returned to Constantinople, where she met Justinian, who fell passionately in love with her.[20]

Procopius's invective sparks many questions and has understandably received more attention than Victor's short account focusing on Julia Domna. Contemporary writings by the Syriac author John of Ephesus describing

Theodora as a 'repentant sinner' from the *porneion* and a 'Mary Magdalene' archetype seem to suggest that parts of Procopius's account of her life were factually correct.[21] Scholars of Late Antiquity have agreed that Theodora probably had a background in *mimos* (μῖμος) acting and performing, which, during Late Antiquity, was often associated with prostitution and pornography. For example, the episode with the geese in the theatre could have been understood to be a humorous pornographic performance of the Leda myth in the *mimos*.[22]

Furthermore, the title of Procopius's writing, *Anekdota* (or *Historia Arcana*), and the author's introductory remarks make clear that he did not intend the writing to be published before the deaths of Theodora and Justinian. Throughout the *Anekdota*, Justinian is also condemned harshly, although not in a sexualised way.[23] Moreover, no surviving accounts confirm that the *Anekdota* was read and circulated during the sixth century. While contemporary writings do mention Procopius's wider historiographical output, there is no mention of the *Anekdota* in Late Antique sources.[24] This has led scholars to believe that, in the 550s, a conservative elite of senators, bureaucrats, and military men might have been plotting against Justinian. In the event of a successful coup, Procopius, who at the time was a renowned court panegyrist and aide-de-camp to Justinian's supreme general Belisarius, might have written the *Anekdota* as proof of his genuine anti-Justinian sentiments.[25] While this explanation holds a certain appeal, it fails to elucidate why Procopius decided to include such a graphic and detailed pornographic portrait of Theodora's supposed disorderly life, especially if he wished only to demonstrate his opposition to Justinian.

Among traditional scholars of Late Antiquity, the writings of the classicising historian Procopius have enjoyed considerable credibility. Compared to contemporary ecclesiastical historiography, Procopius's secular writings might have appeared to be a more reliable source for the period's history. In describing Theodora, these traditionalists have often resorted to modern categories, calling her the first *femme fatale* or a nymphomaniac.[26] Some of these views are still being shared by some more recent scholars who believe that Procopius was recounting a 'truth' that he did not dare articulate publicly until Theodora and Justinian were dead (paradoxically, however, Justinian outlived Procopius).[27] In psychoanalytical interpretations of Procopius's character, others suggest that the educated parvenu hated the uneducated lower class, and especially Theodora, who owed her social ascent to her sexual favours.[28]

Some other scholars have also sought to explain the *Anekdota*'s invective against Theodora by situating its writing in the context of imperial court literature. Like all classicising historians, Procopius was committed to the idea of the imitation (*mimesis*) of classical authors. His writings were thus bound to the rules of the genre of classical Roman historiography, which often operated through invectives against the rulers. At the same time, he also subverted the rules of another genre of classical Roman writing, the *panegyricus*, for the ruler. Instead, he created an anti-*panegyricus* which reads as a precursor for the *psogos* (ψόγος), the Byzantine genre of slander speech against the emperor.[29]

Following such approaches, Anne McClanan has compared Procopius's physical descriptions of Theodora to the later Byzantine descriptions of ideal imperial princesses found in Anna Komnene's writings. McClanan correctly suggests that it was precisely Theodora's public misdeeds (for example, her performances in the theatre in Constantinople) that clashed with the contemporary ideal of the upper-class woman as chaste and secluded, potentially destroying Theodora's imperial-sacred image.[30] However, such readings do not fully explain the functions of Procopius's invective against Theodora, especially since they also fail to take account of earlier fourth-century invectives against imperial women, such as Aurelius Victor's slander of Julia Domna discussed earlier. For this reason, we have to consider other approaches to understand the invectives.

Current debates on ancient sexualities: potentials and inabilities of explaining the empress's sexual transgression

An alternative approach has proven to be more promising. In the last few decades, scholars of Classical Antiquity have presented several studies of gender in the ancient world, contributing to a new perspective in understanding representations of women in the ancient world and perhaps for Late-Antique empresses in classicising historiography too. Emperors, empresses, and their extravagant sex lives had already made an appearance in the historiographical tradition of the early Empire. In the early Roman Empire, sexual anecdotes functioned as a form of character assassination, employed by authors such as the imperial biographer Suetonius to compromise a ruler's moral reputation (*fama*). Depending upon the described sexual practices, sexual anecdotes could function as praise for their assumed masculinity or defamation for their assumed effeminacy.[31] Similar studies operate by recourse to the highly influential 'penetration model' first developed by Kenneth Dover and popularised by Michel Foucault in *The Use of Pleasure*.[32] This model suggests that there was no contemporary understanding of the modern constructions of homosexuality or heterosexuality in Antiquity but that sexual practices were hierarchically ordered according to the active or passive role played by the participant in the sexual act: the person penetrating during the sexual act would be ascribed with typically masculine connotations, while the penetrated person took up a more feminine role. Historians such as Hartmut Ziche have argued that the penetration model can explain Procopius's invective against Theodora.[33] In actively seeking sexual intercourse, Theodora would have acquired male connotations in the eyes of the contemporary Late-Antique public. Therefore, Procopius's invective was directed against a masculine co-emperor ruling next to a diminished Justinian.

Developed initially to describe Greek male homosexuality, the 'penetration model', however, suggests a degree of empowerment through sexual acts that Late-Antique women often did not possess. While Julia Domna was said to have seduced her own son, Caracalla, it was he, according to Aurelius Victor, who ultimately desired the intercourse and took up the penetrating role in the sexual act. By the same token, Procopius may have described Theodora as a 'nymphomaniac', but she did not create the conditions for her renowned sexual performances. Instead, it is suggested that the all-male banquet participants from Constantinople had booked her as an exotic dancer for a sexual performance, and they were the ones who actively performed the act. Similarly, her relationship with the provincial governor Hekebolos was subject to a patriarchal power structure. As feminist anti-pornography scholars have observed in studies of contemporary pornography, Theodora's pornographic performance in the theatre was subordinated to the spectator's gaze and likely happened under coercion.[34] In summary, classicising historians such as Aurelius Victor or Procopius were not particularly concerned with imperial women taking up masculine traits, but rather sought to cast in opposition the two conceptions of femininity of their times: the hyper-sexual woman in her 'natural state' and the chaste, refined, educated, and consequently 'civilised' aristocratic woman.

With reference to the Republican and early Imperial gendered ideal of *pudicitia*, the classical historian Rebecca Langlands has developed an alternative model to explain the moral categorisation to which Roman women were subject.[35] *Pudicitia* is a difficult term to translate and conceptualise, as it rests upon the moralised sexual notion of shame (*pudor*) in Roman society. The transgression of *pudicitia* is usually characterised as a sexual transgression that threatens the social order of the *res publica*. Despite the possible methodological difficulties of applying a model developed for the Roman Republic and early Imperial period to Late Antiquity, it allows us to recognise continuities rather than ruptures in Roman morality. Significantly, Aurelius Victor points out that Julia Domna 'had stripped off her modesty (*pudor*) with her clothes'.[36] Stressing traditional ideas of *pudicitia*, this also downplays the role played by potentially new Christian moral conceptions of sin in Late-Antique invectives against empresses and highlights the continuities between the pagan early Empire and the Christian Late Antiquity, at least, in classicising historiography.[37] For example, in Theodora's case, the Judaeo-Christian tradition that condemns women as Eve(s) who can unleash the devil through their sexuality only plays a very marginal role in the background of her narrative.[38] Somewhat surprisingly, Procopius never draws a similar comparison.[39]

Still, the question of the function of these invectives remains unanswered. Why would Procopius and Aurelius Victor want to attack Theodora's and Julia Domna's *pudicitia* posthumously?

Misogynistic logic: self-assurance and the resistance of a conservative elite

Looking at how classicising historiographers articulated misogynistic ideas can shed new light on the aims and functions of Late-Antique invectives against empresses. The depiction of Julia Domna and Theodora in classicising historiography was motivated by misogynistic ideas shared across the Roman-Byzantine male elite.[40] The term misogyny should not be understood as thoughtless and general hatred against all women, as it is sometimes used now in everyday language. Instead, as Kate Manne has shown in her magistral study of the 'logic' of misogyny, it should be understood primarily as the 'law enforcement' branch of a patriarchal order, which has the overall function of policing and enforcing its governing norms and expectations.[41] Women are thus physically or publicly punished, shamed, and turned into negative examples when they defy the predominant patriarchal order.[42] Simultaneously, supporters of such patriarchal norms can promote positive counter-images of feminine behaviour and sexuality, strengthening the dominant order.[43]

In the denunciation of Julia Domna's and Theodora's sexual lives, Late-Antique classicising historiography also promoted other ideals of femininity and female sexuality. That was the case in the senatorial *Historia Augusta* for Zenobia of Palmyra (r. 267–272), who incorporated such ideals. The *Historia Augusta* was a series of emperor biographies written presumably by a single author in the fourth or fifth century, projecting back pagan-elitist discourses of their own time to the 2nd and 3rd centuries.[44] Here, the anonymous author stated:

> Such was her continence, it is said, that she would not know even her own husband save for the purpose of conception. For when once she had lain with him, she would refrain until the time of menstruation to see if she were pregnant; if not, she would again grant him an opportunity of begetting children.[45]

This image of the Queen of Palmyra and Roman usurper in the *Historia Augusta* was clearly idealised and operated through imaginative depictions of the Orient. The author of the *Historia Augusta* knew relatively little about Zenobia's life. Nevertheless, this construction of Zenobia as an idealised ruler presented her as a legitimate ruler, contrasting her with the contemporary Roman emperor Gallienus, whose rule in Rome was described as weak and unmanly.[46] The fact that Zenobia was allegedly a 'voluntary birthing machine' who had intercourse with her husband only for the purpose of reproduction turned her into a positive example in the eyes of the misogynistic senatorial elite. As such, female rule was not, therefore, necessarily irreconcilable with the patriarchal ideals of the imperial elite.

The descriptions of Julia Domna and Theodora by Aurelius Victor and Procopius served as negative examples of imperial women who had dared to challenge the Late-Antique patriarchy, foregrounding the association of the empress with the notion of *pudicitia*. According to Manne, the sexual-misogynistic invective against the two empresses would therefore represent the posthumous shaming and 'punishment' of two 'rebellious women'. This literary *damnatio memoriae* by means of hyper-sexualisation could have restored the patriarchal order by serving as an admonition for future empresses and as a statement of expectations directed towards imperial women. The aim of the invectives against Julia Domna and Theodora was, consequently, to exclude the two deviant women from the line of empresses and the aristocratic peer group and to confirm and stabilise the order and values of this conservative group. At the same time, partaking in such misogynistic speech also portrayed these authors as members of the same ideological group.[47]

My sense is that these misogynistic elites consisted of two different groups. The first one can be identified with the old Roman senatorial class that had ruled Rome since the expulsion of the kings of Rome around 500 BCE.[48] Despite lamenting their loss of 'liberty' (a euphemism for their own power) at the end of the Republic, the Roman senate continued to exist and constituted the most prominent noble elite even after the establishment of the Empire. As a result, senators were often directly involved in countless conspiracies against the ruling emperors. On the other hand, the emperors tried to present the Empire as a sort of continuation of the Roman Republic. Interestingly, earlier senatorial authors, such as Tacitus, had also written hyper-sexualised invectives against empresses such as Messalina. However, Tacitus's invective against Messalina served a different function in his case. Thomas Späth has demonstrated that Tacitus considered the Roman emperor as a kind of 'super-*pater*' who ruled over his court just as a *pater familias* would over his *domus*. The senators were, in this case, symbolically demasculinised.[49] The hyper-sexualisation of empresses such as Messalina served as a demonstration that her imperial husband was not fulfilling his male duties as the *pater* and was unable to 'tame' his wife; a neglect that destabilised the Imperial order. Female sexual transgression in the writings of early Imperial senatorial authors was interpreted, therefore, as a sign of imperial unmanliness and weakness, resulting in political chaos.[50]

While the genre of misogynistic speech and invective was created by the senatorial authors of the early imperial period, Late-Antique classicising historians no longer questioned the monarchical-imperial order more generally. Instead, the ideal of the emperor as a 'super-*pater*' ruling over his *domus* seems to be transformed into a ruler governing an empire together with the 'best men'. He should only avoid 'unworthy' persons like women or eunuchs. The reforms of Diocletian and Constantine the Great played a crucial role in this shift. They established new forms of monarchical representation and staging in which the emperor was presented as the *dominus*, putting an end to the early imperial fiction of a republic of equals.[51] The senators responded to this new order by 'inventing' a tradition that framed them as the guardians and bearers of ancient Roman values and ideals. These ideals included female *pudicitia*, the rejection of 'autocratic monarchy', and also the rejection of the by-then well-established Christianity in favour of traditional paganism.[52] Constantine the Great also expanded the Roman senate from 600 to 2,000 members and founded a second senate in Constantinople comprising another 2,000 members. This almost sevenfold increase in the number of senators reduced their political importance significantly.[53] While more and more people became eligible for the senatorial honours, senatorial power was also being challenged by an emerging group of new Christian authorities, especially local bishops.

Other groups constituting the Late-Antique elite cannot be clearly defined numerically. They were ambitious status seekers or parvenus, mainly from the provinces, who were able to rise within the ranks of the administrative and military professional elite of the late Roman-Byzantine Empire thanks to a classical education.[54] Aurelius Victor and Procopius, for example, were both part of this group. Sebastian Schmidt-Hofner has characterised such bureaucrats and officers as practising 'a moderate, virtuous lifestyle, and, not least, a cultivated, urban appearance',[55] envisioning 'an empire run not by a monarch but by a professional elite of the "best"'.[56] In this regard, the interests of the 'old' and 'new' elite coincided; for both, an imperial autocracy had to be avoided. Trained in the classical tradition, these bureaucrats were also familiar with classical pieces of senatorial writing. Accordingly, they probably mobilised and shared traditional patterns of senatorial thought. Finally, the case of Aurelius Victor demonstrates that the boundaries between these groups were fluid and porous. By writing his *breviarium*, he managed to become an influential senator. Therefore, it can be argued that classicising historiography allowed the members of a 'new' elite to distinguish themselves amongst the elites of Rome and Constantinople and, in some cases, rise to the rank of the 'old' nobility.[57] By the same token, Procopius of Caesarea need not necessarily have assumed a coup against Justinian, having prepared a statement of his 'true opposition' to him at hand. Perhaps, he was only seeking the patronage of a wealthy and conservative elite and wrote the *Anekdota* as an assurance of his pro-senatorial loyalty. It would have also meant adopting a traditional template of misogynistic speech to achieve this. However, the question remains open in what particular aspect these two empresses deviated from the conservative expectations of the elite to brand them as sexually transgressive.

Misogynistic invectives were, therefore, an expression of senatorial anxieties towards autocratic imperial power. According to Aurelius Victor, the power-hungry Julia Domna seduced her son in order to become his wife and rule at his side.[58] Later, in his *Anekdota*, Procopius describes how Theodora had power over everything, marking the decline of the Roman Empire.[59] The conservative elite feared the 'illegitimate' and 'tyrannical power' of these empresses, which had overturned the Roman patriarchal order. The trope of 'power in the hands of women' is indeed a patriarchal primal fear, but it is not a sufficient explanation for their demonstrative sexualisation.

The rumour surrounding Julia Domna can be traced back to a joke from the Severan period. The inhabitants of the city of Alexandria called her 'Iokaste' after the mythological mother of Oedipus, who had married her own son.[60] Yet, how did this idea originate in the first place? As Caillan Davenport has pointed out, two aspects of Caracalla's rule likely were decisive: Caracalla remained unmarried throughout his reign and decided to represent his mother as complementary to himself in imperial coinage, public monuments, and inscriptions at his side.[61] Particularly striking were the newly introduced *antoniniani*, intended to replace the *denarii*. These were struck either with a depiction of Caracalla as the sun god Sol/Helios or with a portrait of his mother Julia Domna as the moon goddess Luna/Selene.[62] It seems not unlikely that contemporaries also might have misunderstood this kind of imperial representation of an imperial ruling couple as a married couple. The same representation applies to Theodora. McClanan has demonstrated that Theodora herself always appeared together with Justinian at public displays and events like the public ceremonies and rituals in Constantinople and was featured alongside him in 'official media', such as the mosaics of San Vitale in Ravenna, as well as statues, inscriptions, and even on column capitals.[63] By so doing, they presented themselves as an 'imperial couple' to the public sphere. Conservative senatorial elites were not simply concerned with female power but, moreover, with the complementary visibility of the emperor's *and* empress's body in public life, a theme that occurred often in imperial art. In Late Antiquity, the empress was often and demonstratively included in public representations of imperial power as if she were a second (male) emperor. This idea of a joint imperial representation can be characterised as a 'partnership' or κοινωνία/*consortium*.[64] But it was more than that: the senatorial and bureaucratic elite men were triggered by the official representation of femininity and imperial power, complementary to that of the male emperor. By doing this, there was another holder of imperial power, but one who exercised her authority without being influenced by the 'best men' of the state. The empress's body, therefore, functioned as a symbol of imperial autocracy, the very ideal that the senatorial elite rejected. The senatorial elite opposed the Late-Antique visibility of sacralised, imperial femininity in the public sphere with the contrasting image of a hyper-sexualised woman, the exact opposite of these women's official image and sacrality.

Conclusion

The hyper-sexualisation of Late-Antique empresses in classicising historiography has long been considered by scholars as either factually true or merely rhetorical. Empresses such as Theodora have also received greater attention than others. However, no comparative study of sexual invectives directed against certain empresses has been undertaken so far and, therefore, the question of why individual empresses were sexualised by classicising historians remained largely unanswered.

This contribution has interpreted classicising hyper-sexualisation as a discursive strategy of a conservative imperial elite, consisting of senators and learned imperial officials who relied on fragments and rumours from empresses' lives to create misogynistic invectives. These misogynistic invectives served the conservative elite as expressions of their self-definition and self-fashioning, shared values, and of their rejection of 'autocratic emperorship', instead of which they advocated for a more *laissez-faire* style of imperial rule for the 'best men'. Simultaneously, such status seekers and those parvenus who used these literary forms of expression wanted to signal their ideological affiliation to the 'old' senatorial aristocracy. In return, they hoped to receive patronage or to be promoted to the ranks of senators. Working as a form of public punishment and literary *damnatio memoriae*, the misogynistic speech was directed against empresses who had deviated from traditional patriarchal norms. This was aimed at sullying the empresses' *pudicitia*, depicting them as abnormal and estranged from every norm of aristocratic refinement and civility. However, this was not just a consequence of women striving for power in the late Roman Empire. Instead, it was the Late-Antique practice of representing the empress's body as complementary to the emperor's in public displays, depictions, and rituals that triggered so much anxiety within the male nobility. With the female body serving as a symbol of imperial autocracy in Late Antiquity, misogynistic speech may well have functioned as a 'code' for a group of insiders and as a way of challenging imperial authority.

Notes

1 See as a traditional contribution Peter Brown, *The World of Late Antiquity. From Marcus Aurelius to Muhammad (CE 150–750)* (London: Thames & Hudson, 1971). See for a general overview of several aspects Philip Rousseau, ed., *A Companion to Late Antiquity* (Oxford: Blackwell Publishing, 2009) and Scott Fitzgerald Johnson, ed., *The Oxford Handbook of Late Antiquity* (Oxford: Oxford University Press, 2012).
2 Here empresses are neutrally understood as women who bore the title of *Augusta*. However, this could be the wife, sister, or mother of the reigning emperor. On this problem see François Chausson, 'La souveraine en titres et en actes. Une résille de mots et de pouvoirs; un éventail de périodes et de lieux', in *Augusta, Regina, Basilissa. La souveraine de l'Empire romain au Moyen Âge. Entre héritages et metamorphoses*, ed. François Chausson and Sylvain Destephen (Paris: De Boccard, 2018), 7–19.
3 See the contributions in Filippo Carlà-Uhink and Anja Wieber, eds, *Orientalism and the Reception of Powerful Women from the Ancient World* (London: Bloomsbury, 2020).
4 Generally, for the 'classicising historiography' in Late Antiquity, see Michael Kulikowski, 'Classicizing History and Historical Epitomes', in *A Companion to Late Antique Literature*, ed. Scott McGill and Edward J. Watts (Hoboken: Wiley Blackwell, 2018), 143–169.
5 See, for the women in the so-called *Historia Augusta*, Elisabeth Wallinger, *Die Frauen in der Historia Augusta* (Vienna: Österreichische Gesellschaft für Archäologie, 1990); see for Theodora especially Hans-Georg Beck, *Kaiserin Theodora und Prokop. Der Historiker und sein Opfer* (Munich/Zurich: Piper TB, 1986), and Anne McClanan, *Representations of early Byzantine Empresses. Image and Empire* (Basingstoke: Palgrave Macmillan, 2002), 107–120.
6 See Harold W. Bird, *Sextus Aurelius Victor. A Historiographical Study* (Liverpool: Francis Cairns, 1984); David Rohrbacher, *The Historians of Late Antiquity* (London: Routledge, 2002), 42–48.
7 Aurelius Victor, *De Caesaribus* 21.2–3, trans. H.W. Bird (Liverpool: Liverpool University Press, 1994), 26: 'Patiens communis tranquillusque; pari fortuna et eodem matrimonio, quo pater. Namque Iuliam novercam, cuius facinora supra memoravi, forma captus coniugem affectavit, cum illa factiosior aspectui adolescentis, praesentiae quasi ignara, semet dedisset intecto corpore, asserentique:

'Vellem, si liceret, uti', petulantius multo (quippe quae pudorem velamento exuerat) respondisset: 'Libet? plane licet'.
8 See for this Late-Antique legend: Gabriele Marasco, 'Giulia Domna, Caracalla e Geta. Frammenti di tragedia alla corte dei Severi', *L'Antiquité Classique* 65 (1996): 119–134 at 126, and Wallinger, *Die Frauen in der Historia Augusta*, 86–88. For the 'Enmann's Kaisergeschichte' as the main source of the *Historia Augusta*, Aurelius Victor, Eutropius and the *Epitome de Caesaribus*, see A. Enmann, 'Eine verlorene Geschichte der römischen Kaiser und das Buch *De viris illustribus urbis Romae*', *Philologus Supplement* 4:3 (1884): 337–501; Timothy D. Barnes, 'The Lost Kaisergeschichte and the Latin Historical Tradition', in *Bonner Historia Augusta Colloquium 1968/69* (Bonn: R. Habelt Verlag, 1970), 13–43.
9 In the *Historia Augusta* (*Historia Augusta, Life of Caracalla* 10.1–4), Julia Domna even tells him that it is actually forbidden, but that the emperor is above the law; an ironic reference to the legal sentence of the jurist Ulpian (active in the Severan period) concerning the Augustan marriage laws; see *Digest of Justinian*, Volume I, trans. Alan Watson (Philadelphia: University of Pennsylvania Press, 1998), 1.3.31.
10 See Ernst Kornemann, *Große Frauen des Altertums. Im Rahmen 2000 jährigen Weltgeschehens*, 6th edn (Basel: Schibli-Doppler, 1979), 259–264.
11 See Caillan Davenport, 'The sexual habits of Caracalla: Rumour, gossip, and historiography', *Histos* 11 (2017): 75–100; see further Sonja Nadolny, *Die severischen Kaiserfrauen* (Stuttgart: Steiner Verlag, 2016), 186–187 for the parallel discussion with the (nearly the same) description in the *Historia Augusta*.
12 The literature on Procopius is becoming increasingly unmanageable. Averil Cameron, *Procopius and the Sixth Century* (London: Duckworth, 1985) is still considered the most important work; Anthony Kaldellis, *Procopius of Caesarea. Tyranny, History, and Philosophy at the End of Antiquity* (Philadelphia: University of Pennsylvania Press, 2004), in many points against Cameron, is also useful, as is Franz Tinnefeld, *Kategorien der Kaiserkritik in der byzantinischen Historiographie* (Munich: W. Fink, 1971). For a more recent overview, see Mischa Meier and Federico Montinaro, eds, *A Companion to Procopius of Caesarea* (Leiden: Brill 2022).
13 Procopius, *The Anecdota or Secret History*, trans. H.B. Dewing (Cambridge, MA: Harvard University Press, 1935), 9.3–10.
14 Procopius, *Anecdota*, 9.11–15.
15 Procopius, *Anecdota*, 9.17.
16 Procopius, *Anecdota*, 9.16.
17 Procopius, *Anecdota*, 9.18, trans. H.B. Dewing, 109: ἡ δὲ κἀκ τριῶν τρυπημάτων ἐργαζομένη ἐνεκάλει τῇ φύσει, δυσφορουμένη ὅτι δὴ μὴ καὶ τοὺς τιτθοὺς αὐτῇ εὐρύτερον ἢ νῦν εἰσι τρυπῴη, ὅπως καὶ ἄλλην ἐνταῦθα μίξιν ἐπιτεχνᾶσθαι δυνατὴ εἴη. ('And though she made use of three openings, she used to take Nature to task, complaining that it had not pierced her breasts with larger holes so that it might be possible for her to contrive another method of copulation there'.)

18 Procopius, *Anecdota*, 9.19.
19 Procopius, *Anecdota*, 9.20–22.
20 Procopius, *Anecdota*, 9.27–30.
21 John of Ephesus, 'Lives of the Eastern Saints', 13, in *Patrologia Orientalis 17*, 189, trans. Ernest W. Brooks (Paris: Firmin-Didot, 1923). See also David Potter, *Theodora. Actress, Empress, Saint* (New York: Oxford University Press, 2015), 39.
22 See Beck, *Kaiserin Theodora und Prokop*, 71–76.
23 Procopius, *Anecdota*, 1.2.
24 See Cameron, *Procopius and the Sixth Century*, 48.
25 See Henning Börm, 'Procopius, his predecessors, and the genesis of the *Anecdota*. Antimonarchic discourse in late antique historiography', in *Antimonarchic Discourse in Antiquity*, ed. Henning Börm (Stuttgart: Steiner Verlag, 2015), especially 331–333.
26 Edward Gibbon adhered closely to Procopius' account, see Edward Gibbon, *History of the Decline and the Fall of the Roman Empire*, Vol. IV, ed. John B. Bury (London: Methuen, 1909), 225–228. Conversely, the French Byzantinist Charles Diehl took a markedly different approach in his biography of Theodora. Diehl sought to portray her as a lascivious figure, albeit one he perceived as a 'feminist' and 'oriental' foil to Western bourgeois civilization. In doing so, Diehl not only accepted Procopius's accounts but even fabricated additional affairs (!). This narrative contributed significantly to the emergence of the femme fatale archetype associated with Theodora in scholarly discourse, see Charles Diehl, *Théodora. Impératrice de Byzance* (Paris: De Boccard, 1904), 113–122. Similarly also Kornemann, *Große Frauen des Altertums*, 355–397.
27 See Anthony Kaldellis, *Prokopios. The Secret History with Related Texts* (Indianapolis: Hackett, 2010), xxv.
28 See Beck, *Kaiserin Theodora und Prokop*, 70; see also B. Baldwin, 'Sexual Rhetoric in Procopius', *Mnemosyne* 40 (1987): 151 for the classical models of 'mathematical pornography' in ancient literature.
29 See Beck, *Kaiserin Theodora und Prokop*, 153–158. See Sergi Grau and Oriol Febrer, 'Procopius on Theodora: ancient and new biographical patterns', *Byzantinische Zeitschrift* 113.3 (2020): 769–788 for the classical and hagiographical rhetorical traditions in Procopius' *Anekdota*.
30 See McClanan, *Representations of Early Byzantine Empresses*, 112.
31 See Jan Meister, 'Reports about the "Sex Life" of Early Roman Emperors. A Case of Character Assassination?' in *Character Assassination throughout the Ages*, ed. Martijn Icks and Eric Shiraev (New York: Palgrave Macmillan, 2014), 59–81.
32 See Kenneth Dover, *Greek Homosexuality* (London: Duckworth, 1978); Michel Foucault, *The History of Sexuality, Vol. 2: The Use of Pleasure* (London: Penguin, 1992).
33 See Hartmut G. Ziche, 'Abusing Theodora. Sexual and Political Discourse in Procopius', *BYZANTIAKA* 30 (2012–13): at 317–321.
34 See noticeably Catharine MacKinnon, 'Not a Moral Issue', *Yale Law & Policy Review* 2.2 (1983): 321–345.

35 See Rebecca Langlands, *Sexual Morality in Ancient Rome* (Cambridge: Cambridge University Press, 2006).
36 Aurelius Victor, *De Caesaribus* 21.3, trans. H.W. Bird, 26 (see also note 7).
37 For the changes of sexual morality in Late Antiquity, see Kyle Harper, *From Shame to Sin. The Christian Transformation of Sexual Morality in Late Antiquity* (Cambridge, MA: Harvard University Press, 2013).
38 The classical analysis of this is Katharine M. Rogers, *The Troublesome Helpmate. A History of Misogyny in Literature* (Seattle: University of Washington Press, 1966), 3–22.
39 Only the references to Theodora's demonic nature (or that she would be an appropriate partner for the 'prince of demons', Justinian) could be interpreted in this direction, see Procopius, *Anecdota*, 12.28.
40 The 'misogynistic attitude' of Procopius of Caesarea throughout his whole work was especially pointed out by Christoph Schäfer, 'Stereotypen und Vorurteile im Frauenbild des Prokop', in *Frauen und Geschlechter. Bilder – Rollen – Realitäten in den Texten antiker Autoren zwischen Antike und Mittelalter*, ed. Robert Rollinger and Christoph Ulf (Vienna/Cologne/Weimar: Böhlau, 2006), 275–294.
41 See Kate Manne, *Down Girl. The Logic of Misogyny* (Oxford: Oxford University Press, 2017), 78.
42 See Manne, *Down Girl*, 192: 'On my analysis, misogyny's primary function and constitutive manifestation is the punishment of "bad" women, and policing of women's behavior. But systems of punishment and reward – and conviction and exoneration – tend to work together, holistically. So, the overall structural features of the account predict that misogyny as I've analyzed it is likely to work alongside other systems and mechanisms to enforce gender conformity'.
43 See Manne, *Down Girl*, 192: 'We should also be concerned with the rewarding and valorising of women who conform to gendered norms and expectations, enforce the "good" behavior of others, and engage in certain common forms of patriarchal virtue-signaling – by, for example, participating in slut-shaming, victim-blaming, or the Internet analog of witch-burning practices'.
44 In the scholarship of ancient history, the *Historia Augusta* is generally considered to be a source of very little 'factual' historical value; nevertheless, it is by far the most detailed source for the third century and contains valuable insight into Western Roman elite ideologies around 400 AD. See generally for the *Historia Augusta* Hermann Dessau, 'Über Zeit und Persönlichkeit der *Scriptores historiae Augustae*', *Hermes* 24 (1889): 337–392; Ronald Syme, *Emperors and Biography. Studies in the Historia Augusta* (Oxford: Oxford University Press, 1971); and Mark Thomson, *Studies in the Historia Augusta* (Brussels: Latomus, 2012). However, by now the publications on the *Historia Augusta* have become barely manageable even for experts.
45 *Historia Augusta, Volume III. The Thirty Pretenders*, 30.12–13, trans. David Magie (Cambridge, MA: Harvard University Press, 1932), 137/139: 'Cuius ea castitas fuisse dicitur ut ne virum suum quidem scierit nisi temptandis conceptionibus. Nam cum semel concubuisset, exspectatis menstruis continebat se, si praegnans esset, sin minus, iterum potestatem quaerendis liberis dabat'.

46 See generally Anja Wieber, 'Die Augusta aus der Wüste – die palmyrenische Herrscherin Zenobia', in *Frauenwelten in der Antike. Geschlechterordnung und weibliche Lebenspraxis*, ed. Thomas Späth and Beate Wagner-Hasel (Stuttgart/Weimar: J.B. Metzler Verlag, 2000), 281–310; Rex Winsbury, *Zenobia of Palmyra. History, Myth and the Neo-Classical Imagination* (London: Bloomsbury, 2010), 29–41.

47 See further Andrea Geier and Ursula Kocher, 'Einleitung', in *Wider die Frau. Zur Geschichte und Funktion misogyner Rede*, ed. Andrea Geier and Ursula Kocher (Cologne/Weimar/Vienna: Böhlau Köln, 2008), 4: 'Die Ausprägungen misogyner Aussagen sind, so die hier vertretene Auffassung, Kostrukte einer Sprechergemeinschaft, die zu jeweils bestimmten Zeiten in einzelnen Diskursen zur Abgrenzung und Selbstvergewisserung einer Gruppe sowie nichtsprachlicher Inszenierung gedient haben'.

48 See generally Richard Talbert, *The Senate of Imperial Rome* (Princeton: Princeton University Press, 1984).

49 See Thomas Späth, *Männlichkeit und Weiblichkeit bei Tacitus. Zur Konstruktion der Geschlechter in der römischen Kaiserzeit* (Frankfurt: Campus Verlag, 1994), 339–346.

50 See Späth, *Männlichkeit und Weiblichkeit bei Tacitus*, 311–317. The case is similar to Western European monarchies of the Late Middle Ages, where a sexually active queen meant that the king was unable to satisfy her according to the Pauline understanding of marriage and sexuality and so control her, see Henric Bagerius and Christine Ekholst, 'For better or for worse. Royal marital sexuality as political critique in late medieval Europe', in *Routledge History of Monarchy*, ed. Elena Woodacre, Lucinda H.S. Dean, Chris Jones, Russell E. Martin, and Zita Eva Rohr (Abingdon: Routledge, 2019), 636–654.

51 See Frank Kolb, *Herrscherideologie in der Spätantike* (Berlin: De Gruyter, 2001), 38–53; 72–85.

52 See generally for the late Roman senate Michael T.W. Arnheim, *The senatorial aristocracy in the later Roman empire* (Oxford: Oxford University Press, 1972); for their cultural distinctiveness and values see Beat Näf, *Senatorisches Standesbewusstsein in spätrömischer Zeit* (Freiburg: Universitätsverlag, 1995).

53 In the time of emperor Justinian, the number of (Eastern Roman) senators was reduced again. However, new ranks were established, and the senate convened simultaneously with the imperial council, which further decreased the importance of the senate, see Ernst Stein, *Histoire du Bas-Empire. De la disparition de l'Empire d'Occident à la mort de Justinien (476–565 apr. J.-C.)* (Brussels/Paris: Desclée de Brouwer, 1949), 73, 432, and Hartmut Leppin, 'Imperiale Eliten um Justinian', in *Die Interaktion von Herrschern und Eliten in imperialen Ordnungen des Mittelalters*, ed. Wolfram Drews (Berlin: De Gruyter, 2018), 51–55.

54 See generally Sebastian Schmidt-Hofner, 'An Empire of the Best. Zosimus, the monarchy, and the Eastern administrative elite in the fifth century CE', *Chiron* 50 (2020): 217–251.

55 See Schmidt-Hofner, 'An Empire of the Best', 242.

56 See Schmidt-Hofner, 'An Empire of the Best', 247.

57 In scholarship on European Renaissance humanism, similar theories have sometimes been expressed; humanists would have written classicising historiography in order to rise socially in the political order of their own republics and *signorie*, see Gerrit Walther, 'Funktionen des Humanismus. Fragen und Thesen', in *Funktionen des Humanismus. Studien zum Nutzen des Neuen in der humanistischen Kultur*, ed. Thomas Maissen and Gerrit Walther (Göttingen: Wallstein Verlag, 2006), 9–17.

58 See note 7. One might assume that Aurelius Victor's invective would not seem particularly credible to a reader educated in Roman history. He might have known that there had been at least two empresses, Agrippina the Younger and Zenobia, who exercised a kind of female rule without seducing their sons. However, this can be disregarded; Zenobia was portrayed in Roman literature (see above) as an Oriental (as were all other female rulers of the ancient Mediterranean cultures). In the case of 'feminised' Orientals, this did not appear to be very problematic. Agrippina the Younger is a little different; at least in Roman senatorial literature, she was also accused of trying to seduce her son Nero, albeit unsuccessfully, cf. Tacitus, *Annales* 14.2.

59 Procopius, *Anecdota*, 15.16–17.

60 Herodian, *History of the Empire, Volume I: Books 1–4*, trans. C.R. Whittaker (Cambridge, MA: Harvard University Press, 1969), 4.9.3.

61 See Davenport, 'The sexual habits of Caracalla', 79–87.

62 Harold Mattingly and Edward A. Sydenham, eds, *The Roman Imperial Coinage, Vol. IV. Part III: Gordian III – Uranias Antoninus* (London: Spink & Son, 1936), *Caracalla* 379.

63 See McClanan, *Representations of early Byzantine Empresses*, 121–148.

64 See Diliana Angelova, *Sacred Founders. Women, Men, and Gods in the Discourse of Imperial Founding* (Berkeley: University of California Press, 2015), especially 183–202.

Bibliography

Primary sources

Sextus Aurelius Victor. *Liber De Caesaribus*, trans. Harold W. Bird. Liverpool: Liverpool University Press, 1994.

Sextus Aurelius Victor. *Liber De Caesaribus* – Die römischen Kaiser, trans. Kirsten Groß-Albenhausen and Manfred Fuhrmann. Second edition. Darmstadt: Verlag, 2002.

Digest of Justinian, Volume I, trans. Alan Watson. Philadelphia: University of Pennsylvania Press, 1998.

Herodian. *History of the Empire, Volume I: Books 1–4*, trans. C.R. Whittaker. Cambridge, MA: Harvard University Press, 1969.

Historia Augusta, Volume III. The Two Valerians, The Two Gallieni, The Thirty Pretenders, The Deified Claudius, The Deified Aurelian, Tacitus, Probus, Firmus,

Saturninus, Proculus and Bonosus, Carus, Carinus and Numerian, trans. David Magie. Cambridge, MA: Harvard University Press, 1932.
John of Ephesus. 'Lives of the Eastern Saints'. In *Patrologia Orientalis 17*, trans. Ernest W. Brooks. Paris: Firmin-Didot, 1923.
Procopius. *The Anecdota or Secret History*, trans. H.B. Dewing. Cambridge, MA: Harvard University Press, 1935.
Tacitus. *The Annals. The Reigns of Tiberius, Claudius, and Nero*, trans. John C. Yardley. Oxford: Oxford University Press, 2008.

Numismatic Corpora

Mattingly, Harold, and Edward A. Sydenham, eds. *The Roman Imperial Coinage, Vol. IV. Part III: Gordian III – Uranias Antoninus*. London: Spink & Son, 1936.

Secondary sources

Angelova, Diliana. Sacred Founders. Women, Men, and Gods in the Discourse of Imperial Founding. Berkeley: University of California Press, 2015.
Arnheim, Michael T.W. The Senatorial Aristocracy in the Later Roman Empire. Oxford: Oxford University Press, 1972.
Bagerius, Henric, and Christine Ekholst. 'For better or for worse. Royal marital sexuality as political critique in late medieval Europe'. In *The Routledge History of Monarchy*, ed. Elena Woodacre, Lucinda H.S. Dean, Chris Jones, Russell E. Martin, and Zita Eva Rohr, 636–654. Abingdon: Routledge, 2019.
Baldwin, B. 'Sexual Rhetoric in Procopius'. *Mnemosyne* 40 (1987): 151–153.
Barnes, Timothy D. 'The Lost Kaisergeschichte and the Latin Historical Tradition'. In *Bonner Historia Augusta Colloquium 1968/69*, 13–43. Bonn: R. Habelt Verlag, 1970.
Beck, Hans-Georg. Kaiserin Theodora und Prokop. Der Historiker und sein Opfer. Munich/Zurich: Piper TB, 1986.
Bird, Harold W. *Sextus Aurelius Victor. A Historiographical Study*. Liverpool: Francis Cairns, 1984.
Börm, Henning. 'Procopius, his predecessors, and the genesis of the *Anecdota*. Antimonarchic discourse in late antique historiography'. In *Antimonarchic Discourse in Antiquity*, ed. Henning Börm, 305–346. Stuttgart: Steiner Verlag, 2015.
Brown, Peter. *The World of Late Antiquity. from Marcus Aurelius to Muhammad (CE 150–750)*. London: Thames & Hudson, 1971.
Cameron, Averil. *Procopius and the Sixth Century*. London: Duckworth, 1985.
Carlà-Uhink, Filippo and Anja Wieber, eds. Orientalism and the Reception of Powerful Women from the Ancient World. London: Bloomsbury, 2020.
Chausson, François. 'La souveraine en titres et en actes. Une résille de mots et de pouvoirs; un éventail de périodes et de 1lieux'. In *Augusta, Regina, Basilissa. La souveraine de l'Empire romain au Moyen Âge. Entre héritages et metamorphoses*, ed. François Chausson and Sylvain Destephen, 7–19. Paris: De Boccard, 2018.

Davenport, Caillan. 'The sexual habits of Caracalla. Rumour, gossip, and historiography'. *Histos* 11 (2017): 75–100.

Dessau, Hermann. 'Über Zeit und Persönlichkeit der *Scriptores historiae Augustae*'. *Hermes* 24 (1889): 337–392.

Diehl, Charles. *Théodora. Impératrice de Byzance*. Paris: De Boccard, 1904.

Dover, Kenneth. *Greek Homosexuality*. London: Duckworth, 1978.

Enmann, Alexander. 'Eine verlorene Geschichte der römischen Kaiser und das Buch *De viris illustribus urbis Romae*'. *Philologus Supplement* 4:3 (1884): 337–501.

Foucault, Michel. *The History of Sexuality, Volume 2: The Use of Pleasure* London: Penguin, 1992.

Geier, Andrea and Ursula Kocher. 'Einleitung'. In *Wider die Frau. Zur Geschichte und Funktion misogyner Rede*, ed. Andrea Geier and Ursula Kocher, 1–21. Cologne/Weimar/Vienna: Böhlau Köln, 2008.

Gibbon, Edward. *The History of the Decline and the Fall of the Roman Empire*, Volume IV, ed. John B. Bury. London: Methuen, 1909.

Grau, Sergi and Oriol Febrer. 'Procopius on Theodora: ancient and new biographical patterns'. *Byzantinische Zeitschrift* 113.3 (2020): 769–788.

Harper, Kyle. *From Shame to Sin. The Christian Transformation of Sexual Morality in Late Antiquity*. Cambridge, MA: Harvard University Press, 2013.

Johnson, Scott Fitzgerald, ed. *The Oxford Handbook of Late Antiquity*. Oxford: Oxford University Press, 2012.

Kaldellis, Anthony. *Procopius of Caesarea. Tyranny, History, and Philosophy at the End of Antiquity*. Philadelphia: University of Pennsylvania Press, 2004.

Kaldellis, Anthony. *Prokopios. The Secret History with Related Texts*. Indianapolis: Hackett, 2010.

Kolb, Frank. *Herrscherideologie in der Spätantike*. Berlin: De Grutyer, 2001.

Kornemann, Ernst. *Große Frauen des Altertums. Im Rahmen 2000 jährigen Weltgeschehens*, 6th edn. Basel: Schibli-Doppler, 1979.

Kulikowski, Michael. 'Classicizing History and Historical Epitomes'. In *A Companion to Late Antique Literature*, ed. Scott McGill and Edward J. Watts, 143–169. Hoboken, NJ: Wiley Blackwell, 2018.

Langlands, Rebecca. *Sexual Morality in Ancient Rome*. Cambridge: Cambridge University Press, 2006.

Leppin, Hartmut. 'Imperiale Eliten um Justinian'. In *Die Interaktion von Herrschern und Eliten in imperialen Ordnungen des Mittelalters*, ed. Wolfram Drews, 43–62. Berlin/Boston: De Grutyer, 2018.

MacKinnon, Catharine. 'Not a Moral Issue'. *Yale Law & Policy Review* 2.2 (1983): 321–345.

Manne, Kate, *Down Girl. The Logic of Misogyny*. Oxford: Oxford University Press, 2017.

Marasco, Gabriele. 'Giulia Domna, Caracalla e Geta. Frammenti di tragedia alla corte dei Severi'. *L'Antiquité Classique* 65 (1996): 119–134.

McClanan, Anne. *Representations of early Byzantine Empresses. Image and Empire*. Basingstoke: Palgrave Macmillan, 2002.

Meier, Mischa, and Federico Montinaro, eds. *A Companion to Procopius of Caesarea*. Leiden: Brill, 2022.

Meister, Jan. 'Reports about the "Sex Life" of Early Roman Emperors. A Case of Character Assassination?' In *Character Assassination throughout the Ages*, ed. Martijn Icks and Eric Shiraev, 59–81. New York: Palgrave Macmillan, 2014.

Nadolny, Sonja. *Die severischen Kaiserfrauen*. Stuttgart: Steiner Verlag, 2016.

Näf, Beat. *Senatorisches Standesbewusstsein in spätrömischer Zeit*. Freiburg: Universitätsverlag, 1995.

Potter, David. *Theodora. Actress, Empress, Saint*. New York: Oxford University Press, 2015.

Rogers, Katharine M. *The Troublesome Helpmate. A History of Misogyny in Literature*. Seattle: University of Washington Press, 1966.

Rohrbacher, David. *The Historians of Late Antiquity*. London: Routledge, 2002.

Rousseau, Philip. ed. *A Companion to Late Antiquity*. Oxford: Blackwell Publishing, 2009.

Schäfer, Christoph. 'Stereotypen und Vorurteile im Frauenbild des Prokop'. In *Frauen und Geschlechter. Bilder – Rollen – Realitäten in den Texten antiker Autoren zwischen Antike und Mittelalter*, ed. Robert Rollinger and Christoph Ulf, 275–294. Vienna/Cologne/Weimar: Böhlau, 2006.

Schmidt-Hofner, Sebastian. 'An Empire of the Best. Zosimus, the monarchy, and the Eastern administrative elite in the fifth century CE'. *Chiron* 50 (2020): 217–251.

Späth, Thomas. *Männlichkeit und Weiblichkeit bei Tacitus. Zur Konstruktion der Geschlechter in der römischen Kaiserzeit*. Frankfurt: Campus Verlag, 1994.

Stein, Ernst. *Histoire du Bas-Empire. De la disparition de l'Empire d'Occident à la mort de Justinien (476–565 apr. J.-C.)*. Paris: Desclée de Brouwer, 1949.

Syme, Ronald. *Emperors and Biography. Studies in the Historia Augusta*. Oxford: Oxford University Press, 1971.

Talbert, Richard. *The Senate of Imperial Rome*. Princeton: Princeton University Press, 1984.

Thomson, Mark. *Studies in the Historia Augusta*. Brussels: Latomus, 2012.

Tinnefeld, Franz. *Kategorien der Kaiserkritik in der byzantinischen Historiographie*. Munich: W. Fink, 1971.

Wallinger, Elisabeth. *Die Frauen in der Historia Augusta*. Vienna: Österreichische Gesellschaft für Archäologie, 1990.

Walther, Gerrit. 'Funktionen des Humanismus. Fragen und Thesen'. In *Funktionen des Humanismus. Studien zum Nutzen des Neuen in der humanistischen Kultur*, ed. Thomas Maissen and Gerrit Walther, 9–17. Göttingen: Wallstein Verlag, 2006.

Wieber, Anja. 'Die Augusta aus der Wüste – die palmyrenische Herrscherin Zenobia'. In *Frauenwelten in der Antike. Geschlechterordnung und weibliche Lebenspraxis*, ed. Thomas Späth and Beate Wagner-Hasel, 281–310. Stuttgart/Weimar: J.B. Metzler Verlag, 2000.

Winsbury, Rex. *Zenobia of Palmyra. History, Myth and the Neo-Classical Imagination*. London: Bloomsbury, 2010.

Ziche, Hartmut G. 'Abusing Theodora. Sexual and Political Discourse in Procopius'. *BYZANTIAKA* 30 (2012–13): 311–323.

2

Eadwig's coronation scandal: sexuality, rhetoric and the vulnerability of reputation

Matthew Firth

The earliest narrative account of the coronation of the West Saxon King Eadwig (r. 955–59) is found in the earliest *vita* of St Dunstan (d. 988). *Vita S. Dunstani*, written around fifty years after Eadwig's death by a clerical author known only as B, describes a reign that began in ignominy.[1] B reports that, on the day of his coronation, Eadwig absented himself from the celebration feast, prompted by his *lasciuus* (lust) to seek out the company of his two lovers, a mother and daughter. The mother, named Æthelgifu, takes the role of the primary antagonist in B's version of the tale, being variously called *natione precelsa, inepta tamen* (of noble birth, but foolish), *lupa* (a whore), *ganea* (a harlot),[2] and as *Iezabelis flatu uenenifero perfusa* (inspired by Jezebel's poisonous breath).[3] The archbishop of Canterbury, Oda (d. 958), having noted the king's absence, divines its reason, and takes it as affront to the gathered nobles. The nobles, however, wary of attracting the ire of either the king or the two women, prevaricate when Oda beseeches them to seek Eadwig out and return him to the feast. In the end, Bishop Cynesige of Lichfield (d. *c.*964) and Dunstan, then the abbot of Glastonbury, undertake the task. The two clerics find Eadwig, crown cast upon the floor, 'disporting himself disgracefully in between the two women as though they were wallowing in some revolting pigsty'.[4] Taking the lead in what follows, Dunstan chides the king, castigates the women, forcibly separates the lovers, plants the crown on Eadwig's head, and marches him back to the feast. It is small wonder that his actions garner him the enduring animosity of the king and Æthelgifu.

This story is a fiction. Each of its participants is a mere caricature. The hagiographer may be painting a picture of a wanton young king, but his depiction of Dunstan is hardly sympathetic. Unbridled immorality and unbridled morality are juxtaposed. The misguided king and his 'wicked queens' are mere foils for Dunstan's righteousness.[5] Yet there are historical facts here. Oda, Cynesige, and Dunstan were all political figures of Eadwig's reign, as well as those of his predecessor and successors. For her part, Æthelgifu was indeed a presence at Eadwig's court, but not as some inferior, corrupting concubine leading the young king – around fifteen at this time – into sexual immorality. She was, instead, Eadwig's mother-in-law, and her daughter – unnamed in the tale – was Eadwig's consort Ælfgifu.[6] B's story is responding to a factional divide that shaped the English court in the 950s and informed the political milieu of Eadwig's reign. While these factions encompassed numerous named mid-tenth-century political figures, B introduces only a limited cast of characters in his account of events: on one side Dunstan and his allies, on the other Eadwig and his supporters. B correctly delineates which of his characters was on what side of the divide, and these factional alignments are preserved and transmitted within accounts of the drama at Eadwig's coronation in subsequent redactions of *Vita Dunstani*.

There are seven primary texts that relate the coronation scandal: B's *Vita S. Dunstani* (995×1005); Osbern of Canterbury's *Vita S. Dunstani* (1089×1093); Eadmer of Canterbury's *Vita S. Dunstani* (1103×1110); William of Malmesbury's *Vita S. Dunstani* (1126×1130); Eadmer's *Vita S. Odonis* (1093×1100); and William's *Gesta regum Anglorum* (1125×1126). All the accounts are highly intertextual; all versions of Eadwig's infidelities at his coronation share a single source (directly or indirectly): B's *vita*.[7] B's version of *Vita Dunstani* is the nearest to contemporary and, importantly, as Michael Lapidge proves, B was a personal associate of Dunstan during his years at Glastonbury.[8] While this grants him eyewitness authority in some instances, both B's continued reverence for his former abbot and the literary mode of hagiography must be taken into consideration. B is sympathetic to Dunstan's faction, and his account of the coronation scandal at once serves to legitimate the legacies of Dunstan and his allies and denigrate those of Eadwig and his supporters. Moreover, the wider text is a deliberately constructed exemplar of the saint's life genre, purposed above all to emphasise the worthiness and morality of the saint. And B's efforts were not in vain. As the above list of interrelated texts demonstrates, the coronation scandal became deeply embedded within Dunstan's legacy and cult; indeed, more so than within Eadwig's legacy.

Though this account of events on the day of his anointing has a significant and long-term influence on the reception of Eadwig's reign, it is not the only tradition of his kingship that survives. Of England's pre-eminent early twelfth-century histories, only William of Malmesbury's *Gesta regum* reports the event. Moreover, William alone seems to have perceived a need to take sides on any factional divide between Eadwig and Dunstan, firmly placing himself within Dunstan's camp. However, William is something of a unique case, being also a hagiographer who had compiled a *vita* of Dunstan. His contemporaries, John of Worcester, Henry of Huntingdon, and Geffrei

Gaimar, all offer differing visions of the reign, and none report the coronation scandal. John states that Eadwig 'acted foolishly in government', but records little detail to support this beyond noting that Eadwig exiled Dunstan 'for his righteousness'.[9] For his part, Henry pays little attention to Eadwig's reign, but does report that he 'was a praiseworthy holder of the crown'.[10] And finally, Geffrei says almost nothing, recording Eadwig's life and death in just two of the 6,500 lines that comprise his Anglo-Norman verse history.[11] Ultimately, the coronation scandal is a hagiographical tale, not a historical one.

Using B's *Vita Dunstani* as it its starting point, this chapter examines the traditions of inappropriate sexuality associated with Eadwig's legacy. Foremost among these is the coronation scandal, so intimately entwined with St Dunstan's cult, and the chapter first discusses the political context of Eadwig's reign, his conflict with the abbot, and Æthelgifu and Ælfgifu's place within that dispute. It then considers other traditions relating to Eadwig's sexual transgressions, namely those associated with Oda's annulment of his union with Ælfgifu. Primary among these is that the archbishop separated the couple on a charge of consanguinity. However, in certain traditions associated with Oda's cult, an enigmatic alternative explanation is offered, usually interpreted as adultery on Eadwig's part, but argued here to indicate that the couple were never formally married in the first place. Finally, the chapter turns to tenth-century attitudes towards sexuality, sexual transgression, and reputational vulnerability. These can be observed within the comparative portrayals of Eadwig and his brother Edgar (r. 959–975) in the *vitae Dunstani* and related texts, and in those elements of B's account of the coronation scandal that are particularly effective in drawing Eadwig, Ælfgifu, and Æthelgifu's morality into question. Through the examination of these factors, this essay establishes why the trio were vulnerable to charges of inappropriate sexuality, and how such accusations were employed to delegitimise and to disempower.

Factions at the royal court

Eadwig was an orphan when he came to the throne. His mother Ælfgifu, later St Ælfgifu of Shaftesbury, died in 944, while his father King Edmund died in 946. At this time, Eadwig would have been around five years old, his younger brother Edgar only around two. In an era before strict primogeniture, other male scions of the West Saxon royal house could lay claim to the kingship given the support of the *witan*, or king's council. So it was that the two young boys' uncle, Eadred, claimed the throne on Edmund's death. Eadred in turn died childless in 955, clearing the teenaged Eadwig's way to the throne. At least in theory. However, that lack of prescriptive primogeniture once more came into play, and there was another claimant for the throne: Edgar.

There were several powerbrokers at court during Edmund and Eadred's reigns who had also been influential in the reign of their father, King Edward the Elder (r. 899–924). The most relevant among these were Eadgifu (d. c.966), their mother and Edward's third consort; the East Anglian ealdorman Æthelstan Half-King; Abbot Dunstan; and Archbishop Oda. None of these would long retain their influence in Eadwig's court. Æthelstan Half-King retired to Glastonbury in 956, Dunstan was exiled the same year, and Eadwig also confiscated some part of his grandmother's wealth and estates around that time, while by 957 Oda had largely withdrawn his support for the king.[12] In the succession dispute that followed the death of Eadred, all of these figures had supported Edgar rather than Eadwig. This extends to Cynesige who, like Oda, is absent from the witness lists of Eadwigian charters from 957.[13] In their place, Eadwig elevated a new network of elites, many with their own royal connections. This is the context in which Æthelgifu and her daughter Ælfgifu were introduced into the royal court. It is also the context in which their actions during the coronation scandal were framed. The posthumous *vitae* of Dunstan and Oda represent the clerics' absence from Eadwig's court not as a result of political vicissitudes, but as the consequences of a weak king being led by an immoral faction. That factionalism came to a head in 957 when, as John of Worcester recounts:

> Eadwig, king of the English, since he acted foolishly in the government entrusted to him, was abandoned by the Mercians and Northumbrians with contempt, and his brother, the *ætheling* Edgar, was chosen by them as king, and the territory of the kings was divided so the River Thames formed the boundary between their kingdoms.[14]

Despite the division – seemingly a negotiated settlement – occurring some two years after Eadwig ascended the West Saxon throne, it had its foundations in the fact that, from the very outset of his reign, the young king had sought to establish a support base independent of the entrenched advisors of his grandfather, father, and uncle's kingships. In his *Vita Odonis*, Eadmer links the division directly to Eadwig's conflicts with Oda and Dunstan, and goes so far as to state he was driven from his kingdom.[15] While this is a clear exaggeration, there is consensus that Edgar's rise to power saw Dunstan recalled from exile and from 957/8 he, Oda, and Cynesige were all to be found at the northern court.[16]

Notably, not all versions of *Vita Dunstani* place the blame for Eadwig being led astray on Æthelgifu and Ælfgifu. Indeed, B is almost unique in blaming Æthelgifu and Ælfgifu unequivocally by placing them at the heart of his supposed corruption, rather than simply being a symptom of it. Rather, Osbern states that 'he did not listen to the advice of the wise ... [but] followed the advice of boys'.[17] Eadmer follows suit, calling those *pueri* (boys) *iuvenes* and *adolescentes* (youths) in his *Vita Odonis* and *Vita Dunstani*, and indicating that it was their influence in the stead of those *sapientes* (wise men) and *senes* (elders) that brought Eadwig's reign to disaster.[18] The rhetoric here, especially considering its source – panegyric *vitae* of Eadwig's political opponents – is hardly subtle. Eadwig's 'sycophants' were likely no more than members of alternative noble factions elevated to positions of authority by the king,[19] while the ignored 'wise men' are Oda, Dunstan, and Cynesige. In this factional political landscape, Æthelgifu and Ælfgifu sit alongside Eadwig and his 'boys'. The coronation scandal is a demonstration of the dynamic that Dunstan's hagiographers sought to show as characteristic of Eadwig's court. The king is 'young in age and manner',[20] easily led into error and sin, in need of the wise clerics to rescue him from himself and from those leading him astray.

The vaguely referenced 'boys' are hardly as anonymous as the *vitae* make out, and Barbara Yorke and Shashi Jayakumar have identified numerous such Eadwigian allies.[21] To borrow the words of the former, 'Eadwig was inclined to favour his own relations rather than ... the chief counsellors of his father and uncle'.[22] This statement also encompasses Æthelgifu and Ælfgifu, women who, as Pauline Stafford highlights, were 'members of a prominent noble family of southwest England', with familial connections to the dynasty.[23] Dunstan also hailed from this region, which has led to some suggestion that there may have been conflict between the churchman and Æthelgifu's family prior to the events of 955.[24] We are indebted to B for naming Æthelgifu as the mother figure of the coronation scandal. While he does not identify the daughter, his provision of Æthelgifu's name is a significant detail lacking from all other accounts, and it allows for the identification of both women within their historical context. Æthelgifu makes another appearance in the historical record in connection to Eadwig's reign, in a charter dated 956 (discussed further below), where she is named as the mother of Ælfgifu, the wife of Eadwig.[25]

Ælfgifu is more prominent than her mother in the historical record; from her various appearances, commentators have pieced together her identity as the sister of the chronicler and ealdorman Æthelweard.[26] Æthelweard identifies himself as descended from King Æthelred I of Wessex (r. 865–71).[27] Æthelred was an older brother of King Alfred (r. 871–99), from whom Eadwig claimed descent. This means that Ælfgifu too was a scion of the West Saxon dynasty: she and Eadwig shared a great-great-great-grandfather.[28] Or, put more simply, the couple were third cousins once removed. A union between Eadwig and Ælfgifu would then have united two royal lineages, each with direct claims to the throne. The legitimating effect of such a move should not be underestimated, especially for a young king seeking autonomy from the vested interests of the previous reign. With Ælfgifu would have come a new network of kinship: powerful allies that not only sat outside the faction aligned with Edgar, but would have constituted a material threat to its ongoing influence, power, and relevance.

The marital status of Eadwig and Ælfgifu

The possibility that Eadwig and Ælfgifu were related raises questions about the appropriateness of their sexual relationship among medieval authors. Traditions around this matter are broadly separate from the coronation scandal. B makes no mention of Eadwig and Ælfgifu having familial ties in his account of the reign and its scandals, nor does that information appear in either Osbern or Eadmer's *vitae Dunstani*. William is alone in blending the coronation scandal with the idea that the couple were related, but he does so in his history, *Gesta regum*, rather than in his hagiography of St Dunstan.[29] In his history, John of Worcester, who as noted does not engage with the tale of Eadwig's coronation, draws only from this secondary tradition:

> St Oda, archbishop of Canterbury, separated Eadwig, king of the West Saxons, and Ælfgifu, either because, as they say, she was Eadwig's relative, or because, [though they were unwed, Eadwig] loved her as if she was his own wife.[30]

Whereas the coronation scandal is intimately tied to Dunstan's legacy, this tradition of separation or an annulled union is closely connected with Oda's cult. Here, John presents two alternative theories justifying Oda's actions. The first is that Eadwig and Ælfgifu were too closely related, and that their union was annulled on the basis of consanguinity. This is reported in the *Anglo-Saxon Chronicle* D-text against the year 958, and John drew on a progenitor of that text for the framework of his history of the tenth century.[31] This is how the matter of consanguinity enters his text when it is absent in so many other histories and hagiographies that recount the reign. The redaction of the *Chronicle* in which the entry is found was likely composed within decades of Eadwig's reign, and there is no evidence that the 958 entry is a later interpolation.[32] This would make it a near-contemporary assertion, and an eminently plausible one at that. The dissolution of the union can be readily understood within the context of England's fractured political landscape as being a cynical act on Oda's part. Eadwig and Ælfgifu's degree of relationship would not have been unusual for a royal couple at this point in time,[33] and Oda's move to separate them was almost certainly a political one, made more with a view to dividing Eadwig from his support base than correcting any lapse in sexual morality. And, while Eadwig and Ælfgifu's consanguinity is not attested in hagiographical accounts of the scandals of Eadwig's reign, Oda's intervention in their relationship *is* widely told.

The second theory John presents is more opaque, but the essence of it is that the couple were engaging in extra-marital sex. The Oxford Medieval Text translators of John's *Chronicon* render the phrase 'illam sub propria uxore adamauit' as 'the king loved her [Ælfgifu] adulterously as if she were his own wife'. While they do not explain their choice of words here, it is loaded with implications that are not necessarily present in the text, namely the charge of adultery. Adultery would imply that Eadwig was already wed when he began his sexual relationship with Ælfgifu, and the text's use of the accusative feminine singular *illam* leaves little doubt that she is the object of his affections here. Yet, as Richard Getz highlights, Ælfgifu is Eadwig's only known wife and given the king's age, almost certainly his first one.[34] Getz does convincingly demonstrate that the phrase *sub propria uxore* is an idiom referencing sexual transgression, identifying a similar Old English phrase in one of Ælfric's works, and a number of Middle English usages of the phrase *under is wif*. However, he may go astray in presuming that the transgression implied is adultery. Getz hinges this argument on the numerous appearances of the Middle English phrase, and a single use of the Latin formulation from 1375.[35] While he does prove that *these* reference adultery, all this can be said to demonstrate is that the idiom had acquired that meaning by the fourteenth century. Methodologically, this cannot be projected onto the phrase's use some two-and-a-half centuries earlier. Indeed, earlier even than that, given that John owes the expression to Byrhtferth of Ramsey, who recounts Oda's separation of the couple in his *Vita S. Oswaldi* (997×1002) with the phrase 'sub uxore propria alteram adamauit'.[36] While this may sound like adultery if translated literally – 'he loved another under his true wife' – as Michael Lapidge highlights, 'the formulation *sub uxore propria* is Byrhtferth's, [and] its meaning is unclear'.[37] In truth, a charge of adultery makes little sense of John's account of Eadwig's reign considering Ælfgifu is identified by name in the passage on Oda's intervention, and is there implied to be in some sort of union with Eadwig that could be annulled. Evidence for what charge is being laid against Eadwig is most safely sought in contextual clues, and in our knowledge of royal unions in tenth-century England.

Problematically, if parallels are to be sought in Byrhtferth's account of the event, his *Vita Oswaldi* does not name Ælfgifu as the consort from whom Eadwig was separated. This is a broader problem relating to accounts of Eadwig's sexual improprieties, both those connected to Oda's annulment of their union and to the coronation scandal. While B names the mother in the coronation scandal as Æthelgifu, all subsequent accounts are silent on the identities of Eadwig's consort and her mother until William's *Vita Dunstani* over a century later.[38] William is the first to place Ælfgifu at the centre of the scandal by name, yet his account is muddled. William had access to all the *vitae Dunstani* identified here, most closely adhering to B's account of events, but in naming Ælfgifu he identifies *her* as the mother in the story and ascribes to her all the deeds B attributes to Æthelgifu.[39] The identities of the mother and daughter in question as outlined above is relatively secure. William's attempted corrective to B's narrative, possibly intended to reconcile the story with historical knowledge of Ælfgifu as consort, simply introduces error.

The general silence on the identity of Eadwig's consort in hagiographical texts extends to accounts of Oda's separation of Eadwig and his consort. Fortunately, the *Chronicle* D-text makes the clear statement that 'Archbishop Oda separated King Eadwig and Ælfgifu'.[40] This provides some confidence that accounts of Oda's intervention in Eadwig's private life, no matter the narrative detail with which they became embellished, are intended to refer to Ælfgifu. This is important as the lack of names introduces ambiguity as to whether she or her mother is being referenced. Eadmer, for example, recounting the separation in his *Vita Odonis*, identifies the woman being targeted by Oda as 'she who had greater power and more obscene influence'.[41] Following B's narrative, this would be Æthelgifu. However, Eadmer then goes on to state of the woman in question that 'the king had more frequently cavorted with her in extremely rude embraces'.[42] The denigration of her sexuality aside, this more logically points to Eadwig's consort, Ælfgifu, as opposed to her mother. In truth, Eadmer had little interest in distinguishing between the two women – also a feature of Osbern's *Vita Dunstani* – and conflates elements of both into a single antagonist to Oda's protagonist.[43] Nonetheless, in the light of Oda's known intervention in Eadwig and Ælfgifu's relationship, the story that follows is best understood as having developed from that tradition.

Unlike John, Byhrtferth does not offer two explanations for the annulled union in his *Vita Oswaldi*. He reports Oda's separation of the pair *only* on the basis of a relationship *sub uxore propria*. Whatever transgression this entailed, the actions of the king and his consort enraged the archbishop, and the separation here is quite literal.[44] The archbishop arrived at the estate where Ælfgifu was staying with a force of men, abducted her, and forced her into exile beyond the kingdom's borders. Eadmer expanded on Byhrtferth's narrative a century later in his *Vita Odonis*. Firstly, drawing heavily on B (likely via Osbern's *Vita Dunstani*), Eadmer recalls the coronation scandal. He does not identify the women as mother and daughter, though he does so in his *Vita Dunstani*, which leans more directly on B and excludes the story of Oda's intervention.⁴⁵ As noted, neither woman is named (in either text). The *Vita Odonis* then goes on to recount that Oda, observing that Eadwig was not following his advice to repudiate the women, had one of them kidnapped. This time, however, Ælfgifu is not merely expelled from the kingdom (to live in Ireland), but first has her face branded with a hot iron. For having the temerity to later return, Oda's men capture her in Gloucester and cut her hamstrings, from which injuries she dies a few days later.⁴⁶ Eadmer is sure to laud the archbishop for his actions here, calling him *omnium iniquitatum inflexibilis aduersarius* (an unyielding opponent of every evil deed). Oda is here no more sympathetic than his ally Dunstan is in accounts of the coronation scandal. Once again, unbridled immorality is juxtaposed against unbridled morality.

In order to create his account of events, Eadmer drew from B/Osbern and Byrhtferth, creating a story that combines the coronation scandal with Oda's separation of Ælfgifu and Eadwig. This is unique among the texts discussed here, no doubt owing to the fact that this is a *vita* of Oda rather than Dunstan. None of the *vitae Dunstani* of B, William, or even Eadmer himself make mention of Oda's annulment of the royal union. William's *Gesta regum* may mention that the couple were related, but still does this within the context of the coronation scandal and without reference to the separation. While Osbern is the source of the story of the hamstringing, Oda takes no greater role in the overall story than he does in other redactions of the coronation scandal. It seems that Eadmer was likewise unclear on quite what accusation Byhrtferth was levelling at Ælfgifu and Eadwig in *Vita Oswaldi*, and what acts of immorality would warrant Oda exiling the king's consort from the kingdom. He found his answer in the coronation scandal. However, this once again raises the question of what perceived inappropriate sexuality Byhrtferth and John intended to be understood by the phrase *sub propria uxore*.

Broadly speaking, there are two possibilities that fit the literary and historical evidence: either Eadwig and Ælfgifu were having sex before they were married, or they were in a sexual relationship but never married. By this reckoning, *sub uxore propria* is not intended to mean 'under his true wife' in the sense of having a mistress behind the back of a spouse. Rather, the implication of the idiom is that Eadwig loved his consort 'as if she were a true wife', or under the guise of such. In short, they engaged in pre-marital or extra-marital sex. The former ties in well with the coronation scandal. No version of that event records that the couple were married, though B states that it was Æthelgifu's design to have her daughter wed the king.⁴⁷ It seems clear that they were not so at the time of their coronation feast sexual tryst. However, the very inclusion of that detail, accompanied by B's account of Æthelgifu's ascendancy at court and Dunstan's exiling from it, suggest that this subsequently came to pass. Moreover, the transmission context of the coronation scandal within the *vitae* of St Dunstan should be borne in mind. It may in fact be little more than an embellished account of Oda's separation of the couple, designed to place Dunstan at the forefront of events. Both Byrhtferth and Eadmer report that Oda was accompanied by his men when he abducted Ælfgifu. In turn, in their *vitae Dunstani*, B, Osbern, Eadmer, and William each report that Dunstan (and sometimes Cynesige) acted on Oda's orders when intervening in Eadwig's debauchery. The coronation scandal itself, therefore, may reflect (and salaciously exaggerate) rumours that the couple had had a sexual relationship prior to marrying, and it was this that provided Oda with the justification to later separate the couple.

Alternatively, and possibly more likely, the couple were simply never married. It is for this reason that the term 'marriage' has largely been avoided to describe the relationship between them thus far. This is not to say they did not have some sort of acknowledged union in which Oda intervened, but it does not follow that this need have been a marriage *per se*. Eadwig may have taken Ælfgifu as a concubine rather than as a wife. There is no evidence for a marriage, and Ælfgifu was certainly never anointed as queen-consort.[48] Concubinage was a common practice among tenth-century West Saxon kings: monogamous unions recognised by tradition, but lacking the formality of marriage.[49] In fact, the English kings most reputed for this are Eadwig's grandfather, Edward, and brother, Edgar, both of whom had three consorts and are often characterised as serial monogamists.[50] In this context, it would be unsurprising for Eadwig and Ælfgifu's union to be of a similar type. And while this was tolerated for Edward and Edgar, allied as they were with Dunstan and his circle, it was a vulnerability for a king opposed to that powerful clerical faction. As Sheila Sharp highlights, by the tenth century Church sentiment was turning against West Saxon marital practices, though 'the advantages offered by successive marriages and serial monogamy were such that kings and others were difficult to persuade'.[51] Eadwig may have been operating within West Saxon marital norms if he took Ælfgifu as a concubine, but this also offered Archbishop Oda a technicality on which to annul the union and separate the young king from a key factional support base.

In truth, the two theories presented by John are not mutually exclusive. The evidence that Eadwig and Ælfgifu were related, members of different branches of the West Saxon royal line, is compelling. In turn, the only evidence to support the idea the couple were married is found in charter S1292 in which Ælfgifu appears as second witness, titled ðæs cininges wif (this king's wife). As Jayakumar points out, however, this witness list is markedly factionally aligned and thus the statement need not be anything other than aspirational. In theory, Ælfgifu had taken Eadgifu's place at the royal court, and the phrasing *ðæs cininges wif* echoes that used of Eadgifu in her sons' charters: *eiusdem regis mater* (this king's mother).[52] Eadwig's repudiation of his grandmother is only further emphasised by S1292's inclusion of Æthelgifu as its third witness under the title of *ðæs cyninges wifes modur* (this king's wife's mother). There is, moreover, nothing to indicate that royal concubines were not styled as wives during their tenures as the king's bed companion; indeed, granted the number of 'wives' who were repudiated during the century, it seems probable that they often were so styled.[53] Ultimately, no matter if Oda separated the couple for reasons of consanguinity or of marital status (or indeed of both), his underlying rationale for separating them is readily understood. A son of Eadwig and Ælfgifu would not only have represented an alternative heir to Oda and Dunstan's preferred candidate, Edgar, but would have drawn on royal legitimacy from two West Saxon royal lineages, becoming a locus of support from families connected to both.[54]

These fears were ultimately allayed. The union produced no children due to Eadwig's early death and, no doubt, also to Oda's intervention in his relationship with Ælfgifu. Edgar ascended a united throne in 959 and Dunstan and Eadgifu returned to the centre of power (Oda had died by this time). However, the repercussions of Eadwig's reign for the incoming court did not end with the death of the king. He had given significant grants of land to his supporters, he had elevated new men to positions of authority, and his consort Ælfgifu survived him. The simplest way to delegitimise these claims to wealth and to authority was to delegitimise the reign of the king who had granted them. One way in which to do this was to point to transgressive sexuality – whether as pre-marital, extra-marital, or consanguineous sex, or as a lustful, incestuous encounter at a coronation – as symbolic of a more widely immoral character. It is telling that the traditions of these sexual transgressions are transmitted through the *vitae* of Dunstan and Oda, representatives of the faction opposing Eadwig, Ælfgifu, and Æthelgifu. Just as Eadwig and his allies were disempowered by their reputed improprieties, so too were the clerics empowered by their interventions to bring them to a halt, marked out as legitimate and pious defenders of the kingdom.

Sexuality, morality, and the *vitae S. Dunstani*

Returning our focus to the coronation scandal, the question must be why the accusations of sexual impropriety were so effective in this instance. Eadwig was certainly not the only tenth-century king to attract accusations of inappropriate sexuality. Indeed, as noted, Eadwig's brother was one of the period's so-called serial monogamists. While this itself may not have attracted censure, rather more transgressive tales of sexual trysts dog Edgar's legacy. William of Malmesbury, whose inclusive approach to history writing regularly sees him report rumours that other medieval historians eschew, includes several stories of Edgar's lust and its repercussions.[55] In one of these, Edgar abducts and rapes a nun. In another, a girl named Wulfthryth – who would be Edgar's second consort, before becoming abbess of Wilton, and finally a saint – was hiding in an abbey to escape the king's attentions, from where she was abducted and forced into marriage.[56] As Yorke puts it, 'it would appear that various rumours about Edgar's sexual predilections for nuns ... were circulating in the late eleventh and twelfth centuries'.[57] Yet William does not pursue these accusations of inappropriate sexuality with the gusto he brings to those levelled at Eadwig. They are included in part for completeness, and in part to serve as exemplars of transgression and repentance for the rulers of his own day.[58] Certainly, there is no evidence that William believed these stories, and he distances himself from them by introducing them with the statement 'there are those who try to identify blemishes in his immensely distinguished record'.[59] The contrast between the brothers' legacies as presented in the *Gesta regum* is clearly expressed in William's introductions to both their reigns, with Edgar referred to as *honor ac delitiae Anglorum* (the honour and delight of the English), and Eadwig as *petulans adolescens* (a wanton youth).[60]

One would be forgiven for thinking that Edgar's sexual transgressions far outweighed those of his brother, especially in the eyes of clerical authors. However, Edgar's 'sexual predilection for nuns' seems to have had a little long-term repercussion for his legacy. This once more connects to the factionalism of English politics in the 950s. Both of William's stories relating to Edgar's sexual activities with nuns connect directly to Dunstan. In that relating to Wulfthryth, we are told that 'it is also certain that St Dunstan was indignant at [Edgar] casting eyes of desire over one who had passed even through the shadow of religious life'.[61] William's account relating to the other nun is, however, perhaps more interesting:

> Hearing of the beauty of a nun under vows, he removed her by violence from her convent and, having done so, he raped her and forced her to his bed more than once. But when this reached the ears of St Dunstan, [Edgar] was greatly rebuked by him, and did not refuse seven years' penance, submitting, king though he was, to be ordered to fast, and at the same time to forego the wearing his crown for seven years.[62]

The two stories of the nuns are, in fact, one and the same. William's sources are again Osbern and Eadmer's *vitae Dunstani*, where this is reported as a single story, but the differences between them seem to have recommended them to William as distinct tales (at least in his *Gesta regum*). Osbern reports that she was a nun, Eadmer that she was a noblewoman posing as a nun (albeit a lay affiliate).[63] Eadmer and William in fact take quite some exception to Osbern's implication that Wulfthryth was a nun with whom Edgar had a child – King Edward the Martyr according to Eadmer, St Edith of Wilton according to William.[64] This was clearly a sexual transgression too far, irreconcilable with the king's positive legacy. This explains William's reporting them as separate stories in *Gesta regum*, as he seeks to preserve information relating to both the seven-year penance and Edgar's abduction of Wulfthryth without the one being causal to the other. Notably, the seven-year penance reflects an attempt to make sense of the fact that Edgar had two coronations – an anointing at the start of his reign, and a remarkable coronation ceremony at Bath in 973 connected to the Church reforms being promoted by Dunstan and his allies.[65]

In its origins, the 973 coronation has no association with any purported sexual transgressions on Edgar's part. Nor is there any report of Edgar's inappropriate sexuality or of his second coronation in B's *Vita Dunstani*. This tradition of the king's seven-year penance entered St Dunstan's legacy at a later stage, possibly drawing from the *vitae* of the various saintly women of Wilton Abbey.[66] But it is the framing of the episode within the *vitae Dunstani* more so than its source that is important to this discussion. Edgar's inappropriate sexuality is then turned to an entirely different purpose to that of Eadwig, with the brothers serving as opposing exemplars. Even if B makes no report of Edgar's sexuality, his statement that Edgar 'did not forget how much respect his predecessors felt [for Dunstan]' is telling.[67] Edgar's obedience and respect stand in distinct opposition to the characterisation of his brother's relationship with the abbot.

Many traditions relating to Eadwig and Edgar's legacies have been preserved through a Dunstanian lens. Certainly, their names and deeds are preserved across an array of sources, but in narrative histories of their kingships the influence of Dunstan's legacy should not be underestimated. Eadwig exiled Dunstan, Edgar recalled him. Eadwig marginalised Dunstan's allies, Edgar brought them into his court. Eadwig showed limited support for Dunstan's programmes of Church reform, Edgar supported them and elevated Dunstan first to the bishoprics of Worcester and of London, then the archbishopric in Canterbury. Eadwig responded to Dunstan's admonitions of his sexual transgression with anger and retribution, Edgar responded with contrition and obedience. And herein lies the main difference between the brothers regarding their inappropriate sexuality according to the *vitae* of St Dunstan. Edgar repented his sinfulness and reformed his ways, accepting Dunstan's guidance. This had the dual effect of absolving the king of his transgressions and augmenting the reputation and sanctity of the saint. In contrast, Eadwig rejected all such advice, from Dunstan and from Oda, and continued his lascivious ways until his death. Of course, it should again be pointed out that this is a politicised perspective of the brothers' reigns. The ascendancy of a new political faction during Eadwig's rule is an anomaly of mid-tenth century English history. Dunstan and his allies were influential court advisors in the reigns of Eadwig's three predecessors, and of his three successors. In essence, Dunstan and his faction won, and their acolytes and admirers wrote the history of Eadwig's reign.

In this context, as Katherine Weikert argues, the coronation scandal is a carefully constructed framework of transgression designed to contravene numerous cultural-religious norms. Weikert points to escalating layers of sexual transgression as latent within the story of the coronation scandal, constituting what she terms 'dangerous sexuality'.[68] In the first instance, Eadwig's sex at the coronation has no procreative purpose. It is extra-marital sex for pleasure's sake, an undesirable expression of sexuality in the eyes of the Church.[69] This sits in contrast to the ideal sexuality of the chaste figures of Dunstan and Cynesige who interrupted the affair. Moreover, Eadwig's status must be recalled. He was king, and with that came an expectation for productive sex, the creation of heirs. In this light, his sex for pleasure becomes symbolic of his wider abandonment of the duties of his office.

Second is incest and consanguinity. It is important, however, not to conflate the various accusations against Eadwig's sexuality. As discussed above, different accusations belong to distinct hagiographical traditions; Dunstan and Oda's cults codify different charges of sexual impropriety that have inherent within them distinct transgressions. No *vita* of St Dunstan reports the couple's consanguinity. However, incest can be reasonably contested; Eadwig's sexual liaison at his coronation was with a mother and daughter. Weikert identifies an extensive list of prohibitions on incest, each entailing significant periods of penance.[70] The coronation scandal therefore entails an expression of sexuality that was at once extra-marital (twice over), intended for pleasure and the satiation of lust, and incestuous. This is intended to be a shocking moment, and it seems appropriate to allow William to give his impression of the event:

> And the story went that Eadwig played around with both mother and daughter, satisfying himself with each in turn. But belief in this must rest in the hands of the old writers. Would that I was wrong in this, and that none will credit my story that a Christian man ever subjected himself to such reproaches.[71]

William's seemingly shocked sensibilities were no doubt what B hoped for when he wrote the tale. As noted, the coronation scandal is a hagiographical story, not a historical one. But more even than this, it is a political tale. Its motivations are evident.

Dunstan found himself relegated to the periphery of court life by Eadwig, his factional allies likewise replaced as royal power was invested in a new network of elites. Eadwig had sought to free himself of the constraints of the entrenched political interests of his uncle, father, and grandfather's reigns. As an element of this programme of change, Eadwig surrounded himself with loyal relatives, including a consort who was also a descendant of the West Saxon royal house. The legitimating effect of uniting two royal lineages in the Eadwig–Ælfgifu union could have constituted an existential threat to the Dunstan-led faction coalescing around Eadwig's more compliant younger brother, Edgar. And so that union needed to be delegitimated, its associated faction disempowered. One element of this was Oda's annulment of their union, an historical event irrespective of Eadmer's embellishments. This was a cynical move, almost certainly justified by their consanguinity, but also perhaps by a less than formal marriage arrangement. However, after the deaths of the key figures in the dramas of Eadwig's reigns, another story emerged: the coronation scandal. Here, Dunstan's hagiographers constructed a story designed to shock and discredit, accessing ideas of inappropriate sexuality. It was a story intended to tarnish the king's legacy, to delegitimate and disempower his factional allies, while at the same time augmenting the sanctity and morality of Cynesige, Oda, and Dunstan, and legitimating the political faction they represented.

Notes

1 B, 'Vita S. Dunstani', in *The Early Lives of St Dunstan*, ed. and trans. Michael Lapidge and Michael Winterbottom (Oxford: Clarendon Press, 2012), 66–73. Latin quotes are taken from the cited editions of texts, English translations are vetted and adapted from those provided in these texts where available.
2 For the medieval uses of the term *ganea* as meaning 'harlot', see *Dictionary of Latin from Medieval British Sources*, s.v. 'ganea', at www.dmlbs.ox.ac.uk/web/online.html (accessed 27 November 2023).
3 B, 'Vita S. Dunstani', 66–71. For further discussion of the Jezebel motif in tenth- to twelfth-century Anglo-Latin hagiography, see Matthew Firth, 'The Character of the Treacherous Woman in the *passiones* of Early Medieval English Royal Martyrs', *Royal Studies Journal* 7.1 (2020): 1–21. On this passage in particular, see Matthew Firth, 'Deconstructing the Female Antagonist of the Coronation Scandal in B's *Vita Dunstani*', *English Studies* 103.4 (2022): 527–546. See also Jan Ziolkowski, *Jezebel: A Norman Latin Poem of the Early Eleventh Century* (New York: Peter Lang, 1989), 15–26.
4 B, 'Vita S. Dunstani', 68–69. 'ipsum more maligno inter utrasque, uelet in uili suillorum uolutabro'.
5 Firth, 'The Character', 11–12; Firth, 'Deconstructing', 533–539.

6 Firth, 'Deconstructing', 528–533; Barbara Yorke, 'Æthelwold and the Politics of the Tenth Century', in *Bishop Æthelwold: His Career and Influence*, ed. Barbara Yorke (Woodbridge: Boydell, 1988), 76–77.
7 Shashi Jayakumar, 'Eadwig and Edgar: Politics, Propaganda, Faction', in *Edgar, King of the English 959–975: New Interpretations*, ed. Donald Scragg (Woodbridge: Boydell, 2008), 102.
8 Michael Lapidge, 'B. and the *Vita Dunstani*', in *St Dunstan: His Life, Times and Cult*, ed. Nigel Ramsay, Margaret Sparks, and Tim Tatton-Brown, 251–257.
9 R.R. Darlington and P. McGurk, eds, *The Chronicle of John of Worcester. Volume II: The Annals from 450–1066*, trans. Jennifer Bray and Patrick McGurk (Oxford: Clarendon Press, 1995), 406–409: 'in commisso regimine insipienter egit'; 'pro iustitia'. My translations.
10 Henry of Huntingdon, *Historia Anglorum*, ed. and trans. Diana E. Greenway (Oxford: Clarendon Press, 1996), 318–319. 'Rex autem predictus Eadwi non inlaudabiliter regulam infulam tenuit'. My translation.
11 Geffrei Gaimar, *Estoire des Engleis*, ed. and trans. Ian Short (Cambridge: Cambridge University Press, 2009), 194–195.
12 Mary Elizabeth Blanchard, 'A New Perspective on Family Strategy in Tenth- and Eleventh-Century England: Ealdorman Status and the Church', *Historical Research* 92.256 (2019): 247–248; M. Firth, *Early English Queens, 850–1000: Potestas Reginae* (London: Routledge, 2024), 106–109; Dominik Wassenhoven, 'The Role of Bishops in Anglo-Saxon Succession Struggles, 955×978', in *Leaders of the Anglo-Saxon Church: From Bede to Stigand*, ed. Alexander R. Rumble (Woodbridge: Boydell, 2012), 100–102; Yorke, 'Æthelwold', 74–75.
13 Wassenhoven, 'Role of Bishops', 100–101.
14 Darlington and McGurk, *John of Worcester*, 406–407. 'Rex Anglorum Edwius, quoniam in commisso regimine insipienter egit, a Mercensibus et Norðhymbrensibus contemptus relinquitur, et suus germanus clito Eadgarus ab eis rex eligitur, sicque res regum seiuncta es tut flumen Tamense regnum disterminaret amborum', though cf. the *Anglo-Saxon Chronicles* (*ASC*) B- and C-text entries for 957 which ascribe no popular rejection of Eadwig's reign to Edgar's succession to the Mercian throne. For commentary on the division of the kingdom, see Jayakumar, 'Eadwig and Edgar', 84–90; Wassenhoven, 'Role of Bishops', 100–101. Throughout this chapter the *ASC* is cited by manuscript and year, taken from the respective volumes of *The Anglo-Saxon Chronicle: A Collaborative Edition*, general eds D. Dumville and S. Keynes (Cambridge: Brewer, 1983–2004).
15 Eadmer of Canterbury, 'Vita S. Odonis', in *Lives and Miracles of Saints Oda, Dunstan and Oswald*, ed. and trans. A.J. Turner and B.J. Muir (Oxford: Oxford University Press, 2006), 28–29.
16 See for example, Adelard, 'Lectiones in depositione S. Dunstani', in *The Early Lives of St Dunstan*, 128–129; *ASC* D 958; B, *Vita S. Dunstani*, 74–77; Darlington and McGurk, *John of Worcester*, 406–407; S 674–679. See also Wassenhoven, 'Role of Bishops', 101–102.

17 Osbern of Canterbury, 'Vita S. Dunstani', in *Memorials of St Dunstan*, ed. William Stubbs (London: Longman, 1874), 99: 'neque sapientium consilio adquiescens ... puerorum consilia seetabatur'.
18 Eadmer of Canterbury, 'Vita S. Dunstani', in *Lives and Miracles*, 92–93; Eadmer, 'Vita S. Odonis', 24–25. William of Malmesbury hews more closely to B's narrative in his account of the reign in both his *Vita S. Dunstani* and *Gesta regum*.
19 Firth, 'Deconstructing', 533. See also Blanchard, 'A New Perspective', 247–248.
20 Eadmer, 'Vita S. Odonis', 24–25: 'moribus et aetate iuuenculus'; cf. B, 'Vita S. Dunstani', 66–67. My translation.
21 Jayakumar, 'Eadwig and Edgar', 84–90; Yorke, 'Æthelwold', 76–80.
22 Yorke, 'Æthelwold', 76.
23 Pauline Stafford, *Queens, Concubines and Dowagers: The King's Wife in the Early Middle Ages* (London: Batsford Academic, 1983), 16.
24 Nicholas Brooks, 'Career of St Dunstan', in *St Dunstan: His Life, Times and Cult*, 15; Wassenhoven, 'Role of Bishops', 99–100.
25 S 1292. Charters are cited thus (S 000) per P.H. Sawyer, ed., *Anglo-Saxon Charters: An Annotated List and Bibliography*, revd by Simon Keynes, Susan Kelly, et al. See https://esawyer.lib.cam.ac.uk (accessed 27 November 2023).
26 Jayakumar, 'Eadwig and Edgar', 87–88; Katherine Weikert, 'Eadwig has a Threesome: Gender, Sex and the Breaking of Authority in the Tenth Century', in *The Reigns of Edmund, Eadred and Eadwig, 939–959: New Interpretations*, ed. Mary Blanchard and Christopher Riedel (Woodbridge: Boydell & Brewer, 2024), 227–252. Yorke, 'Æthelwold', 77.
27 *The Chronicle of Æthelweard*, ed. and trans. Alistair Campbell (London: Thomas Nelson, 1962), 38–39.
28 Pauline Stafford presents an alternative genealogy via the Mercian royal family, which changes the degree of Ælfgifu and Eadwig's familial relationship, but not the fact of it. See Pauline Stafford, 'Ælfgifu (fl. 956–966)', *ODNB* at https://doi.org/10.1093/ref:odnb/179 (accessed 27 November 2023); Pauline Stafford, 'Political Women in Mercia, Eighth to Early Tenth Centuries', in *Mercia: An Anglo-Saxon Kingdom in Europe*, ed. Michelle P. Brown and Carol A. Farr (London: Continuum, 2001), 35, 46.
29 William of Malmesbury, *Gesta regum Anglorum. Volume I*, ed. and trans. R.A.B. Mynors, R.M. Thomson, and M. Winterbottom (Oxford: Clarendon Press, 1998), 236–237.
30 'Sanctus Odo Dorubernie arciepiscopus regem Wessaxonum Eduuium et Ælfgiuam, uel quia, ut fertur, propinqua illius exstitit uel quia illam sub propria uxore adamauit ab inuicem separauit'. Darlington and McGurk, *John of Worcester. Vol. II*, 408–409. [My translation].
31 Pauline Stafford, *After Alfred: Anglo-Saxon Chronicles and Chroniclers, 900–1150* (Oxford: Oxford University Press, 2021), 135–142.
32 Stafford, *After Alfred*, 135–145.
33 Stafford, *Queens, Concubines and Dowagers*, 75–76; Yorke, 'Æthelwold', 76–77. See also, Nicholas Brooks, *Anglo-Saxon Myths: State and Church, 400–1066* (London: Hambledon, 2000), 171; Weikert, 'Eadwig has a Threesome'.

34 Robert Getz, '*Sub uxore proproa / under is wif*: The Alleged Adultery of Eadwig', *Notes & Queries* 59.1 (2012): 21–22.
35 Getz, '*Sub uxore proproa*', 21–22.
36 Byrhtferth of Ramsey, 'Vita S. Oswaldi', in *The Lives of St Oswald and St Ecgwine*, ed. M. Lapidge (Oxford: Clarendon Press, 2009), 12–13.
37 Byrhtferth, 'Vita S. Oswaldi', 13 (n.30).
38 B, 'Vita S. Dunstani', 68–69.
39 William of Malmesbury, 'Vita S. Dunstani', in *Saints' Lives*, ed. and trans. M. Winterbottom and R.M. Thomson (Oxford: Clarendon Press, 2002), xvii–xxv, 224–229. In describing the women's role in Dunstan's exile, William also draws on the rhetoric of Adelard, 'Lectiones', 114–145.
40 'Oda arcebiscop totwæmde Eadwi cyning 7 Ælgyfe'.
41 Eadmer, 'Vita S. Odonis', 28–29: 'quam et amplior potentia et obscenior impudentia dehonestabat'. My translation.
42 Eadmer, 'Vita S. Odonis', 28–29: 'nimium contumeliosis amplexibus rex frequentius abutebatur'.
43 Eadmer, 'Vita S. Odonis', 28–29; cf. Osbern, 'Vita S. Dunstani', in *Memorials of St Dunstan*, ed. William Stubbs (London: Longman, 1874), 100–102.
44 Byhrtferth, '*Vita S. Oswaldi*', 12–13. Byhrtferth draws connections between Eadwig's actions and the sins of King David, but it does not follow that this indicates adultery so much as general inappropriate sexuality. David took numerous concubines (2 Sam 2:2, 3:3–5; 5:13), and Byrhtferth references Oda's response in connection to a biblical story of Israelites' *fornicatus* (having fornicated), not *moechatus* (having committed adultery) (Num 25). Bible references are per the Vulgate.
45 Eadmer, 'Vita S. Odonis', 28–29, cf. Eadmer, 'Vita Dunstani', 97–101.
46 Eadmer, 'Vita S. Odonis', 24–29. Eadmer borrows the story of the hamstringing in Gloucester from Osbern, *Vita Dunstani*, 102.
47 B, *Vita Dunstani*, 66–67.
48 Weikert, 'Eadwig has a Threesome'.
49 Margaret Clunies Ross, 'Concubinage in Anglo-Saxon England', *Past & Present* 108 (1985): 7, 10; Matthew Firth, 'Identifying Queenship in Pre-Conquest England', in *Norman to Early Plantagenet Consorts: Power, Influence and Dynasty*, ed. Aidan Norrie et al. (London: Palgrave Macmillan, 2023), 17–45.
50 See Clunies Ross, 'Concubinage', 5–6, 11–13; Kathrin Prietzel, 'Appetite for power: the Anglo-Saxon *regina gratia dei*', *English Studies* 93 (2012): 553; Pauline Stafford, 'The King's Wife in Wessex 800–1066', *Past and Present* 91 (1981): 7. See also Sheila Sharpe, 'The West Saxon Tradition of Dynastic Marriage', in *Edward the Elder, 899–924*, ed. N.J. Higham and D.H. Hill (London: Routledge, 2001), 79–88.
51 Sharpe, 'The West Saxon Tradition', 81.
52 See for example, S 523, S 526, S 532.
53 Stafford, 'The King's Wife', 7–15.
54 Firth, 'Deconstructing', 533; Jayakumar, 'Eadwig and Edgar', 88–90; Yorke, 'Æthelwold', 77.

55 William, *Gesta regum*, 257–261. One of these is also recorded (and embellished) in some detail in Geffrei Gaimar, *Estoire*, 196–213. Edgar's purported vices of lust and anger are discussed in detail in Matthew Firth, 'Rage and Lust in the Afterlives of King Edgar the Peaceful', in *Emotional Alterity in the Medieval North Sea World*, ed. Erin Sebo, Matthew Firth, and Daniel Anlezark (Basingstoke: Palgrave Macmillan, 2023), 201–230.
56 William, *Gesta regum*, 258–261.
57 Barbara Yorke, 'The Women in Edgar's Life', in *Edgar, King of the English 959–975: New Interpretations*, 155.
58 Firth, 'Rage and Lust'.
59 William, *Gesta regum*, 256–257: 'sunt qui ingenti eius gloriae neuum temptent apponere'. Adapted translation.
60 William, *Gesta regum*, 236–239.
61 William, *Gesta regum*, 260–261: 'unde offensum beatum Dunstanum, quod illam concupisset quar uel umbratice sanctimonialis fuisset'.
62 William, *Gesta regum*, 258–259: 'Virginis Deo dicatae audiens pulchritudinem, uiolenter eam a monasterio abstraxit, abstractae pudorem rapuit et non semel thoro suo collacauit. Quod cum aures beati Dunstani offendisset, uehmenter ab eo increpitus, septennem penitentiam non fastidiuit, dignatus rex affligi ieiunio simulque diademate carere septennio'. My translation.
63 Eadmer, 'Vita S. Dunstani', 134–135.
64 Eadmer, 'Vita S. Dunstani', 44–45; William of Malmesbury, *Gesta pontificum Anglorum*, ed. M. Winterbottom and R.M. Thomson (Oxford: Clarendon Press, 2007), 300–301. Though William recounts the stories in *Gesta regum* and acknowledges them in *Gesta Pontificum*, they are absent from his *Vita S. Dunstani*.
65 ASC A–E 973. For detailed analysis of the second coronation, see Julia Barrow, 'Chester's Earliest Regatta? Edgar's Dee Rowing Revisited', *Early Medieval Europe* 10 (2001): 81–93; Ann Williams, 'An Outing on the Dee: King Edgar at Chester, A.D. 973', *Mediaeval Scandinavia* 14 (2004): 229–243.
66 Susan Ridyard, *The Royal Saints of Anglo-Saxon England* (Cambridge: Cambridge University Press, 1988), 42–44.
67 B, *Vita Dunstani*, 74–77: 'non inmemor quantae reuerentiae fuerit antecessoribus ipsius'. My translation.
68 Weikert, 'Eadwig has a Threesome'.
69 Christopher Monk, 'In Bed with the Anglo-Saxons: The Sensuality of Sex in Early English Culture', in *Sense and Feeling in Daily Living in the Early Medieval English World*, ed. M. Clegg-Hyer and G.R. Owen-Crocker (Liverpool: Liverpool University Press, 2020), 123.
70 Weikert, 'Eadwig has a Threesome'.
71 William, *Vita Dunstani*, 226–227. 'Ferebaturque Edwius lasciuire tam in matrem quam in filiam et in ambabus satiare uoluptatem uicariam. Sed huius dicti credulitas penes antiquos auctores sit. Utinam in hoc dumtaxat sim uanus, nullusque ad imitandum michi fidem accommodet, quod umquam Christianus se tali probro subiecerit'. My translation.

Bibliography

Primary texts

Adelard. 'Lectiones in depositione S. Dunstani'. In *The Early Lives of St Dunstan*, ed. and trans. Michael Lapidge and Michael Winterbottom, 114–145. Oxford: Clarendon Press, 2012.

Æthelweard. *The Chronicle of Æthelweard*, ed. and trans. Alistair Campbell. London: Thomas Nelson, 1962.

The Anglo-Saxon Chronicle: A Collaborative Edition, general editors David Dumville and Simon Keynes (MSS A-F, various editors). Cambridge: Brewer, 1983–2004.

B. 'Vita S. Dunstani'. In *The Early Lives of St Dunstan*, ed. and trans. Michael Lapidge and Michael Winterbottom, 1–109. Oxford: Clarendon Press, 2012.

Byrhtferth of Ramsey. 'Vita S. Oswaldi'. In *The Lives of St Oswald and St Ecgwine*, ed. Michael Lapidge, 1–204. Oxford: Clarendon Press, 2009.

Eadmer of Canterbury. 'Vita S. Dunstani'. In *Lives and Miracles of Saints Oda, Dunstan and Oswald*, ed. and trans. Andrew J. Turner and Bernard J. Muir, 41–159. Oxford: Clarendon Press, 2006.

Eadmer of Canterbury. 'Vita S. Odonis'. In *Lives and Miracles of Saints Oda, Dunstan and Oswald*, ed. and trans. Andrew J. Turner and Bernard J. Muir, 1–40. Oxford: Clarendon Press, 2006.

Geffrei Gaimar. *Estoire des Engleis / History of the English*, ed. and trans. Ian Short. Cambridge: Cambridge University Press, 2009.

Henry of Huntingdon. *Historia Anglorum*, ed. and trans. Diana E. Greenway. Oxford: Clarendon Press, 1996.

John of Worcester. *The Chronicle of John of Worcester. Volume II: The Annals from 450–1066*, ed. R.R. Darlington and P. McGurk, trans. Jennifer Bray and P. McGurk. Oxford: Clarendon Press, 1995.

Osbern of Canterbury. 'Vita S. Dunstani'. In *Memorials of St Dunstan*, ed. William Stubbs, 69–128. London: Longman, 1874.

Sawyer, P.H., ed., *Anglo-Saxon Charters: An Annotated List and Bibliography*, rev. by Simon Keynes, Susan Kelly, et al. Cited as S, available at https://esawyer.lib.cam.ac.uk (accessed 27 November 2023).

William of Malmesbury. *Gesta pontificum Anglorum*, ed. M. Winterbottom with R.M. Thomson. Oxford: Clarendon Press, 2007.

William of Malmesbury. *Gesta regum Anglorum. Volume I*, ed. and trans. R.A.B. Mynors, R.M. Thomson, and M. Winterbottom. Oxford: Clarendon Press, 1998.

William of Malmesbury. 'Vita S. Dunstani'. In *Saints' Lives*, ed. and trans. M. Winterbottom and R.M. Thomson, 165–304. Oxford: Clarendon Press, 2002.

Secondary sources

Barrow, Julia. 'Chester's Earliest Regatta? Edgar's Dee rowing revisited'. *Early Medieval Europe* 10 (2001): 81–93.

Blanchard, Mary Elizabeth. 'A New Perspective on Family Strategy in Tenth- and Eleventh-Century England: Ealdorman status and the Church'. *Historical Research* 92.256 (2019): 244–266.

Brooks, Nicholas. *Anglo-Saxon Myths: State and Church, 400–1066*. London: Hambledon, 2000.

Brooks, Nicholas. 'The Career of St Dunstan'. In *St Dunstan: His life, times and cult*, ed. Nigel Ramsay, Margaret Sparks, and Tim Tatton-Brown, 1–23. Woodbridge: Boydell, 1992.

Clunies Ross, Margaret. 'Concubinage in Anglo-Saxon England'. *Past & Present* 108 (1985): 3–34.

Firth, Matthew. 'The Character of the Treacherous Woman in the *passiones* of Early Medieval English Royal Martyrs'. *Royal Studies Journal* 7.1 (2020): 1–21.

Firth, Matthew. 'Deconstructing the Female Antagonist of the Coronation Scandal in B's *Vita Dunstani*'. *English Studies* 103.4 (2022): 527–546.

Firth, Matthew. 'Identifying Queenship in Pre-Conquest England'. In *Norman to Early Plantagenet Consorts: Power, influence and dynasty*, ed. Aidan Norrie, Carolyn Harris, J.L. Laynesmith, Danna R. Messer, and Elena Woodacre, 17–45. London: Palgrave Macmillan, 2023.

Firth, Matthew. 'Rage and Lust in the Afterlives of King Edgar the Peaceful'. In *Emotional Alterity in the Medieval North Sea World*, ed. Erin Sebo, Matthew Firth and Daniel Anlezark (Basingstoke: Palgrave Macmillan, 2023), 201–230.

Getz, Robert. '*Sub uxore proproa / under is wif*: The alleged adultery of Eadwig'. *Notes & Queries* 59.1 (2012): 19–25.

Jayakumar, Shashi. 'Eadwig and Edgar: Politics, propaganda, faction'. In *Edgar, King of the English 959–975: New Interpretations*, ed. Donald Scragg, 83–103. Woodbridge: Boydell, 2008.

Lapidge, Michael. 'B. and the Vita Dunstani'. In *St Dunstan: His life, times and cult*, ed. Nigel Ramsay, Margaret Sparks, and Tim Tatton-Brown, 247–259. Woodbridge: Boydell, 1992.

Monk, Christopher. 'In Bed with the Anglo-Saxons: The sensuality of sex in early English culture'. In *Sense and Feeling in Daily Living in the Early Medieval English World*, ed. Maren Clegg-Hyer and Gale R. Owen-Crocker, 113–133. Liverpool: Liverpool University Press, 2020.

Prietzel, Kathrin. 'Appetite for Power: The Anglo-Saxon *regina gratia dei*'. *English Studies* 93 (2012): 549–558.

Ridyard, Susan. *The Royal Saints of Anglo-Saxon England*. Cambridge: Cambridge University Press, 1988.

Sharpe, Sheila. 'The West Saxon Tradition of Dynastic Marriage'. In *Edward the Elder, 899–924*, ed. N.J. Higham and D.H. Hill, 79–88. London: Routledge, 2001.

Stafford, Pauline. 'The King's Wife in Wessex 800–1066'. *Past and Present* 91 (1981): 3–27.

Stafford, Pauline. *Queens, Concubines and Dowagers: The king's wife in the early middle ages*. London: Batsford Academic, 1983.

Stafford, Pauline. 'Political Women in Mercia, Eighth to Early Tenth Centuries'. In *Mercia: An Anglo-Saxon kingdom in Europe*, ed. Michelle P. Brown and Carol A. Farr, 35–49. London: Continuum, 2001.

Stafford, Pauline. 'Ælfgifu (fl. 956–966)'. *Oxford Dictionary of National Biography (ODNB)*, Oxford: Oxford University Press, 2004. See https://doi.org/10.1093/REF:ODNB/179 (accessed 27 November 2023).

Stafford, Pauline. *After Alfred: Anglo-Saxon Chronicles and Chroniclers, 900–1150*. Oxford: Oxford University Press, 2021.

Wassenhoven, Dominik. 'The Role of Bishops in Anglo-Saxon Succession Struggles, 955 × 978'. In *Leaders of the Anglo-Saxon Church: From Bede to Stigand*, ed. Alexander R. Rumble, 97–108. Woodbridge: Boydell, 2012.

Weikert, Katherine. 'Eadwig has a Threesome: Gender, Sex and the Breaking of Authority in the Tenth Century'. In *The Reigns of Edmund, Eadred and Eadwig, 939–959: New interpretations*, ed. Mary Blanchard and Christopher Riedel, 227–252 (Woodbridge: Boydell & Brewer, 2024).

Williams, Ann. 'An Outing on the Dee: King Edgar at Chester, A.D. 973'. *Mediaeval Scandinavia* 14 (2004): 229–243.

Yorke, Barbara. 'Æthelwold and the Politics of the Tenth Century'. In *Bishop Æthelwold: His Career and Influence*, ed. Barbara Yorke, 65–89. Woodbridge: Boydell, 1988.

Yorke, Barbara. 'The Women in Edgar's Life'. In *Edgar, King of the English 959–975: New interpretations*, ed. Donald Scragg, 143–157. Woodbridge: Boydell, 2008.

Ziolkowski, Jan. *Jezebel: A Norman Latin poem of the early eleventh century*. New York: Peter Lang, 1989.

3

Scandal, romance, political affairs: Walter Map's 'Portuguese king' and Anglo-Flemish relations in the twelfth century

Fabrizio De Falco

In the twelfth century, the court of the Plantagenet kings of England was a famous centre of cultural production, scandal, and intrigue. For almost a century, this court – representing the core of a heterogeneous system of dominions under the authority of the kings of England – became one of the principal political actors in Europe. Henry II (r. 1154–1189) and his sons Richard I (r. 1189–1199) and John (r. 1199–1216) ruled or controlled territories spanning from southern France to Ireland. Therefore, the literary production of the Plantagenet court merged the interests of its rulers and the Anglo-Norman literary tradition with the transformations arising in continental Europe over the last decades of the twelfth century.[1] Authors writing at court studied at universities, held administrative functions in the government, and participated actively in both the cultural and political life of the kingdom. Neither they nor their patrons underestimated the political value of courtly writing and literature and their possible usages.[2] In this context, reporting – or inventing – scandals was often an explicit way of launching a political offensive.

In a culture of honour, personal reputation was essential for conducting public affairs.[3] The loss of *bona fama* could result in legal and social impediments, and gossip was one of the perfect tools for bringing down a person's *fama*. In a world defined by men, women's *bona fama* was bound in particular to the submission of wives to their husbands.[4] Rumours of sexual misbehaviour and adultery could thus be used to weaken a woman's standing and, in many cases, to misconstrue her political actions; indeed, medieval authors often explained women's actions by referring to their irrational, sentimental and libidinous natures, thereby also minimising female agency. At the Plantagenet court, the use and effects of *mala fama* on women found a famous example in Eleanor, the duchess of Aquitaine and queen of England.[5] Eleanor's choice to divorce her first husband, the king of France Louis VII, to marry Henry II changed the political balance in France and was a pivotal point for the Plantagenet family's rising political importance in Europe. When Eleanor supported her sons in opposition to Henry II, authors close to the king accused her of a long list of adulterous relations and irrational behaviours, depicting her decisions as driven by typical female inconstancy rather than political motivations.[6] Her insistence on a political range of action and her support for Henry the Young King and Richard I gained Eleanor fame as one of the most scandalous queens of all time.

Rumours and scandals were an integral part of political language at the Plantagenet court, and the case of Eleanor of Aquitaine is perhaps only the most notorious of many examples. Various chronicles and reports of the Plantagenet space document treacherous queens acting against their husbands. Some infamous acts covered a great distance, like the actions of Sichelgaita, Robert Guiscard's wife, who held expertise in poisoning her relatives.[7] Other scandals directly affected the survival of men and institutions. Hugh of Nonant reported William Longchamp's attempt to flee England, for instance, highlighting that the archbishop made the attempt dressed as a prostitute, an adventure that marked the end of William's influence in England.[8] When in 1150 a nun at Watton announced her miraculous pregnancy, her sisters were worried that this evidence of sexual activity might affect the monastery's reputation and, ultimately, survival. Only the miraculous intervention of the ghost of the Archbishop of York resolved this unfortunate situation, and the child disappeared over the course of a single night.[9]

The cases described above show the convergence of scandals, romance, and politics in the cultural production of the twelfth-century Plantagenet court. The documented use and reporting of scandals, particularly women's sexual misbehaviour, illustrates how important this subject was at court and points to the possibility of analysing less explicit texts in this same manner. In the following pages, I take the political use of rumours as the interpretative key for analysing *De nugis curialium*'s Chapter I.12.

The adultery of the Portuguese queen

Walter Map was a royal cleric at the court of Henry II, a canon of Hereford, archdeacon of Oxford in the diocese of Lincoln, and bishop-elect of Hereford. *De nugis curialium* is Map's only surviving work, contained in a single fourteenth-century manuscript. Walter Map wrote this text in the second half of the twelfth century, originally between 1172 and 1189 (at least), a temporal uncertainty that stems from the drifting structure of the text and the corrections made by both the author (during the writing process) and later copyists.[10] The scholarly debate about the composition of *De nugis curialium* is longstanding and, in line with Joshua Byron Smith's latest study of the text, I consider *De nugis curialium* to be a work 'frozen in revision': Walter Map was still reviewing the text in the last decade of the twelfth century, revising stories he had previously written during his stay at Henry II's court.[11] *De nugis curialium* is presented as a collection of anecdotes and narratives in which the writer touches on almost all the topics near and dear to the Plantagenet court, reporting his personal experiences at court in a kaleidoscope of styles and themes designed to entertain the courtiers. Specifically, *De nugis curialium* is famous for its folkloristic stories and satirical attacks.[12] Walter Map's biting words often reveal rumours or report malicious stories about contemporary *potentes*, as for instance with his tales about Geoffrey, Archbishop of York, the illegitimate son of Henry II.[13]

However, talking explicitly about the misdeeds of lords and ladies was a dangerous game, and this danger gave rise to another characteristic of Walter Map's writing style: allusiveness. In the *prologus* of the fifth distinction of *De nugis curialium*, Walter Map explains the circumstances that would lead an author to conceal real names under fictitious identities, and his own choice to present some reports as ancient tales.[14] To be effective, this communicative strategy presumes that readers share with the writer a common background of information: the public is supposed to possess the necessary references to decrypt the message.

Chapter I.12 reports a story that Walter Map claims happened during his own time.[15] The tale is about the king of Portugal and Map does not provide any other identifying information, avoiding calling the king by his name. The narrative opens with the king of Portugal welcoming to his court a young knight who had saved the king's life during a fierce battle and states that the knight, brave and noble, entered into the good graces of the king to become the closest of his *familiares*. This rise in the king's favour caused envy among the other courtiers, and they decided to act against the newcomer. Knowing of the king's jealousy, the courtiers forged a scandalous story and whispered into their king's ears rumours of an adulterous relationship between the queen and the knight. The king's reaction was furious: he ordered the knight to be put to death, an act promptly carried out by the courtiers, and killed his pregnant wife. When the whole story became public, the king began to fear for his own good name. It was only at this point that the king realised the courtiers' dishonesty and punished them.[16]

In reading the story of the king of Portugal, we have to consider the public that was involved in and addressed by this narrative. Walter Map was renowned for his ability as a storyteller in Anglo-Norman, so famous in fact that after his death the *Lancelot-Graal* cycle was attributed to him.[17] Readers/listeners expected to be amused by the tale, but it also had the potential to serve as a didactic tool. Walter Map combined these two aspects by constructing a story that has all the characteristics of medieval romance and offers insight into the way rumour-spreading could be used at court and in politics. The narrative structure of the tale of the king of Portugal includes the usual topics and characters of twelfth-century romance.[18] An adulterous relationship between a valiant knight and the queen was the core subject of the *amour Courtois*.[19] In particular, the story created by the Portuguese courtiers closely recalls the love triangle involving King Arthur, Queen Guinevere, and the knight Lancelot. The treason of the courtiers who lied to the king and provoked his anger is another typical element of medieval romances. Traitors are characters occupying a position near the protagonist of the tale and they are usually part of a circle of companions or advisors to the king, as their social position allows them the level of credibility necessary for the protagonist to trust them so they can carry out the treasonous action.[20] In some medieval romances, adultery, intrigue and political unrest – such as the discontent of the population in Walter Map's tale – are woven together as signs of deeper institutional crises. In these cases, the narrative events present the king as being unable to maintain the integrity of his kingdom and carried away by multiple forces.[21]

Chapter I.12 develops arguments and writing techniques that are coherent with the rest of *De nugis curialium* and that Walter Map also used in other chapters. The choice to organise the tale according to the narrative steps and setting of a romance was made for other stories in *De nugis curialium* as well, like the one about Sadio and Galo.[22] In the statement that 'the queen was the Portuguese king's only weakness' there is an echo of *Dissuasio Valerii*, the epistle in which Walter Map illustrates the reasons for avoiding marriage.[23] Moreover, the political use of the adultery scandal tells us something about Walter Map's own methods: he also reported that Eleanor of Aquitaine had sexual intercourse with Geoffrey of Anjou before marrying his son Henry II.[24] Besides the narrative structure of the tale, Walter Map claimed that the story was real and that the king of Portugal was a live, reigning king. Various passages of the text shore up this claim of reality by resolving the narrative knots in a manner that was not typical of the romances to which Walter Map and his public were accustomed. By murdering his wife, the king presents himself as a real person gripped by a – tremendous and unjustifiable – attack of jealousy. As an example of how unusual this reaction was, King Arthur – the archetype of the cuckolded prince of twelfth-century romances – would hardly do such a thing, and indeed he did not, even when the relationship between Lancelot and Guinevere was exposed before his eyes.[25] Since the courtiers in Map's story were blinded and castrated, only the punishment allotted to the traitors is more coherent with the literary canon. In medieval romances, felony was mostly met with severe corporal punishment or death, while in twelfth-century England exile was an increasing common sentence meted out to felons charged with harsh crimes.[26] The claimed reality of the tale makes this chapter a vivid example of how the invention and spread of a scandal could be used at court to eliminate a political opponent and more broadly to turn a population against its ruler.[27]

Echoes of a Flemish scandal

The writing strategies, views, and assertions are coherent with the *De nugis curialium* style and Walter Map's explicit intent to report a scandal rather than spin a tale. Unusually, Walter Map does not refer to any of the protagonists of Chapter I.12 by name. The protagonist himself is called simply the 'king of Portugal' which, in Walter Map's time, could mean Alfonso I or one of his sons. However, the historical record does not provide any rumours or stories about these rulers like the one reported by Chapter I.12, as is also noted by the editors of *De nugis curialium*.[28]

Given the fact that Walter Map's Portuguese king cannot be identified with the contemporary kings of Portugal, the analysis should consider the literary and political space in which *De nugis curialium*'s allusiveness, rumour-spreading, and courtly literature operated. As Laura Ashe's study of William Marshal's life and Lancelot shows, it is possible to find a combination of romance and biographical accounts of famous men and women in English courtly literature.[29] Authors and the public shared a common store of knowledge regarding people, events, and recognisable narrative structures. Focusing on the peculiar narrative plot of Chapter I.12, the research can be enlarged to entail a comparison with other texts produced in the cultural and political milieu of the Plantagenet court. Widening the research field to twelfth-century texts written in Latin for a courtly public, a large number of scandals and rumours surface. In particular, Roger of Howden and Ralph de Diceto reported a scandal concerning Count Philip of Alsace the development of which very closely resembles Map's tale of the Portuguese king.[30] In 1175, Philip accused Walter de Fontaines, a knight of his court, of having had an affair with his wife, Elisabeth de Vermandois. Walter de Fontaines professed his innocence, but the king had him clubbed to death and dumped in a drainage ditch. This unjust and cruel death sparked a popular revolt led by James of Avesnes that spread ferociously across the county of Flanders.[31]

As Ruth Harvey has noted, it was only the English authors of the Plantagenet court who wrote about this scandal and its outcomes.[32] There is nothing to confirm this story in the Flemish chronicles of Gislebert of Mons and André de Marchiennes; these latter cover the revolt of James of Avesnes in 1174 and 1176 in great detail and explain that the cause of the revolt was the murder of Robert, Bishop of Cambrai.[33] More than a documented report, then, Map's story was probably an item of gossip intended to point to the political struggle of the county of Flanders.

Comparing the plots of this Anglo-Flemish gossip and the Portuguese king's scandal, we see that both rumours unfold through the same recognisable narrative points – the adulterous relationship between the knight and the lady, the brutal murder of the lover, the discontent of the population. Both scandals were written up in the same milieu and addressed to a similar public, an audience that would have been able to recognise the similar narrative structure of the two stories easily. To proceed with the analysis and identify the possible political implication of Chapter I.12, Walter Map's peculiar style and marked allusiveness must be considered. In writing *De nugis curialium*, Walter Map used literary themes, narratives, cultural references and genealogical information that were part of the cultural context and knowledge of the Plantagenet court.[34] In 1184, Philip of Alsace married Theresa, the daughter of the Portuguese king, Alfonso I. The historians of the Plantagenet court were aware of this marriage. The event was reported by Roger of Howden and Ralph de Diceto, the same authors who wrote about the Anglo-Flemish gossip regarding Philip of Alsace's wife, describing vividly how Count Philip fell in love the first time he saw the Portuguese princess.[35] The description of Philip of Alsace's profound love of Theresa recalls the emotions the Portuguese king felt for his wife but, in reporting the event, Henry II's courtiers were not moved by romanticism. The marriage of Philip of Alsace and Theresa of Portugal had particular importance for the king of England: Henry II had been active in arranging this union and paid for the ship that brought Theresa from Portugal to Flanders[36] because his intermediation confirmed the English king's role as a recognised mediator between the Iberian kingdom and northern Europe and generated friendly new relations with Philip of Alsace, a ruler who had supported Henry II's sons' efforts to revolt against their father.[37]

Philip of Alsace's marriage to Theresa of Portugal was thus a significant event for the kingdom of England and part of the common knowledge of the authors at the Plantagenet court. Considering the similarity between Chapter I.12 of *De nugis* and the Anglo-Flemish gossip involving Philip of Alsace, as well as the English interest in this ruler's marriage to the princess of Portugal, Walter Map was pointing to the count of Flanders when talking about the king of Portugal and his public could easily have read between the lines of his allusiveness.

Rumours and heiresses: a road to Vermandois

In writing the story of the Portuguese king, Walter Map merged two events concerning Philip of Alsace that were well known at the Plantagenet court. The first was the English gossip about Elisabeth de Vermandois, Philip of

Alsace's first wife, and her adultery; the second was the marriage of the same Philip of Alsace with the Portuguese princess Theresa, organised with the support of Henry II.

The two events were closely related. The marriage between Philip and Theresa was part of the negotiations that took place to resolve the dispute arising around the inheritance of Vermandois after Elisabeth de Vermandois died in 1182 without heirs.[38] Elisabeth de Vermandois was the daughter of Ralph I de Vermandois and Petronilla of Aquitaine, Eleanor of Aquitaine's younger sister. Her marriage with Philip of Alsace in 1159 marked a significant alliance between two important houses of northern France: the size of Vermandois and its geographic proximity to the county of Flanders were important resources to fuel Philip of Alsace's ambitions. It is not clear if Elisabeth's brother Raoul was dead or too ill to rule the county, but at any rate in 1164 Elizabeth inherited the vast territories belonging to the counts of Vermandois.[39] These territories consisted of Valois and the province of Vermandois, which included Amiens, Saint-Quentin, Péronne, Montdidier, Ribemont, and Chauny. This development represented an unforeseen event that strengthened Philip of Alsace's political influence over north-eastern France. The couple had no heir, however, and on the death of Elisabeth in 1182 the lack of children therefore gave rise to a crisis regarding her inheritance.[40]

The king of France, Philip II, intervened to support the claim of Elisabeth's younger sister, Eleanor de Vermandois. Eleanor was married to Matthew, Count of Beaumont-sur-Oise and Grand Chamberlain of the king of France. Ensuring that Eleanor inherited Vermandois presented King Philip II with a two-fold occasion to contain the increasing influence of Philip of Alsace across the northern border and, at the same time, reward one of his most trusted men. Philip of Alsace battled to retain control of at least some part of the county but was forced to surrender. It took two years for the conflict to be resolved and, in the end, Vermandois was separated into three parts and divided between Eleanor, Philip of Alsace, and Philip II. Philip of Alsace was permitted to maintain much of Vermandois and the title 'count of Vermandois' for the remainder of his life, while Eleanor came out of the deal with possession of Valois.[41] Henry II's role in these events was ambiguous, as was his involvement in the dispute. Eleanor of Aquitaine was the aunt of the two heiresses of Vermandois, and the king's half-brother Hamelin was able to advance claims over Vermandois on behalf of his wife in that Hamelin had married Isabel de Warenne, Countess of Surrey, who was part of the Vermandois lineage.[42]

The political importance of the matter of the Vermandois inheritance for the Plantagenet court during Walter Map's lifetime is confirmed by the report detailing the English king's diplomatic efforts to resolve the dispute, whereas no mention of these activities is made by the French sources, and by the reports about the destiny of the county of Vermandois after Philip of Alsace's death in 1191.[43] Walter Map's choice to be allusive suited the changeable political scenario of the Plantagenet dominions during the second half of the twelfth century, a period in which openly targeting Philip of Alsace could have put Walter Map in danger. Although both Philip of Alsace and the heiresses of Vermandois had supported Henry the Young King's revolt against Henry II, after the victory of the English king relations with the county of Flanders became significant enough for Count Philip and the heiresses to oppose King Philip II's political action.[44] The false account of Elisabeth of Vermandois's adultery stemmed from English chroniclers' hostility to the role Philip and Elisabeth played in the Young King's 1173–1174 rebellion but, after the death of Henry II, the king's rebel son Richard was crowned and so many former enemies gained significant positions in his court. At this point Walter Map, who was close to Henry II even in the hardest moments of his reign and had harsh words for his enemy, fled from the court.

Although the impossibility, to date, of assessing how widely Chapter I.12 was disseminated at the time precludes further analysis of the tale of the Portuguese king, it is possible to sketch a brief conclusion. At the Plantagenet court, scandal and tales of sexual misbehaviour were largely used as weapons of political attack on the *fama* of political opponents. Studying *De nugis curialium*'s Chapter I.12 confirms the potential strength and use of such rumours even beyond the texts that explicitly name a specific person. Considering the political value of courtly writing and the allusiveness that often characterises Walter Map's work, this analysis has proceeded on the grounds that the rumour would have been recognisable in the milieu of the Plantagenet court, looking at both its narrative structure and its references to major events. It has been argued that Walter Map wove together two stories about Philip of Alsace that were familiar to contemporary English authors. In so doing, Chapter I.12 uses the tale of the Portuguese king to imply a precise issue of Plantagenet European politics: the inheritance of the county of Vermandois, a matter in which the English king acted as an interested mediator between Philip of Flanders, Philip II and Eleanor of Vermandois.

These conclusions point to the possibility of further investigating Walter Map's and his public's personal reasons for being interested in the county of Vermandois. It is crucial to bear in mind that the countesses of Vermandois were rulers and possessed of political weight independent of their role as wives.[45] As shown by the famous case of Eleanor of Aquitaine, accusations of adultery were used to minimise, reject, or discredit women's agency and political action. Considering the political use of scandal and gossip, Walter Map's tale of the Portuguese king assumes the form of a counter-narrative, rehabilitating Countess Elisabeth de Vermandois' *bona fama*. Since Elisabeth in fact continued to govern her territories and the gossip of her adulterous relations was an English invention, it is in England that we must look for the actors interested in denying or affirming the validity of her rule and actions.

Further studies might thus set off from an analysis of the network systems operating in both England and Flanders at the end of the twelfth century, systems which involved magnates and properties and had supporters at the court of the count of Flanders.[46] In the last decades of twelfth century, the inheritance of Vermandois and female agency continued to be a delicate issue. After the death of Philip of Alsace (1191), Philip II of France attempted to add Vermandois and Valois to his dominions. In 1192, Eleanor of Vermandois and Philip II signed a treaty, by virtue of which the countess continued to rule as lord of Saint-Quentin/Peronne and Valois until she died in 1213. This was a very concrete rule: over those years, Eleanor of Vermandois settled disputes, collected taxes, confirmed donations, and minted coins.[47] Walter Map had personal networks who could keep him informed on the state of affairs in the county of Flanders. Chapter IV.1 reports that he had a young relative who was a versatile diplomat and had served at the court of Philip of Alsace.[48]

The accuracy shown by Walter Map in writing the tale of the Portuguese king prompts a reassessment of the *De nugis curialium*, which is often considered as an informal memoir without a public.[49] Joshua Byron Smith has remarked that the *De nugis curialium* was probably on its way to becoming a book through the careful revisions of its author.[50] Moreover, Chapter I.11 merges the histories of two renowned events in order to forge a chivalrous scandal that parodies the reputation of the court of Flanders as a centre of chivalric literature, while alluding to specific political matters. All this appears to point to a degree of commitment, which is consistent with the composition of a text with an intended public. Walter Map's chosen allusiveness in proposing a confutation of the official reports on Elisabeth's adultery appears to be coherent with the serious involvement of English interests in Flanders and with the changes that took place in Plantagenet space after the death of Henry II. Following the whispers of adultery and other scandals has proven a useful tool for revealing the political value of works usually conceived as literary fiction, works that need to be contextualised in terms of the interaction between authors, readers, and their times.

Notes

1 Martin Aurell, *L'Empire des Plantagenêt, 1154–1224* (Paris: Perrin, 2003); Robert Bartlett, *England under the Norman and Angevin kings, 1075–1225* (Oxford: Oxford University Press, 2000).

2 Ruth Kennedy and Simon Meecham-Jones, eds, *Writers of the Reign of Henry II: Twelve Essays* (New York: Palgrave Macmillan, 2006); Nancy Partner, *Serious Entertainments: The Writing of History in Twelfth-Century England* (Chicago: University of Chicago Press, 1977); Susan Crane, *Insular Romance: Politics, Faith, and Culture in Anglo-Norman and Middle English Literature* (Berkeley: University of California Press, 1986).
3 Myriam Soria and Maïté Billoré, eds, *La rumeur au Moyen Âge: Du mépris à la manipulation, Ve-XVe siècle* (Rennes: Presses Universitaires de Rennes, 2011); Thelma Fenster and Daniel Lord Smail, eds, *Fama: The Politics of Talk and Reputation in Medieval Europe* (Ithaca, NY: Cornell University Press, 2003).
4 Elisabeth Van Houts, *Married Life in the Middle Ages, 900–1300* (Oxford: Oxford University Press, 2019), 124–131.
5 Ralph V. Turner, *Eleanor of Aquitaine: Queen of France, Queen of England* (London: Yale University Press, 2009); Jean Flori, *Aliénor d'Aquitaine: La reine insoumise* (Paris: Editions Payot & Rivages, 2004); Catherine Léglu and Marcus Bull, eds, *The World of Eleanor of Aquitaine: Literature and Society in Southern France between the Eleventh and Thirteenth Centuries* (Woodbridge: Boydell Press, 2005); John Carmi Parsons and Bonnie Wheeler, eds, *Eleanor of Aquitaine: Lord and Lady* (New York, Palgrave Macmillan, 2003).
6 John Gillingham, 'Events and Opinions: Norman and English Views of Aquitaine, c. 1152–c. 1204', in *The World of Eleanor of Aquitaine: Literature and Society in Southern France between the Eleventh and Thirteenth Centuries*, ed. Catherine Léglu and Marcus Bull (Woodbridge: Boydell Press, 2005), 57–81; Ursula Vones Liebenstein, 'Aliénor d'Aquitaine, Henri le Jeune et la révolte de 1173: un prélude à la confrontation entre Plantagenêt et Capétiens?' in *Plantagenêts et Capétiens. Confrontations et héritages*, ed. Martin Aurell and Noël-Yves Tonnerre (Turnhout: Brepols, 2006), 75–93; Martin Aurell, 'Aux origines de la légende noire d'Aliénor d'Aquitaine', in *Royautés imaginaires (XIIe-XVIe siècles), Colloque de l'Université de Paris X-Nanterre du 26 au 27 septembre 2003*, ed. Anne-Hélène Allirot, Gilles Lecuppre and Lydwine Scordia (Turnhout: Brepols, 2005), 89–102.
7 Elisabeth Van Houts, *Medieval Memories: Men, Women and the Past, 700–1300* (London/New York: Routledge, 2014), 43. Regarding Sichelgaita's career, see Patricia Skinner, "Halt! Be Men!': Sikelgaita of Salerno, Gender and the Norman Conquest of Southern Italy', *Gender & History* 12 (2000): 622–641.
8 Egbert Türk, 'La chute de Guillaume de Longchamp (1191) ou la rumeur instrumentalisée', in *La Rumeur au Moyen Âge: Du mépris à la manipulation, Ve-XVe siècle*, ed. Myriam Soria and Maïté Billoré (Rennes: Presses Universitaires de Rennes, 2011), 195–212.
9 Giles Constable, 'Aelred of Rievaulx and the Nun of Watton: An Episode in the Early History of the Gilbertine order', *Studies in Church History. Subsidia* 1 (1978): 205–226; Raymonde Foreville, 'Heurs et malheurs de la cohabitation. Un cas exemplaire de service au XIIe siècle: l'ordre de Sempringham', in *Les religieuses dans le cloître et dans le monde des origines à nos jours. Actes du Deuxième Colloque International du C.E.R.C.O.R. Poitiers, 29 Septembre-2*

Octobre 1988, ed. Nicole Bouter (Saint-Etienne, Publications de l'Université de Saint-Etienne, 1994), 353–365.
10. See James Hinton, 'Walter Map's *De nugis curialium*. Its Plan and Composition', *Publications of the Modern Language Association of America* 32.1 (1917): 81–132, available at www.jstor.org/stable/456912; Arthur George Rigg, '[Review of] *De nugis curialium; Courtiers' Trifles* by Walter Map, ed. James, Brooke and Mynors', *Speculum* 60.1 (1985): 177–182.
11. See Joshua Byron Smith, *Walter Map and the Matter of Britain* (Philadelphia: University of Pennsylvania Press, 2017), 76–82.
12. Robert Levine, 'How to Read Walter Map', *Mittellateinisches Jahrbuch* 23 (1988): 91–105.
13. Walter Map, *De nugis curialium*, ed. and trans. M.R. James, C.N.L. Brooke, and R. Mynors (Oxford: Oxford University Press, 1983), 478 and 494–499.
14. Walter Map, *De nugis curialium*, 406–407: 'Certe si Henricum uel Gauterum uel eciam tuum ipsius nomen aliquis nouus karacter subnotatum prestiterit, uilipendis et rides; at non eorum uicio, et utinam non tuo. Quod si Hannibalem uel Menestratem uel aliqod prisce suauitatis nomen inspexeris, errigis animum et prementita etatis auree secula ingressus gestis et exultas ... audi priscam de nostris malignitatem, ut Neronis et similium soles ... Hanc tibi uitandam proponimus pro ueneficiis, ellam eligendam pro beneficiis; neutri tibi est omnis pagina quam uideris et examinanda, nec sit ulla neclecta nisi perlecta' (Certain it is that if any new writing shows you Henry or Walter or even your own name recorded, you set it at naught and mock it; but through no fault of theirs, and I hope through not of your own. If, however, you see Hannibal or Menestrates, or any name sweet with the perfume of antiquity, your spirits rise and you learn and exult at the thought of entering on the golden ages of old fable ... listen at least to tales of ancient wickedness in our people, as you will to those of Nero and the like ... This we hold up to you to be shunned for its banes, the other to be chosen for its boons: withdraw not your eye from either unless you have thoroughly viewed it and taken it in; for you should read and scrutinize every page you see, and not one should be disused without being perused).
15. Walter Map, *De nugis curialium*, I.12, 30–31: 'Portigalensis rex, qui uiuit, et adhuc suo modo regnat' (The king of Portugal who yet lives, and still reigns after his manners).
16. Walter Map, *De nugis curialium*, I.12, 30–35.
17. Neil Cartlidge, 'Masters in the Art of Lying? The Literary Relationship between Hugh of Rhuddlan and Walter Map', *Modern Language Review* 106.1 (2011): 1–16; Gilda Caiti-Russo, 'Situation actuelle de Gautier Map, écrivain fantastique', *Revue des langues Romanes* 102.2 (1997): 55–80; Richard Trachsler, 'Gautier Map, une vieille connaissance', in *Façonner son personnage au Moyen Âge*, ed. Chantal Connochie-Bourgne (Aix-en-Provence: Presses universitaires de Provence, 2007), 319–328.
18. Cf Norris J. Lacy, ed., *Text and Intertext in Medieval Arthurian Literature* (New York: Garland, 1996); Eugene Dorfman, *The Narreme in the Medieval Romance Epic* (Toronto: University of Toronto Press, 1969).

19 Cf the sociologic interpretation given in George Duby, 'Dans la France du Nord-Ouest au XIIe siècle: Les « jeunes » dans la société aristocratique', *Annales. Economies, sociétés, civilisations* 19.5 (1964): 835–846; Erich Köhler, *L'Aventure chevaleresque: Idéal et réalité dans le roman courtois, études sur la forme des plus anciens poèmes d'Arthur et du Graal* (Paris: Gallimard, 1974 or 1956). See also Peggy McCracken, 'The body politic and the queen's adulterous body in french romance', in *Feminist Approaches to the Body in Medieval Literature*, ed. Linda Lomperis and Sarah Stanbury (Philadelphia: University of Pennsylvania Press, 1993), 38–64.

20 Albrecht Classen, 'Outsiders, Challengers, and Rebels in Medieval Courtly Literature: The Problem with the Courts in Courtly Romances', *Arthuriana* 26.3 (2016): 67–90.

21 J.M. Stary, 'Adultery as a symptom of political crisis in two Arthurian romances', *Parergon* 9.1 (1991): 63–73.

22 Roger E. Bennett, 'Walter Map's Sadius and Galo', *Speculum* 16.1 (1941): 34–56; Kathryn Hume, 'The Composition of a Medieval Romance: Walter Map's Sadius and Galo', *Neuphilologische Mitteilungen* 76.3 (1975): 415–423; Smith, *Walter Map and the Matter of Britain*, 28–36.

23 Walter Map, *De nugis curialium*, I.12, 32–33: 'qua parte dominum suum inermem senciunt et nudum, attemptant' (They directed their aim to the spot in which they knew their lord to be bare and open to attack). The *Dissuasio Valerii* is in Walter Map, *De nugis curialium*, IV.3, 288–311, and had a great diffusion as a separate work; see Gérard Blangez, '« Dissuasio Valerii » ou la dissuasion de mariage de Gautier Map', in *Mélanges d'études anciennes offerts à Maurice Lebel, Professeur émérite et doyen honoraire de la Faculté des Lettres de l'Université Laval*, ed. Jean-Benoît Caron, Michel Fortin, and Gilles Maloney (St.-Jean-Chrysostôme: Éditions du Sphinx, 1980), 385–394; Neil Cartlidge, 'Misogyny in a Medieval University? The «Hoc contra malos» Commentary on Walter Map's «Dissuasio Valerii»', *Journal of Medieval Latin* 8 (1998): 156–91; Gregory Hays, 'The «Dissuasio Valerii» and Its Commentators: Some Supplementary Notes', in *Teaching and Learning in Medieval Europe. Essays in Honour of Gernot R. Wieland*, ed. Greti Dinkova-Bruun and Tristan Major (Turnhout: Brepols, 2017), 173–202.

24 Walter Map, *De nugis curialium*, 474.

25 Inna Matyushina, 'Treacherous Women at King Arthur's Court: Punishment and Shame', in *Treason. Medieval and Early Modern Adultery, Betrayal, and Shame*, ed. Larissa Tracy (Leiden: Brill, 2019), 288–319; Peggy McCracken, 'Love and adultery: Arthur's affairs', in *The Cambridge Companion to the Arthurian Legend*, ed. Elizabeth Archibald and Ad Putter (Cambridge: Cambridge University Press, 2009), 188–200.

26 William R.J. Barron, 'The Penalties for Treason in Medieval Life and Literature', *Journal of Medieval History* 7.2 (1981): 187–202; William Chester Jordan, *From England to France: Felony and Exile in the High Middle Ages* (Princeton: Princeton University Press, 2015).

27 Walter Map, *De nugis curialium*, I.12, 34–35: 'Huiusmodi sunt lusus curie, et tale ibi demonum illusiones' (Such are the tricks of the court, and such the deceits of devils that have place there).

28 'Presumably Alfonso, the first king of Portugal; the story does not seem to be recorded elsewhere', Walter Map, *De nugis curialium*, 30, note 2.
29 Laura Ashe, 'William Marshal, Lancelot and Arthur: Chivalry and Kingship', *Anglo-Norman Studies* 30 (2007), 19–40.
30 Roger of Howden, *Chronica*, ed. William Stubbs, 4 vols. (London: Longman, 1884–1885) 2: 82–83; Roger of Howden, *Gesta regis Henrici Secundi*, ed. William Stubbs, 2 vols. (London: Longman, 1867) 1: 99–101, Ralph de Diceto, *Ymagines historiarum*, ed. William Stubbs, 2 vols. (London: Longman, 1876) 1: 402.
31 Roger of Howden, *Chronica*, 2: 83.
32 Ruth Harvey, 'Cross-Channel Gossip in the Twelfth Century', in *England and the Continent. Essays in Memory of Professor Andrew Martindale*, ed. John Mitchell (Stamford: Paul Watkins Press, 2000), 48–59.
33 Nonetheless, even allowing the possibility that both authors chose to not report the adultery and the cruel execution, it has to be noted that Walter de Fontaines existed and peacefully died as a monk. Gislebert of Mons, *Chronicon Hanoniense*, ed. Laura Napran (Woodbridge: Boydell Press, 2005), 106, 84. For a precise analysis on Flemish authors see Harvey, 'Cross-Channel Gossip', 54–57.
34 Walter Map used a similar combination of genealogical references and literature to stage an attack on the Earl of Gloucester; see Fabrizio De Falco, 'I capitoli melusiniani del De nugis curialium: ribaltamento dell'ideologia cavalleresca e uso politico', *Studi Medievali* 58.1 (2017): 76–80.
35 Walter Map, *De nugis curialium*, I. 12, 32. Ralph de Diceto, *Ymagines historiarum*, 2: 28–29; Roger of Howden, *Chronica*, 2: 283; Roger of Howden, *Gesta regis*, 1: 310.
36 *Pipe Roll, vol. 33, The Great roll of the pipe for the thirtieth year of the reign of King Henry the Second, A.D. 1183–1184* (London: Pipe Roll Society, 1912), xxv and 155. Cf. Pierre Chaplais, ed., *Diplomatic documents preserved in the Public Record Office, I, 1101–1272* (London: Public Record Office, 1964), 10; Patricia Odber de Baubeta, 'Some early English sources of Portuguese History', *Estudos Medievais* 9 (1988): 203–206.
37 Anne Duggan, 'Aspects of Anglo-Portuguese Relations in the Twelfth Century. Manuscripts, Relics, Decretals and the Cult of St Thomas Becket at Lorvão, Alcobaça and Tomar', *Portuguese Studies* 14 (1998): 6–7; Stephen Lay, *The Reconquest Kings of Portugal: Political and Cultural Reorientation on the Medieval Frontier* (Basingstoke: Palgrave Macmillan, 2008), 168–169. On the friendship between Philip of Alsace and Henry the Young, see Matthew Strickland, 'On the instruction of a prince: the upbringing of Henry, the young king', in *Henry II: New Interpretations*, ed. Christopher Harper-Bill and Nicholas Vincent (Woodbridge: Boydell Press, 2007), 184–214.
38 Karen Nicholas, 'Countesses as Rulers in Flanders', in *Aristocratic Women in Medieval France*, ed. Theodore Evergates (Philadelphia: University of Pennsylvania Press, 1999), 124–125; Louis Duval-Arnould, 'Les aumônes d'Aliénor dernière comtesse de Vermandois et dame de Valois', *Revue Mabillon* 60 (1984): 395–463.
39 For Raoul I: André Moreau-Néret, 'Le comte de Vermandois Raoul IV de Crépy et Peronelle d'Aquitaine soeur de la Reine Aliénor', *Mémoires de la Fédération de la Société d'histoire et d'archéologie de l'Aisne* 18 (1972): 82–116. For

Raoul II, Louis Duval-Arnould, 'Les dernières années du comte lépreux Raoul de Vermandois (v. 1147–ca.1167) et les dévolutions des ses provinces à Philippe d'Alsace', *Bibliothèque d'École des chartes* 142 (1984): 81–92.

40 Heather Tanner, 'Elisabeth and Eleanor of Vermandois: Succession and Governance in the Counties of Vermandois, Valois, and Amiens', *Medieval Prosopography* 34 (2019): 85–118.
41 John W. Baldwin, *The Government of Philip Augustus: Foundations of French Royal Power in the Middle Ages* (Berkeley: University of California Press, 1986), 18; Thérèse de Hemptinne, 'Aspects des relations de Philippe Auguste avec la Flandre au temps de Philippe d'Alsace', in *La France de Philippe Auguste: le temps des mutations: actes du colloque international*, ed. Robert-Henri Bautier (Paris: Editions du CNRS, 1982), 259.
42 See Diana Greenway and Leslie Watkiss, eds, *Liber de fundatione cenobii de Waldena* (Oxford: Clarendon Press, 1999), 107–112.
43 Rigord did not mention Henry II: Rigord, *Gesta Philippi Augusti*, ed. Henri-François Delaborde (Paris: Renouard, 1885), 43. On the other side of the Channel, Gerald of Wales did report on Henry II's diplomatic activity: Gerald of Wales, *De principis instructione*, ed. Robert Bartlett (Oxford: Oxford University Press, 2018), 88–90.
44 John Gillingham, *The Angevin Empire* (London: Edward Arnold, 1984), 30; Theodore Evergates, *Henry the Liberal: Count of Champagne* (Philadelphia: University of Pennsylvania Press, 2016), 133–136.
45 Heather Tanner, 'Elisabeth and Eleanor of Vermandois', 99–114.
46 Regarding these networks, see: Eljas Oksanen, *Flanders and the Anglo-Norman World*, 82–113; Gaston Dept, *Les Influences anglaise et française dans le comté de Flandre au début du XIIIe siècle* (Paris: Champion, 1928).
47 Heather Tanner, 'Elisabeth and Eleanor of Vermandois', 112.
48 Walter Map, *De nugis curialium*, IV.1, 478–479.
49 Michael Staunton, *The Historians of Angevin England* (Oxford: Oxford University Press, 2017), 142: 'This is a book without an audience, without an intended audience, and without a contract between author and reader'.
50 Joshua Byron Smith, *Walter Map and the Matter of Britain*, 42–43.

Bibliography

Primary sources

Diplomatic documents preserved in the Public Record Office, Vol. I, 1101–1272, ed. Pierre Chaplais. London: Public Record Office, 1964.

Gerald of Wales. *De principis instructione*, ed. Robert Bartlett. Oxford: Oxford University Press, 2018.

Gislebert of Mons. *Chronicon Hanoniense*, ed. Laura Napran. Woodbridge: Boydell Press, 2005.

Liber de fundatione cenobii de Waldena, ed. Diana Greenway and Leslie Watkiss. Oxford: Clarendon Press, 1999.

Pipe Roll, vol. 33, The Great roll of the pipe for the thirtieth year of the reign of King Henry the Second, A.D. 1183–1184. London: Pipe Roll Society, 1912.
Rigord. *Gesta Philippi Augusti*, ed. Henri-François Delaborde. Paris: Renouard, 1885.
Roger of Howden. *Chronica*, ed. William Stubbs. 4 vols. London: Longmans, 1884–1885.
Roger of Howden. *Gesta regis Henrici Secundi*, ed. William Stubbs. 2 vols. London: Longmans, 1867.
Ralph de Diceto. *Ymagines Historiarum*, ed. William Stubbs. 2 vols. London: Longmans, 1876.
Walter Map. *De nugis curialium*, ed. and trans. Montague Rhodes James, Christopher Nugent Lawrence Brooke, and Roger Mynors. Oxford: Oxford University Press, 1983.

Secondary sources

Ashe, Laura. 'William Marshal, Lancelot and Arthur: Chivalry and Kingship'. *Anglo–Norman Studies* 30 (2007): 19–40.
Aurell, Martin. 'Aux origines de la légende noire d'Aliénor d'Aquitaine'. In *Royautés imaginaires (XIIe-XVIe siècles), Colloque de l'Université de Paris X-Nanterre du 26 au 27 septembre 2003*, ed. Anne-Hélène Allirot, Gilles Lecuppre and Lydwine Scordia, 89–102. Turnhout: Brepols, 2005.
Aurell, Martin. *L'Empire des Plantagenêt, 1154–1224*. Paris: Perrin, 2003.
Baldwin, John W. *The Government of Philip Augustus: Foundations of French Royal Power in the Middle Ages*. Berkeley: University of California Press, 1986.
Barron, Wiliam R.J. 'The Penalties for Treason in Medieval Life and Literature'. *Journal of Medieval History* 7.2 (1981): 187–202.
Bartlett, Robert. *England under the Norman and Angevin kings, 1075–1225*. Oxford: Oxford University Press, 2000.
Baubeta, Patricia Odber de. 'Some early English sources of Portuguese History'. *Estudos Medievais* 9 (1988): 201–210.
Bennett, Roger. 'Walter Map's Sadius and Galo'. *Speculum* 16.1 (1941): 34–56.
Blangez, Gérard. '« Dissuasio Valerii » ou la dissuasion de mariage de Gautier Map'. In *Mélanges d'études anciennes offerts à Maurice Lebel, Professeur émérite et doyen honoraire de la Faculté des Lettres de l'Université Laval*, ed. Jean-Benoît Caron, Michel Fortin and Gilles Maloney, 385–394. St.-Jean-Chrysostôme: Éditions du Sphinx, 1980.
Caiti-Russo, Gilda. 'Situation actuelle de Gautier Map, écrivain fantastique'. *Revue des langues Romanes* 102.2 (1997): 55–80.
Cartlidge, Neil. 'Masters in the Art of Lying? The Literary Relationship between Hugh of Rhuddlan and Walter Map'. *The Modern Language Review* 106.1 (2011): 1–16.
Cartlidge, Neil. 'Misogyny in a Medieval University? The «Hoc contra malos» Commentary on Walter Map's «Dissuasio Valerii»'. *Journal of Medieval Latin* 8 (1998): 156–191.
Classen, Albrecht. 'Outsiders, Challengers, and Rebels in Medieval Courtly Literature: The Problem with the Courts in Courtly Romances'. *Arthuriana* 26.3 (2016): 67–90.

Constable, Giles. 'Aelred of Rievaulx and the Nun of Watton: An Episode in the Early History of the Gilbertine order'. *Studies in Church History. Subsidia* 1 (1978): 205–226.

Crane, Susan. *Insular Romance: Politics, Faith, and Culture in Anglo-Norman and Middle English Literature*. Berkeley: University of California Press, 1986.

De Falco, Fabrizio. 'I capitoli melusiniani del De nugis curialium: ribaltamento dell'ideologia cavalleresca e uso politico'. *Studi Medievali* 58.1 (2017): 45–92.

De Falco, Fabrizio. *Authors, Factions, and Courts in Angevin England. A Literature of Personal Ambition (12th–13th Century)*. Cham: Palgrave Macmillan, 2023.

Dept, Gaston. *Les influences anglaise et française dans le comté de Flandre au début du XIIIe siècle*. Paris: Champion, 1928.

Dorfman, Eugene. *The Narreme in the Medieval Romance Epic*. Toronto: University of Toronto Press, 1969.

Duby, George. 'Dans la France du Nord-Ouest au XIIe siècle: Les « jeunes » dans la société aristocratique'. *Annales: Economies, sociétés, civilisations* 19.5 (1964): 835–846.

Duggan, Anne. 'Aspects of Anglo-Portuguese Relations in the Twelfth Century. Manuscripts, Relics, Decretals and the Cult of St Thomas Becket at Lorvão, Alcobaça and Tomar'. *Portuguese Studies* 14 (1998): 1–19.

Duval-Arnould, Louis. 'Les aumônes d'Aliénor dernière comtesse de Vermandois et dame de Valois'. *Revue Mabillon* 60 (1984): 395–463.

Duval-Arnould, Louis. 'Les dernières années du comte lépreux Raoul de Vermandois (v. 1147–ca.1167) et les dévolutions des ses provinces à Philippe d'Alsace'. *Bibliothèque d'École des chartes* 142 (1984): 81–92.

Evergates, Theodore. *Henry the Liberal: Count of Champagne*. Philadelphia: University of Pennsylvania Press, 2016.

Fenster, Thelma and Daniel Lord Smail, eds. *Fama: The Politics of Talk and Reputation in Medieval Europe*. Ithaca, NY: Cornell University Press, 2003.

Flori, Jean. *Aliénor d'Aquitaine: La reine insoumise*. Paris: Editions Payot & Rivages, 2004.

Foreville, Raymonde, 'Heurs et malheurs de la cohabitation. Un cas exemplaire de service au XIIe siècle: l'ordre de Sempringham'. In *Les religieuses dans le cloître et dans le monde des origines à nos jours. Actes du Deuxième Colloque International du C.E.R.C.O.R. Poitiers, 29 Septembre-2 Octobre 1988*, ed. Nicole Bouter, 353–365. Saint-Etienne, Publications de l'Université de Saint-Etienne, 1994.

Gillingham, John. 'Events and Opinions: Norman and English Views of Aquitaine, c. 1152–c. 1204'. In *The World of Eleanor of Aquitaine: Literature and Society in Southern France between the Eleventh and Thirteenth Centuries*, ed. Catherine Léglu and Marcus Bull, 57–81. Woodbridge: Boydell Press, 2005.

Gillingham, John. *The Angevin Empire*. London: Edward Arnold, 1984.

Harvey, Ruth. 'Cross-Channel Gossip in the Twelfth Century'. In *England and the continent in the Middle Ages: studies in memory of Andrew Martindale: proceedings of the 1996 Harlaxton Symposium*, ed. John Mitchell and Matthew Moran, 48–59. Stamford: Shaun Tyas, 2000.

Hays, Gregory. 'The «Dissuasio Valerii» and Its Commentators: Some Supplementary Notes'. In *Teaching and Learning in Medieval Europe. Essays in Honour of Gernot*

R. Wieland, ed. Greti Dinkova-Bruun and Tristan Major, 173–202. Turnhout: Brepols, 2017.
Hemptinne, Thérèse de. 'Aspects des relations de Philippe Auguste avec la Flandre au temps de Philippe d'Alsace'. In *La France de Philippe Auguste: le temps des mutations: actes du colloque international*, ed. Robert-Henri Bautier, 255–262. Paris, Editions du CNRS, 1982.
Heng, Geraldine. *Empire of Magic: Medieval Romance and the Politics of Cultural Fantasy*. New York: Columbia University Press, 2003.
Hinton, James. 'Walter Map's De nugis curialium: Its Plan and Composition'. *Publications of the Modern Language Association of America* 32.1 (1917): 81–132.
Hinton, James, 'Notes on Walter Map's *De nugis curialium*, *Studies in Philology* 20.4 (1923): 448–468, available in facsimile at www.jstor.org/stable/4171874?seq=2.
Hume, Kathryn. 'The composition of a medieval romance: Walter Map's Sadius and Galo'. *Neuphilologische Mitteilungen* 76.3 (1975): 415–423.
Jordan, William Chester. *From England to France: Felony and Exile in the High Middle Ages*. Princeton: Princeton University Press, 2015.
Kennedy, Ruth and Simon Meecham-Jones, eds, *Writers of the Reign of Henry II: Twelve Essays*. New York: Palgrave Macmillan, 2006.
Köhler, Erich, *L'Aventure chevaleresque: Idéal et réalité dans le roman courtois, études sur la forme des plus anciens poèmes d'Arthur et du Graal*. Paris: Gallimard, 1974 or 1956.
Lacy, Norris J. *Text and Intertext in Medieval Arthurian Literature*. New York: Garland, 1996.
Lay, Stephen *The Reconquest Kings of Portugal: Political and Cultural Reorientation on the Medieval Frontier*. Basingstoke: Palgrave Macmillan, 2008.
Léglu, Catherine and Marcus Bull, eds. *The World of Eleanor of Aquitaine: Literature and Society in Southern France between the Eleventh and Thirteenth Centuries*. Woodbridge: Boydell Press: 2005.
Levine, Robert. 'How to read Walter Map'. *Mittellateinisches Jahrbuch* 23 (1988): 91–105.
Matyushina, Inna. 'Treacherous Women at King Arthur's Court: Punishment and Shame'. In *Treason: Medieval and Early Modern Adultery, Betrayal, and Shame*, ed. Larissa Tracy, 288–319. Leiden: Brill, 2019.
McCracken, Peggy. 'Love and adultery: Arthur's affairs'. In *The Cambridge Companion to the Arthurian Legend*, ed. Elizabeth Archibald and Ad Putter, 188–200. Cambridge: Cambridge University Press, 2009.
McCracken, Peggy. 'The body politic and the queen's adulterous body in french romance'. In *Feminist Approaches to the Body in Medieval Literature*, ed. Linda Lomperis and Sarah Stanbury, 38–64. Philadelphia: University of Pennsylvania Press, 1993.
Moreau-Néret, André. 'Le comte de Vermandois Raoul IV de Crépy et Peronelle d'Aquitaine soeur de la Reine Aliénor'. *Mémoires de la Fédération de la Société d'histoire et d'archéologie de l'Aisne* 18 (1972): 82–116.
Nicholas, Karen. 'Countesses as Rulers in Flanders'. In *Aristocratic Women in Medieval France*, ed. Theodore Evergates, 111–137. Philadelphia: University of Pennsylvania Press, 1999.

Oksanen, Eljas. *Flanders and the Anglo-Norman World: 1066–1216*. Cambridge: Cambridge University Press, 2012.

Parsons, John Carmi and Bonnie Wheeler, eds. *Eleanor of Aquitaine: Lord and Lady*. New York: Palgrave Macmillan, 2003.

Partner, Nancy. *Serious Entertainments: The Writing of History in Twelfth-Century England*. Chicago: University of Chicago Press, 1977.

Rigg, Arthur George. '*De nugis curialium; Courtiers' Trifles* by Walter Map, ed. M.R. James, C.N.L. Brooke, R.A.B. Mynors'. *Speculum* 60.1 (1985): 177–182.

Ruth, Kennedy and Simon Meecham-Jones, eds. *Writers of the Reign of Henry II: Twelve Essays*. New York, Palgrave Macmillan, 2006.

Skinner, Patricia. '"Halt! Be Men!": Sikelgaita of Salerno, Gender and the Norman Conquest of Southern Italy'. *Gender & History* 12 (2000): 622–641.

Smith, Joshua Byron. *Walter Map and the Matter of Britain*. Philadelphia: University of Pennsylvania Press, 2017.

Soria, Myriam and Maïté Billoré, eds. *La rumeur au Moyen Âge: Du mépris à la manipulation, Ve-XVe siècle*. Rennes, Presses Universitaires de Rennes, 2011.

Stary, J.M. 'Adultery as a symptom of political crisis in two Arthurian romances'. *Parergon* 9.1 (1991): 63–73.

Staunton, Michael. *The Historians of Angevin England*. Oxford, Oxford University Press, 2017.

Strickland, Matthew. 'On the instruction of a prince: the upbringing of Henry, the young king'. In *Henry II: New Interpretations*, ed. Christopher Harper-Bill and Nicholas Vincent, 184–214. Woodbridge: Boydell Press, 2007.

Tanner, Heather. 'Elisabeth and Eleanor of Vermandois: Succession and Governance in the Counties of Vermandois, Valois, and Amiens'. *Medieval Prosopography* 34 (2019): 85–118.

Trachsler, Richard. 'Gautier Map, une vieille connaissance'. In *Façonner son personnage au Moyen Âge*, ed. Chantal Connochie-Bourgne, 319–328. Aix-en-Provence, Presses universitaires de Provence, 2007.

Türk, Egbert. 'La chute de Guillaume de Longchamp (1191) ou la rumeur instrumentalisée'. In *La Rumeur au Moyen Âge: Du mépris à la manipulation, Ve-XVe siècle*, ed. Myriam Soria and Maïté Billoré, 195–212. Rennes, Presses Universitaires de Rennes, 2011.

Turner, Ralph V. *Eleanor of Aquitaine: Queen of France, Queen of England*. London: Yale University Press, 2009.

Van Houts, Elisabeth. *Married Life in the Middle Ages, 900–1300*. Oxford: Oxford University Press, 2019.

Van Houts, Elisabeth. *Medieval Memories: Men, Women and the Past, 700–1300*. London/New York: Routledge, 2014.

Vones Liebenstein, Ursula. 'Aliénor d'Aquitaine, Henri le Jeune et la révolte de 1173: un prélude à la confrontation entre Plantagenêt et Capétiens?' In *Plantagenêts et Capétiens. Confrontations et héritages*, ed. Martin Aurell and Noël-Yves Tonnerre, 75–93. Turnhout: Brepols, 2006.

4

Isabella of France and Roger Mortimer: lovers or allies?

Michael Evans

It is a truth (almost) universally acknowledged that Isabella of France was an adulterous queen. She united with the nobleman Roger of Mortimer to overthrow her husband, England's King Edward II, in 1327, and the two assumed *de facto* rulership of the kingdom for three years before being overthrown in turn by Isabella's son, Edward III, in whose name they had previously governed. The partnership between the two has been assumed to be both sexual and political, an assumption that has rarely been challenged. In Christopher Marlowe's *Edward II*, the king describes her as 'that unnaturall Queene false Isabell / ... my unconstant Queene / Who spots my nuptiall bed with infamie'.[1] The Strickland sisters, writing in the nineteenth century, helped establish the moralistic Victorian image of Isabella and 'her ferocious paramour Mortimer' as rebels and adulterers:[2]

> she came attended by her paramour, an outlawed traitor, and at the head of a band of foreign mercenaries, to raise the standard of revolt against her husband and sovereign, having abused her maternal influence over the mind of the youthful heir of England to draw him into a parricidal revolt.[3]

Even recent historians continue to assume Isabella and Mortimer's adultery, such as Chris Given-Wilson arguing that Isabella was expelled from the court of her brother, Charles IV of France, because of the 'scandalising' nature of her relationship with Mortimer.[4] The assumption of Isabella's adultery with Mortimer has been challenged all too infrequently, whereas Edward II's sexuality has been subject of much debate. In the words of Kathryn Warner, biographer of both Edward and Isabella,

> Every piece of evidence that Edward II might have loved Piers Gaveston and Hugh Despenser romantically and/or sexually ... is placed under a microscope, examined in isolation, and nitpicked out of existence. By contrast, the notion that Roger Mortimer was Queen Isabella's 'lover' and that she was a 'certain adulteress' is treated with the unquestioning reverence that some people accord to Holy Writ.[5]

This double standard may reflect heteronormative prejudices (a heterosexual adultery is assumed to be true by default, but a homosexual one is not), or it may represent a tradition of criticism of adulterous queens.

A more sober assessment of Isabella's reign shows her to have fulfilled the traditional roles of medieval queenship, with no suggestion of the 'rebel and adulteress' image before her break with Edward in 1325. For example, she acted as Edward's partner, deputy and ally;[6] played the role of diplomat and intercessor;[7] and was a pious benefactor of religious houses.[8] If we are to use chronicle accounts as the basis for claims of Isabella's adultery, we must contextualise these alongside contemporaries' praise of her. For example, John Trokelowe, a chronicler of St Albans Abbey and a contemporary source, described her as a 'nurse of peace and concord' between the king and the barons,[9] while one contemporary song described her as 'generous, prudent, beautiful, and virtuous.'[10]

It is probably futile, based on sources that say little about the nature of Mortimer and Isabella's relationship, to determine if they were 'really' lovers. It is, however, worth our while to question the traditional narrative that their relationship must have been a sexual one, and to locate accusations of Isabella's adultery in a tradition of invective against (supposedly) adulterous queens. We should also decentre the salacious focus on the nature of her relationship with Mortimer and listen more carefully to what criticisms of Isabella were actually raised by early-fourteenth-century chroniclers.

Contemporary or near-contemporary chroniclers say remarkably little about Isabella's supposed adultery with Roger Mortimer. The most hostile source is Geoffrey le Baker, who was writing in the 1340s or 1350s, at some distance from the period of Isabella's seizure of power, and following her fall from grace. According to the modern editor of his chronicle, he was intent on 'the blackening of Isabella's character'.[11] For Le Baker, Isabella was a 'Jezebel' and a 'an enraged virago',[12] both fairly standard epithets used by medieval chroniclers against women who were viewed as displaying excessive or illegitimate authority.[13] Le Baker was also anti-French, complaining (for example) of 'Gallic guile and greed'.[14] Le Baker makes perhaps the most unambiguous accusations of adultery, claiming that 'she had found comfort in the unlawful embraces of Roger Mortimer'.[15] Even then, he hedges it with the preface that some 'guessed that' she had done so. We should also note that the reference to Isabella as 'Jezebel' need not have any sexual implications; as well as being a pun on the name Isabel(la), it also portrays her as an enemy of the faith, in association with clerical allies who Le Baker dubs 'priests of Baal'.[16] This was a reference to the original, biblical Jezebel, whose bad reputation was based not on adultery, but on her bringing the priests of Baal and her Canaanite religion to Israel. The Bible makes no accusations of sexual impropriety against Jezebel, and her reputation in that regard derives solely from the fact that she painted her face before confronting her enemy Jehu.[17]

Le Baker is also the source for the story that, during Edward III's seizure of personal power in 1330, Mortimer was captured in Isabella's bedchamber at Nottingham Castle, leading her to beg her son to 'have pity on gentle Mortimer'.[18] This does not in itself prove or even imply that they were lovers; firstly, because the chronicle evidence on this point is ambiguous at best, and second, because the queen's bedchamber was a political as well as a private space.

Le Baker's source for Mortimer's presence in Isabella's chamber, the Middle English *Brut*, omits the much-quoted 'gentle Mortimer' line and says nothing about Isabella and Mortimer being lovers, and instead has her say 'Now, fair sires, y ӡow praye þat ӡe done non harme vnto his body; a worþi knyӡt, our wel bilouede frende and our dere cosyn'.[19] In the words of the modern editor of Le Baker's chronicle, '[t]he scene is changed [by Baker] from an attack on Mortimer to a confrontation between the king and his adulterous mother'.[20] The presence of Mortimer in Isabella's chamber does not imply any sexual relationship; yes, Mortimer was there, but so were others, including the bishop of Lincoln, who tried to escape through a latrine. The *Annales Paulini* lists Mortimer among Isabella's adherents without commenting on the nature of their relationship, and records that he was captured 'in Queen Isabella's chamber' without suggesting any sexual implications.[21] The *Scalacronica*, whose author was far from sympathetic to the regime of Isabella and Mortimer, states that 'the Queen, Mortimer, and their confidential adherents were holding a council' in a 'hall' before 'pass[ing] forward into the chamber' where Mortimer was seized.[22]

Adam Murimuth, who was a source for Le Baker's chronicle,[23] complained about Isabella's 'excessive familiarity' with Mortimer.[24] Natalie Fryde finds 'no reason to doubt Murimuth's statement … since he was, in the years 1327–30, a close confidant of Mortimer and Isabella'.[25] However, his chronicle is generally laconic and descriptive, and does not single out Isabella for particular condemnation. He lists the charges made against Mortimer following his fall, but they include no mention of adultery with the queen.[26] The *Vita Edwardi Secundi*, which ends in 1325, so was presumably written just as Isabella's breach with Edward was occurring, makes no mention of Mortimer or any suggestion that Edward suspected her of adultery. The author cites a letter in which the king says Isabella left for France on good terms with him, '[b]ut now someone has changed her mind; someone has filled her mind with extraordinary stories', but that 'someone' is not identified, nor is sexual impropriety implied.[27]

The only other chronicle references to Isabella's adultery are the Lanercost Chronicler's claim that 'there was a liaison suspected between [Mortimer] and the lady queen-mother, as according to public report',[28] and Jean Le Bel's statement that Mortimer, 'rumour had it, was intimate with the king's mother both in secret and otherwise' and that 'a dreadful rumour started – whether it was true I don't know – that the Queen Mother was pregnant, and Lord Mortimer more than anyone was suspected of being the father', a rumour repeated by Froissart, who used Le Bel as his source.[29] As Kathryn Warner argues, these are late references (the Lanercost chronicler in about 1346, and Jean Le Bel in the 1350s, although he was in England at the time of Isabella's and Mortimer's invasion) and hedge their claims by referring to the fact that these were rumours – as do Le Baker and Murimuth. Likewise, Laura Slater argues that '[t]he basic narrative of the interregnum period in contemporary English chronicles minimises the involvement and appearance of Isabella wherever possible. Later, c.1340s chronicles such as Lanercost and the hostile writings of Geoffrey le Baker go into the greatest detail about the queen's political activity and adultery with Mortimer'.[30] This might imply that the adultery was only reported after it was politically safe to do so, but could equally suggest it was a later invention or exaggeration. Warner goes on to identify five chronicles that say nothing about any adultery between Mortimer and Isabella, or which make ambiguous claims that could be interpreted simply as meaning that Mortimer was a chief counsellor of the queen, such as the *Brut*'s statement that he 'was wonder priuee with þe Quene Isabell'.[31] Warner (correctly, in my view) interprets *priuee* to mean 'that Roger [Mortimer] was Isabella's close confidant and trusted adviser'.[32]

Accusations of closeness, secrecy or privacy are ambiguous; they could be used to openly accuse a ruler of adultery, or to accuse them of excessive reliance on a single 'favourite'. For example, before openly saying Isabella and Mortimer were lovers, Le Baker stated that 'Roger Mortimer ... by this time [early 1327] was the most secret and influential person in the queen's private household'.[33] In this, they resemble complaints about Edward II and his male 'intimates' such as Piers Gaveston and Hugh Despenser.[34] As we have observed above, the question of whether these relationships were sexual has been debated to an extent that has not been applied to the relationship of Isabella and Mortimer. Alternatively, accusations of privacy or secrecy might carry no sexual innuendo, but rather imply disapproval of government by a clique around the ruler, as in the *Scalacronica*'s reference to 'confidential adherents' of Isabella.[35]

In fact, it was more common for chroniclers simply to portray Mortimer as Isabella's chief ally or counsellor: the *Scalacronica* refers to 'Roger de Mortimer, then chief of her council'[36] and the Bridlington chronicle states that Roger Mortimer 'adhered to the queen'.[37] Furthermore, Warner points out that none of the charges made by Edward in the months leading up to Isabella's invasion say anything about her adultery with Mortimer.[38] For example, a proclamation of 8 February 1326 complains that 'the queen is adopting the counsel of the Mortimer, the king's notorious enemy and rebel, and of other rebels, and that she is making alliances with the men of those parts and other strangers'.[39] Again, we see Mortimer portrayed as a chief ally or counsellor rather than a lover of the queen.

It this context, it is worth us returning to our discussion of the presence of Mortimer in Isabella's bedchamber, which Geoffrey le Baker used to imply adultery. Isabella's chamber was an ambiguous space. It was 'private', and therefore made her subject to the suspicion of adultery when men were present there; places of privacy were often viewed as locations where men could take sexual advantage of women.[40] The architecture and geography of royal residences in late medieval England was trending toward the creation of separate spaces for the queen, suggesting her removal from the 'public' world of political authority.[41] But Isabella's bedchamber was also a 'public' space when it was the location for meetings of the ruler and his or her advisors; and Mortimer and Isabella were effectively the rulers of England in 1330. There was a trend in the fourteenth century toward the king's chamber becoming the location for matters of state.[42] In the words of Henric Bagerius and Christine Ekholst, '[t]he king's chamber was a key political space; it was here that important strategies were drawn up and momentous decisions taken'.[43] By holding meetings in her chamber, Isabella may have been making herself vulnerable to chroniclers' accusations of sexual impropriety, but she was also staking a claim to 'kingship' and regendering her private space as public and 'male'. Moreover, we could even challenge this interpretation, based as it is on a male-public / female-private dichotomy. In the words of Thomas Kuehn and Anne Jacobson Schutte, there was in practice no 'neat equation of public space gendered as male space and private space gendered as female'.[44]

If there is little contemporary chronicle evidence that Isabella and Mortimer were lovers, then how should we account for the emergence and longevity of the claim? It may reflect the unpopularity of their rulership, and resentment of the Mortimers' favoured position. As we have seen, the claim that Isabella and Mortimer were lovers was (unsurprisingly) more prominent in chronicle accounts after their fall from power, and the same applies to criticism of their rulership in the period 1327–30, with contemporary chroniclers not 'censur[ing] Isabella's actions', in the words of Lisa Benz St John.[45] Among those chroniclers who were critical, commentary on their government featured more prominently than criticisms of their sexual relationship. Le Baker accused Isabella of adultery, but had more to say about Isabella's cruelty toward her opponents during her seizure of power.⁴⁶ The *Brut* complained about the power of Mortimer and Isabella during the minority of her son, Edward III: 'ffor þe Kyng and alle þe lordes þat shulde gouerne him, were gouernede and reulede after þe Kyngus moder, Dame Isabel, and by Sir Roger þe Mortymer'.⁴⁷ The *Scalacronica* states that 'Queen Isabella and Mortimer governed all England in such a fashion as to displease the nobles of the realm' and that 'the Queen, with the advice of [Roger Mortimer] the Earl of March, had everything in her governance'.⁴⁸

Of course, the absence of contemporary evidence for Isabella and Mortimer having a sexual relationship is not necessarily evidence of absence. Joanna Laynesmith, in an article on claims of adultery by English queens, remarks that 'it is the striking lack of contemporary tales of her [Isabella's] adultery that is puzzling'.⁴⁹ She argues that, in a conversation with Bishop Hamo of Rochester, Edward complained about Isabella's disobedience rather than adultery.⁵⁰ Laynesmith interprets this as Edward not wishing to draw attention to adultery on the part of the queen, because it was traditionally associated with failing kingship.⁵¹ But I would argue that disobedience was the real cause of concern to the king, and that maybe no adultery had even occurred, and therefore there is no need to explain the 'puzzling' lack of contemporary evidence of it. As Kathryn Warner argues, maybe 'a majority of fourteenth-century chronicles are "silent" on Isabella's adultery because they hadn't heard that she'd committed adultery, or even, perhaps, just maybe, ... there was no adultery'.⁵²

It could be argued in favour of the claims of adultery that, while Isabella and Mortimer's affair was not mentioned in contemporary written sources, later accounts reflect an oral tradition of popular rumour. As we have seen, accusations of adultery were often prefaced by claims that these things were 'rumoured' or 'said', in order for the writer to distance themselves a little from such incendiary claims or to maintain a tone of objectivity. This was standard practice among medieval chroniclers. We see this, for example, in claims made about a former allegedly adulterous queen of England, Eleanor of Aquitaine. According to Gervase of Canterbury, 'People said' that she had contrived the dissolution of her marriage to Louis VII of France and 'it was said' that she instigated her son's rebellion against her second husband, Henry II of England.⁵³ Richard of Devizes alluded cryptically to claims that she committed adultery with her uncle, Raymond, prince of Antioch: 'many know what I would that none of us knew ... Let no one say any more about it. I know it well. Keep silent!'⁵⁴

As we have seen, the Lanercost chronicler cited rumour as the basis for their claim that Isabella and Mortimer had a 'liaison', as did Jean le Bel for the story that Isabella was pregnant by him. The author of the Lanercost chronicle referred to rumour elsewhere, in his account of Isabella's rebellion, where he states that 'there were contradictory rumours in England about the queen, some declaring that she was the betrayer of the king and the kingdom, others that she was acting for peace and the common welfare of the kingdom'.[55] So we can see how rumour was often employed as a strategy by chroniclers, not always in a defamatory way; in this example, the Lanercost chronicler was taking a balanced approach to the 'contradictory rumours'.

The 'it is said' formulation is therefore a literary device on the part of the chroniclers, but might it reflect a world of popular rumour that occasionally found its way into written accounts, but is otherwise largely invisible to the historical record? Laura Slater draws on visual sources that may reflect rumours about Isabella, focusing on a window in St Frideswide's Abbey in Oxford (now Christ Church Cathedral).[56] The window depicts a king and queen with the English and French coats of arms; presumably Isabella and her husband Edward II or son Edward III. Beneath this respectful depiction however, are satirical images of woman–animal hybrids that plausibly comment upon female sexual sin.

If the window was produced roughly contemporaneously with the years of the deposition and interregnum, c.1327–30, there are obvious resonances here with recent political events in England: the marital troubles and rumoured sexual sins of Isabella of France, and the hopes for a fresh start vested in the reign of Edward III.[57]

Slater goes on the argue that Geoffrey le Baker's comments about Isabella's 'unlawful embraces' may derive from rumours circulating among Oxford clerics, as le Baker was at one time a cleric at the Augustinian house at Osney near Oxford.[58]

However, Slater also notes that none of the satirical female figures in the Oxford window are crowned, so 'there is no explicit visual condemnation of the sinful activities of queens, and no unambiguous reference to Isabella of France'.[59] Furthermore, the existence of rumour does not necessarily reflect reality; in today's politics, rumour 'tells' us that Hillary Clinton ran a child-trafficking ring out of a pizza restaurant in Washington, DC, that Covid vaccinations implant monitoring chips in our arms, and that chemicals in the water turn frogs gay.[60]

I would therefore argue that, while we can never disprove that Isabella and Mortimer were lovers, there are no compelling reasons to assume that they were, or to imagine that rumours of adultery reflected a 'real' oral history that could not be expressed openly in writing until after their fall from power in 1330. Furthermore, regardless of whether Mortimer was the lover of Isabella, our scepticism should be heightened by the existence of a tradition of criticising queens through accusations of adultery. Therefore, claims that Isabella and Mortimer were lovers may simply be a topos employed to attack Isabella as a woman who had rebelled against her king and husband, who ruled (at least in the eyes of her critics) without legitimate authority, and whose rule was increasingly unpopular.

Examples of queens accused of adultery are almost too many to list; we have already addressed the claims that Eleanor of Aquitaine had an affair with her uncle while in Antioch on the Second Crusade. She was also accused by Walter Map of sleeping with her father-in-law, Geoffrey of Anjou.[61] In the Tour de Nesle affair Isabella's sisters-in-law, Blanche and Margaret of Burgundy, were brought down (ironically, partly at Isabella's instigation) over claims that they committed adultery with a pair of knights.[62] As well as general claims of adultery, the specific accusation that the queen was pregnant with her lover's child was common, and particularly damning as it raised questions about the royal succession. Jean le Bel made this claim about Isabella, and similar accusations were made against Isabeau of Bavaria (the wife of Charles VI of France),[63] Margaret of Anjou (wife of England's Henry VI), and Joanna of Portugal (wife of Enrique IV of Castile).[64] In the case of Joanna of Portugal, it was said that her husband King Enrique had persuaded his favourite, Beltrán de la Cueva, to sleep with the queen because the king himself was unable to consummate his marriage.[65] The trope of a wife cuckolding an unmanly king and bearing another man's child has such longevity that it appears in *Braveheart*, where Isabella conceives a child with William Wallace.[66] During the Wars of the Roses, we see claims of adulterous pregnancy made against the king's or male heir's mother more than against the queen herself, as such rumours worked to cast doubt on the king's legitimacy (such accusations were raised to dispute the legitimacy of Henry VI and Margaret of Anjou's son, and of Edward IV).[67] Maybe Jean Le Bel's claim about Isabella reflected pro-Valois rumours that cast doubt on the legitimacy of Edward III's claim to the French throne in the opening decades of the Hundred Years' War; if Edward were illegitimate, arguments over whether his mother could pass on the crown of France to him would become moot.

We can see some common contexts to these accusations of adultery by queens. They were mainly aimed at women who were seen as asserting an inappropriate level of authority supplanting that of their husbands or sons. They often occurred at times of political turmoil, such as Isabella's removal of Edward, the disputed succession of Isabeau of Bavaria's son Charles VII, or Margaret of Anjou's role in the Wars of the Roses. As well as critiquing over-powerful queens, such rumours also drew attention to the weakness of kings such as Edward II, Charles VII, or Henry VI. In the words of Joanna Laynesmith, '[t]ales of Margaret [of Anjou]'s adultery were to become more elaborate and more common as her husband's hold on power collapsed'.[68] Laynesmith argues that there was a strong association between

Isabella and Mortimer: lovers or allies? 97

queenly adultery and failing kingship, seen, for example, in Arthurian romance, where Arthur's power begins to collapse when Mordred seizes both his kingdom and his queen. She points out that three royal depositions in late medieval England – those of Edward II, Richard II, and Henry VI – are 'associated with tales of queenly adultery'.[69]

If we are duly sceptical of the assumption that Mortimer and Isabella were lovers, it frees us to reconsider what early-fourteenth-century chroniclers actually did say about Isabella, and it reveals an alternative candidate for the role of Isabella's chief partner in crime. Even Geoffrey le Baker, one of the few chroniclers who openly accused Isabella of adultery with Mortimer, reserved most of his wrath for Adam Orleton, the bishop of Hereford, and the other bishops who supported Isabella's coup d'état. The rebels were described as 'priests of Baal, pupils of Jezebel' and Orleton specifically as 'that priest of Baal the bishop of Hereford'.[70] His account may contain hints that Baker sees Orleton as her lover. He claims (immediately preceding his reference to the queen's 'unlawful embraces' with Mortimer) that Orleton was upset 'that Roger Mortimer ... ha[d] usurped his place as [Isabella's] friend' and refers to her moving against Edward 'on the advice of her lovers [plural]'.[71] Orleton, not Mortimer, was viewed as the prime mover behind Isabella's rebellion, 'the principal plotter of this great disaster' and 'the instigator of the whole of her wicked plot' and Isabella's 'master'.[72]

Intriguingly, if we accept Slater's interpretation of the imagery in the St Lucy window at St Frideswide's as commentary upon Queen Isabella, she is not paired with a symbol of Mortimer but with clerical figures. The satirical images of women are accompanied by similar human–animal hybrids of bishops or other churchmen. They include a 'creature with female head and bishop's head' and '[t]aken as a whole, the eight grotesques immediately below the arms of France and England form a series of derisive allusions to the animal desires of men, women and clerics'.[73] Slater argues that, while the meanings of such images are not fixed,

> spectators could read the female hybrids below the arms of France as figures for the sexual sins of Isabella of France. Similarly, the monstrous bishops in the tracery zone might be identified with Adam Orleton ... The monstrous combinations in the St Lucy window and [similar iconography in] the Luttrell Psalter both evoke the diabolic alliance between Isabella and Adam Orleton narrated by [Geoffrey le] Baker in his *Chronicon*.[74]

I am not, of course, suggesting that Orleton and Isabella were lovers; rather, that Mortimer was not the only person accused of being her lover, or at least of being a malign influence upon her, which should in turn make us question how seriously to take similar accusations about him and Isabella.

No serious historian today believes rumours that Orleton and Isabella were lovers, or that Isabella was made pregnant by Mortimer, yet her alleged adultery with the latter is too often taken for granted.

The almost universal assumption that Isabella committed adultery with Roger Mortimer should therefore be challenged. There is some contemporary or near contemporary evidence for it, but no more so than for other allegations of adultery against medieval queens that have been treated more sceptically by historians. If we accept claims that Isabella was an adulteress, why are we more cautious about similar rumours about – for example – Eleanor of Aquitaine or Margaret of Anjou? Likewise, why do we believe that Isabella had an affair with Roger Mortimer, but not give such credence to contemporary innuendo about her relationship with Bishop Orleton, or her pregnancy by Mortimer? These accusations reflect well-established traditions and *topoi* of adulterous queens, which does not necessarily make them false, but should lead us to treat them with caution.

More generally, I would argue against becoming fixated on the 'did they or didn't they?' argument and argue instead for considering why accusations of adultery emerged at times of political crisis, and what meaning they carried. To quote Laynesmith one last time:

> [t]ales told of adulterous queens in late medieval England rarely referred to events that actually happened. Rather their fascination is in what they reveal about ideas. They illustrate popular perceptions about the power of noble blood and about poor government consequent on non-noble blood.[75]

In the case of Isabella, I would argue that they were deployed in an attempt to explain her subversive action of rebelling against her husband and king, and to retrospectively denigrate her rule after the coup of 1327 by casting the shadow of adultery over her political alliance with Roger Mortimer.

Notes

1 Christopher Marlowe, *Edward II*, Perseus Digital Library, act 5, scene 1, lines 17, 30–31, available at www.perseus.tufts.edu/hopper/text?doc=Perseus:text:1999.03.0007 (accessed 27 November 2023).
2 Agnes Strickland, *Lives of the Queens of England*, 16 vols (Philadelphia: George Barrie & Son, 1902–3) 2: 167–168.
3 Strickland, *Lives of the Queens of England*, 2: 190.
4 Chris Given-Wilson, *Edward II: The Terrors of Kingship* (London: Penguin, 2016), 92.
5 Kathryn Warner, 'The Relationship of Queen Isabella and Roger Mortimer (2)', *Edward II*, available at http://edwardthesecond.blogspot.com/2021/02/the-relationship-of-queen-isabella-and.html (accessed 27 November 2023).

6 Lisa Benz St John, *Three Medieval Queens. Queenship and the Crown in Fourteenth-Century* (New York: Palgrave MacMillan, 2012) 135–136.
7 Benz St. John, *Three Medieval Queens*, 33–43.
8 Michael Robson, 'Queen Isabella (c.1295/1358) and the Greyfriars: An example of royal patronage based on her accounts for 1357/1358', *Franciscan Studies* 65 (2007): 325–348.
9 John de Trokelowe, *Johannes de Troklowe et Henrici de Blaneforde Chronica et Annales*, ed. T.H. Riley (London; Her Majesty's Stationery Office, 1865), 110.
10 Anne Rudloff Stanton, 'The Psalter of Isabelle, Queen of England 1308–1330: Isabelle as the Audience', *Word & Image* 18.4 (2002): 25.
11 Geoffrey le Baker, *The Chronicle of Geoffrey le Baker*, trans. David Preest, ed. Richard Barber (Woodbridge: Boydell, 2012), xiii.
12 Le Baker, *Chronicle*, 21, 24.
13 See, for example, Janet L. Nelson, 'Queens as Jezebels: The Careers of Brunhild and Balthild in Merovingian History', *Studies in Church History Subsidia* 1 (1978): 31–77; Kimberley A. LoPrete, 'Gendering Viragos: Medieval Perceptions of Powerful Women', in *Studies on Medieval and Early Modern Women 4: Victims or Viragos?*, ed. Christine Meek and Catherine Lawless (Dublin: Four Courts Press, 2005), 17–38.
14 Le Baker, *Chronicle*, 19.
15 Le Baker, *Chronicle*, 19–20.
16 Le Baker, *Chronicle*, 21.
17 2 Kings 9:30 (Bible, New International Version).
18 Le Baker, *Chronicle*, xix.
19 *The Brut or the Chronicles of England*, ed. Friedrich W.D. Brie, 2 vols (London: Early English Text Society, 1880), 2: 271.
20 Le Baker, *Chronicle*, xix.
21 Anonymous, 'Annales Paulini, 1307–1340', in *Chronicles of the Reigns of Edward I and Edward II*, ed. William Stubbs, 2 vols (London: Her Majesty's Stationery Office, 1882–1883), 1: 314, 352.
22 Thomas Grey, *Scalacronica: The Reigns of Edward I, Edward II and Edward III*, ed. and trans. Herbert Maxwell (Glasgow: James MacLehose, 1907), 86–87.
23 Le Baker, *Chronicle*, xiii–xvi.
24 Adam Murimuth, *Continuatio chronicarum Robertus de Avesbury de gestis mirabilibus regis Edwardi Tertii*, ed. Edward Maunde Thompson (London: Her Majesty's Stationery Office, 1889), 45–46.
25 Natalie Fryde, *The Tyranny and Fall of Edward II* (Cambridge: Cambridge University Press, 1979), 180.
26 Kathryn Warner, 'The Relationship of Queen Isabella and Roger Mortimer (1)', *Edward II*, available at http://edwardthesecond.blogspot.com/2014/02/isa-and-rm-relationship.html (accessed 27 November 2023).
27 *Vita Edwardi Secundi: The Life of Edward the Second*, ed. and trans. Wendy R. Childs (Oxford: Oxford University Press, 2005), 244–247.
28 *The Chronicle of Lanercost*, ed. and trans. Herbert Maxwell (Glasgow: James MacLehose & Sons, 1913), 266–267.

29 Jean le Bel, *The True Chronicles of Jean le Bel, 1290–1360*, ed. and trans. Nigel Bryant (Woodbridge: Boydell, 2011), 58–59; Jean Froissart, 'Translation of Book I, Folio 23r', The Online Froissart, The Digital Humanities Institute, 20 December 2013, available at www.dhi.ac.uk/onlinefroissart/browsey.jsp?pb0=BookI-Translation_23r&img0=&div0=ms.f.transl.BookI-Translation&panes=1&GlobalMode=facsimile&img0=&disp0=pb&GlobalWord=0&GlobalShf=&pb0=BookI-Translation_23v (accessed 27 November 2023); Warner, 'Relationship (1)'.
30 Laura Slater, 'Defining Queenship at Greyfriars London, c.1300-58', *Gender & History* 27.1 (2015): 64.
31 *Brut*, 2: 268.
32 Warner, 'Relationship (2)'.
33 Le Baker, *Chronicle*, 20.
34 Antonia Gransden, *Historical Writing in England, vol. 2, c. 1307 to the Early Sixteenth Century* (London: Routledge, 1997), 21. Gransden cites the chronicle of Robert of Reading, who was sympathetic to Isabella and hostile to Edward.
35 *Scalacronica*, 86.
36 *Scalacronica*, 72.
37 'Gesta Edwardi de Carnarvon', in *Chronicles of the Reigns of Edward I and Edward II*, ed. William Stubbs, 2 vols (London: Longman, 1883) 2: 86–87.
38 Warner, 'Relationship (1)'.
39 *Calendar of the Close Rolls Preserved in the Public Record Office, Edward II, A.D. 1323-7* (London: Her Majesty's Stationery Office, 1898), 543.
40 Sarah Rees Jones, 'Public and Private Space and Gender in Medieval Europe', in *The Oxford Handbook of Women and Gender in Medieval Europe*, ed. Judith M. Bennett and Ruth Mazo Karras (Oxford: Oxford University Press, 2013), 253.
41 Rees Jones, 'Public and Private', 249.
42 Rees Jones, 'Public and Private', 251.
43 Henric Bagerius and Christine Ekholst, 'Kings and Favourites: Politics and Sexuality in Late Medieval Europe', *Journal of Medieval History* 43.3 (2017): 309.
44 Quoted in Rees Jones, 'Public and Private', 249.
45 Benz St John, Three Medieval Queens, 160.
46 Le Baker, *Chronicle*, 23–24.
47 *Brut*, 254. Paul R. Dryburgh, 'The Career of Roger Mortimer, first earl of March (c.1287-1330)', (PhD thesis, University of Bristol, 2002), 110.
48 *Scalacronica*, 84.
49 Joanna Laynesmith, 'Telling Tales of Adulterous Queens in Medieval England: From Olympias of Macedonia to Elizabeth Woodville', in *Every Inch a King: Comparative Studies on Kings and Kingship in the Ancient and Medieval Worlds*, ed. Lynette Mitchell and Charles Melville (Leiden: Brill, 2013), 196. I would like to thank Dr Laynesmith for providing me with a copy of her chapter.
50 Laynesmith, 'Telling Tales', 198.
51 Laynesmith, 'Telling Tales', 199.
52 Warner, 'Relationship (2)'.

53 Gervase of Canterbury, *Historical Works, the Chronicle of the Reigns of Stephen, Henry II, and Richard I*, ed. William Stubbs, 2 vols (London: Her Majesty's Stationery Office, 1879–1880), 1: 149; 1: 242.
54 Jean Flori, *Eleanor of Aquitaine: Queen and Rebel*, ed. and trans. Olive Classe (Edinburgh: Edinburgh University Press, 2007), 69, 109; Richard of Devizes, *The Chronicle of Richard of Devizes*, ed. and trans. J.T Appleby (London: Thomas Nelson, 1963), 25–26.
55 *Chronicle of Lanercost*, 250.
56 Laura Slater, 'Rumour and reputation management in fourteenth-century England: Isabella of France in text and image', *Journal of Medieval History* 47.2 (2021): 257–292, available at www.tandfonline.com/doi/full/10.1080/03044181.2021.1891449 (accessed 27 November 2023). I would like to thank Dr Slater for pointing me toward her article.
57 Slater, 'Rumour and Reputation', 282.
58 Slater, 'Rumour and Reputation', 287.
59 Slater, 'Rumour and Reputation', 282.
60 Michael E. Miller, 'Pizzagate's Deadly Legacy', *Washington Post* (Washington, DC), 16 Feb. 2021; 'Is it true? Do COVID-19 vaccines contain a microchip or any kind of tracking technology?' Australian Government Department of Health, updated 10 May 2022, available at www.health.gov.au/initiatives-and-programs/covid-19-vaccines/is-it-true/is-it-true-do-covid-19-vaccines-contain-a-microchip-or-any-kind-of-tracking-technology (accessed 27 November 2023); Bruce Y. Lee, 'Alex Jones' Top 10 Health Claims and Why they are Wrong', *Forbes*, 16 Aug. 2018, available at www.forbes.com/sites/brucelee/2018/08/16/alex-jones-top-10-health-claims-and-why-they-are-wrong/?sh=451f24583e7f (accessed 27 November 2023).
61 Walter Map, *De Nugis Curialium: Courtiers' Trifles*, ed. and trans. M.R. James, C.N.L. Brooke, and R. Mynors (Oxford: Clarendon Press, 1983), 453.
62 Kathryn Warner, *Isabella of France. The Rebel Queen* (Stroud: Amberley, 2016), Kindle Edition, chapter 3.
63 Rachel Gibbons, 'Isabeau of Bavaria, Queen of France (1385–1422): The Creation of an Historical Villainess', *Transactions of the Royal Historical Society*, 6th Series 6 (1996): 62.
64 Bagerius and Ekholst, 'Kings and Favourites', 316
65 Bagerius and Ekholst, 'Kings and Favourites', 316.
66 Mel Gibson, *Braveheart* (Los Angeles: Icon Productions, The Ladd Company / Paramount, 1995).
67 Laynesmith, 'Telling Tales', 206–207.
68 Laynesmith, 'Telling Tales', 195.
69 Laynesmith, 'Telling Tales', 200.
70 Le Baker, *Chronicle*, 21, 28.
71 Le Baker, *Chronicle*, 19–20.
72 Le Baker, *Chronicle*, 22, 24, 30.
73 Slater, 'Rumour and Reputation', 273, 280.
74 Slater, 'Rumour and Reputation', 285.
75 Laynesmith, 'Telling Tales', 212.

Bibliography

Primary sources

Anonymous. 'Annales Paulini, 1307–1340'. In *Chronicles of the Reigns of Edward I and Edward II*, ed. William Stubbs. 2 vols. London: Her Majesty's Stationery Office, 1882–1883.

Anonymous. 'The Brut or the Chronicles of England', ed. Friedrich W.D. Brie. 2 vols. London: Early English Text Society, 1880.

Anonymous. 'The Chronicle of Lanercost', ed. and trans. Herbert Maxwell. Glasgow: James MacLehose and Sons, 1913.

Anonymous. 'Gesta Edwardi de Carnarvon'. In *Chronicles of the Reigns of Edward I and Edward II*, ed. William Stubbs. 2 vols. London: Her Majesty's Stationery Office, 1882–1883.

Australian Government Department of Health. 'Is it true? Do COVID-19 vaccines contain a microchip or any kind of tracking technology?' Australian Government Department of Health, updated May 10, 2022, at www.health.gov.au/initiatives-and-programs/covid-19-vaccines/is-it-true/is-it-true-do-covid-19-vaccines-contain-a-microchip-or-any-kind-of-tracking-technology (accessed 27 November 2023).

Braveheart. Amazon online. Directed by Mel Gibson. Los Angeles: Icon Productions, The Ladd Company / Paramount, 1995.

Calendar of the Close Rolls Preserved in the Public Record Office, Edward II, A.D. 1323–7. London: Her Majesty's Stationery Office, 1898.

Froissart, Jean. 'Translation of Book I, Folio 23 r'. *The Online Froissart*. The Digital Humanities Institute, December 20, 2013, available at www.dhi.ac.uk/onlinefroissart/browsey.jsp?pb0=BookI-Translation_23r&img0=&div0=ms.f.transl.BookI-Translation&panes=1&GlobalMode=facsimile&img0=&disp0=pb&GlobalWord=0&GlobalShf=&pb0=BookI-Translation_23v (accessed 27 November 2023).

Gervase of Canterbury, *Historical Works: The Chronicle of the Reigns of Stephen, Henry II, and Richard I*, ed. William Stubbs. 2 vols. London: Her Majesty's Stationery Office, 1879–1880.

Grey, Thomas. *Scalacronica: The Reigns of Edward I, Edward II and Edward III*, ed. and trans. Herbert Maxwell. Glasgow: James MacLehose, 1907.

Le Baker, Geoffrey. *The Chronicle of Geoffrey le Baker*. Trans. David Preest, ed. Richard Barber. Woodbridge: Boydell, 2012.

Le Bel, Jean. *The True Chronicles of Jean le Bel, 1290–1360*, ed. and trans. Nigel Bryant. Woodbridge: Boydell, 2011.

Lee, Bruce Y. 'Alex Jones' Top 10 Health Claims and Why they are Wrong.' *Forbes*, Aug. 16, 2018, available at www.forbes.com/sites/brucelee/2018/08/16/alex-jones-top-10-health-claims-and-why-they-are-wrong/?sh=451f24583e7f (accessed 27 November 2023).

Map, Walter. *De Nugis Curialium: Courtiers' Trifles*, ed. and trans. M.R. James, C.N.L. Brooke, and R. Mynors. Oxford: Clarendon Press, 1983.

Marlowe, Christopher. *Edward II*. Perseus Digital Library, available at www.perseus.tufts.edu/hopper/text?doc=Perseus:text:1999.03.0007 (accessed 27 November 2023).

Miller, Michael E. 'Pizzagate's Deadly Legacy.' *The Washington Post* (Washington, DC), Feb. 16, 2021.

Murimuth, Adam. *Continuatio chronicarum Robertus de Avesbury de gestis mirabilibus regis Edwardi Tertii*, ed. Edward Maunde Thompson. London: Her Majesty's Stationery Office, 1889.

Richard of Devizes. *The Chronicle of Richard of Devizes*, ed. and trans. J.T Appleby. London: Thomas Nelson, 1963.

Trokelowe, John de. *Johannes de Troklowe et Henrici de Blanneforde Chronica et Annales*, ed. Thomas Henry Riley. London; Her Majesty's Stationery Office, 1865.

Secondary sources

Bagerius, Henric, and Christine Ekholst. 'Kings and Favourites: Politics and Sexuality in Late Medieval Europe'. *Journal of Medieval History* 43.3 (2017): 298–319.

Benz St. John, Lisa. *Three Medieval Queens. Queenship and the Crown in Fourteenth-Century England*. New York: Palgrave Macmillan, 2012.

Dryburgh, Paul R. 'The Career of Roger Mortimer, first earl of March (c.1287–1330).' PhD thesis, University of Bristol, 2002.

Flori, Jean. *Eleanor of Aquitaine: Queen and Rebel*, ed. and trans. Olive Classe. Edinburgh: Edinburgh University Press, 2007.

Fryde, Natalie. *The Tyranny and Fall of Edward II*. Cambridge: Cambridge University Press, 1979.

Gibbons, Rachel. 'Isabeau of Bavaria, Queen of France (1385–1422): The Creation of an Historical Villainess'. *Transactions of the Royal Historical Society*, 6th Series 6 (1996): 51–73.

Given-Wilson, Chris. *Edward II: The Terrors of Kingship*. London: Penguin, 2016.

Gransden, Antonia. *Historical Writing in England, Volume 2, c. 1307 to the Early Sixteenth Century*. London: Routledge, 1997.

Laynesmith, Joanna. 'Telling Tales of Adulterous Queens in Medieval England: From Olympias of Macedonia to Elizabeth Woodville'. In *Every Inch a King: Comparative Studies on Kings and Kingship in the Ancient and Medieval Worlds*, ed. Lynette Mitchell and Charles Melville, 195–214. Leiden: Brill, 2013.

Lo Prete, Kimberley A. 'Gendering Viragos: Medieval Perceptions of Powerful Women'. In *Studies on Medieval and Early Modern Women 4: Victims or Viragos?*, ed. Christine Meek and Catherine Lawless, 17–38. Dublin: Four Courts Press, 2005.

Nelson, Janet L. 'Queens as Jezebels: The Careers of Brunhild and Balthild in Merovingian History'. *Studies in Church History Subsidia* 1 (1978): 31–77.

Rees Jones, Sarah. 'Public and Private Space and Gender in Medieval Europe'. In *The Oxford Handbook of Women and Gender in Medieval Europe*, ed. Judith M. Bennett and Ruth Mazo Karras, 246–261. Oxford: Oxford University Press, 2013.

Robson, Michael. 'Queen Isabella (c.1295/1358) and the Greyfriars: An example of royal patronage based on her accounts for 1357/1358'. *Franciscan Studies* 65 (2007): 325–48.

Slater, Laura. 'Defining Queenship at Greyfriars London, c.1300–58'. *Gender & History* 27.1 (2015): 53–76.

Slater, Laura. 'Rumour and Reputation Management in Fourteenth-Century England: Isabella of France in Text and Image'. *Journal of Medieval History*

47.2 (2021): 257–292, available at www.tandfonline.com/doi/full/10.1080/03044181.2021.1891449 (accessed 27 November 2023).

Stanton, Anne Rudloff. 'The Psalter of Isabelle, Queen of England 1308–1330: Isabelle as the Audience'. *Word & Image* 18.4 (2002): 1–27.

Strickland, Agnes. *Lives of the Queens of England*. 16 volumes. Philadelphia: George Barrie and Son, 1902–1903.

Warner, Kathryn. *Isabella of France. The Rebel Queen*. Stroud: Amberley, 2016. Kindle Edition.

Warner, Kathryn. 'The Relationship of Queen Isabella and Roger Mortimer (1).' *Edward II*. February 5, 2021, available at http://edwardthesecond.blogspot.com/2014/02/isa-and-rm-relationship.html (accessed 27 November 2023).

Warner, Kathryn. 'The Relationship of Queen Isabella and Roger Mortimer (2).' *Edward II*. February 20, 2021, available at http://edwardthesecond.blogspot.com/2021/02/the-relationship-of-queen-isabella-and.html (accessed 27 November 2023).

5

Isabel of Castile and her images: viewing sex, scandal, and sanctity in fifteenth-century Spain[1]

Jessica Weiss

The reign of Isabel of Castile was marked by the continual promotion of her legitimacy, due to the scandals that plagued her ascent to the throne. Her older half-brother, Enrique IV, had been crowned during Isabel's childhood. However, a faction of nobles dissatisfied with Enrique's rule pressured the king to repudiate his own daughter, Juana, and instead recognise his half-brother, Alfonso, as heir. The death of Alfonso in 1468 caused Isabel to become the face of the rebellion, and Enrique agreed to name her as his successor shortly thereafter.[2] When Enrique returned his support to Juana, the country was thrown into civil war. Even after Isabel's coronation in 1474, Juana's claim continued to be pressed by her husband, Afonso V of Portugal.[3]

While the underlying causes of discontent with Enrique were social and economic tensions between noble factions, the outrage was articulated through sexual slander coloured by the patriarchal gender-binary of the time.[4] Enrique's transgressions were asserted in the *Carta-Protesta*, an anonymous open letter circulated among the aristocracy. The critique included a homosexual relationship with Beltrán de la Cueva, impotence, and enabling Beltrán to engage in a sexual relationship with the queen.[5] These charges conflated Enrique's own supposed sexual activities with those of his wife and questioned the legitimacy of their daughter.[6] Enrique was also accused of failing to conform to the correct performance of normative gender roles, describing his effeminate behaviour and his inability to control his wife, resulting in cuckoldry.[7] This sexual slander was also used to repudiate Juana's claim by casting the princess as the illegitimate daughter of a lascivious queen who was married to an impotent, emasculated king.[8] The inclusion of these critiques against Enrique and Juana within the texts produced by Isabel's royal chroniclers reveals the importance these events and characterisations had on the framing of Isabel's reign and the explicit use of sexual slander as a political weapon, even after Isabel's consolidation of power.[9]

The casting of Enrique and Juana as unfit to rule because of effeminacy and sexual deviance had the potential to also undermine Isabel's own position by perpetuating the dominant belief that women were weak, unable to control their emotions and desires, leading them to indulge in sexual activities. These traits were understood to be innate to all women because of Eve's secondary creation from Adam's rib and her primary role in the downfall of humankind in the Garden of Eden.[10] In order to combat this, Isabel was shrewdly cast as not just a political alternative but as the moral opposite of her predecessor and rival who embodied the specifically female virtues of chastity, humility, and piety.[11] Like the female saints and the Virgin Mary, Isabel could transcend her womanly nature and transform her sexuality into a vehicle for redemption, even as her position necessitated the public display of her sexual activities through her role as wife and mother in the literal embodiment of sovereignty.[12] This was explicitly articulated by authors such as Fray Martín de Córdoba who, in his *Jardín de nobles donzellas*, argued that Isabel could be transfigured from a mere woman into the Queen of Castile in order to heal the body politic through the control of her desires.[13] Throughout her reign, Isabel and her supporters continued to argue for her legitimacy by positioning her within a series of binaries: Isabel/Enrique, female/male, virtuous rule/immoral rule. This reliance on sexual slander as a pointed critique of political rivals and the counterbalance of Isabel as a virtuous, legitimate ruler certainly impacted Isabel's own self-fashioning and identity construction.

Royal images and Isabel's position as viewer

Isabel's identity was created not only through texts but also through the creation and reception of images. Careful consideration of illuminated images in Isabel's book of hours at the Cleveland Museum of Art (Leonard C. Hanna, Jr. Fund 1963.256) and in Isabel's breviary in the British Library (Add. Ms. 18851) reveals the nuanced ways in which imagery, when considered in terms of self-reflective consumption, may have participated in Isabel's self-conception as the legitimate queen-regnant of Castile due to her virtuous sexuality and pure femininity.[14] By considering these image cycles in the context of Isabel's life, it is possible to hypothesise how they may have been interpreted by Isabel as reflecting her personal experiences and perspectives. This interpretive approach is similar to reader-response criticism as theorised by Louise Rosenblatt. Rosenblatt has argued for a view of the process of reading as 'a unique coming-together of a particular personality and a particular text at a particular time and place under particular circumstances'.[15] This process is transactional, with the construction of meaning occurring through the co-constituted conditions of the individual and the text.[16] During the reading act, the reader's experience is constituted of both the response evoked by the text and their reactionary response to this evocation. This process is impacted not only by creative process of the author and the stance of the reader, but by the reader's own knowledge and beliefs, including their personal, social, and cultural contexts. Rosenblatt articulates the summation of experience that leads to individualised meaning as 'the residue of an individual's past transactions ... what can be termed a linguistic-experiential reservoir'.[17] Rosenblatt emphasises that the construction of meaning is not a linear or mechanical operation of decoding, but a fluid and organic process in which the reader responds both to the text itself and to their 'lived through current of ideas, sensations, images, tensions' experienced during the reading act and therefore is incorporated into their interpretive construct.[18] The result of this process, when captured, is a series of related thoughts, observations, and questions synthesised by the reader.[19]

Considering the book of hours in Cleveland, and the breviary in London, within this framework enables the conceptualisation of Isabel as an active viewer constructing her own personalised meaning. While it is impossible to replicate her direct experience, imagining the queen as transacting with these images enables the consideration of how the events of her life and prerogatives of her reign, analogous to her linguistic-experiential reservoir, may have participated in her response to these visual messages. As the viewer, Isabel would have brought to the transaction a complex network of lived experiences and ideological constructs that included the sexual scandals that were used to critique her political rivals and the need to dissociate herself from Enrique and Juana. Elements of these ideas and remembered experiences may have been incorporated into the queen's chain of thought process. By enabling the construction of meaning through the lens of Isabel as the imagined viewer, we can consider how these images might have participated in her self-conception as the moral counter to Enrique, as the chaste (not lascivious) legitimate (though female) Queen of Castile.

Centring Isabel as viewer

When envisioning Isabel as the imagined viewer, the first consideration is how she may have understood the imagery subjectively. While neither the Cleveland hours nor the London breviary include a portrait of Isabel, the inclusion of her emblems and coats of arms (Figures 5.1–2) would have similarly contextualised her experience of the texts and images within a subjective framework. The heraldry in the book of hours occurs on the first

108 *Part I: Scandal, perception and representation*

5.1 Armorial, Hours of Queen Isabel, c. 1500 (ink, tempera, and gold on vellum, codex is 23.5 × 17.3 cm). Cleveland Museum of Art 1963.256., fol. 1v.

5.2 Armorial, Breviary of Queen Isabel, c. 1497 (ink, tempera, and gold on parchment, codex is 23 × 16 cm). British Library Additional MS 18851, fol. 436v.

opening and therefore serves as a prelude to the entire experience of the object. The shield is presented with a yoke and bundle of arrows, the personal devices of Isabel and Fernando. Below, two banderols undulate across the space, inscribed with the motto of the queen and king and an excerpt from the Psalms.[20] Each of the elements in this illumination contributes to the invocation of Isabel's individual identities as queen and wife. In contrast, the heraldry illumination in the breviary, located in the sanctoral, emphasises her familial connections. Her and Fernando's coat of arms is joined by those of Prince Juan and Margaret of Austria on the left and Isabella's daughter Juana and her husband, Philip the Handsome, on the right.[21] Again, banderols encircle the armorials with excerpts from the Psalms.[22]

Isabel's engagement with the images as corresponding to her own experiences and identities also extends to other areas of the codices.[23] For example, both Isabel's breviary and her book of hours include St Elizabeth of Hungary within the sanctoral (Figures 5.3–4). These images show the saint clutching two crowns, symbolising her dual status as both an earthly queen and heavenly saint. Like many female Christian saints, the sanctity of St Elizabeth was based in part on her sexuality. In the *Golden Legend,* her *vita* is constructed to celebrate the safeguarding of her virginity until 'she was constrained to enter into the degree of marriage, for her father constrained her thereto, because she should bring forth fruit'.[24] As a noble woman who lived her life according to the Christian values of piety, humility, and chastity within marriage, the thirteenth-century saint was not only the namesake of Isabel and a distant relative but also a model for the very qualities necessary for Isabel's presentation as the righteous counterpart to her brother Enrique. Similarly, Isabel may have reflected more explicitly on the importance of sexual chastity, especially for a female ruler, while transacting with the representations of St Catharine of Alexandria (Figures 5.5–6). Like Isabel, Catharine was a noble woman who rose to become queen regnant. In both images, Catharine plunges a large sword into the body of Maxentius who lies at her feet. This corporeal penetration is a visual counterpoint to the saint's hagiography as articulated in *The Golden Legend*, where Catharine's sexuality, specifically her virginal status, is a central theme.[25] Her refusal of Maxentius's offer of a sexual relationship is due in part to her previous mystical marriage to Christ. This event is predicated on Catharine's virginal state, with Mary saying 'she had a great conflict and battle to keep her virginity, and [… my son] desireth her beauty and loveth her chastity among all the virgins on the earth'.[26]

Isabel may have considered the connection between female virtue and female rule, and how her own position as benefactor to her subjects intersected with conceptions of 'proper' sexual behaviour while transacting with the images of St Elizabeth and St Catharine. They may have conjured for Isabel

5.3 St Elizabeth of Hungary, Breviary of Queen Isabel. British Library Additional MS 18851, fol. 488v.

112 Part I: Scandal, perception and representation

5.4 St Elizabeth of Hungary, Hours of Queen Isabel. Cleveland Museum of Art 1963.256, fol. 197v.

5.5 St Catharine of Alexandria, Hours of Queen Isabel. Cleveland Museum of Art, 1963.256, fol. 189v.

5.6 St Catharine of Alexandria, Breviary of Queen Isabel. British Library Additional MS 18851, fol. 495v.

Isabel of Castile and her images

memories of her own marriage negotiations and the gendered articulation of her queenship.[27] Even as Isabel's supporters advanced her position as heir to the throne, there was also a recognition of the need for an advantageous marriage that produced legitimate heirs.[28] Texts such as Martín de Cordoba's *Jardín de nobles donzellas* attempted to prepare Isabel for this inevitability by instructing her on the proper behaviour of wives.[29] The questions over the selection of a spouse were settled by the marriage contract with Fernando of Aragon, completed in March 1469, which protected Isabel's interests as primary ruler of Castile.[30] Isabel then usurped the traditionally masculine attribute of the unsheathed sword during her coronation in Segovia on 13 December 1474, conducted in Fernando's absence.[31] The prominent placement of the sword in the depiction of St Catharine in both the Cleveland hours and the London breviary, and its use by a sexually virtuous woman to subjugate a male ruler, may have resonated with Isabel's own history, both in her triumph over the licentious Enrique and in her success in maintaining control of her kingdom within her own marriage. This political reality differed from the public presentation of Isabel and Fernando's political and conjugal union as between equals, symbolised by the motto 'Tanto Monta' and their chivalric emblems including the yoke or *yugo* (Figure 5.1), which reinforced their heteronormative relationship and emphasised their sexuality as within the sanctity of Christian marriage.[32]

Mary as exemplar and avatar

One of the most poignant ways Isabel may have interacted with these images is through contemplation of the Virgin Mary, who is a prominent figure in both manuscripts. The Virgin provided a visual guide to proper female behaviour by exemplifying chastity, humility, and devotion.[33] When Isabel transacted with these images, the reflection of herself through the image of Mary may have encouraged her to mirror this sexless love. While Isabel's emulation would have been limited by the dynastic need for legitimate children, she may have recognised the necessity for her to minimise her bodily passions in the wake of the moral depravity of her predecessor.

While the function of Mary as devotional model is not unique to Isabel, Castile, or even the fifteenth century, the predominance of political propaganda that equated Isabel with the Virgin may have further nuanced Isabel's response to these images. Even before Isabel ascended the throne as queen, Martín de Córdoba encouraged Isabel to prepare for the role by cultivating the Virgin's modesty, piety, and compassion in his *Jardín de nobles donzellas*.[34] In order to foster these qualities, Isabel should emulate the chastity of the Virgin, who was similar to her in that both were maidens of royal descent who were expected to be queen.[35] This framework was especially poignant, as it differentiated between Isabel and her niece Juana, who was associated with the sexual misconduct of her father, Enrique. Isabel's chroniclers repeatedly utilised sexual slander as a form of political critique by invoking Enrique's licentious behaviour and cuckolding before describing the events of their patron's reign.[36] For example, Pulgar explicitly describes Juana as the daughter of Beltran de la Cueva throughout the text;[37] Alonso de Palencia suggests the salaciousness of Enrique's activities saying that to describe them 'makes me blush and embarrasses me',[38] and Valera describes how Enrique's failings have led to an era of lawlessness and spiritual decline including the pillaging of churches and rampant sexual assault.[39] The writers continued to emphasise this Enrique/Isabel dichotomy even after she was recognised as the sole ruler of Castile and explicitly connected Isabel's healing of the body politic as resulting from her sexual and spiritual control.[40] This shift was compared to Mary's role in human redemption through her Immaculate Conception and as the mother of Christ.[41] Just as Mary redeemed the world through the birth of Christ, Isabel's production of a male heir would demonstrate divine favour by unifying the Spanish kingdoms within Christendom.[42] For example, Pulgar suggests that the birth of Prince Juan reveals that God has chosen Isabel specifically over her brother Enrique.[43] Alfonso de Palencia compared the conception of Juana to the fall of humanity which only the Virgin, and by extension Isabel, could rectify, saying

> the weakness of woman and principal instrument to the disgrace of humanity, for whose repair was chosen a Virgin and most singular mother, so that by the extraordinary and renowned virtue of one woman the original sin that by the corruption of another was introduced into the world since the beginning might be remedied.[44]

Diego de Valera pushed the comparison even further, writing in a letter to the queen

> that just as our Lord wanted our glorious Lady to be born into the world, because from her would come the Universal redeemer of the human race, so he determined that, you, my lady, were born to reform and restore these kingdoms and bring them out from the tyrannical government in which they have been for so long.[45]

This context certainly impacted Isabel's self-conception and transactions with texts and images of the Virgin. This reception may have been heightened by additional compositional elements, such as the location of her coats of arms in her breviary. As stated previously, this illumination was added into the manuscript during the finalisation of the project to the middle of the sanctoral, directly across from prayers for the Feast of the Assumption of the Virgin (Figure 5.7). The conceptual echo between the Queen of Heaven

5.7 The Coronation of the Virgin, Breviary of Queen Isabel. British Library Additional MS 18851, fol. 437r.

and the Queen of Castile is a plausible reason for Francisco de Roja's decision to place his own arms and dedicatory inscription in this location and attests to the prevalence of the comparison between Isabel and the Virgin at the Castilian Court. When viewed by Isabel, this opening would have invited her to reflect on this connection between herself and Mary. Perhaps it even reminded her of the *Jardín de nobles donzellas* and Martín's urging that the success of her rule was predicated on her ability to embody the qualities of the Virgin. Mary's presentation in the illumination, kneeling with her head bowed in prayer while God the Father and Christ concurrently place the crown on her head, would have encouraged such contemplation by combining humility with the act of coronation.

Similarly, the image of the coronation of the Virgin from Isabel's book of hours (Figure 5.8) may have also led Isabel to see reflections of herself. Unlike the coronation in the breviary, this depiction has Mary standing while two angels, created with thin strokes of gold paint, place the crown upon the Virgin's head. While the iconography of the Immaculate Conception was still being developed, the inclusion of a radiating, golden mandoral and the crescent moon conflates Mary with the Apocalyptic Woman from Revelations.[46] These qualities were already incorporated into the textual articulation of the Immaculate Conception and the image, therefore, may have evoked for Isabel contemplation of this construct. As the doctrine centred on the Virgin's spiritual and physical purity, the depiction within the book of hours may have spurred Isabel to consider her own state. When transacting with this image, Isabel may have used the textual arguments of her reign that connected her own purity with her rightful position as ruler to the purity of the Virgin Mary, whose Immaculate state was a necessary precursor to the divine grace offered to humanity and her elevation to Queen of Heaven.[47]

Remembering the danger inherent to women

A consideration of the ways in which Isabel's experiences may have impacted her transactions with the visual cycles in her breviary in London and her book of hours in Cleveland reveals how the queen's collection of images may have reinforced the Castilian queen's self-conception as an embodiment of sanctity and sexual virtue. However, because of the ideological gender construction of the fifteenth century, Isabel's femininity was also a liability.[48] Even as texts such as the *Jardín de nobles donzellas* argued for the possibility of female rule, they also articulated the potential danger of women. Their inherent weaknesses not only included sexual deviancy, but also vanity and financial mismanagement. Even the gendered critique of Enrique IV as effeminate

5.8 The Coronation of the Virgin, Hours of Queen Isabel. Cleveland Museum of Art 1963.256, fol. 159v.

was articulated in part through his ostentatious display and the economic turbulence of his rule.[49] Isabel herself was not immune to criticism of her personal expenditures and supposed trivialities. In 1492, Talavera wrote to Isabel to condemn the excesses of the courtly celebrations held to mark a new treaty with France and the return of contested territories to Aragon.[50]

This countering ideology may have also influenced the ways in which Isabel interpreted her images. In the marginalia in the depiction of *All Saints* from her breviary (Figure 5.9) a small, hybrid creature crouches in the lower left corner among the scattering of flowers, berries, bird and butterfly. Combining a green lizard with the face, long hair, and breasts of a woman, this fantastical beast gazes into a hand mirror. The placement of the creature in the margins of *All Saints* provides a counterpoint to the central image. Even while the deep, ultramarine blue of Mary's robes creates visual emphasis on the Virgin's place within the heavenly sphere, the repetition of blues and greens throughout the border guide the eye towards the hybrid creature. The golden crown upon the creature's head and honey-coloured hair further unite the two figures while the circular form of the mirror echoes the circular view into heaven. The connection between the creature and the Virgin is also suggested by a similar marginal figure in Isabel's book of hours (Figure 5.10). This reptilian female accompanies the *O Intermerata* prayer, an intercessory prayer to the Virgin Mary. These creatures' visual prominence interpellates the viewer and may have evoked a complex network of associations and intersecting realms of knowledge as part of the transaction.

If Isabel's experiential reservoir may have enabled her to see her own identity reflected in images of the Virgin during her visual transaction, to be reminded of the importance of emulating Mary's sexuality in order to embody a counterpoint to the lasciviousness of her predecessor, these small figures may have nuanced this construction of meaning by reminding Isabel of the danger of her own femininity. The mirror held by the creatures and their steady act of self-gazing denotes the vices of vanity, pride, and lust.[51] These sins, as well as the mirror itself, were often associated with femininity.[52] Mirrors also symbolised amorous relationships as they were common gifts from male lovers.[53] The creatures' connection to sinfulness might also be connoted by the combination of an animal body and human face. Polycorporality often signifies both a creature's demonic origins and association with bodily, earthly existence.[54] Moreover, the combination of specifically female visage and reptilian body may have evoked images of the serpent from the Garden of Eden who was often depicted with the torso and face of a woman because, in the words of Petrus Comestor, 'like attracts like'.[55] A depiction of Adam and Eve in the garden from the book of hours owned by Isabel's daughter (Figure 5.11) is representative of this iconographic trend.[56] The similarity between the creature in the corner of Isabel's manuscript

5.9 The Feast of All Saints, Breviary of Queen Isabel. British Library Additional MS 18851, fol. 477v.

5.10 O Intemerata prayer, Hours of Queen Isabel. Cleveland Museum of Art 1963.256, fol. 262r.

Isabel of Castile and her images

5.11 The Mirror of Conscience, Hours of Joanna of Castile, 1486–1506 (ink, tempera, and gold on parchment, codex is 11 × 8 cm). British Library Additional MS 18852, fols 14v–15r.

and the serpent in the Tree of Knowledge may have enabled Isabel to conceptually link the creature to Eve and to the vice inherent in women through Eve's punishment.[57] The Curse of Eve, specifically 'I will greatly multiply your pain in childbearing; in pain you shall bring forth children, yet your desire shall be for your husband, and he shall rule over you', was explicitly tied to both female sexual experience and female subjugation.[58] The connection between Eve and all women was central to texts such as the *Jardín de nobles donzellas* and was often invoked by Isabel.[59]

The combined invocation of the Virgin Mary and Eve would have invited Isabel to consider herself within this binary of female sexuality. Mary was the theological opposite of Eve and her role in salvation was articulated by God when he said to the serpent 'I will put enmity between you and the woman, and between your seed and her seed; [s]he shall bruise your head, and you shall bruise their heel'.[60] This passage was understood to express the redemptive power of Mary, through whom the reclamation of humanity is made possible. The articulation of Mary as the new Eve is also presented in the London breviary, located at the beginning of the prayer 'Nunc, Sancte, nobis Spiritus' based on Psalm 118:33 and marking Terce (Figure 5.12).

5.12 Expulsion from Paradise and Pentecost, Breviary of Queen Isabel. British Library Additional MS 18851, fol. 177v.

This prayer was closely associated with Pentecost, which is depicted on the right of the miniature with the Virgin Mary prominently placed in the centre. This image is combined with the Garden of Eden; Adam and Eve are expelled through the gate in the background, but they are guided back towards an open gate by Mary in the foreground. The connection between sin and redemption is also expressed by Juana's manuscript through the pairing of the Garden of Eden with a *Mirror of Conscience* on the opposite folio. The illumination marks the opening of a section dedicated to explaining the elements of the Christian faith and the danger to the soul if they are disregarded.[61] The appearance of the skull in the mirror combined with the prominent 'speculum consciencie' on the frame functions as a *momento mori* in alignment with the text.[62] The mirror encourages the transactor to reflect on the state of their own soul, to consider if they are on the path to damnation or salvation. The *Mirror of Conscience* problematises the understanding of the object as inherently associated with vanity and lust; mirrors were also symbolic of the diametrically opposite virtues of prudence and truthfulness.[63]

This conflation of meaning further ties the small creature in Isabel's breviary to the central illumination (Figure 5.9), as the doctrine of the Immaculate Conception in particular emphasised Mary's redemption of Eve's sins.[64] The purity of the Virgin Mary as one born without the stain of original sin was described as the mirror without blemish, and this state enabled salvation through the very function articulated in the Curse of Eve, childbirth. This association is also implicated in Isabel's book of hours, where the placement of the hybrid creature alongside an intercessory prayer to Mary is paired with a full-page miniature of the lamentation (Figure 5.13). The fig being grasped in the Virgin and Child in the same manuscript (Figure 5.8) further condenses Mary's immaculate condition, her identification with the woman from Revelations, and her position as the second Eve in a single image.[65] Mary's conception of Christ occurred without the penetration of sexual intercourse and her virginity was safeguarded through the pregnancy, birth, and postpartum processes. The reclamation of a female body before the pollution of original sin conjures the memory of creation and God's edict to 'Be fruitful and multiply'.[66] This message of progenation and Mary's recasting of childbirth as a redemptive process may have enabled Isabel to insert her own sexuality, sanctified through a heteronormative marriage and producing numerous children, into the dichotomy between virginity and carnality.

In addition to this network of theological and iconographical concepts, the creature's reptilian features and long, golden hair topped by a crown may have instead reminded Isabel of the character Melusine from the popular romance written by Jean d'Arras (Figure 5.14).[67] In this narrative,

126 Part I: *Scandal, perception and representation*

5.13 Lamentation, Hours of Queen Isabel. Cleveland Museum of Art 1963.256, fol. 261v.

5.14 Title woodcut with Melusine and her descendants, Thüring von Ringoltingen, *Melusine* (Augsburg: Bämler, 1480), fol. A1v.

Raymond of Poitou comes across a beautiful woman next to a fountain in the woods. She is Melusine, a half-human, half-fairy who transforms into a serpent every Saturday.[68] Raymond falls in love with Melusine and, by following her guidance, garners wealth, power, and reputation. One of the conditions of their marriage, however, is that Raymond must promise never to view his wife on Saturday and, if perchance he does, to never speak of it. After years of marriage, during which Melusine and Raymond establish the castle at Lusignan and produce ten sons, Raymond's brother arrives one Saturday and says 'it is rumored hither and yon that every Saturday your wife dishonors you by lying in carnal sin with another man'.[69] Raymond is filled with jealousy and, forgetting his promise, proceeds to spy on Melusine in the bath (Figure 5.15). He saw combing her hair 'a woman who from the navel down took the form of a massive serpent's tail, extremely long and thick as a herring keg, and splashing the water so hard that it splattered the vaulting of the chamber'.[70] This betrayal eventually led to the revelation of Melusine's secret and her flight from the castle in the form of a large dragon.[71]

Written in the later fourteenth century, the text was translated into Castilian and published in 1489 in Toulouse as *Historia de la linda Melosina*, an edition that included numerous woodcuts.[72] Many of the romance's themes may have resonated with the Castilian queen.[73] Like Isabel's, Melusine's gender and sexuality form an intrinsic component of her social advancement and they both work to establish a familial dynasty while expanding the associated political-spatial holdings.[74] Her transformations, even during gestation, into an animal form focus the reader's attention upon her lower body while the progression of the narrative hinges on her marriage and creation of progeny. Nor did Melusine's fairy nature preclude her desire for Christian salvation.[75] Throughout the text, Melusine encourages her children to cultivate their devotion and her final lament is not only for the separation from her love but also that 'if only [Raymond] had not betrayed me, I would have been redeemed, exempted from pain and torment ... I would have received all the sacraments and been buried in the Church of Our Lady in Lusignan ... and now I must endure and suffer [penance] until Judgment Day'.[76] Melusine's longing for salvation and her engagement with Christian practices is further emphasised in the Castilian translation printed in Toulouse. The passage describing the wedding ceremony between Melusine and Raymond was significantly expanded into a detailed account of the ritual.[77] Throughout the text, Melusine's assistance to Raymond is also framed as part of God's plan. Like the Virgin Mary, Melusine serves an intermediary between the people of Lusignan and the divine.[78]

The small creatures in the London breviary (Figure 5.7) and the Cleveland book of hours (Figure 5.10) mimic Melusine in the corporal hybridity of feminine and reptilian features. The clutching of the mirror and unbound

Isabel of Castile and her images 129

5.15 Raymond spies on Melusine in the bath, Thüring von Ringoltingen, *Melusine* (Augsburg: Bämler, 1480), fol. 51r reused in *La historia de la Linda Melosina* (Toulouse: Juan Parix and Estevan Cleblat, 1489), fol. 119v.

hair may signify a woman in repose, just as Melusine is witnessed in her bath by Raymond. The surrounding flowers and fruit, while appearing throughout both manuscripts, may in this context have evoked the fecundity and success of Lusignan under Melusine's guidance.[79] The location of the figure, in the lower corner separated from the heavenly depiction above, evokes Melusine's exclusion from Christian salvation due to her nonhumanity. Even when successfully hiding her serpentine body, the birth of Melusine's sons with bodily difference, such as a lion's paw complete with fur and claws on the cheek of the fourth son Antoine and a large tooth that projected through the mouth of the sixth son Geoffroy, reveal her nonhumanity through her progeny.[80] While her sons are pious and successful despite their physical difference, it is Geoffroy's monstrous actions of fratricide and destruction of the monastery at Maillezais that spur Raymond to reveal Melusine's secret.[81] Therefore the association of the small creature in the breviary with Melusine may have conjured for Isabel both the aspirational aspects of the romance and the tragedy of the heroine's ultimate transformation into a dragon. This conceptual devolution of the creature in the London breviary from polycorporality to nonhuman monstrosity is suggested by a similar creature in the Spinola Hours (Figure 5.16).[82] While greyish-brown instead of green, the creature is similarly featured and positioned. This creature is joined by five other similarly coloured monsters entwined throughout the decorative acanthus, creating a visual echo between the feminine beast and the hideous dragons. The border decoration of the Spinola Hours indicates the ability of the small creature in the London breviary to evoke, like Melusine, a spectrum of physical forms.

Transacting with the images

Similarly to Rosenblatt's theory of transactional reader-response, Isabel may have constructed a conceptual network of associated ideas when viewing the imagery of the Feast of All Saints in her breviary along with its marginal decoration: I am a queen like the Virgin, because I am a woman I am like Mary, Mary is the opposite of Eve, because I am a woman I am like Eve, like Eve I must be fruitful for the security of my kingdom, like Melusine I am establishing a dynasty, in order to perpetuate my dynasty I must produce heirs, to produce children I must engage in sexual relations, producing children is the curse Eve received in the Garden of Eden, Melusine was cursed and betrayed by her husband, like Melusine I must control my base nature, because I am a woman I am prone to lust and vanity, I must overcome my womanly nature and be pure like the Virgin, as queen of Castile I must be chaste unlike my brother Enrique, my brother Enrique was criticised for

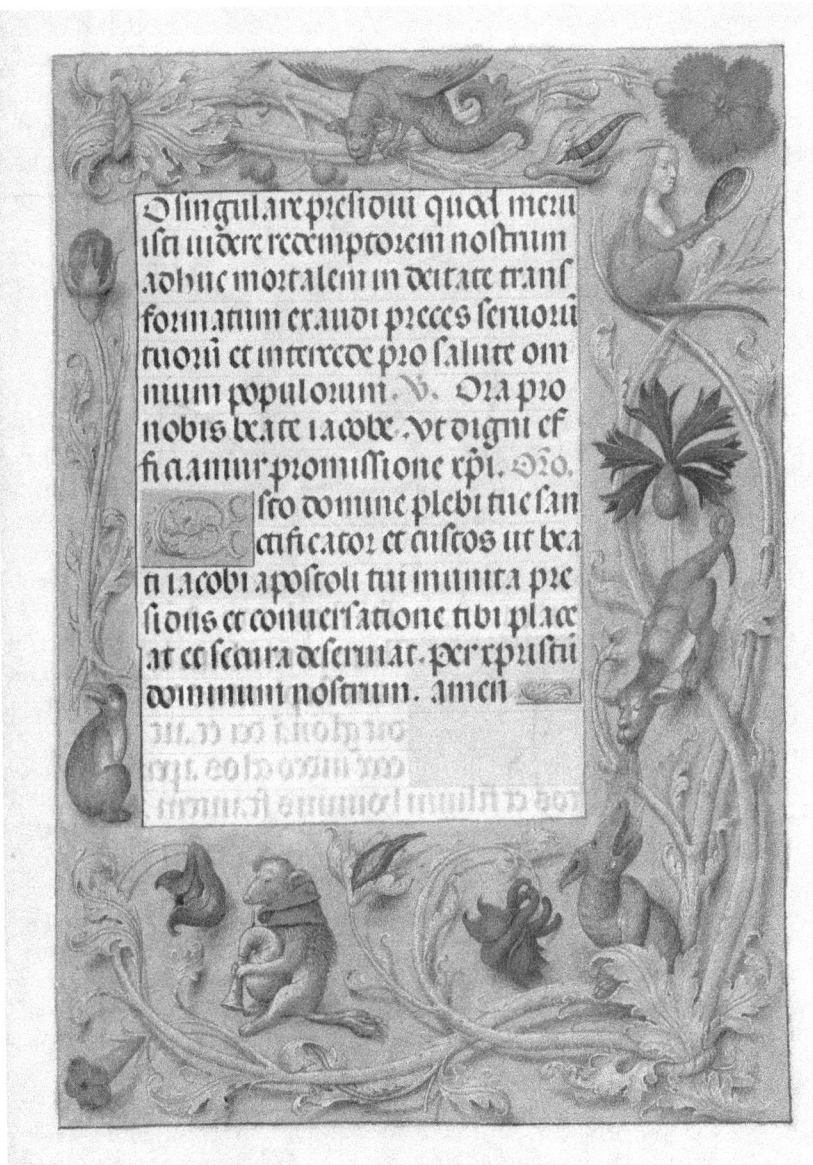

5.16 Prayer to St. James the Greater, Spinola Hours, c. 1510–1520 (ink, tempera, and gold on parchment, codes is 23.2 × 16.7 cm). Getty Museum MS Ludwig IX 18 (83.ML.114), fol. 253r.

his immorality and his vanity, I must be a queen of Castile modelled on the virtue of the queen of heaven. This organic shifting of ideas, associations, and interpretations, based on her reservoir of experiences but also responding to visual components during the transactional process of engaging with the work, reveals the potentially nuanced responses that Isabel may have had as viewer and the ways in which these images may have reinforced her self-conception as the legitimate queen regnant.

Notes

1 This project would not have been possible without the assistance of Michelle Burns, Leejay Guyton, Lacey Manuel, Rebekah Sokol, and Jolie Voss at Metropolitan State University of Denver, Ariella Hartstein at the Ingalls Library at the Cleveland Museum of Art, and the amazing interlibrary loan team at the Auraria library, Denver. Research support was provided by the Metropolitan State University of Denver College of Letters, Arts, and Sciences.
2 Tariscio de Azcona, *Isabel la Católica: Estudio crítico de su vida y su reinado*, 3rd edn (Valladolid: Instituto Isabel la Católica de Historia Eclesiástica, 1993), 142–143; Peggy Liss, *Isabel the Queen: Life and Times* (Philadelphia: University of Pennsylvania Press, 2004), 55, 71–72; Cristina Guardiola-Griffiths, *Legitimizing the Queen: Propaganda and Ideology in the Reign of Isabel I of Castile* (Lanham, MD: Rowman & Littlefield, 2010), 54.
3 Liss, *Isabel the Queen*, 118–140; Susannah Humble Ferreira, 'Juana La Beltraneja, Dynastic Fears, and Threats of Marriage (1475–1506)', *Renaissance and Reformation / Renaissance et Réforme*. Special Issue: Spaces and Power of the Spanish Nobility (1480–1750) 43.4 (2020): 85–87.
4 Feminist historians who have utilised gender theory to analyse Isabel's rise to power and the use of sexual slander in her legitimisation include Barbara Weissberger, "A tierra, puto!' Alfonso de Palencia's Discourse on Effeminacy', in *Queer Iberia: Sexualities, Cultures, and Crossings from the Middle Ages to the Renaissance*, ed. Josiah Blackmore and Gregory S. Hutcheson (Durham, NC: Duke University Press, 1999), 291–324; Elizabeth Lehfeldt, 'Ruling Sexuality: The Political Legitimacy of Isabel of Castile', *Renaissance Quarterly* 53.1 (2000): 31–56; Barbara Weissberger, *Isabel Rules: Constructing Queenship, Wielding Power* (Minneapolis: University of Minnesota Press, 2003), 69–95; Guardiola-Griffiths, *Legitimizing the Queen*, 45–68. The impact of constructions of gender and sexuality have been important lenses for understanding the complexities and nuance of power within queenship studies. For an introduction to the topic and historiography, see Regina Schulte, 'Introduction: Conceptual Approaches to the Queen's Body', in *The Body of the Queen: Gender and Rule in the Courtly World, 1500–2000*, ed. Regina Schulte (New York: Berghahn Books, 2000), 1–15; Theresa Earenfight, 'Where Do We Go From Here? Some Thoughts on Power and Gender in the Middle Ages', *Medieval Feminist Forum: A Journal of Gender and Sexuality* 5.2 (2015): 116–131; Theresa Earenfight, 'A

Lifetime of Power: Beyond Binaries of Gender', in *Medieval Elite Women and the Exercise of Power, 1100–1400: Moving Beyond the Exceptionalist Debate*, ed. Heather Tanner (Basingstoke: Palgrave Macmillan, 2019), 271–293; Anke Gilleir, 'On Gender, Sovereignty and Imagination: An Introduction', in *Strategic Imaginations: Women and the Gender of Sovereignty in European Culture*, ed. Anke Gilleir and Aude Defurne (Leuven: Leuven University Press, 2020), 7–26. The power of queens and other elite women in the Spanish world has also been closely studied within this framework. For example, see Theresa Earenfight, *Queenship and Political Power in Medieval and Early Modern Spain* (Aldershot: Ashgate, 2005); Grace Coolidge, *Guardianship, Gender, and the Nobility in Early Modern Spain* (Aldershot: Ashgate, 2010); Martha Hoffman, *Raised to Rule: Educating Royalty at the Court of the Spanish* (Baton Rouge: Louisiana State University Press, 2011); Ann Cruz and Maria Galli Stampino, eds, *Early Modern Habsburg Women: Transnational Contexts, Cultural Conflicts, Dynastic Continuities* (London: Routledge, 2013); María Cristina Quintero, 'Royal Players: Habsburg Women, Border Crossings, and the Performance of Queenship', in *Beyond Spain's Borders: Women Players in Early Modern National Theaters*, ed. Anne Cruz and María Cristina Quintero (Abingdon: Routledge, 2017), 129–151.

5 Liss, *Isabel the Queen*, 41–47. This critique of Enrique followed an historical precedent of using sexual slander as a political weapon to justify regime change in medieval Iberia, including the institution of the Umayyad caliphate of Al-Andalus and the founding of the Trastámara dynasty. For an analysis of the historiographical use and interpretation of these scandals in later periods, see Robert Tate, *Ensayos sobre la historiografía peninsular del siglo XV*, trans. Jesús Díaz (Madrid: Gredos, 1970); Richard Kagan, *Clio and the Crown: The Politics of History in Medieval and Early Modern Spain* (Baltimore: Johns Hopkins University Press, 2009); Samuel Claussen, 'Royal Punishment and Reconciliation in Trastámara Castile', in *Treason: Medieval and Early Modern Adultery, Betrayal, and Shame*, ed. Lariss Tracy (Leiden: Brill, 2019), 110–118. A rich assessment of the legend of La Cava, which explains the fall of the Visogothic King Rodrigo and the creation of Al-Andalus, has been conducted by Patricia Grieve, who traced the telling of this story through the centuries in order to assess the ways in which the political ramifications of female sexuality and sexual assault have participated in the formation of national identity; Patricia Grieve, *The Eve of Spain: Myths of Origins in the History of Christian, Muslim, and Jewish Conflict* (Baltimore: Johns Hopkins University Press, 2009). The use of sexual scandal as a political weapon is certainly not limited to fifteenth-century Iberia. For an example from tenth-century England, see Matthew Firth's chapter in this volume.

6 On the comparison between Juana's succession and other examples of perceived female adultery in fourteenth-century France, see Emily Lalande's chapter in this volume.

7 William D. Phillips, *Enrique IV and the Crisis of Fifteenth-Century Castile (1425–1480)* (Cambridge, MA: Medieval Academy of America, 1978), 1–16; Weissberger, "A tierra, puto!", 300–303; Lehfeldt, 'Ruling Sexuality', 32–34;

Weissberger, *Isabel Rules*, 77–81; Thomas Devaney, 'Virtue, Virility, and History in Fifteenth-Century Castile', *Speculum* 88.3 (2013): 243–245. It is important to note that the criticisms targeted at Enrique's sexuality, with their reliance on a specific construction of masculinity, also intersect with fifteenth-century Iberian conceptions of religious identity. Enrique's less than overwhelming success in martial pursuits against Granada was therefore evidence of his ineffectual rule, his effeminacy, and his compromised Christianity. For the long history of anxiety about sexual relations between Christians and non-Christians in Iberia, see Chapter 9 by David Cantor-Echols in this volume.

8 For a thorough examination of the claim of Juana's illegitimacy, see Óscar Villarroel González, *Juana la Beltraneja: La construcción de una ilegitimidad* (Madrid: Silex Ediçiones, 2014).

9 For the inclusion of the *Carta-Protesta* into Isabel's chronicles, see Hernando Pulgar, *Crónica de los Señores Reyes Católicos Don Fernando y Doña Isabel de Castilla y de Aragon* (Valencia: Benito Monfort, 1780), 3–4; Mosén Diego de Valera, 'Memorial de diversas hazañas', in *Crónicas de los reyes de Castilla*, eds Cayetano Rosell, Biblioteca de Autores Españoles (Madrid: Atlas, 1953), 33. Alfonso de Palencia elaborated on Enrique's follies in his *Crónica de Enrique IV*, written in 1477 under the patronage of Isabel. Alfonso de Palencia, *Cronica de Enrique IV*, 3 vols (Madrid: Ediciones Atlas, 1973–1975). For analysis of this text, see Weissberger, *Isabel Rules*, 72–95. The propagandistic force of Isabel's reign has long been noted. The existence of multiple versions of Enríquez de Castillo's *Crónica del rey don Enrique el Cuartro*, in order to insert the criticisms against Enrique, reveals the revision of existing texts to justify her assumption to the throne. Gemma Avenoza, 'Un nuevo manuscrito de las *Generaciones y semblanzas*: la *Crónica de Enrique IV* y la propaganda isabelina', *Anuario medieval* 3 (1991): 7–22; María del Pilar Carceller Cerviño, 'Álvaro de Luna, Juan Pacheco y Beltrán de la Cueva: un estudio comparativo del privado regio a fines de la Edad Media', *En la España Medieval* 32 (2009): 85–112, at 103–106. Jaime Vicens Vives has suggested that Isabel went so far as to forge documents, including the treaty between Isabel and Enrique that recognised her as his heir presumptive. Jaime Vicens Vives, *Historia crítica de la vida y reinado de Fernando II de Aragón* (Zaragoza: Institudión "Fernando el Católico", 1962), 209–243. It is important to note that a counternarrative also exists in chronicles produced in Portugal, where Juana continued to hold political influence throughout her life. Humble Ferreira, 'Juana La Beltraneja, Dynastic Fears, and Threats of Marriage', 79–100.

10 Patricia Parker, *Literary Fat Ladies: Rhetoric, Gender, Property* (New York: Methuen, 1987), 178–233; Howard Bloch, *Medieval Misogyny and the Invention of Western Romantic Love* (Chicago: University of Chicago Press, 1991), 37–38.

11 Lehfeldt, 'Ruling Sexuality', 44–54; Weissberger, *Isabel Rules*, 71; Liss, *Isabel the Queen*, 236–263; Miriam Shadis, 'Women, Gender, and Rulership in Romance Europe: The Iberian Case', *History Compass* 4.3 (2006): 1–3. While the necessity of dynastic heir limited chastity to within marriage, the institution of policies related to the observance of enclosure for nuns enable Isabel to shaper her own

chaste image through the control of the sexuality of others. Lehfeldt, 'Ruling Sexuality', 47–49.

12 Isabel had seven pregnancies between 1470 and 1485, with five children surviving to adulthood. The political reality of reproduction and motherhood also impacted the life of Enrique's daughter Juana. Because of her ability to produce a collateral dynastic line, Juana remained a threat to Castilian political stability throughout Isabel's lifetime. In order to mediate this threat, Juana was forced to enter a cloister after Isabel consolidated power. Humble Ferreira, 'Juana La Beltraneja, Dynastic Fears, and Threats of Marriage', 80.

13 Fray Martín de Córdoba, *Jardín de nobles donzellas*, ed. Harriet Goldberg (Chapel Hill, NC: University of North Carolina Department of Romance Studies, 1974). For an introduction to the construction of gender within this text, see Jacob Ornstein, 'Misogyny and Pro-Feminism in Early Castilian Literature', *Modern Language Quarterly* 3.2 (1942): 221–234; Catherine Soriano, 'Conveniencia política y tópico literario en el *Jardín de nobles doncellas* (1468?) de Fray Martín Alonso de Córdoba', in *Actas del VI Congreso Internacional de la Associación Hispánica de Literatura Medieval (Alcalá de Henares, 12–16 de septiembre de 1995)* (Alcalá de Henares: Universidad de Alcalá, 1997), 1457–1466; Blas Sánchez Dueñas, 'Una particular visión de la mujer en el siglo XV: Jardín de nobles doncellas de Fray Martín de Córdoba', *Boletín de la Real Academia de Córdoba de Ciencias, Bellas Letras y Nobles Artes* 80 (2001): 291–300; Vanesa Regalado de Valle, 'El tratado de Jardín de nobles doncellas y su influencia en la personalidad de Isabel la Católica', *Digilec: Revista internacional de lenguas y culturas* 6 (2019): 1–13. For analysis of this text within the framework of Isabel's self fashioning as queen, see Lehfeldt, 'Ruling Sexuality', 35–37; Weissberger, *Isabel Rules*, 29–44; Guardiola-Griffiths, *Legitimizing the Queen*, 23–39.

14 Digitisation of the book of hours in Cleveland is available at www.clevelandart.org/art/1963.256 (accessed 27 November 2023); digitisation of the breviary in London is available at www.bl.uk/manuscripts/FullDisplay.aspx?ref=Add_MS_18851 (accessed 27 November 2023). Neither of these manuscripts was initiated with the queen's ownership in mind. The royal emissary Francisco de Rojas acquired the unbound, incomplete breviary as a luxurious gift for Isabel. Bodo Brinkmann, *Die flämische Buchmalerie am Ende des Burgunderreichs: Der Meister des Dresdener Gebetbuchs und die Miniaturisten seiner Zeit*, 2 vols (Turnhout: Brepols, 1997), 134–139; Thomas Kren and Scot McKendrick, eds, *Illuminating the Renaissance: The Triumph of Flemish Manuscript Painting in Europe* (Los Angeles: J. Paul Getty Museum, 2003), cat. no. 100, 347–351; Nigel Morgan and Scot McKendrick, 'Contents and Authorship', in *The Isabella Breviary: The British Library, London, Add. Ms. 18851*, ed. Mónica Miró (Barcelona: M. Moleiro, 2012), 99–110; Joni M. Hand, *Women, Manuscripts and Identity in Northern Europe, 1350–1550* (Burlington, VT: Ashgate, 2013), 83–85. Similarly, the book of hours recast as a royal gift. See Patrick de Winter, 'A Book of Hours of Queen Isabel la Católica', *Bulletin of the Cleveland Museum of Art* 68.10 (1981): 347–350; Kren and McKendrick, *Illuminating the Renaissance*, cat. no. 105, 361, n.13; Lieve de Kesel, *The Hours of Queen Isabella the Catholic:*

the Cleveland Museum of Art, Cleveland/Ohio, Leonard C. Hanna Jr. Fund 1963.256. (Gütersloh: Faksimile Verlag, 2014), 20.

15 Louise M. Rosenblatt, 'Viewpoints: Transaction versus Interaction – A Terminological Rescue Operation', *Research in the Teaching of English* 19 (1985): 104. Rosenblatt returned to and revised her theory throughout her career, see Louise M. Rosenblatt, *The Reader, the Text, the Poem: The Transactional Theory of the Literary Work* (Carbondale, IL: Southern Illinois University Press, 1978); Louise M. Rosenblatt, *Litterature as Exploration*, 3rd edn (New York: Modern Language Association of America, 1995); Louise M. Rosenblatt, 'The Transactional Theory of Reading and Writing', in *Theroetical Models and Processes of Literacy*, ed. Donna Alvermann et al. (New York: Routledge, 2018), 451–479.

16 Rosenblatt, 'The Transactional Theory of Reading and Writing', 455–457. Rosenblatt's concept of transaction is heavily indebted to John Dewey and Arthur Bently. Rosenblatt, 'Viewpoints', 98–100; Rosenblatt, 'The Transactional Theory of Reading and Writing', 452. Rosenblatt also views her theory as derived from Charles Sanders Peirce's triadic formulation of linguistic meaning. Rosenblatt, 'The Transactional Theory of Reading and Writing', 453–454.

17 Rosenblatt, 'The Transactional Theory of Reading and Writing', 454.

18 Rosenblatt, 'Viewpoints', 103.

19 Louise M. Rosenblatt, 'Toward a Transactional Theory of Reading', *Journal of Reading Behavior* 1, no. 1 (1969), 31–34.

20 The banderols contain 'Tanto Monta' (just as one, so as the other) and a variation on Psalm 16:8 'Sub umbra alaru[m] tuaru[m] protege nos' (protect us under the shadow of your wings). All biblical quotations are from the Revised Standard Version. For an analysis of the motto, see Weissberger, *Isabel Rules*, 47–55; Theresa Earenfight, 'Two Bodies, One Spirit: Isabel and Fernando's Construction of Monarchical Partnership', in *Queen Isabel I of Castile: Power, Patronage, Persona*, ed. Barbara Weissberger (New York: Tamesis, 2008), 3–18; Barbara Weissberger, '*Tanto monta*: The Catholic Monarchs' Nuptial Fiction and the Power of Isabel I of Castile', in *The Rule of Women in Early Modern Europe*, ed. Anne J. Curz and Mihoko Sukuki (Urbana: University of Illinois Press, 2009), 43–62.

21 It is possible that the London breviary was acquired by Juana after Isabel's death. Hand, *Women, Manuscripts and Identity in Northern Europe*, 41. The emphasis on the marriage of Isabel's children, across the opening from Rojas's dedication, would have reminded the queen of his role in negotiating this double match. For analysis of the opening within this context, see Hand, *Women, Manuscripts and Identity in Northern Europe*, 83–85, 140–142.

22 One banderol contains Psalm 44:17 'Pro patribus tuis nati sunt tibi filii; constituisti eos principes super omnem terram' (Your children are born to you instead of your parents; you have made them princes of all the earth) and the other Psalm 111:2 'Potens in terra erit semen eius: generatio rectorum benedicetur' (Powerful is his seed over the earth; blessed be the generation of the righteous).

23 Joni Hand has investigated the impact a patron's identity had on the sanctoral in books of hours owned by women, though they do not include codices owned

by Isabel in their analysis. Hand, *Women, Manuscripts and Identity in Northern Europe*, 85–92.

24 Jacobus de Voragine, *The Golden Legend or Lives of the Saints*, trans. William Caxton, 7 vols. (London: Temple Classics, 1900), 6: 100–106. Available at https://sourcebooks.fordham.edu/basis/goldenlegend/GoldenLegend-Volume6.asp#Elizabeth (accessed 27 November 2023). This presentation is in contrast to the general themes of the text which present Virginity as the ultimate goal and marriage as a hindrance to salvation. Sherry Reames, *The Legenda Aurea: A Reexamination of its Paradoxical History* (Madison: University of Wisconsin Press, 1983), 98–99, 106–107; Linda Burke, 'A Sister in the World: Saint Elizabeth of Hungary in the "Golden Legend"', *Hungarian Historical Review* 5.3 (2016): 8–9, 515. Isabel owned multiple collections of saints' lives, which likely included two extant volumes based on Voragine's text. Emma Gatland, *Women from the Golden Legend: Female Authority in a Medieval Castilian Sanctoral* (London: Tamesis, 2011), 4–6.

25 Voragine, *The Golden Legend or Lives of the Saints*, 7: 4–16. Available at https://sourcebooks.fordham.edu/basis/goldenlegend/GoldenLegend-Volume7.asp#Katherine (accessed 27 November 2023).

26 Voragine, *Golden Legend*, 9.

27 Isabel's role as queen regnant and Fernando's as consort were articulated in the marriage capitulations. Earenfight, 'Two Bodies, One Spirit', 3–18.

28 Vicente Rodríguez Valencia, *Artículos del postulador* (Valladolid: Institución Isabel la Católica de Historia Eclesiástica, 1972), 61.

29 Lehfeldt, 'Ruling Sexuality', 36.

30 Vicens Vives, *Historia crítica de la vida y reinado de Fernando II de Aragón*, 247–248; Liss, *Isabel the Queen*, 106–107.

31 Diego de Valera, see Valera, 'Memorial de diversas hazañas', 4. See also, Liss, *Isabel the Queen*, 86–87. Isabel's coronation was not without criticism. Pulgar, *Cronica de los senores Reyes Catolicos*, 34; Valera, 'Memorial de diversas hazañas', 4; Palencia, *Cronica de Enrique IV*, 2: 162. For analysis of the gendered implications of this response, see Lehfeldt, 'Ruling Sexuality', 34–35; Weissberger, *Isabel Rules*, 45–46; Guardiola-Griffiths, *Legitimizing the Queen*, 46–47.

32 On the rich connections between the motto, emblems, and propaganda of Isabel's reign, see Weissberger, *Isabel Rules*, 47–55; Barbara Weissberger, 'Patronage and Politics in the Court of the Catholic Monarchs: The "Cancionero de Pedro Marcuello"', *Studies in Iconography* 26 (2005): 181–183; Earenfight, 'Two Bodies, One Spirit', 3–18; Weissberger, 'Tanto monta', 43–62.

33 Isabel's reflection on the need to emulate Mary may have been heightened by the location of the images themselves, within the pages of books. The iconography of the Virgin interacting with books was very common. When Isabel transacted with these images, she would have been embodying a similar position. On the prevalence of images of the Virgin and female saints interacting with books, see Joaquín Yarza Luaces, 'La santa que lee', in *Luchas de género en la Historia a través de la imagen*, ed. María Teresa Sauret Guerrero and Amparo Quiles Faz (Málaga: Centro de Ediciones de la Disputación de Málaga, 2001), 421–468.

34 Soriano, 'Conveniencia política y tópico literario', 1457–1466; Lehfeldt, 'Ruling Sexuality', 35–37; Weissberger, *Isabel Rules*, 28–68; Guardiola-Griffiths, *Legitimizing the Queen*, 23–44; Regalado de Valle, 'El tratado de Jardín de nobles doncellas', 5–8.
35 Córdoba, *Jardín de nobles donzellas*, 164.
36 As the goal of the critique was legitimising Isabel's reign, the veracity of the claims against Enrique were less important than the propagandistic effect of repeating them. The success of this smear campaign is perhaps best marked by the continued reference to Enrique IV as 'el impotente' and Juana as 'la Beltraneja' by historians centuries later. María del Pilar Carceller Cervino has attempted to untangle historical realities from Isabel's propaganda by assessing the future fortunes of Beltrán de la Cueva. María del Pilar Carceller Cerviño, 'Realidad y representación de la nobleza en el siglo XV: El linaje de la Cueva y la casa ducal de Alburquerque' (PhD diss., Universidad Complutense de Madrid, 2006); Carceller Cerviño, 'Álvaro de Luna, Juan Pacheco y Beltrán de la Cueva: un estudio comparativo del privado regio a fines de la Edad Media', 102–107.
37 Pulgar, *Cronica de los senores Reyes Catolicos*, 5; 7–8; 56; 73.
38 'me sonroja y me apena' in Palencia, *Cronica de Enrique IV*, 1: 83.
39 Mosén Diego de Valera, *Crónica de los Reyes Católicos*, Anejos de la Revista de Filología Española (Madrid: Consejo Superior de Investigaciones Cietíficas, 1927), 5.
40 The success of this counter-campaign can similarly be marked by the repeated invocation of Isabel's virtue, and even saintliness, as well as her good governance throughout the subsequent centuries. For recent assessment of this phenomenon, see David Boruchoff, 'Isabel, Her Chroniclers, and the Inquisition: Self-Fashioning and Historical Memory', in *A Companion to the Queenship of Isabel la Católica*, ed. Hilaire Kallendorf (Leiden: Brill, 2023), 58–71; Caroline Travalia, 'The Legend of Isabel la Católica, Founder of Spain', in *A Companion to the Queenship of Isabel la Católica*, ed. Hilaire Kallendorf (Leiden: Brill, 2023), 299–338. It is important to note that an alternative view of Isabel is presented in Jewish and Islamic writings from the period. Michelle M. Hamilton, 'Hostile Histories: Isabel and Fernando in Jewish and Muslim Narratives', in *A Companion to the Queenship of Isabel la Católica*, ed. Hilaire Kallendorf (Leiden: Brill, 2023), 213–231.
41 On the Immaculate Conception more generally, see Marina Warner, *Alone of All Her Sex: The Myth and Cult of the Virgin Mary* (New York: Knopf, 1976), 236–254; Suzanne Stratton, *The Immaculate Conception in Spanish Art* (Cambridge: Cambridge University Press, 1994), 5–34; Lesley Twomey, *The Serpent and the Rose: The Immaculate Conception and Hispanic Poetry in the Late Medieval Period* (Leiden: Brill, 2008). On the promotion in Spain and comparison to Isabel, see Lehfeldt, 'Ruling Sexuality', 49–53; Weissberger, *Isabel Rules*, 69–95, 112–124; Liss, *Isabel the Queen*, 157–161; R.E. Surtz, 'The Reciprocal Construction of Isabelline Book Patronage', in *Queen Isabel I of Castile: Power, Patronage Persona*, ed. Barbara Weissberger (New York: Tamesis, 2008), 56–57.

42 Azcona, *Isabel la Católica*, 396–400; Liss, *Isabel the Queen*, 157–161; Lehfeldt, 'Ruling Sexuality', 50–52; Weissberger, *Isabel Rules*, 112–120; Guardiola-Griffiths, *Legitimizing the Queen*, 16–23; Núria Silleras-Fernández, *Chariots of Ladies: Francesc Eiximenis and the Court Culture of Medieval and Early Modern Iberia* (Ithaca, NY: Cornell University Press, 2015), 151–202. The death of Prince Juan in 1497 was similarly noted by some as evidence of divine disfavour. Núria Silleras-Fernández, 'Isabel's Years of Sorrow: Consoling the Catholic Queen', in *A Companion to the Queenship of Isabel la Católica*, ed. Hilaire Kallendorf (Leiden: Brill, 2023), 254–278.
43 Fernando del Pulgar, *Letras. Glosa a las "Complas de Mingo Revulgo"* (Madrid: La Lectura, 1929), 54.
44 Palencia, *Cronica de Enrique IV*, 1: 132. 'frágil mujer y antiguo principal instrumento de la desgracia de la humanidad, para cuya reparación fue escogida una Virgen y madre singularísima, a fin de que por la extraordinaria e insigne virtud de una mujer se remediase el pecado original que la corrupción de otra introdujo en el mundo desde sus comienzos'.
45 Mosén Diego de Valera, *Epístolas de Mosen Diego de Valera: Embiadas en diversos tiempos é á diversas personas* (Madrid: Impr. de M. Ginesta, 1878), épis. 13: 46. 'que asy commo nuestro Señor quiso en este mundo naciese la gloriosa Señora nuestra, porque della procediese el vniuersal Redintor del linaje humano, asy determinó, vos, Señora, nasciésedes para reformar é restaurar estos reynos é sacarlos de la tyránica gouernacion en que tan luenga mente han estado'. For analysis of this passage, see Weissberger, *Isabel Rules*, 56–57; Cristina Guardiola-Griffiths, 'Isabel I of Castile and Saintly Propaganda: Interpreting the St Anne Retable in the *Capilla del Condestable*', in *A Companion to the Queenship of Isabel la Católica*, ed. Hilaire Kallendorf (Leiden: Brill, 2023), 103.
46 Mirella Levi d'Ancona, *The Iconography of the Immaculate Conception in the Middle Ages and Early Renaissance* (New York: College Art Association, 1957), 46–58; Stratton, *The Immaculate Conception in Spanish Art*, 5–34.
47 Contemporary writers made similar connections, going so far as to suggest that Isabel herself was not tainted by the acts of conception and childbirth. Lehfeldt, 'Ruling Sexuality', 51–53; Liss, *Isabel the Queen*, 185–161.
48 Lehfeldt, 'Ruling Sexuality', 40–41; Weissberger, *Isabel Rules*, 124–133; Guardiola-Griffiths, *Legitimizing the Queen*, 24–39.
49 Weissberger, *Isabel Rules*, 75–76; Guardiola-Griffiths, *Legitimizing the Queen*, 49–52; Devaney, 'Virtue, Virility, and History', 243–244. On the financial failures of Enrique IV, see Pablo Ortego Rico, '"Sy algunas quiebras en ellas oviese …": crisis de liquidez y quiebras financieras en Castilla a fines de la Edad Media', *Cuadernos de Historia Moderna* 42.2 (2017): 421–436.
50 Rafael García y García de Castro, *Virtudes de la reina católica* (Granada: Consejo Superior de Investigaciones Científicas, 1961), 364.
51 Katharine Jewett and Sabine Melchoir-Bonnet, *The Mirror: A History* (New York: Routledge, 1994), 193–195; 200–201.
52 Jewett and Melchoir-Bonnet, *The Mirror*, 201–203. Many medieval preachers and moralists denounced the vain and lecherous women who primp in mirrors.

John Block Friedman, 'L'iconographie de Vénus et de son miroir à la fin du moyen âge', in *Érotisme au moyen âge*, ed. Bruno Roy (Montreal: Aurore, 1977), 68–82; Herbert Grabes, *The Mutable Glass: Mirror-imagery in Titles and Texts of the Middle Ages and English Renaissance* (Cambridge: Cambridge University Press, 1982), 135–141.

53 Susan Smith, 'The Gothic Mirror and the Female Gaze', in *Saints, Sinners, and Sisters: Gender and Northern Art in Medieval and Early Modern Europe*, ed. Jane Carroll and Alison Stewart (Burlington, VT: Ashgate, 2003), 74.

54 Reptilian and amphibious creatures, such as frogs and snakes, are particularly common components in the iconography of hellscapes, Christ's torment, the last judgment, and other scenes that include demons or evil forces.

55 For analysis of this iconography, see John Bonnell, 'The Serpent with a Human Head in Art and in Mystery Play', *American Journal of Archaeology* 21.3 (1917): 255–291; Robert Koch, 'The Salamander in van der Goes' *Garden of Eden*', *Journal of the Warburg and Courtauld Institutes* 28 (1965): 323–326; J.B. Trapp, 'The Iconography of the Fall of Man', in *Approaches to Paradise Lost*, ed. C.A. Patrides (London: Edward Arnold, 1968), 223–265; Nona Cecilia Flores, '"Virgineum Vultum Habens": The Woman-Headed Serpent in Art and Literature from 1300–1700' (PhD diss., University of Illinois at Urbana-Champaign, 1981); Sydney Higgins, 'Playing the Serpent: Devil, Virgin or Mythical Beast?', *European Medieval Drama* 2 (1998): 207–214; Frances Gussenhoven, 'The Serpent with a Matron's Face: Medieval Iconography of Satan in the Garden of Eden', *European Medieval Drama* 4 (2000): 207–230; Shulamit Laderman, 'Two Faces of Eve: Polemics and Controversies Viewed Through Pictorial Motifs', *IMAGES* 2.1 (2008): 1–5. An interesting iconographical variant is the depiction of the woman/serpent with coiffured and covered hair, indicating that the creature is simulating a matron and not a virgin and therefore the form most conducive to deception is that of a wife. Gussenhoven, 'The Serpent with a Matron's Face', 229.

56 Kren and McKendrick, *Illuminating the Renaissance*, cat. no. 114, 385–387; Hand, *Women, Manuscripts and Identity in Northern Europe*, 140–142; Lesley Twomey, 'Juana of Castile's Book of Hours: An Archduchess at Prayer', *Religions* 11.4 (2020): 1–31. doi.org/10.3390/rel11040201. A digitised version of this manuscript is available at www.bl.uk/manuscripts/FullDisplay.aspx?ref=Add_MS_18852 (accessed 27 November 2023). Other examples include the sculpture on the right portal of the west façade of Notre Dame de Amiens, the *Morgan Picture Bible* (Morgan Library Ms. 638 fol. 1v), the *Tres Riches Heures de Duc de Berry* (Musée de Condé Ms. 65 fol. 25v), the left panel of the diptych by Hugo van der Goes now in Vienna (Kunsthistorisches Museum Gemäldegalerie 5822a), and the depiction by Michelangelo in the ceiling fresco of the Sistine Chapel in Rome. Several of the creatures in these examples also have a variety of limbs. This is perhaps in response to the curse of the serpent after the fall that forced it to crawl on its belly, so therefore it would have originally had appendages in the Garden of Eden.

57 Ian Maclean, *The Renaissance Notion of Women: A Study in the Fortunes of Scholasticism and Medical Science in European Intellectual Life* (Cambridge: Cambridge University Press, 1980), 220.

58 Genesis 3:16. For analysis, see Jerome Gellman, 'Gender and Sexuality in the Garden of Eden', *Theology & Sexuality* 12.3 (2006): 324–325; Renate Mariam van Dijk-Coombes, 'Towards a New Understanding of the Curse of Eve: Female Sexual Pain in Genesis 3:16 and Other Ancient Texts', *Scriptura* 119.1 (2020): 7–8.
59 Liss, *Isabel the Queen*, 173–175; Weissberger, *Isabel Rules*, 113–114.
60 Genesis 3:15. In Jerome's translation, the referent 'he' was mistranslated as 'she' and the prophecy was therefore understood to be doubly focused on Mary. Warner, *Alone of All Her Sex*, 245. The description of a woman with serpent underfoot was combined with the Woman of the Apocalypse described in Revelations in order to visually express the Virgin of the Immaculate Conception. Stratton, *The Immaculate Conception in Spanish Art*, 48.
61 Kren and McKendrick, *Illuminating the Renaissance*, 386; Hand, *Women, Manuscripts and Identity in Northern Europe*, 74–76.
62 James Marrow, '"*In desen speigell*": A New Form of *Memento Mori* in Fifteenth-Century Netherlandish Art', in *Essays in Northern European Art: Presented to Egbert Haverkamp-Begemann on his Sixtieth Birthday*, ed. Anne-Marie Logan (Groningen: Davaco, 1983), 157.
63 Jewett and Melchoir-Bonnet, *The Mirror*, 135–136.
64 Warner, *Alone of All Her Sex*, 50–67; 236–237. For the use of this framework among Isabel's circle, see Lehfeldt, 'Ruling Sexuality', 51–52.
65 For analysis of the fruit held by Eve and the significance of the fig, see James Snyder, 'Jan van Eyck and Adam's Apple', *Art Bulletin* 58.4 (1976): 512–513.
66 Genesis 1:28.
67 Although no version of this text is listed in the inventories taken of Isabel's books upon her death, the inclusion of multiple Arthurian romances indicates her engagement with this genre. Moreover, it is possible that a version of the text printed in 1512 was posthumously dedicated to Isabel, or alternatively to her daughter-in-law Margaret of Austria. Margaret did own a copy of the 1489 Castilian edition printed in Toulouse, which survives in Brussels (Royal Library of Belgium, INC B 840). Lydia Zeldenrust, *The Mélusine Romance in Medieval Europe: Translation, Circulation, and Material Contexts* (Woodbridge: D.S. Brewer, 2020), 112–114.
68 Frederika Bain, 'The Tail of Melusine: Hybridity, Mutability, and the Accessible Other', in *Melusine's Footprint: Tracing the Legacy of a Medieval Myth*, ed. Misty Urban, Deva Kemmis, and Melissa Ridley Elmes (Leiden: Brill, 2017), 17–20.
69 Jean d'Arras, *Melusine; Or the Noble History of Lusignan*, trans. Donald Maddox and Sara Sturm-Maddox (University Park, PA: Pennsylvania State University Press, 2012), 181.
70 d'Arras, *Melusine*, 181.
71 d'Arras, *Melusine*, 194–195.
72 A.D. Deyermond, 'La historia de la linda Melosina: Two Spanish Versions of a French Romance', in *Medieval Hispanic Studies Presented to Rita Hamilton*, ed. A.D. Deyermond (London: Tamesis, 1976), 57–65; Isidro Rivera, 'The 'Historia de la linda Melosina' and the Construction of Romance in Late Medieval Castile',

Modern Language Notes 112.2 (1997): 131–146; Zeldenrust, *The Mélusine Romance in Medieval Europe*, 102–145. On the accompanying woodcuts, see Lydia Zeldenrust, 'Serpent of Half-Serpent? Bernhard Richel's Melusine and the Making of a Western European Icon', *Neophilologus* 100 (2016): 23–25; Zeldenrust, *The Mélusine Romance in Medieval Europe*, 107–110.

73 Scholars have long noted the resonances between the tale of Melusine and the politics of Isabel's reign, including the emphasis on crusading, territorial expansion, and redemption through Christianity. Ivy Corfis, 'Beauty, Deformity, and the Fantastic in the Historia de la linda Melosina', *Hispanic Review* 55.2 (1987): 559–575; Rivera, "The 'Historia de la linda Melosina" and the Construction of Romance in Late Medieval Castile', 141–144; Zeldenrust, *The Mélusine Romance in Medieval Europe*, 128–131.

74 Jan Shaw, *Space, Gender, and Memory in Middle English Romance: Architecture of Wonder in Melusine* (New York: Palgrave Macmillan, 2016), 144–147; Jane Bonsall, 'Whose Sword? Materiality, Gender Subversion and the Fairy Women of Middle English Romance', *Medieval Feminist Forum: A Journal of Gender and Sexuality* 56.1 (2020): 124–132. For the way these architectural constructions may have resonated in Isabelline Iberia, see Anna Casas Aguilar, 'Architecture and Empire in *Historia de la linda Melosina*', in *Melusine's Footprint: Tracing the Legacy of a Medieval Myth*, ed. Misty Urban, Deva Kemmis, and Melissa Ridley Elmes (Leiden: Brill, 2017), 112–114.

75 Chera Cole, 'Passing as a 'Humayn Woman': Hybridity and Salvation in the Middle English *Melusine*', in *Melusine's Footprint: Tracing the Legacy of a Medieval Myth*, ed. Misty Urban, Deva Kemmis, and Melissa Ridley Elmes (Leiden: Brill, 2017), 240–241. While later Castilian editions minimise Melusine's liminal positionality between human and fairy as well as her existence as a marvel of God's creation, the Castilian translation printed during Isabel's lifetime maintains this framing from the original text. Zeldenrust, *The Mélusine Romance in Medieval Europe*, 118–119.

76 d'Arras, *Melusine*, 191–192. The Spanish translation further emphasised Melusine's desire for Christian salvation. Zeldenrust, *The Mélusine Romance in Medieval Europe*, 122–131. On the relationship between physiognomy and interior character in the Spanish translation, see Corfis, 'Beauty, Deformity, and the Fantastic int he Historia de la linda Melosina', 182–183.

77 Zeldenrust, *The Mélusine Romance in Medieval Europe*, 124–128.

78 Zeldenrust, *The Mélusine Romance in Medieval Europe*, 129. Rivera similarly remarks on the intersections between Christianity and Melusine's governance in the context of the fifteenth century. Rivera, 'The 'Historia de la linda Melosina' and the Construction of Romance in Late Medieval Castile', 140–141.

79 Shaw, *Space, Gender, and Memory in Middle English Romance*, 129–164; Bonsall, 'Whose Sword? Materiality, Gender Subversion and the Fairy Women of Middle English Romance', 127–130.

80 d'Arras, *Melusine*, 70–71. For analysis, see Gabrielle Spiegel, 'Maternity and Monstrosity: Reproductive Biology in the *Roman de Mélusine*', in *Melusine of Lusignan: Founding Fiction in Late Medieval France*, ed. Donald Maddox and Sara Sturm-Maddox (Athens, GA: University of Georgia Press, 1996), 108–109.

The alterity of Melusine's sons is poignantly highlighted by the manipulation of the woodcut images in the Castilian translation produced by Parix and Clebat in Toulouse. Zeldenrust, *The Mélusine Romance in Medieval Europe*, 134–142.
81 d'Arras, *Melusine*, 191.
82 Getty Museum 83.ML.114, available at www.getty.edu/art/collection/object/103RVJ (accessed 27 November 2023). Kren and McKendrick, *Illuminating the Renaissance*, cat. no. 124; 414–417.

Bibliography

Primary sources

Córdoba, Fray Martín de. *Jardín de nobles donzellas*. Chapel Hill, NC: Romance, 1974.
d'Arras, Jean. *Melusine; Or the Noble History of Lusignan*. Trans. Donald Maddox and Sara Sturm-Maddox. University Park, PA: Pennsylvania State University Press, 2012.
Palencia, Alfonso de. *Cronica de Enrique IV*. 3 vols. Madrid: Ediciones Atlas, 1973–1975.
Pulgar, Hernando. *Crónica de los Señores Reyes Católicos Don Fernando y Doña Isabel de Castilla y de Aragon*. Valencia: Benito Monfort, 1780.
Valera, Mosén Diego de. *Epístolas de Mosen Diego de Valera: Embiadas en diversos tiempos é á diversas personas*. Madrid: Impr. de M. Ginesta, 1878.
Valera, Mosén Diego de. *Crónica de los Reyes Católicos*. Anejos de la Revista de Filología Española. Madrid: Consejo Superior de Investigaciones Cietíficas, 1927.
Vicens Vives, Jaime. *Historia crítica de la vida y reinado de Fernando II de Aragón*. Zaragoza: Institudión 'Fernando el Católico', 1962.
Voragine, Jacobus de. *The Golden Legend or Lives of the Saints*. Trans. William Caxton. 7 vols. London: Temple Classics, 1900.

Secondary sources

Avenoza, Gemma. 'Un nuevo manuscrito de las *Generaciones y semblanzas*: la *Crónica de Enrique IV* y la propaganda isabelina'. *Anuario medieval* 3 (1991): 7–22.
Bain, Frederika. 'The Tail of Melusine: Hybridity Mutability, and the Accesible Other'. In *Melusine's Footprint: Tracing the Legacy of a Medieval Myth*, ed. Misty Urban, Deva Kemmis and Melissa Ridley Elmes, 17–35. Leiden: Brill, 2017.
Bloch, Howard. *Medieval Misogyny and the Invention of Western Romantic Love*. Chicago: University of Chicago Press, 1991.
Bonnell, John. 'The Serpent with a Human Head in Art and in Mystery Play'. *American Journal of Archaeology* 21.3 (1917): 255–291.
Bonsall, Jane. 'Whose Sword? Materiality, Gender Subversion and the Fairy Women of Middle English Romance'. *Medieval Feminist Forum: A Journal of Gender and Sexuality* 56.1 (2020): 107–133.

Boruchoff, David. 'Isabel, Her Chroniclers, and the Inquisition: Self-Fashioning and Historical Memory'. In *A Companion to the Queenship of Isabel la Católica*, ed. Hilaire Kallendorf, 34–71. Leiden: Brill, 2023.

Brinkmann, Bodo. *Die flämische Buchmalerei am Ende des Burgunderreichs: Der Meister des Dresdener Gebetbuchs und die Miniaturisten seiner Zeit*. 2 vols. Turnhout: Brepols, 1997.

Burke, Linda. 'A Sister in the World: Saint Elizabeth of Hungary in the "Golden Legend"'. *The Hungarian Historical Review* 5.3 (2016): 509–535.

Carceller Cerviño, María del Pilar. 'Realidad y representación de la nobleza en el siglo XV: El linaje de la Cueva y la casa ducal de Alburquerque.' PhD diss., Universidad Complutense de Madrid, 2006.

Carceller Cerviño, María del Pilar. 'Álvaro de Luna, Juan Pacheco y Beltrán de la Cueva: un estudio comparativo del privado regio a fines de la Edad Media'. *En la España Medieval* 32 (2009): 85–112.

Casas Aguilar, Anna. 'Architecture and Empire in *Historia de la linda Melosina*'. In *Melusine's Footprint: Tracing the Legacy of a Medieval Myth*, ed. Misty Urban, Deva Kemmis and Melissa Ridley Elmes, 109–131. Leiden: Brill, 2017.

Claussen, Samuel. 'Royal Punishment and Reconciliation in Trastámara Castile'. In *Treason: Medieval and Early Modern Adultery, Betrayal, and Shame*, ed. Lariss Tracy, 100–118. Leiden: Brill, 2019.

Cole, Chera. 'Passing as a 'Humayn Woman': Hybridity and Salvation in the Middle English *Melusine*'. In *Melusine's Footprint: Tracing the Legacy of a Medieval Myth*, ed. Misty Urban, Deva Kemmis and Melissa Ridley Elmes, 240–258. Leiden: Brill, 2017.

Coolidge, Grace. *Guardianship, Gender, and the Nobility in Early Modern Spain*. Aldershot: Ashgate, 2010.

Corfis, Ivy. 'Beauty, Deformity, and the Fantastic int he Historia de la linda Melosina'. *Hispanic Review* 55.2 (1987): 181–193.

Cruz, Ann, and Maria Galli Stampino, eds. *Early Modern Habsburg Women: Transnational Contexts, Cultural Conflicts, Dynastic Continuities*. London: Routledge, 2013.

de Azcona, Tariscio. *Isabel la Católica: Estudio crítico de su vida y su reinado*. 3rd edn. Valladolid: Instituto Isabel la Católica de Historia Eclesiástica, 1993.

de Kesel, Lieve. *The Hours of Queen Isabella the Catholic: the Cleveland Museum of Art, Cleveland/Ohio, Leonard C. Hanna Jr. Fund 1963.256*. Gütersloh: Faksimile Verlag, 2014.

de Winter, Patrick. 'A Book of Hours of Queen Isabel la Católica'. *The Bulletin of the Cleveland Museum of Art* 68.10 (1981): 342–427.

Devaney, Thomas. 'Virtue, Virility, and History in Fifteenth-Century Castile'. *Speculum* 88.3 (2013): 721–749.

Deyermond, A.D. 'La historia de la linda Melosina: Two Spanish Versions of a French Romance'. In *Medieval Hispanic Studies Presented to Rita Hamilton*, ed. A.D. Deyermond, 57–65. London: Tamesis, 1976.

Earenfight, Theresa. *Queenship and Political Power in Medieval and Early Modern Spain*. Aldershot: Ashgate, 2005.

Earenfight, Theresa. 'Two Bodies, One Spirit: Isabel and Fernando's Construction of Monarchial Partnership'. In *Queen Isabel I of Castile: Power, Patronage, Persona*, ed. Barabara Weissberger, 3–18. New York: Tamesis, 2008.

Earenfight, Theresa. 'Where Do We Go From Here? Some Thoughts on Power and Gender in the Middle Ages'. *Medieval Feminist Forum: A Journal of Gender and Sexuality* 5.2 (2015): 116–131.

Earenfight, Theresa. 'A Lifetime of Power: Beyond Binaries of Gender'. In *Medieval Elite Women and the Exercise of Power, 1100–1400: Moving Beyond the Exceptionalist Debate*, ed. Heather Tanner, 271–93. Basingstoke: Palgrave Macmillan, 2019.

Flores, Nona Cecilia. "Virgineum Vultum Habens': The Woman-Headed Serpent in art and Literature from 1300–1700.' PhD diss., University of Illinois at Urbana-Champaign, 1981.

Friedman, John Block. 'L'iconographie de Vénus et de son miroir à la fin du moyen âge'. In *Érotisme au moyen âge*, ed. Bruno Roy, 53–82. Montreal: Aurore, 1977.

García y García de Castro, Rafael. *Virtudes de la reina católica*. Granada: Consejo Superior de Investigaciones Científicas, 1961.

Gatland, Emma. *Women from the Golden Legend: Female Authority in a Medieval Castilian Sanctoral*. London: Tamesis, 2011.

Gellman, Jerome. 'Gender and Sexuality in the Garden of Eden'. *Theology & Sexuality* 12.3 (2006): 319–35.

Gilleir, Anke. 'On Gender, Sovereignty and Imagination: An Introduction'. In *Strategic Imaginations: Women and the Gender of Sovereignty in European Culture*, ed. Anke Gilleir and Aude Defurne, 7–26. Leuven: Leuven University Press, 2020.

Grabes, Herbert. *The Mutable Glass: Mirror-imagery in Titles and Texts of the Middle Ages and English Renaissance*. Cambridge: Cambridge University Press, 1982.

Grieve, Patricia. *The Eve of Spain: Myths of Origins in the History of Christian, Muslim, and Jewish Conflict*. Baltimore: Johns Hopkins University Press, 2009.

Guardiola-Griffiths, Cristina. *Legitimizing the Queen: Propaganda and Ideology in the Reign of Isabel I of Castile*. Lanham, MD: Rowman & Littlefield, 2010.

Guardiola-Griffiths, Cristina. 'Isabel I of Castile and Saintly Propaganda: Interpreting the St Anne Retable in the *Capilla del Condestable*'. In *A Companion to the Queenship of Isabel la Católica*, ed. Hilaire Kallendorf, 91–112. Leiden: Brill, 2023.

Gussenhoven, Frances. 'The Serpent with a Matron's Face: Medieval Iconography of Satan in the Garden of Eden'. *European Medieval Drama* 4 (2000): 207–230.

Hamilton, Michelle M. 'Hostile Histories: Isabel and Fernando in Jewish and Muslim Narratives'. In *A Companion to the Queenship of Isabel la Católica*, ed. Hilaire Kallendorf, 213–231. Leiden: Brill, 2023.

Hand, Joni M. *Women, Manuscripts and Identity in Northern Europe, 1350–1550*. Burlington, VT: Ashgate, 2013.

Higgins, Sydney. 'Playing the Serpent: Devil, Virgin or Mythical Beast?' *European Medieval Drama* 2 (1998): 207–214.

Hoffman, Martha. *Raised to Rule: Educating Royalty at the Court of the Spanish.* Baton Rouge: Louisiana State University Press, 2011.

Humble Ferreira, Susannah. 'Juana La Beltraneja, Dynastic Fears, and Threats of Marriage (1475–1506)'. *Renaissance and Reformation / Renaissance et Réforme.* Special Issue: Spaces and Power of the Spanish Nobility (1480–1750) 43.4 (2020): 79–100.

Jewett, Katharine, and Sabine Melchoir-Bonnet. *The Mirror: A History.* New York: Routledge, 1994.

Kagan, Richard. *Clio and the Crown: The Politics of History in Medieval and Early Modern Spain.* Baltimore: Johns Hopkins University Press, 2009.

Koch, Robert. 'The Salamander in van der Goes' *Garden of Eden*'. *Journal of the Warburg and Courtauld Institutes* 28 (1965): 323–326.

Kren, Thomas, and Scot McKendrick, eds. *Illuminating the Renaissance: The Triumph of Flemish Manuscript Painting in Europe.* Los Angeles: The J. Paul Getty Museum, 2003.

Laderman, Shulamit. 'Two Faces of Eve: Polemics and Controversies Viewed Through Pictorial Motifs'. *IMAGES* 2.1 (2008): 1–20.

Lehfeldt, Elizabeth. 'Ruling Sexuality: The Political Legitimacy of Isabel of Castile'. *Renaissance Quarterly* 53.1 (2000): 31–56.

Levi d'Ancona, Mirella. *The Iconography of the Immaculate Conception in the Middle Ages and Early Renaissance.* New York: College Art Association, 1957.

Liss, Peggy. *Isabel the Queen: Life and Times.* Philadelphia: University of Pennsylvania Press, 2004.

Maclean, Ian. *The Renaissance Notion of Women: A Study in the Fortunes of Scholasticism and Medical Science in European Intellectual Life.* Cambridge: Cambridge University Press, 1980.

Marrow, James. '*In desen speigell*': A New Form of '*Momento Mori*' in Fifteenth-Century Netherlandish Art'. In *Essays in Northern European Art: Presented to Egbert Haverkamp-Begemann on his Sixtieth Birthdat*, ed. Bitite Vinklers, 153–163. Groningen: Davaco, 1983.

Morgan, Nigel, and Scot McKendrick. 'Contents and Authorship'. In *The Isabella Breviary: The British Library, London, Add. Ms. 18851*, ed. Mónica Miró, 75–113. Barcelona: M. Moleiro, 2012.

Ornstein, Jacob. 'Misogyny and Pro-Feminism in Early Castilian Literature'. *Modern Language Quarterly* 3.2 (1942): 221–234.

Ortego Rico, Pablo. "Sy algunas quiebras en ellas oviese …': crisis de liquidez y quiebras financieras en Castilla a fines de la Edad Media'. *Cuadernos de Historia Moderna* 42.2 (2017): 411–439.

Parker, Patricia. *Literary Fat Ladies: Rhetoric, Gender, Property.* New York: Methuen, 1987.

Phillips, William D. *Enrique IV and the Crisis of Fifteenth-Century Castile (1425–1480).* Cambridge, MA: Medieval Academy of America, 1978.

Pulgar, Fernando del. *Letras. Glosa a las 'Complas de Mingo Revulgo'.* Madrid: La Lectura, 1929.

Quintero, María Cristina. 'Royal Players: Habsburg Women, Border Crossings, and the Performance of Queenship'. In *Beyond Spain's Borders: Women Players in Early Modern National Theaters*, ed. Anne Cruz and María Cristina Quintero, 129–151. Abingdon: Routledge, 2017.

Reames, Sherry. *The Legenda Aurea: A Reexamination of its Paradoxical History*. Madison: University of Wisconsin Press, 1983.

Regalado de Valle, Vanesa. 'El tratado de Jardín de nobles doncellas y su influencia en la personalidad de Isabel la Católica'. *Digilec: Revista internacional de lenguas y culturas* 6 (2019): 1–13.

Rivera, Isidro. 'The 'Historia de la linda Melosina' and the Construction of Romance in Late Medieval Castile'. *Modern Language Notes* 112.2 (1997): 131–146.

odríguez Valencia, Vicente. *Artículos del postulador*. Valladolid: Institución Isabel la Católica de Historia Eclesiástica, 1972.

Rosenblatt, Louise M. 'Toward a Transactional Theory of Reading'. *Journal of Reading Behavior* 1.1 (1969): 31–49.

Rosenblatt, Louise M. *The Reader, the Text, the Poem: The Transactional Theory of the Literary Work*. Carbondale, IL: Southern Illinois University Press, 1978.

Rosenblatt, Louise M. 'Viewpoints: Transaction versus Interaction-A Terminological Rescue Operation'. *Research in the Teaching of English* 19 (1985): 96–107.

Rosenblatt, Louise M. *Litterature as Exploration*. 3rd ed. New York: Modern Language Association of America, 1995.

Rosenblatt, Louise M. 'The Transactional Theory of Reading and Writing'. In *Theroetical Models and Processes of Literacy*, ed. Donna Alvermann, Norman Unrau, Misty Sailros and Robert Ruddell, 451–479. New York: Routledge, 2018.

Sánchez Dueñas, Blas. 'Una particular visión de la mujer en el siglo XV: Jardín de nobles doncellas de Fray Martín de Córdoba'. *Boletín de la Real Academia de Córdoba de Ciencias, Bellas Letras y Nobles Artes* 80 (2001): 291–300.

Schulte, Regina. 'Introduction: Conceptual Approaches to the Queen's Body'. In *The Body of the Queen: Gender and Rule in the Courtly World, 1500–2000*, ed. Regina Schulte, 1–15. New York: Berghahn Books, 2000.

Shadis, Miriam. 'Women, Gender, and Rulership in Romance Europe: The Iberian Case'. *History Compass* 4.3 (2006): 1–7.

Shaw, Jan. *Space, Gender, and Memory in Middle English Romance: Architecture of Wonder in Melusine*. New York: Palgrave Macmillan, 2016.

Silleras-Fernández, Núria. *Chariots of Ladies: Francesc Eiximenis and the Court Culture of Medieval and Early Modern Iberia*. Ithaca, NY: Cornell University Press, 2015.

Silleras-Fernández, Núria. 'Isabel's Years of Sorrow: Consoling the Catholic Queen'. In *A Companion to the Queenship of Isabel la Católica*, ed. Hilaire Kallendorf, 254–278. Leiden: Brill, 2023.

Smith, Susan. 'The Gothic Mirror and the Female Gaze'. In *Saints, Sinners, and Sisters: Gender and Northern Art in Medieval and Early Modern Europe*, ed. Jane Carroll and Alison Stewart, 73–93. Burlington, VT: Ashgate, 2003.

Snyder, James. 'Jan van Eyck and Adam's Apple'. *Art Bulletin* 58.4 (1976): 511–515.

Soriano, Catherine. 'Conveniencia política y tópico literario en el *Jardín de nobles doncellas* (1468?) de Fray Martín Alonso de Córdoba'. In *Actas del VI Congreso Internacional de la Associación Hispánica de Literatura Medieval (Alcalá de Henares, 12–16 de septiembre de 1995)*, 1457–1466. Alcalá de Henares: Universidad de Alcalá, 1997.

Spiegel, Gabrielle. 'Maternity and Monstrosity: Reproductive Biology in the *Roman de Mélusine*'. In *Melusine of Lusignan: Founding Fiction in Late Medieval France*, ed. Donald Maddox and Sara Sturm-Maddox, 100–124. Athens, GA: University of Georgia Press, 1996.

Stratton, Suzanne. *The Immaculate Conception in Spanish Art*. Cambridge: Cambridge University Press, 1994.

Surtz, R.E. 'The Reciprocal Construction of Isabelline Book Patronage'. In *Queen Isabel I of Castile: Power, Patronage Persona*, ed. Barbara Weissberger, 55–70. New York: Tamesis, 2008.

Tate, Robert. *Ensayos sobre la historiografía peninsular del siglo XV*. Trans. Jesús Díaz. Madrid: Gredos, 1970.

Trapp, J.B. 'The Iconography of the Fall of Man'. In *Approaches to Paradise Lost*, ed. C.A. Patrides, 223–282. London: Edward Arnold, 1968.

Travalia, Caroline. 'The Legend of Isabel la Católica, Founder of Spain'. In *A Companion to the Queenship of Isabel la Católica*, ed. Hilaire Kallendorf, 299–338. Leiden: Brill, 2023.

Twomey, Lesley. *The Serpent and the Rose: The Immaculate Conception and Hispanic Poetry in the Late Medieval Period*. Leiden: Brill, 2008.

Twomey, Lesley. 'Juana of Castile's Book of Hours: An Archduchess at Prayer'. *Religions* 11.4 (2020): 1–31.

Valera, Mosén Diego de. 'Memorial de diversas hazañas'. In *Crónicas de los reyes de Castilla*, ed. Cayetano Rosell. Biblioteca de Autores Españoles, 3–95. Madrid: Atlas, 1953.

van Dijk-Coombes, Renate Mariam. 'Towards a New Understanding of the Curse of Eve: Female Sexual Pain in Genesis 3:16 and Other Ancient Texts'. *Scriptura* 119.1 (2020): 1–14.

Villarroel González, Óscar. *Juana la Beltraneja: La construcción de una ilegitimidad*. Madrid: Silex Ediçiones, 2014.

Warner, Marina. *Alone of All Her Sex: The Myth and Cult of the Virgin Mary*. New York: Knopf, 1976.

Weissberger, Barbara. "A tierra, puto!' Alfonso de Palencia's Discourse on Effeminacy'. In *Queer Iberia: Sexualities, Cultures, and Crossings from the Middle Ages to the Renaissance*, ed. Josiah Blackmore and Gregory S. Hutcheson, 291–324. Durham, NC: Duke University Press, 1999.

Weissberger, Barbara. *Isabel Rules: Constructing Queenship, Wielding Power*. Minneapolis: University of Minnesota Press, 2003.

Weissberger, Barbara. 'Patronage and Politics in the Court of the Catholic Monarchs: The 'Cancionero de Pedro Marcuello". *Studies in Iconography* 26 (2005): 175–204.

Weissberger, Barbara. '*Tanto monta*: The Catholic Monarchs' Nuptial Fiction and the Power of Isabel I of Castile'. In *The Rule of Women in Early Modern Europe*, ed. Anne J. Curz and Mihoko Sukuki, 43–62. Urbana: University of Illinois Press, 2009.

Yarza Luaces, Joaquín. 'La santa que lee'. In *Luchas de género en la Historia a través de la imagen*, ed. María Teresa Sauret Guerrero and Amparo Quiles Faz, 421–468. Málaga: Centro de Ediciones de la Disputación de Málaga, 2001.

Zeldenrust, Lydia. 'Serpent of Half-Serpent? Bernhard Richel's Melusine and the Making of a Western European Icon'. *Neophilologus* 100 (2016): 19–41.

Zeldenrust, Lydia. *The Mélusine Romance in Medieval Europe: Translation, Circulation, and Material Contexts*. Woodbridge: D.S. Brewer, 2020.

Part II

Gender, morality, and desire

6

Gender, moral, and sexual warfare in the *Roman de Silence*

Kathleen M. Blumreich

The *Roman de Silence*,[1] a thirteenth-century French romance, concentrates on the adventures of Silence, a girl reared as a boy in consequence of a royal ban on female inheritance. A quick study who soon excels at traditionally masculine activities such as jousting, wrestling, and skirmishing, Silence is forced at puberty to choose whether to continue the charade or to exchange her lances for sewing needles. Rebelling against a 'natural' order that would deem her worthy only for feminine pursuits, she runs away with a pair of minstrels in hopes of learning a marketable skill. Silence gains fame as a talented *jongleur*, is reunited with her parents, and makes her way to the English court. There, she becomes a favourite of the king, Ebain, and, to her detriment, his queen, Eufeme. Sent to serve the King of France, and narrowly escaping death, Silence continues to hone her skills in battle and chivalry; she is knighted in Paris at the age of seventeen. When civil war erupts in England, our heroine returns to fight against Ebain's foes. Yet, despite abundant proof of Silence's loyalty, the king capitulates to the demands of his wicked wife and sends his vassal on a quest to capture Merlin. Having completed this impossible mission, Silence returns to court where she is unmasked, her biological sex revealed. Simultaneously, the queen's treachery is exposed, and she and her secret lover are summarily executed. The king lifts the ban on female inheritance, takes Silence to wife, and the poem moves toward its close, with its author commenting on the appropriateness of censure for a bad woman and praise for a good one.

While Master Heldris of Cornwall,[2] the putative author, was clearly interested in composing a romance rather than a sermon, there is nevertheless an important thematic concern with morality that emerges. At nearly every turn, the poet presents his characters – and by extension, his readers – with moral choices, some easy, some fraught. A quasi-Ramist quality pervades the narrative structure, for each time a problem is introduced, the characters affected are confronted with (or imagine there to be) essentially two options:

follow truth or follow desire. Successive choices are further broken into dichotomies requiring deeper reflection on the part of the character, regardless of age, sex, or status. At the centre of this schematic is our heroine, Silence. As we shall see, she is in some respects little more than a pawn, moved about a politically, emotionally, and sexually charged chessboard by those with authority over her. Ironically, she is simultaneously the character with the greatest agency, for she is the only one who actively seeks to follow a righteous path.[3] That is, Silence is careful to balance what is expected or demanded of her against what she believes to be morally just and refuses to be ruled by her own passions or proclivities. From a modern position, we may chafe at her literal silence when she is forced from the prison of gender concealment to the prison of royal duty and its attendant domestic obligations.[4] Yet Heldris makes clear that Silence is heroic, stalwart throughout her journey, remaining above the fray even while she is in the thick of it. Disguises and war-gear help her to survive in the world and on the physical battlefield; honesty, a sense of personal honour, and assiduous exercise of right reason sustain her on the moral battlefield. In the context of a work concerned with the perils of revealing one's true self, this is no mean feat.

Indeed, the poem comprises a guidebook to right living, emphasising the triumph of virtue over vice.[5] And not surprisingly, in a work whose plot is catalysed and sustained by a cross-dressing trope, licit sexuality is often a crucial subtext. Although Cador and Eufemie, Silence's parents, emblematise heteronormativity, and Ebain and Eufeme reflect the realities of loveless royal unions as well as 'unnatural' appetites, Silence herself never seems to express desire for physical intimacy. Perhaps this is because she is the perfect 'maid' whose character cannot be sullied by base carnality; perhaps this is because she prefers asexuality; or perhaps this is because she must direct her energies toward maintaining the epicenity forced upon her by legal exigencies and filial duty. The poem, focused as it is on Silence's travails, is thus less about the protagonist's own sexuality than it is about the effect of her biological sex, appearance, and gender performativity on others.

The *Roman de Silence* opens rather conventionally, with Master Heldris speaking to his skill as a poet. He tells us that he 'is writing these verses strictly to measure' and remarks that 'A learned man might study long | to fashion rhyme and verse'.[6] Surprisingly, however, the author entreats anyone possessing his work to burn it rather than share it with people 'who don't know a good story | when they hear one'.[7] He further clarifies that he does not wish to have his poetry circulate 'among those who prize money more than honor, | or among people who want to hear everything | but do not care to make a man happy | with some reward they might wish to give'.[8] Heldris continues to rage against a contemporary milieu in which parsimoniousness reigns and where 'greedy, nasty, petty people' are 'intoxicated with Avarice', eschewing honour and generosity in favour of wealth and false praise.[9] The reason for this jeremiad? Heldris confides:

> Before I begin my story for you,
> I really have to let it all out a little
> in order to get into the proper frame of mind.
> I want to get it all out of my system beforehand,
> so that when it's time to tell the tale,
> there'll be nothing left in me to spoil the telling.[10]

Although this prefatory material may initially strike us as divorced from the narrative proper, Heldris is here providing the ethical framework for his tale. When at line 107 the poet writes, 'Once upon a time Ebain was king of England',[11] we are already deep in a world where greed, the will to power, spite, and every kind of vice trump basic human decency.[12] By the time Heldris introduces Silence (*in utero*) at line 1671, we have met the majority of the romance's key players, all of whom have been or shortly will be presented with tests of their own moral fibre. These characters function as foils, sometimes to one another, but always to Silence herself. To fully appreciate Silence's comportment, then, we might begin by considering the degree to which her caregivers, travelling companions, and royal role models are successful in abjuring vice.

Following a textbook romance courtship, Cador and Eufemie marry for love and set up a household where they live in mutual respect. When Eufemie becomes pregnant and delivers a girl, however, the couple's entire focus shifts to economic matters.[13] The parents are delighted to have a perfectly formed, beautiful daughter, but they realise that their estates are at risk, given King Ebain's ban on female inheritance. And since they do not know whether they will later have a male heir, or whether Ebain will reverse his judgment, Cador enlists the aid of a trusted cousin to serve as midwife and announce the birth of a son. With this lady's help, Cador and Eufemie further succeed in lying about the newborn's health and tricking a chaplain into christening their allegedly dying son with the name Silentius. The child is then sent to live with the lady and a loyal seneschal in the forest, where 'she' is raised as 'he'.[14]

On the surface, it appears that Cador and Eufemie behave as concerned parents: they wish to circumvent an unjust edict and thus protect their child's fortune.[15] Yet the strategy they employ is as morally untenable as the ban on female inheritance itself. Not only do Cador and Eufemie conflate parental responsibility and personal desire, they flout the law and seek to deprive the king of his rightful authority. Cador acknowledges that what they plan is wrong, but he brushes it off, claiming that if they do happen to have a son in the future, 'we'll turn this one back into a girl. | That way, no one can accuse us | of treason or felony, | of wickedness or villainy'.[16] To compound their disloyalty, they engage conspirators to abet them. The lady and the seneschal may elect to render aid out of a sense of duty, but the ease with which they lie, accept monetary compensation for their efforts, and swear 'solemn oaths' not to reveal the deception is troubling.[17] Perhaps most problematic is that Cador and Eufemie seem not to consider how their duplicity might affect Silence, the very person for whose benefit they set their contingency plan in motion. Although her physical and educational needs are met by her caregivers, she is kept isolated, restrained from venturing beyond her lodging in the woods for fear that she might reveal her birth sex. In fact, when Silence 'was old enough | to understand he was a girl, | his father sat down to reason with him | and explain the circumstances | which had led them to conceal his identity this way'.[18] Assuring his 'Dear sweet precious son' that 'we are not doing this | for ourselves, but for you', Cador admonishes Silence: 'As you cherish honor, | you will continue to conceal yourself from everyone'.[19] The burden of her parents' decision – as well as her father's definition of honour – is thus put squarely on Silence's shoulders. More importantly, the literal security of all involved in the scheme depends upon how well Silence plays her role. What Silence feels about living as a boy, eschewing sexual intimacy altogether, and whether she might wish for a different life doesn't figure into the equation.[20]

The moral calibre of Silence's role models does not improve as the story develops. Having decided to run away from her sylvan prison, Silence is taken in by a pair of itinerant entertainers, one a harpist and the other a *jongleur*. At first, they treat her kindly, allowing her to serve as valet as they travel from performance to performance. Before three years pass, however, Silence – under the pseudonym 'Malduit' – has learned to play and sing so well that she surpasses her masters in skill and artistry; soon, she is the centre of attention and is earning the trio great sums.[21] Instead of being appreciative of Silence's continued service, proud of her rapid progress, or even grateful for her enrichment of their coffers, the men feel humiliated and grow increasingly envious of their protégé. Convinced that Silence's talent somehow diminishes their own, they contrive to murder her under cover of darkness, 'for such deeds are better done unseen'.[22] Interestingly, in keeping with Heldris's earlier diatribe on avarice, much of their conversation focuses on money, and they rationalise their plan by imagining that Silence will eventually rob them of their livelihood altogether.[23] Warned in a dream that her companions are dangerous, Silence manages to escape and makes her way back home, where she is reunited with Cador and Eufemie. Soon thereafter, she is summoned to court.

Whereas the *jongleurs* are motivated by pecuniary interests (and bruised egos), Queen Eufeme is motivated by desire of another sort, though one that consumes her equally: lust, or more precisely, greed for sexual dalliance.[24] As queen, Eufeme should be the quintessential role model for women throughout the realm, demonstrating the virtues of honesty, integrity, and fidelity. What she manifests are their opposites. Trapped in a stultifying, sterile marriage to Ebain, Eufeme attempts to stave off boredom. When Silence is pressed into service as the queen's page and personal musician, the relationship is initially above board, Silence keeping Eufeme company and entertaining her by playing the harp. Rather than continuing to engage in such innocent pursuits, however, Eufeme determines that she must have the love of this 'boy', and her courtly façade rapidly deteriorates. The queen demonstrates her longing for this epicene figure clearly and aggressively, kissing and embracing Silence and exposing her own body to tempt 'him'. Her efforts at seduction failing again and again, Eufeme variously accuses Silence of acting coy, of being a prostitute trying to negotiate a higher price, and of being homosexual.[25] Utterly rebuffed, Eufeme then plots revenge, fabricating evidence of attempted rape and insisting that the king put his vassal to death for treason. When Ebain balks, Eufeme enlarges the constellation of her crimes through forgery, theft and illicit appropriation of the royal seal, breaking and entering, and attempted murder by proxy.

As noted earlier, Eufeme's activities eventually come to light and she is punished horribly for them. For this reason, we might view Eufeme as exemplifying how not to conduct oneself; certainly, her actions do not merit imitation. But given the bad behaviour of practically everyone that Silence has come into contact with, it is equally possible to see the queen as merely one more negative object lesson in the romance. Yet if the moral choices of Cador and Eufemie, the lady and seneschal, the *jongleurs*, and Eufeme leave much to be desired, nowhere is the contrast between right action and personal gratification more sharply drawn than in the character of King Ebain. The literal and metaphorical embodiment of duty and justice, Ebain actually spends much of his energy satisfying his own desires, manufacturing excuses to avoid responsibility, and engaging in ethically questionable activities.[26]

Heldris's initial depiction of King Ebain is nothing short of glowing: he is second only to Arthur, a generous ruler intent on maintaining chivalry and determined to ensure peace and justice in his kingdom through law and order. Shortly after we are told of the king's many virtues, we learn that he has been at war with King Begon of Norway, and that the Norwegian people have suffered tremendously as a result. While international conflict would certainly not have been unusual for the time period – and is a frequent *topos* in romance – what is striking is that the clash between Ebain and Begon started 'over something trivial'.[27] Suddenly, Ebain appears less the good king than the petty tyrant who, insulted over a slight of some kind, goes on a rampage, laying waste to another country.[28] Only after Ebain's wise counsellors contract a marriage between their lord and Begon's daughter, Eufeme, does the war end. Significantly, Ebain's response to the offer of a political union is quite in keeping with his hasty desire to settle the score with Norway. Apparently forgetting his earlier bellicosity, he behaves like a giddy adolescent, and in an unwittingly telling statement, Ebain remarks,

> Now I have fought a good fight indeed:
> it was well worth the hard work
> if I can have this woman to wife,
> for there is no greater treasure on earth:
> I want to wed and bed her properly.
> I have suffered long for love of her.[29]

Ebain's idea of what it is to fight a good fight is hardly Pauline.[30] It is even more peculiar because, prior to this moment, we have heard nothing of Eufeme or of Ebain's burning desire for her. By the time we reach line 220 of the poem, we have already seen the king behaving less than nobly. While he may not have broken any laws or treaties, his conduct suggests that justice was not foremost in his mind either when he declared war on Norway or when he agreed to accept Eufeme as peace-weaver. That Eufeme is left to her own devices following the nuptials might also imply that once Ebain had wedded and bedded her, he lost interest. Or perhaps the bride-elect's reluctance to kiss Ebain when they first meet – 'for her heart was a little bitter | from the tiring journey across the sea'[31] – carries over into the marriage. In either case, this royal union does not appear to go much beyond a business transaction.

Ebain next re-frames justice following the episode in which two counts, having wed twin daughters, quarrel over the inheritance. Since neither is willing to negotiate or to compromise, they resort to a duel. Each is 'so severely wounded in the fight | that they both died trying to prove themselves right'.[32] Upon hearing this news, the king is enraged, for he has lost good men; however, he places blame not on the obstinate counts but on the 'two orphaned girls'[33] and swears by Saint Peter that thenceforth, women shall be barred from inheriting. Although Ebain purports to be righting a terrible wrong, his knee-jerk response is a grossly abusive exercise of royal authority. Because two males could not settle their claims reasonably and civilly, all females will suffer discriminatory treatment under the law. Like the now-deceased counts, Ebain reacts with a distinct lack of reasonableness and civility and fails to consider the impact of his actions on others – his loyal, but son-less subjects included. Ironically, the king has inscribed on each of the counts' tombs: 'Greed has robbed many a man of his freedom, | and more than that if he gets hooked – | she makes him trot until he is dead'.[34]

Ebain remains blind to the fact that his edict serves no purpose other than as a means through which to vent his anger.

If the preceding examples give us a portrait of regal power guided by self-interest and acquisitive sexual desire, others further cement that perception. While on a journey from Chester to Winchester, Ebain and his men are attacked by a dragon. Unable to defeat the fire-drake himself, and mourning the loss of thirty of his entourage, Ebain offers a handsome reward – the warrior's *guerdon* – to any knight successful in slaying the dragon: 'I will give him a county | And let him have his choice | Of any woman in the kingdom. | Let him take the one he likes best, | Except, of course, if she's already pledged'.[35] On its face, this appears a clearly worded, unambiguous oath. Embedded in the king's promise, however, is a shrewdly crafted escape clause. 'Sans calenge', as translated by Sarah Roche-Mahdi, refers exclusively to the marriageability of the prospective bride. Since one meaning of *chalengen* is 'to claim (something) as one's right, due, privilege, or property',[36] we can appreciate Ebain's clarification: the prize-winner may not simply take another man's betrothed for his own. A second definition is 'to accuse (somebody), bring charges against';[37] therefore, we might translate 'sans calenge' as 'without accusations or charges pending against', which shifts the focus: if the knight were to select a bride whose reputation were less than spotless, Ebain could renege. It is also possible that Ebain is giving himself an out with respect to the dragon-slayer. If we read 'Mais solement soit sans calenge' as modifying the entire passage, we see that should there be any dispute as to who actually killed the dragon, or should the victor be of dubious integrity, Ebain could withdraw his proffered reward. What if, for instance, a mercenary or an individual hostile to the realm killed the dragon? Surely Ebain would not wish to bestow lands and a title upon or establish a political alliance with someone deemed unworthy or dangerous. A third gloss of the infinitive – 'to object or take exception to (a person, for example, as a candidate for jury or office)'[38] – is similarly important to our reading of Ebain's hidden caveats, for the phrase 'Mais solement soit sans calenge' could actually refer to either the chosen bride or the successful warrior. That is, objections by family, members of the court, or Ebain himself could be invoked to prevent the union. The king's oath is thus less a straightforward if–then verbal contract with any valiant man bold enough to risk his life than a shaky agreement filled with loopholes and fine print.

Not surprisingly, when Cador battles the dragon and emerges seriously injured but victorious, the king is slow to act. To some extent, of course, Heldris decelerates the narrative to a snail's pace in order to develop the relationship between Cador and Eufemie as well as to underscore the exquisite pain and anxiety that accompany romantic longing.[39] Yet even after the lovers tell him of their mutual consent to marry, the king delays, assembling a council to advise him. The extended debate heightens dramatic tension and gives Ebain time to ascertain whether Cador and Eufemie are a socially acceptable match. Perhaps more significantly, the prolonged proceedings afford Ebain an opportunity to wash his hands of the matter should that become necessary: he can appear to have acted in good faith but still blame others for any negative outcome. By relying on the counsel of his nobles, Ebain also gains the advantage of seeming to be a disinterested party with respect to the distribution of wealth in England. Eufemie, as the only child of Count Renald of Cornwall, would stand to gain a substantial sum were it not for Ebain's earlier ban. In the absence of a legitimate heir, Renald's estate will revert to the crown upon his death; if Eufemie marries, all goods and chattels become the property of her husband. What better way for the king to retain control of this fortune than to accept the advice of his council and marry her to Cador, the king's own nephew? For Ebain, this is a win–win situation: he can maintain his image as the generous, thoughtful king while simultaneously satisfying his own greed.[40]

With age comes wisdom, or so we are told. As the years pass in the pages of *Silence*, however, this proves not to be the case with King Ebain. His moral compass never points true north. Indeed, Ebain's understanding of 'good' or 'right' continues to be influenced by whether he perceives some personal or political advantage to be had. When Eufeme accuses Silence of assault and attempted rape, Ebain sidesteps the matter, briefly consoling his queen and observing that boys will be boys.[41] It would be too bad, Ebain asserts, to ruin the reputation of a perfectly good vassal for one youthful indiscretion. Pressing the matter, Eufeme demands justice, arguing that Silence has committed treason and therefore deserves the death penalty. Ebain, with a measure of exasperation, finally addresses his real concern: his own reputation, and secondarily Eufeme's, would suffer. The king thus determines instead to send Silence to France, letter of introduction in hand. Nor does Ebain's penchant for expedience change after Silence has returned to England to fight against the baronial uprising. Following Merlin's revelations about Silence's true sex and Eufeme's adultery, Ebain once more turns the situation to his benefit. Instead of punishing Cador, Eufemie, and/or Silence for their disobedience, he listens carefully to Silence's history and immediately reverses the law barring female inheritance. By telling Silence 'I give you my friendship and protection',[42] Ebain effectively renders his former vassal untouchable. In essence, Ebain moves Silence into position for her later role as queen even while Eufeme still holds the title. By contrast, Ebain refuses to hear a word of defence from Eufeme or her transvestite-nun-lover, and immediately has the offenders put to death.

It may be no wonder that Ebain is drawn to Silence, for she is everything that Eufeme is not: young, beautiful, loyal, and, we might assume, capable of bearing children. Yet given the swiftness with which Ebain abandons one royal edict for another, we might pause to consider the possibility that the king – like his queen – has found Silence sexually appealing all along. Only after Silentius has proved to be Silentia is it 'safe' for Ebain to act on any latent erotic impulses. When Ebain's courtiers bless the warrior–maiden, and his most trusted advisors urge him to marry her, once again the king's focus is on himself, on his own material and carnal desires. He neatly overlooks the fact of his and Silence's consanguinity and ignores procedures required by canon law.[43] Silence remarks that 'It is by his acts that one knows who is truly king'.[44] If this is the case, what we've seen of Ebain's kingship does not inspire confidence.

The foregoing may seem a long prelude to discussion of Silence herself, but to understand who a character is, it is often helpful to understand who that character is not. By exploring the context in and out of which Silence develops, we can gain deeper appreciation for how she emerges from the moral quagmire that threatens to swallow her. A further benefit of this approach is that it allows us to see more clearly what Silence represents beyond the fictional boundaries of the narrative. Medieval romance generally

> serves as a virtual guidebook, a manual of instruction for the integration of the hidden self within the public sphere. The romance hero is precisely he who, having lived through a series of internal crises, either achieves ... a balance between personal desire and social necessity, or who ... is excluded from society altogether.[45]

On at least two occasions, Silence is referred to as 'the mirror of the world'; as such, she is the glass in which we are invited to check our reflections.[46] Both character and poem function in a way similar to other medieval literary 'mirrors' which give us images of ideal behaviours and attitudes, for '[b]y looking into such a mirror the addressee can measure him/herself against the 'ideal' in order (at least in principle) to ameliorate his/her behavior'.[47] Silence is the 'mirror of ideal female form and apogee of male chivalric prowess [that] also demonstrates the inward beauty of moral rectitude'.[48] Thus, while the particulars of characters' experiences may be their own, the lessons taught through them are intended for Heldris's readership. The paramount lesson is that we should see Silence as our exemplar and reject the models of comportment embodied by her parents, companions, and social superiors, all of whom are ruled by and fall prey to desire.

From the moment Silence is introduced, we are made aware that she is extraordinary, set apart from run-of-the-mill humanity in terms of both external and internal qualities. Created from a special mould, Silence is lovely: from her bright blonde hair to her little ears to her slender fingers to her shapely thighs to her perfectly proportioned feet and toes, Silence is

Nature's masterpiece. As Heldris informs us, 'there is absolutely nothing wrong with this girl – | except that she's too beautiful. | ... Nature will never work so well | on any mortal being again'.[49] To be sure, in fashioning Silence's beauty, Nature is fastidious. But Heldris de-emphasises the importance of the physical by drawing attention to Nature's use of only the most purified raw materials in her crafting of Silence. Nature's goal is to make a noble person, which is only possible if the clay is finely sifted, for 'this coarse matter attacks the heart right away. | ... | The body is mere sackcloth, | even if it's made from the finest clay, | and the heart made of coarse mixed with fine | isn't worth a crab-apple'.[50] Purity of heart is, ultimately, Silence's most notable feature. She can – and does – disguise her beauty so as to appear more boyish: she chops off her hair, often gets sunburned or resorts to smearing her face with berry juice, covers her feminine contours with male clothing, and, no doubt, re-shapes her body through the exercise required for knightly endeavours. What she cannot hide, from herself or from readers, is a conscience that refuses to allow her to behave badly. This is not to say that Silence appears to us in holy illumination; Heldris's protagonist is not on the verge of sainthood, nor is she superhumanly good.[51] Over the course of the romance, Silence manifests a broad range of emotions, from happiness to anger to hope to confusion, and she is certainly motivated by survival instinct more than once.

During battle against the rebel barons, Silence gets caught up in the bloodlust and behaves every bit an Achilles to Hector or an Odysseus vis-à-vis the suitors:

> Silence didn't feel like fooling around,
> he didn't want to stop fighting;
> he kept slicing off enemy legs and feet and fists.
> The French came and helped him.
> There was not one who failed to respond
> to his cry of 'Montjoie!':
> the enemy fled; the French pursued.
> God was on Silence's side, as you can plainly see,
> for he won the war.[52]

Nevertheless, in contrast to the other characters populating the narrative landscape, Silence consistently puts a premium on morality, elevating proper action over personal desire. Even in his description of Silence's frenzy, Heldris is quick to point out that God is on the side of our heroine and thus her rage is appropriately – even righteously – directed. The arming scene just prior to battle confirms this through images reminiscent of Paul's in his letter to the Ephesians: Silence is dressed in a tunic of padded silk, followed by a light, flawless hauberk, leggings, and hood of fine mesh. On her head is laced a helmet: 'There wasn't another like it anywhere. | It was covered with precious stones and a golden circlet | that were worth a fortune. | ... | The nose-piece held a deep-red ruby'.[53] At her side is girt a good sword. On her feet are fastened spurs crafted of beautiful gold. After mounting her war-horse without having to grip the saddle-bow, Silence, 'as an experienced leader',[54] addresses the thirty Frenchmen in her company:

> Lords, you have consented
> to follow me to this land.
> Now I should like to urge you
> to conduct yourselves in such a way
> that none may accuse us
> of arrogance, excess, or folly
> unless they do it out of sheer envy.
> I am pledged to you and you to me.[55]

Instead of goading her men to violent slaughter, Silence encourages them to fight honourably – with justice, moderation, and reason.

Silence's inherent goodness comes to the fore early in Heldris's recounting of her history. As a child, Silence is an excellent student, easily learning her letters as well as practical skills like hunting and riding. But she takes equally to tougher knowledges: she is schooled to be respectful, humble, obedient, loyal, kind, generous, and honourable. Heldris writes, 'The child was not ungrateful; | he was very glad of such learning – | that was the effect of his good nature. | The child's innate qualities were such | that he taught himself'.[56] And when given good advice and urged to be good, 'He was receptive to their teaching | and heeded their admonitions well. | ... | His heart itself schooled him | to eschew foolish behavior'.[57] Regardless of their motives for keeping Silence hidden away in the forest, the lady, seneschal, Cador, and Eufemie are effective teachers. They strengthen the naturally solid moral foundation upon which Silence will stand throughout her adventures, even when minor cracks appear.

During her twelfth year, Silence experiences her first crisis of conscience, represented via a debate among Nature, Nurture, and Reason.[58] Having bested her male peers to the point that 'none was his master any more. | ... | Silence was deeply disturbed about this, | for her conscience told her | that she was practicing deception by doing this'.[59] Scolding Silence for ruining her feminine beauty, running around like a savage, and tricking women into falling in love with her, Nature demands that Silence abandon her masculine ways. Nurture then asserts that her claim on the 'boy' is firmer since she has already undone Nature's work. When Reason steps in, she first warns Silence that giving up the only identity she has ever known would be tantamount to suicide. Reason then reminds Silence of what is at stake: should anyone discover her birth sex, Silence would lose her chance to train for knighthood and her rightful inheritance. Most importantly, though, Silence realises on her own that betraying the secret would prove her father a liar; it is this fact, not merely the fear of losing male prerogative, that convinces her to remain a 'boy'. For Silence, obedience to her father's – and mother's – wishes, and ensuring their continued safety must take precedence over everything else, Nature included.

As the plot of the romance continues to unfold, we see that it is Silence's commitment to moral behaviour that sustains her. When our heroine decides to run away with the *jongleurs*, she does so out of a sense of social obligation: should she prove 'slow at chivalry',[60] she would have no useful employment. Should King Ebain die and women become eligible to inherit again, Silence would be deficient in the skills necessary to run a household. While in service to the musicians, Silence performs her duties with care and courtesy, demonstrating respect for her tutors as well as taking every opportunity to learn. And even when the *jongleurs* prove to be full of malice and envy, she does not respond in kind. Instead, she shames them into remorse by reminding them of the Golden Rule. Similarly, when Queen Eufeme shows her true colours, Silence remains unflaggingly loyal and deferential; never is she intent upon getting revenge, though one could hardly blame her if she were. The same holds true when Silence learns that her king is in danger. Although she has become a renowned knight in France, she does not hesitate to leave that behind and go to the aid of her lord – a lord who has not shown her the same level of fidelity or love. Finally, at the close of the romance, it is out of a sense of responsibility to her parents that Silence relates the tale of her upbringing and strange adolescence: her aim is not to defend herself for having engaged in a masquerade, but to ensure that Ebain knows why her parents chose to defy the law.

Feminist readers of the *Roman de Silence* have found the conclusion to the poem troubling. When Silence is stripped of her masculine attire, dressed in queenly garb, and taken to wife by her great-uncle, King Ebain, she is simultaneously stripped of her male identity and the freedom that she enjoyed as a boy. Her days as a fierce knight are over; we fear that she will be truly silenced, her armour relegated to some dusty closet. This seems all the more likely because 'After Nature I had recovered her rights, I she spent the next three days refinishing I Silence's entire body, removing every trace I of anything that being a man had left there'.[61] Yet, Silence has run away before, first to preserve her sense of self and later to save her own life. Why, then, does she not seek escape now? Perhaps she stays because she has been defeated, by Nature as well as by a patriarchal system that would have her lovely, obedient, and voiceless. But equally possible is that Silence realises that in a very real sense she has won. She has proved her physical, emotional, and moral mettle, and as queen, she will have more power, more influence than she had as a knight. As Silentius, she was in constant fear of discovery; as Silentia, she can exercise the kind of royal prerogative that might keep Ebain in check and might improve circumstances for women throughout the kingdom. If she has always been aggressive – not merely assertive – in doing the right thing, why should we imagine that she would suddenly reverse direction? Even if during the Middle Ages women were taught to abjure traditionally masculine behaviours, including adopting leadership roles and engaging in battle, history demonstrates that at times such action was deemed not only necessary but admirable.[62] Before she is made queen, Silence is fully capable of determining when conditions are right for her to be Silentia and when to be Silentius. It is difficult to imagine her retreating to a serene domesticity merely because her personal circumstance has changed.

In the end, the *Roman de Silence* has much to tell us about right living, about appropriate sexual and gendered behaviour, about morality itself. As we have seen, alongside instances of physical conflict and combat there are numerous examples of invisible warfare throughout the poem. At some point, every character – major or minor – must decide whether to allow ethical behaviour or greedy, sometimes lust-driven, self-interest to prevail. Where we would expect to find exemplars of rectitude, however, we encounter very few. Those granted the most authority are precisely the ones who exercise it most poorly, proving themselves incapable of rendering good decisions; most often, we find them resorting to expedience or succumbing to their own egocentric desires.

Through the character of Silence, Heldris encourages us to seek a different pattern of action. Rather than embrace appetite or desire, we should weigh our choices carefully, act with purity of intention, and prefer reason to either the pull of nature or the conditioning of nurture. This does not mean that the cultivation of virtue should be construed as a passive exercise. Were that the case, Silence's adventure might well have ended before it could begin, with Silence heeding Nature's warning and heading off to learn sewing. On the contrary, throughout the romance Silence examines her situation thoughtfully and plans accordingly, adopting a strategy that mediates between blind obeisance and equally blind desire. When the occasion demands, she is unafraid to be assertive, transgressive, aggressive, or all three. At the close of the poem, Silence's chainmail, jewelled helmet, and sword may be hidden away, but her moral armour remains. As queen, Silence will be able to show women how to reclaim their 'masculinity' despite the strictures of a socially constructed notion of 'femininity'. For Heldris, and for his readers, it is not merely that Silence fought, but that she continues to fight a good fight and will do so until she finishes the course, regardless of others' imperfections, failings, and inability to rule themselves.

Notes

1. All textual quotations are from the facing-page translation, Heldris de Cornuälle *Silence: A Thirteenth-Century French Romance*, ed. and trans. Sarah Roche-Mahdi (East Lansing, MI: Colleagues Press, 1992).
2. Nothing more is known about the poet. For the purposes of this essay, I will not distinguish between 'Master Heldris' and the 'narrator' as some critics have. Sources and analogues of the romance are discussed in Heldris, *Silence*, xii–xvii and Michèle Perret, 'Travesties et transsexuelles: Yde, Silence, Grisandole, Blanchandine', *Romance Notes* 25 (1985): 328–340.
3. An exception might be the King of France who, intuiting the goodness and nobility of Silence, refuses to execute her at Ebain's alleged direction. Since the *lettre de cachet* has been forged by Eufeme, the king's perspicacity is especially fortunate.
4. See Jane Tolmie, 'Silence in the Sewing Chamber: *Le Roman de Silence*', *French Studies* 63.1 (2009): 14–26. Whereas I read the poem as offering a series of branching choices, Tolmie argues compellingly that the romance invites us 'to investigate the collapse of binary systems' and conflates images 'of a woman's life with images of death and captivity', 14.
5. For a discussion of didactic messages within the romance, see Suzanne Kocher, 'Narrative Structure of the *Roman de Silence*: Lessons in Interpretation', *Romance Notes* 42 (2002): 349–358.
6. 'Escrist ces viers trestolt a talle', l. 2; 'Uns clers poroit lonc tans aprendre | Por rime trover et por viers', ll. 14–15.
7. 'Que, quant il oënt un bon conte, | Ne sevent preu a quoi il monte', ll. 7–8.
8. 'par gent | Qui proisent mains honor d'argent, | N'a gent qui tolt voellent oïr | Que si n'ont soing c'om puist joïr', ll. 10–13.
9. 'Avere gent, honi et las', l. 31; 'enbevré en Avarisse', l. 39.
10. 'Ainz que jo m'uevre vus conmence, | M'estuet un petit que jo tence | Por moi deduire en bien penser, | Car jo me voel tost desivrer, | Que quant venra al conte dire | N'ait en moi rien qui m'uevre enpire', ll. 77–82.
11. 'Ebans fu ja rois d'Engletiere', l. 107.
12. The spelling of the king's name – anglicised to Evan by Roche-Mahdi – varies within the text, from Ebans to Ebains to Ebain. For consistency, I have adopted the third spelling throughout this essay.
13. Significantly, this is the point at which Euphemie adopts a traditional gender role, yielding to her husband's judgement in matters of import.
14. Much has been written about gender 'slippage' in the romance, including the way in which Heldris refers to Silence with both masculine and feminine pronouns. See, for example, Kate Mason Cooper, 'Elle and L: Sexualized Textuality in *Le Roman de Silence*', *Romance Notes* 25 (1985): 341–360; Simon Gaunt, 'The Significance of Silence', *Paragraph* 13.2 (1990): 202–216; Edward J. Gallagher, 'The Modernity of *Le Roman de Silence*', *University of Dayton Review* 21.3 (1992): 31–42; Peggy McCracken, '"The Boy Who Was a Girl": Reading Gender in the *Roman de Silence*', *Romanic Review* 85.4 (1994): 517–536; Kathleen M. Blumreich, 'Lesbian Desire in the Old French *Roman de Silence*', *Arthuriana* 7.2

(1997): 47–62; Elizabeth A. Waters, 'The Third Path: Alternative Sex, Alternative Gender in *Le Roman de Silence*', *Arthuriana* 7.2 (1997): 35–46; Emma Campbell, 'Translating Gender in Thirteenth-Century French Cross-Dressing Narratives: *La Vie de Sainte Euphrosine* and *Le Roman de Silence*', *Journal of Medieval and Early Modern Studies* 49.2 (2019): 233–264.

15 Ironically, when Cador later believes that Silence has been abducted, he banishes minstrels from his land, on pain of death.

16 'Cesti ferons desvaleter. | Nus ne nos en pora reter | De traïson, de felonie, | De malvaistié, de vilonie', ll. 2046–2050.

17 See lines 2175–2200. Since the seneschal builds what is tantamount to a fortress in the woods and the lady has to lie about why she is living there, we have greater reason to suspect their motives. It is also worth noting that once Silence has gone missing, her caregivers are greatly distressed, though less for her absence than for fear of what their lax security might cost them.

18 'est de tel doctrine | Qu'il entent bien qu'il est mescine, | Ses pere l'a mis a raison, | Se li demostre l'oquoison | Por que on le coile si et cuevre', ll. 2439–2443.

19 'Bials dols ciers fils, n'est pas por nos | Cho que faisons, ainz est por vos … Si chier come l'onor avés, | Si vos covrés viers tolte gent', ll. 2453–54, 2456–2457.

20 A brief overview of the relationship between Cador and Silence appears in Catherine White, 'Not So Dutiful Daughters: Women and Their Fathers in Three French Medieval Works: *Le Roman de Silence*, *Erec et Enide* and *Le Livre de la cité des dames*', *Cincinnati Romance Review* 18 (1999): 189–198.

21 Silence chooses this alias, Malduit, 'Car il se tient moult por mal duit, | Moult mal apris lonc sa nature. | Et sil refait par coverture' ('because he thought himself very badly brought up, | very badly educated with regard to his nature, | and also to conceal his identity'), ll. 3178–3180. Discussion of Silence's re-naming and the importance of 'jonglerie' in the poem can be found in R. Howard Bloch, 'Silence and Holes: The *Roman de Silence* and the Art of the Trouvère', *Yale French Studies* 70 (1986): 81–99; Cooper, 'Elle and L', 341–360; Gallagher, 'Modernity', 31–42; Perret "Travesties et transsexuelles', 328–340; and Loren Ringer, 'Exchange, Identity and Transvestism in *Le Roman de Silence*', *Dalhousie French Studies* 28 (1994): 3–13.

22 'Car tels fais n'a soig c'on le voie', l. 3402.

23 On more than one occasion, Heldris suggests that the minstrels have been incited to evil by the devil. This is doubly ironic since the pair are wont to swear by various saints and often call on God for blessings and protection. As we see later, Eufeme similarly asks for divine aid both when she is lusting after and when she is seeking to destroy Silence.

24 Eufeme's function as a direct contrast to Eufemie is fairly obvious. The latter is depicted as noble, good, compassionate, and faithful to her husband; she is also a trained physician with a talent for healing others. Eufeme, on the other hand, is of royal lineage, but she is wicked, spiteful, and unfaithful to Ebain. Eufeme is also more intent on destruction than on conservation or creation. Scholarly appraisals of the poem's female characters abound. See, for instance, Kathleen J. Brahney, 'When Silence was Golden: Female Personae in the *Roman de Silence*', in *The Spirit of the Court: Selected Proceedings of the Fourth Congress of the*

International Courtly Literature Society, ed. Glyn S. Burgess and Robert A. Taylor (Woodbridge: Boydell & Brewer, 1985), 52–61; Heather Lloyd, 'The Triumph of Pragmatism – Reward and Punishment in *Le Roman de Silence*', in *Rewards and Punishments in Arthurian Romance and Lyric Poetry of Mediaeval France: Essays Presented to Kevin Varty on the Occasion of his Sixtieth Birthday*, ed. Peter W. Davies and Angus J. Kennedy (Woodbridge: D.S. Brewer, 1987), 77–88; Sharon Kinoshita, 'Male-Order Brides: Marriage, Patriarchy, and Monarchy in *Le Roman de Silence*', *Arthuriana* 12.1 (2002): 64–75; Kristin Burr, 'A Question of Honor: Eufeme's Transgressions in *Le Roman de Silence*', *Medieval Feminist Forum* 38 (2004): 28–37; Katie Keene, '"Cherchez Eufeme": The Evil Queen in *Le Roman de Silence*', *Arthuriana* 14.3 (2004): 3–22.

25 Cf. Guenevere's similar accusation against the hero in Marie de France's *Lanval*.
26 Portions of the argument below are taken from my unpublished paper: Kathleen M. Blumreich, '"Sans calenge": Legal Technicalities in the *Roman de Silence*', delivered at a meeting of the International Courtly Literature Society, Vancouver, British Columbia, July 1998.
27 'par petite oquoison', l. 149.
28 Interestingly, Heldris alludes to Ebain's hot temper when he says that lawbreakers, whether right or wrong, would not get out of prison alive. See Heldris, *Silence*, ll. 115–118.
29 'Or ai ge moult bien guerriié / Et bien mon traval emploié / Se jo a feme puis avoir; / Il n'a el mont si chier avoir, / Que jo tant aim et tant desir / Par us d'eglise od li gesir. / Piece a l'amors de li me poinst', ll. 179–185.
30 Cf. Ephesians 6:11–17; II Timothy 4:6–7.
31 'Car son cuer ot un poi amer / De la lasté et de la mer', ll. 245–246.
32 'En la bataille si blecié / Qu'il en sunt mort par lor verté', ll. 302–303.
33 '.ii. orphenes pucieles', l. 310.
34 '... Par covoitise / Tolt a maint home sa francise, / Et plus avoec – quant s'i amort / Troter le fait jusque a la mort', ll. 329–332.
35 'Jo li donroie une conté: / Et feme li lairai coisir / En mon roiame par loisir. / Ki miols li plaira, celi prengne, / Mais solement soit sans calenge', ll. 382–386.
36 John A. Alford, *Piers Plowman: A Glossary of Legal Diction* (Woodbridge: D.S. Brewer, 1988), 23.
37 Alford, *Piers Plowman*, 23.
38 Alford, *Piers Plowman*, 24.
39 Like Tristan and Isolde, Cador and Eufemie privately agree that exile together would be preferable to the agony of separation. See Heldris, *Silence*, ll.1345–1389. For discussion of the ways in which the *bos* offers freedom from the patriarchal constraints of life at court, see Jessica Barr, 'The Idea of the Wilderness: Gender and Resistance in *Le Roman de Silence*', *Arthuriana* 3.1 (2020): 3–25. See also Miranda Griffin, 'Figures in the Landscape: Encounters and Entanglements in the Medieval Wilderness', *Journal of Medieval and Early Modern Studies* 49.3 (2019): 501–520.
40 Ebain's penchant for land- and power-grabbing has been discussed by numerous critics. See, for instance, Sharon Kinoshita, 'Heldris de Cornuälle's *Roman de*

Silence and the Feudal Politics of Lineage', *PMLA* 110.3 (1995): 397–409; Kinoshita, 'Male-Order Brides', 64–75; Craig A. Berry, 'What Silence Desires: Female Inheritance and the Romance of Property in the *Roman de Silence*', in *Translating Desire in Medieval and Early Modern Literature*, ed. Craig A. Berry and Heather Richardson Hayton (Tempe: Arizona Center for Medieval and Renaissance Studies, 2005), 217–34; Erika E. Hess, 'Inheritance Law and Gender Identity in the *Roman de Silence*', in *Law and Sovereignty in the Middle Ages and the Renaissance*, ed. Robert S. Sturges (Turnhout: Brepols, 2011), 217–235.

41 See Brahney, 'When Silence was Golden', 59.
42 'Amer te voel et manaidier', l. 6639.
43 See Christopher Callahan, 'Canon Law, Primogeniture, and the Marriage of Ebain and Silence', *Romance Quarterly* 49.1 (2002): 12–21. We might also recall that Ebain's trusted advisors have not proved very trustworthy: among those urging the union between Cador and Eufemie was the count of Chester, one of the rebel leaders.
44 'al fait pert quels est li sire', l. 6646.
45 R. Howard Bloch, *Etymologies and Genealogies: A Literary Anthropology of the French Middle Ages* (Chicago: University of Chicago Press, 1983), 226; quoted in Heldris, *Silence*, ed. and trans. Roche-Mahdi, xxiii.
46 See ll. 3061–3065 and 3115–3116.
47 Kathy M. Krause, '"Li Mireor du Monde": Specularity in the *Roman de Silence*', *Arthuriana* 12.1 (2002): 85–91, 86.
48 Krause, '"Li Mireor du Monde"', 89.
49 'En li n'a nïent a blasmer | Fors solement qu'ele est trop biele. | ... | Ainc n'ovra mais si bien Nature | A rien ki morir doive vivre', ll. 1950–1951, 1956–1957. Heldris devotes more than 150 lines to Nature's artistry in the creation of Silence.
50 'Cil gros se trait al cuer en oire. | ... | Li cors n'est mais fors sarpelliere, | Encor soit de la terre chiere; | Mais li cuers ne valt une alie | K'est fais de grosse et de delie', ll. 1839, 1845–1848. See also Heldris, *Silence, ed. and trans.* Roche-Mahdi, xix.
51 Apparently, Silence's only blemish is a cruciform birthmark on her right shoulder, ll. 3647–3648. The symbolism here is understated, but nevertheless important. The cross appears on the right side of her body – as opposed to the left, or 'sinister' side; moreover, it literally marks her as a Christian in need of God's grace, protection, and guidance. It also underscores her role as a Christian warrior.
52 'Silences n'a soig de juër: | Ne violt pas le guerre atriuër, | Cui colpe jambe, u piet, u puig. | Li Franchois vienent al besoig; | A "Monjoie!" que il escrie | N'i a un seul qui se detrie, | Cil de fuïr, cil del cacier. | Savoir poés que Dex l'a cier, | Silence, ki le guerre fine', ll. 5639–5647.
53 'N'en a si bon en nul roialme. | Pieres i a et cercle d'or | Ki valent bien tolt un tressor. | ... | El nasal a un escarboncle', ll. 5336–5360. Perhaps it is not pushing the matter too far to suggest that the 'cercle d'or' is intended to call to

mind a halo. The function and significance of the arming *topos* in the poem is discussed by Lorraine Koschanske Stock, '"Arms and the (Wo)man" in Medieval Romance: The Gendered Arming of Female Warriors in the *Roman d'Enéas* and Heldris's *Roman de Silence*', *Arthuriana* 5.4 (1995): 56–83.

54 'com senés', l. 5375.
55 'Segnor, jo vos ai amenés | Par vos mercis en ceste tiere. | Or si vos voel jo moult requierre | Que vos soiés ensi par vos | Que nus ne puist dire de nos | Orguel, oltrage, ne folie, | Se il nel dist par droite envie. | Jo sui a vos et vos a mi', ll. 5376–83.
56 'Li enfes pas ne la desdegne, | Ainz est moult liés de l'apresure | Car cho li fait bone nature. | Li enfes est de tel orine | Que il meïsmes se doctrine', ll. 2382–2386.
57 'Il est de tel entendement | Qu'il croit bien lor castiement. | ... | Ses cuers meïsmes bien l'escole | Al deguerpir maniere fole', ll. 2467–2468, 2489–2490.
58 If Reason here is the equivalent of the medieval 'ratio', the character allegorises the God-given faculty through which human beings discern right from wrong.
59 'N'i a un seul de lui plus maistre. | ... | Silences forment s'enasprist, | Car ses corages li aprist | Ke si fesist par couverture', ll. 2493, 2497–2599.
60 'lens ... en chevalerie', l. 2863.
61 'D'illuec al tierc jor que Nature | Ot recovree sa droiture | Si prist Nature a repolir | Par tolt le cors et a tolir | Tolt quanque ot sor le cors de malle', ll. 6669–6673.
62 See, for instance, Megan McLaughlin, 'The Woman Warrior: Gender, Warfare and Society in Medieval Europe', *Women's Studies* 17 (1990) 193–209; Katrin E. Sjursen, 'Weathering Thirteenth-Century Warfare: The Case of Blanche of Navarre', *Haskins Society Journal* 25 (2013): 205–222; V.S. Sergeeva, 'The Feminine and the Masculine in *Roman de Silence*', *Studia Litterarum* 3.4 (2018): 116–139 (in Russian).

Bibliography

Primary sources

Heldris de Cornuälle. *Silence: A Thirteenth-Century French Romance*, ed. and trans. Sarah Roche-Mahdi. East Lansing MI: Colleagues Press, 1992.

Secondary sources

Alford, John A. *Piers Plowman: A Glossary of Legal Diction*. Woodbridge: D.S. Brewer, 1988.
Barr, Jessica. 'The Idea of the Wilderness: Gender and Resistance in *Le Roman de Silence*'. *Arthuriana* 3.1 (2020): 3–25.
Berry, Craig A. 'What Silence Desires: Female Inheritance and the Romance of Property in the *Roman de Silence*'. In *Translating Desire in Medieval and Early*

Modern Literature, ed. Craig A. Berry and Heather Richardson Hayton, 217–234. Tempe AZ: Arizona Center for Medieval and Renaissance Studies, 2005.

Bloch, R. Howard. *Etymologies and Genealogies: A Literary Anthropology of the French Middle Ages*. Chicago: University of Chicago Press, 1983.

Bloch, R. Howard. 'Silence and Holes: The *Roman de Silence* and the Art of the Trouvère'. *Yale French Studies* 70 (1986): 81–99.

Blumreich, Kathleen M. 'Lesbian Desire in the Old French *Roman de Silence*'. *Arthuriana* 7.2 (1997): 47–62.

Blumreich, Kathleen M. "*Sans calenge*': Legal Technicalities in the *Roman de Silence*.' Unpublished paper, delivered at a meeting of the International Courtly Literature Society, Vancouver, British Columbia, July 1998.

Brahney, Kathleen J. 'When Silence was Golden: Female Personae in the *Roman de Silence*'. In *The Spirit of the Court: Selected Proceedings of the Fourth Congress of the International Courtly Literature Society*, ed. Glyn S. Burgess and Robert A. Taylor, 52–61. Woodbridge: Boydell and Brewer, 1985, 52–61.

Burr, Kristin. 'A Question of Honor: Eufeme's Transgressions in *Le Roman de Silence*'. *Medieval Feminist Forum* 38 (2004): 28–37.

Callahan, Christopher. 'Canon Law, Primogeniture, and the Marriage of Ebain and Silence'. *Romance Quarterly* 49.1 (2002): 12–21.

Campbell, Emma. 'Translating Gender in Thirteenth-Century French Cross-Dressing Narratives: *La Vie de Sainte Euphosine* and *Le Roman de Silence*'. *Journal of Medieval and Early Modern Studies* 49.2 (2019): 233–264.

Cooper, Kate Mason. 'Elle and L: Sexualized Textuality in *Le Roman de Silence*'. *Romance Notes* 25 (1985): 341–360.

Gallagher, Edward J. 'The Modernity of *Le Roman de Silence*'. *University of Dayton Review* 21.3 (1992): 31–42.

Gaunt, Simon. 'The Significance of Silence'. *Paragraph* 13.2 (1990): 202–216.

Gilmore, Gloria Thomas. '*Le Roman de Silence*: Allegory in Ruin or Womb of Irony?' *Arthuriana* 7.2 (1997): 111–123.

Griffin, Miranda. 'Figures in the Landscape: Encounters and Entanglements in the Medieval Wilderness'. *Journal of Medieval and Early Modern Studies* 49.3 (2019): 501–520.

Hess, Erika E. 'Inheritance Law and Gender Identity in the *Roman de Silence*'. In *Law and Sovereignty in the Middle Ages and the Renaissance*, ed. Robert S. Sturges, 217–235. Turnhout: Brepols, 2011.

Keene, Katie. "Cherchez Eufeme': The Evil Queen in *Le Roman de Silence*'. *Arthuriana* 14.3 (2004): 3–22.

Kinoshita, Sharon. 'Heldris de Cornuälle's *Roman de Silence* and the Feudal Politics of Lineage'. *PMLA* 110.3 (1995): 397–409.

Kinoshita, Sharon. 'Male-Order Brides: Marriage, Patriarchy, and Monarchy in *Le Roman de Silence*'. *Arthuriana* 12.1 (2002): 64–75.

Kocher, Suzanne. 'Narrative Structure of the *Roman de Silence*: Lessons in Interpretation'. *Romance Notes* 42 (2002): 349–358.

Krause, Kathy M. "Li Mireor du Monde': Specularity in the *Roman de Silence*'. *Arthuriana* 12.1 (2002): 85–91.

Lloyd, Heather. 'The Triumph of Pragmatism – Reward and Punishment in *Le Roman de Silence*'. In *Rewards and Punishments in Arthurian Romance and Lyric Poetry of Medieval France: Essays Presented to Kevin Varty on Occasion of his Sixtieth Birthday*, ed. Peter W. Davies and Angus J. Kennedy, 77–88. Woodbridge: D.S. Brewer, 1987.

McCracken, Peggy. "The Boy Who Was a Girl': Reading Gender in the *Roman de Silence*'. *Romanic Review* 85.4 (1994): 517–536.

McLaughlin, Megan. 'The Woman Warrior: Gender, Warfare and Society in Medieval Europe'. *Women's Studies* 17 (1990): 193–209.

Perret, Michèle. 'Travesties et transsexuelles: Yde, Silence, Grisandole, Blanchandine'. *Romance Notes* 25 (1985): 328–340.

Ringer, Loren. 'Exchange, Identity and Transvestism in *Le Roman de Silence*'. *Dalhousie French Studies* 28 (1994): 3–13.

Sergeeva, V.S. 'The Feminine and the Masculine in *Roman de Silence*'. *Studia Litterarum* 3.4 (2018): 116–139. In Russian.

Sjursen, Katrin E. 'Weathering Thirteenth-Century Warfare: The Case of Blanche of Navarre'. *Haskins Society Journal* 25 (2014): 205–222.

Stock, Lorraine Koschanske. "Arms and the (Wo)man' in Medieval Romance: The Gendered Arming of Female Warriors in the *Roman d'Enéas* and Heldris's *Roman de Silence*'. *Arthuriana* 5.4 (1995): 56–83.

Tolmie, Jane. 'Silence in the Sewing Chamber: *Le Roman de Silence*'. *French Studies* 63.1 (2009): 14–26.

Waters, Elizabeth A. 'The Third Path: Alternative Sex, Alternative Gender in *Le Roman de Silence*'. *Arthuriana* 7.2 (1997): 35–46.

White, Catherine. 'Not So Dutiful Daughters: Women and Their Fathers in Three French Medieval Works: *Le Roman de Silence, Erec et Enide* and *Le Livre de la cité des dames*'. *Cincinnati Romance Review* 18 (1999): 189–198.

7

Muslim caliphs and homosexuality: al-Amin (787–813) and al-Hakam II (915–976). Two men in pursuit of *hubb al-walad*

Fatima Rhorchi

The history of Muslim rulers is not composed solely of royal glory and conquest. There are less studied and more controversial areas that in the past most Arabic historians avoided revealing, particularly that of (homo) sexuality. By the same token, as one of its primary lacunae, medieval history more generally is also acknowledged as having a lack of conspicuous source material concerning homosexuality. Yet Arab monarchs, like rulers of other kingdoms and societies, are known to have recruited boys for pleasure. This practice was viewed as a natural consequence when rulers and the elite circles surrounding them indulged themselves, opening opportunities for elite and royal men to search for and partake in different forms of sexual gratification. Regardless of the strict prohibition of sodomy in all its forms in the religious system, including intercourse with *al-ghilmān* (slave-soldiers), its practice is testified to in the Islamic East with the Abbasids in Baghdad, persisting into the era of the Umayyads in al-Andalus.[1] Islam's stance on homosexuality is well defined in its jurisprudence, and not least in the Qur'an, with punishment varying according to the *hadiths* (reported records of what the Prophet Muhammed thought, said, and did), and recognised by each different school of jurisprudence, in Islamic history.[2]

Notwithstanding this, numerous high-ranking men, especially rulers, philosophers, scholars, and poets, are known to have taken male lovers, or to have celebrated male love in their poetry. Records from Abbasid royal courts from the classical era are typically more abundant than those from the lives of monarchs of the Umayyad Andalusian courts. As a result, there tends to be less evidence available to support claims of homosexual practices among the Umayyad courtiers than the Abbasids.[3] According to Joseph Massad, extant records of such practices nevertheless remain taboo, ignored by historians and not even mentioned in Arabic educational curricula.[4] Instead, throughout the historiography of Islamic caliphates, the focal points of historians and chroniclers were the caliphs' glories and their accomplishments rather than their ruling, and at times, complicated sexualities.

In this context, Jamal Jum'a mentions Ahmad al-Tifashi as the only scholar daring enough to excavate the history of the forbidden Arab erotic; other historians tended to overlook the intimate details of their rulers' lives, whether in fear or in shame, relegating sexuality to the unspoken side of Muslim court culture.[5] For Massad, Arabic historians and intellectuals must shoulder the blame for disregarding and failing to portray these hidden facets of their chosen caliphs' histories. Between the self-evident facts reported by Western chroniclers such as Lévi-Provençal, Crompton, and others, coupled with the blatant silence with which Arabic historians tend to deal with the caliphs, this chapter explores the portrayals of two caliphs in particular, al-Amin (r. 809–813) and al-Hakam II (r. 961–976), and how representations of their sexual orientations varied from the overtly queer for the former to covert and ambiguous for the latter. It asks how their authority and successions might have been jeopardised by *hubb al-ghulam* (love of boys).[6] The primary focus here is to examine the impact of homosexuality upon the stability of these two Muslim caliphates and shed light on the societal guidelines of both epochs to reveal some of the paradoxical realities of historical homosexuality in Islam.

hubb al-ghulam *in the Islamic caliphates*

Contrary to modern perceptions that Islam is implacably opposed to homosexuality, the history of Islamic culture provides considerable factual affirmation of a more nuanced point of view.[7] In his book *nouzhat al-albāb fīmā lā yūjadu fī kitab* (The Delight of Hearts: or What you will not find in any Book), al-Tifashi records the prevalence of new sexual patterns among members of the Islamic aristocracy as a type of sexual luxury in which they lived, the heroes of the tale being their concubines or enslaved boys (*ghilman*), or both. He presents a comprehensive survey of the hidden sexual phenomena prevalent in Islamic society until the middle of the seventh century.[8] Scholars such as Crompton note that popular attitudes in Islam concerning homosexuality appeared less hostile than was the case in Christendom. For him, Arabs, Turks, and Persians tended to find relations between men and boys, or other men, unremarkable.[9] Although the Qu'ran explicitly condemns homosexual acts, it does so without indicating specific punishments. Some traditions of the prophet (*hadith*) display tolerance of homoerotic desires, while others report the prophet to have said that both active and passive partners must be put to death. Muslim jurists themselves differed in their opinions as to the severity of the punishment, ranging from flagellation to death by stoning.[10]

Medieval historian ibn Hazm includes a chapter on sexual sins and sets forth the various penalties prescribed by religious tradition, recounting a story of Abū Bakr burning a man alive for playing a merely passive role in a homosexual act.[11] The same caliph is said to have struck and killed a man 'who had merely pressed himself against a youth until he had an orgasm'.[12] The jurist Malik praised an emir for beating a young man to death for allowing another man to embrace him similarly.[13] While admitting his heterodox stance, ibn Hazm considered such responses excessive, concluding that ten lashes might have sufficed. In the case of penetrative sodomy, he cites only Malik's opinion that parties should be stoned, omitting to share overtly what his actual point of view might be.[14] Ibn Hazm's anecdotes and his poems, from which he quotes unabashedly in his treatise, *tawq al-ḥamāmah* (The Ring of the Dove), reveal something of his own erotic sensibility.[15] He argues that lovers should keep their love secret and not divulge it, even to the beloved. Ibn Hazm mentions that a man allowed 'his harem to be violated, and exposed his family to dishonour, all for the sake of gratifying his amorous whim for a boy'.[16] Such an outcome might account for ibn Hazm amply illustrating the case for discretion in his tales of men who kept silent about the women or the men they loved. Not all Arabs were as censorious as ibn Hazm, however. We are told by the anthologist Al-Fath ibn Khāqān that ibn Bājja penned a series of lamentations on the death of 'a black slave with whom he was infatuated ... who died at Barcelona, much to his grief'.[17]

Earlier recorded Arabic medieval sexual practices were refuted and condemned by Muslim intellectuals of the nineteenth-century enlightenment, otherwise termed the awakening, *an-nahda*. In his book, *tārikh attamadun al-Islami*, Jurji Zaydan expressed his disapproval of certain sexual desires, stating that 'one of the ugliest forms of that debauchery (*tahattuk*) during this process of civilisation was the flirtation (*taghazul*) with youthful boys and their being taken as slave boys'.[18] In the palaces of the Abbasid and Umayyad caliphs, the courtly sovereigns of Baghdad and Córdoba convened their courtiers, princes, and the wealthy elite in expressly acquired 'appropriate' settings for their interactions, most of which were centred around the *majlis al-uns* (intimate salons).[19] These spaces were used as a setting where *hubb al-walad* or *al-ghulam* (the love of boys) was revealed as a trait of extravagance and luxury – an indulgence practised by the elite. Such pederastic indulgence is not reported overtly by Arabic historians but is well attested in a variety of *ādab* (courtesy literature) sources, including prose and romance poetry – most strikingly among the poets known as *al-ghulamiyyāt* (female youths) – as well as in the narratives of judges and jurists. Poets and poetry in Arabic social history are of historiographical importance because creators and their compositions provide us with a realistic picture of what might have happened in historical caliphate courts, allowing us the opportunity to examine the intricacies of all the various contexts of their existence in considerable detail.[20] For example, Thomas Bauer quotes this:

> 'ruhifida'u'idharin halla wajnata man fāq al-kawākiba shamsan thumma aqmāra' (I would give everything for the sprouting beard that settled on the cheeks of one who – being a sun – is superior to stars and even moons).[21]

In Arabic literature, young boys are presented in many forms, and serve various literary purposes. They are often associated with other archetypes such as the beardless (al-murd) or the cupbearer (al-Sāqi). In the Eastern Islamic medieval world, a Sufi meditation that survived in practice until recently, after centuries of condemnation by theologians, was the contemplation of beardless boys by the Sufi mystics, known as nazar ila'lmurd. Meditations such as this were considered haram (forbidden) by Islam. During the Abbasid era, those charged with electing al-ghilman to the Abbasid caliphs, whether from acquisition or captivity, chose the best of them and handed them over to the caliphs' chamberlains where they were included among their inner entourages. Some were freed and would be known as 'atiiq (liberated), coupled with the name of their previous master, 'atiiq fulān, that is 'freed by so and so'.[22] It seems that this practice was common in diverse Muslim dynasties. The Fatimids also took care of raising boys, and it seems that sultans followed the same approach, adding what they saw as appropriate for their era in raising their slave boys.[23] According to Robinson, these androgynous fityān (boys) were depicted as 'gifted with night vision and deadly glances, bearers of the sweet agonies of lovesickness'.[24]

In addition to their mien, the age of these boys also mattered. Khaled al-Rouauheb notes that it is not a straightforward affair to determine the age at which a male youth was sexually attractive to adult men. The relevant terms, such as al-murd or ghulam, tend to be impressionistic and somewhat loosely employed in the sources. For example, the term murd (beardless boy) could be used to refer to prepubescent, completely smooth-cheeked boys, as opposed to adolescent, downy-cheeked youths, but it could also refer to all youths who did not yet have a fully developed beard.[25] So, infatuation and passionate love was metaphorically expressed by the elite towards those of lithesome figure and sweet smile and from those who were in their teens (awlad al-'ashr). During Sayf al-Dawla's reign (r. 945–967), with many courtiers themselves the authors of poems using metaphors likening boys' lips to myrtles, and their slim waists to banyan trees.[26]

al-Amin and the penchant for eunuchs

The Abbasid Caliphate was the third caliphate to succeed the Prophet Mohammed. As kinsmen to the Prophet, through the line of his uncle al-'Abbas ibn Abd al-Muttaleb (566–653), they held messianic titles that pointed to their spiritual gifts as imams, emphasising their distinct historical role in guiding the mission of government – one totally out of keeping with any non-heteronormative orientation. Titles such as *al-Mansur* (the victorious), *al-Mahdi* (the guided by God), *al-Hādi* (the guide), *al-Rashid* (the upright), *al-Amin* (the trustworthy), and *al-Ma'mun* (the trusted) were varying expressions of their claims to a divine right to rule.[27]

The Abbasid caliphate witnessed its golden age during the reign of Harun al-Rashid (r. 786–809) who had three sons, Mohammed (*al-Amin*), Abdullah (*al-Ma'mun*), and al-Qassim. Mohammed, the future al-Amin, was born in April 787 to Harun al-Rashid and Zubaida, who was herself descended from the second Abbasid caliph, al-Mansur (r. 754–775).[28] The favourite of Harun al-Rashid, she was a royal Hashemite Arab who wielded enormous influence within the Abbasid court. Consequently, al-Amin's pure Abbasid lineage gave him seniority over his elder half-brother.[29] A royal prince born of a royal Arab mother was a rarity in early Islam. In 791–792, al-Amin was five years old when he was designated heir to his father's throne, al-Ma'mun having been passed over due to al-Amin's superior lineage. Expressing his concerns about the adult al-Amin's homosexuality, the caliph Harun disclosed his predicament to his *wazir* (advisor) Yahya, stating that he was more inclined to grant the succession to al-Ma'mun whose common sense and insight into the management of the caliphate were reassuring, rather than al-Amin whose conduct was daunting and unpredictable.[30]

Despite his misgivings, he conceded that the Hashemites favoured al-Amin, even though al-Amin was captive to his non-heteronormative passions and whims as well as being much given to the influence of slave boys in his affairs, with Harun pleading: 'Should I incline to Abdallah, I will displease the Hashemites; and should I leave Mohammed as my sole heir, I fear he will cause disturbances in the state'.[31] According to Abbott, Zubaida was to blame for the lack of self-discipline and weakness in her only son.[32] After Harun's death, al-Amin, the new caliph, 'assigned the burden of government to his *wazir*', losing no time in giving in to his own pleasures and preferences.[33] According to Mohammed ibn Ishāq, when the caliphate devolved to al-Amin and the people of Baghdad became calm, he rose on Saturday morning, a day after allegiance had been sworn to him, and ordered the building of a *maydan* (parade ground) for polo and games with his eunuchs.[34] A Baghdad poet wrote:

> God's Amin built a parade ground,
> and turned the tract into a garden
> The gazelles in it were banyan trees
> that were brought to him in it as gazelles.[35]

What is exceptional about the case of al-Amin is that records of homosexuality exist not only from his reign as caliph, but also from his younger years in the royal court. They indicate that homosexual practices touched even the highest levels of the court during his reign.[36] Eunuchs were often the way in which the elite engaged in sodomy, as was the case with al-Amin. As a young crown prince, al-Amin had separated himself early from the company and influence of his family, both men and women, giving himself wholly over to debauched pleasure in the company of his eunuchs. He dressed some of these as girls and organised them into a group of the black-clad whom he named 'The Ravens' and another group of the white-clad who were called 'The Grasshoppers'.[37] His relationships with these eunuchs became a major scandal, first in the capital city, Baghdad, and later throughout the empire.[38] As caliph, al-Amin's obsession with eunuchs was not simply an element of his adult life. Records indicate that while al-Amin's father Harun al-Rashid was caliph, al-Amin's mother, Zubaida, had resorted to deception to 'tame' her son's predilection for eunuchs. She recruited pretty, young girls of slim stature, had their hair cut like boys, dressed them in jackets with tight belts, and had them presented to the young Amin'.[39] The fact that Zubaida felt compelled to suppress her son's homosexual tendencies at a young age implies that homosexuality was not acceptable in this royal court, even at the highest levels.

Perhaps this was for religious reasons, or perhaps instead it was a pragmatic reaction to the existential threat posed by a homosexual caliph to the continuity of the royal dynasty since al-Amin, as caliph, had abandoned his obligations not only to his family, but also to his empire.[40] He became the popular target of court poets as well as the subject of scandalous gossip throughout the empire, particularly for his infatuation with his eunuch Kauthar.[41] By acting so brazenly upon his predilection for eunuchs, al-Amin brought shame and disgrace to his court and his caliphate through the scorn and gossip it generated. Once sodomy had breached the highest levels of his court it was no longer tolerated by his people and was instead the subject of ridicule by all levels of society. Any weakening of a caliph's power, whether actual or merely perceived due to the growth of criticism, eventually jeopardised his caliphate's stability. In general, a caliph was responsible for perpetuating the glory and honour of his realm. As an *amir al-mu'minin* (prince of the believers), in the name of God, a caliph advocated for the protection of the *umma* (Muslim community). He was expected to display exemplary and irreproachable behaviour rather than attract the condemnation and ridicule of others, specifically within his society and more broadly across other societies.[42] Al-Amin's overt sexual orientation did not comply with the requirements and expectations of a commander of the faithful.

Putting all of that to one side, al-Amin's homosexuality was brushed off not only by some of his contemporaries, but also by later Arabic historians. Massad notes that Jurji Zaydan and many Arab intellectuals of the nineteenth-century Arabic Renaissance tend to dismiss the caliph's sexual desires as being of little relevance to Arabic historiography. According to Massad, Zaydan hardly mentions the infamous sexual life of the caliph al-Amin except for a cursory note that the latter had overindulged in purchasing eunuchs (*Khysyān*), spending colossal amounts of money to enjoy their constant presence in his private quarters. While deploring his inclination for 'excess' in whimsy as well as ardent love for eunuchs and his playful, quaint and fanciful behaviour, Zaydan describes al-Amin as a 'courageous' and 'muscular' young man who would wrestle with a lion and as an 'articulate' man of letters'.[43] Zaydan alludes to the poems of erotic love *ghazal* and poetry praising wine as both being manifestations of the 'vice' that prevailed in the Abbasid court, which he ascribed to its preference by al-Amin, and the *fitnah* (temptation) caused by the youthful boys he owned who pushed the poets themselves strongly towards the vice.[44]

In his novel *al-'abbāssa ukhtu al-rachid*, Zaydan meticulously describes one of the parties hosted by al-Amin at his palace before he assumed the throne. The famous poet Abu Nuwas, who wrote poems celebrating love between men, had been invited to the event. The love of boys shared by al-Amin and Abu Nuwas is obvious in the florid descriptions of their encounters. Abu Nuwas in his collected poetry (*diwan*) wrote one thousand couplets of *al-ghazal* in the masculine (*al-ghazal fi al-muthakkar*). In his poem 'I am a reprobate' he recalls:

> Abdelah blames my choice, a boy smooth as an Oryx,/ leave me alone, I said, don't blame me,/ I am committed to what you hate and until death do us part,/ did not the book of Allah instruct to prefer boys over girls?

Abu Nuwas became the drinking companion of the caliph. His verses display the joys of wine and boys.[45] The further al-Amin went down the path of debauchery and profligacy, the more his half-brother al-Ma'mun took note of these factors and made use of them in the propaganda he deployed against al-Amin.[46] The years 809–810 witnessed a growing deterioration in the relationship between the two brothers: al-Amin had the succession documents of his brothers al-Ma'mun and al-Qasim, documents that their father Harun had so ceremoniously publicised and displayed on the walls of the holy Ka'bah, brought to Baghdad, where he tore them to pieces.[47] The brothers retaliated by publicly denouncing the debaucheries of al-Amin and his favourite, the poet Abu Nuwas.[48]

Zubaida's patience is said to have been sorely tried on account of her son's private life. This is inferred from both her words and her deeds at the outbreak of the subsequent fraternal civil war in 811. She revealed her pain to al-Amin's general 'Ali ibn 'Isa, saying: 'Oh Ali! Though the commander of the believers is my own son, my pity for him has reached its limits and my cautiousness on his behalf is ended'.[49] When the news of 'Ali's beheading reached al-Amin, he was fishing in the company of his eunuch Kauthar. He pushed away the messenger and said: 'Woe to you! Leave me alone. Kauthar has hooked two fishes and I have caught none as yet'.[50] Following 'Ali's death, al-Ma'mun claimed the caliphate and declared al-Amin deposed; al-Amin reacted by confiscating al-Ma'mun's assets and holdings administered by his agent, taking al-Ma'mun's wife and two of his sons hostage.[51] As the long siege that al-Ma'mun imposed on the *Khulud* ('Eternity') palace in Baghdad hardened, al-Amin realised the hopelessness of his cause. He took refuge in his mother's quarters to await further developments, but even then he continued to fall back upon his obsessive pleasures.[52]

Eventually, faced with catastrophe, the fallen caliph offered his surrender. According to the sources, his boat capsized, and al-Amin swam ashore, where he was discovered and killed.[53] His head was cut off and displayed on a spear at the city gate. Other sources report, however, that al-Amin met his serious moments of despair with philosophic verses of his own composing:

> O Soul! must thou beware/ For where is there a refuge from fate?/ Every man, of what he feareth/and hopeth, is in peril/He who sippeth the sweets of life/ Shall one day be choked by affliction.[54]

After his death, anarchy, chaos, and vandalism took temporary hold of the city of the caliphs. And, in the aftermath of the crisis between al-Amin and his brother al-Ma'mun, the Abbasid caliphate never fully recovered. By the early 900s, the Abbasid caliphs only ruled definitively in central and southern Iraq.[55] Mohammed al-Amin's records serve to illustrate the way in which the royal court would deal with a caliph who displayed homosexual tendencies at various stages in his life, which had proved scandalous given his position as *amir al-mu'minin* (commander of the faithful). Among the poems written in derision (*al-hija'*) of him after his assassination, al-Tabbari quotes the following:

> Why should we weep for you? Why? – because of [your] raptures, Abu Musa [al-Amin], because of [your] promoting of amusement? Because of [your] omission of the five [prayers] in their times, in your eagerness for the juice of the grape? For Shanif I do not weep; as for Kauthar, the thought of his death gives me no grief. You did not know what was the measure of [God's] pleasure, nor did you know the measure of [His] wrath. You were not fit to rule, and the Arabs did not grant you obedience as ruler.[56]

Male love in al-Andalus

The history of homosexuality in al-Andalus is riddled with frustrating lacunae. Although the political and economic aspects of al-Andalus are now quite well understood by current historians, its history of homosexuality remains obscured. John Boswell, in researching homosexuals in western Europe from the beginning of the Christian era to the fourteenth century, recorded that in al-Andalus every variety of homosexual relationship was common – from prostitution to idealised love. Boswell asserts that 'erotic verse about homosexual relationships constitutes the bulk of published Hispano-Arabic poetry', a source which might help us to fill some of the lacunae on male love in this era.[57] Medieval Spain, unlike other parts of the Islamic world, offers a wide body of poetry and songs by and about members of many different social classes, and a large portion of the writings reflect the homosexual practices of the royal courts.

In al-Andalus, indulgence in homosexual pleasures was revealed by rulers openly keeping male harems. In an atmosphere of overcharged romanticism, men loved and expressed their feelings openly in fervent verse, all the while loudly protesting their chastity. Most of these homosexual affairs involved well-known rulers. For instance, caliph 'Abd ar-Rahmān III, who ruled Córdoba at its political and cultural zenith (929–961) is said to have been attracted to a young Christian hostage, who rejected the amorous intentions of the caliph, causing 'Abd ar-Rahmān to have him mercilessly executed. The young man became a hero–martyr cited in a poem by his contemporary, the tenth-century German nun Hrosvitha, who condemned Arab lust and glorified Christian chastity.[58] However, this event is not mentioned in any Arabic sources. In his memoirs, Badis, the last Zirid king of Granada, makes references to male prostitutes who charged higher fees and had a higher class of clientele than their female counterparts. Abdelwahab Bouhdiba notes that the outskirts of the cities contained several taverns, mostly frequented by homosexuals of both sexes, where many kinds of entertainment were provided to pleasure seekers without constraint or awkwardness.[59]

According to Daniel Eisenberg, homosexuality was a key symbolic issue throughout the Middle Ages in Iberia, as it was in many places until at least the nineteenth century. Evidence for this includes the behaviour of rulers, such as 'Abd ar-Rahmān III, al-Hakam II, Hisham II, and al-Mu'tamid, who openly kept boy slaves in their harems.[60] These caliphs were no more intolerantly cruel than Christian laws and many of their Christian subjects (and certainly Spain's Jews) preferred these infidel rulers to the illiberal Visigoths.[61] The *taifa* kings (*mulūk al-tawā'if*) (1031–1086) were just as given to pleasure as their predecessors, the Ummayyads.[62] And their court cultures were tolerant and hedonistic. The eleventh-century Muslim king of Seville, al-Mu'tamid (1040–1095), is recorded as having exhibited homosexual proclivities on more than one occasion. Al-Mu'tamid expressed his love for various men through poetry as well as by bestowing political power upon the men he favoured. Such was the case of his prime minister, ibn Ammar, who after a night of poetry and wine, reported that al-Mu'tamid had insisted that they sleep together on the same pillow.⁶³ Bold behaviour such as this ignited the anger of his father who sent him into exile to put an end to this relationship. Al-Mu'tamid also wrote of a cupbearer:

> They named him Sword; two other swords: his eyes! Both he and those two are ready to slay me! Would not one slaying by sword have quite sufficed? Yet by his eyebrows two further blows were dealt! I made him captive and his charming eyes in turn made me his captive: now we both are masters, both slaves! Oh Sword, be kind toward a captive of love, who asks not, as a favour, to be freed by you!⁶⁴

This poetic expression of his infatuation with his page suggests that the king feared neither condemnation by the people nor chastisement by the religious leaders for his overt statement of homosexual lust, reinforcing evidence of the prevailing hedonism of the period.⁶⁵

al-Hakam II *and* hubb al-walad

Caliph al-Hakam II (r. 961–976), also known as al-Mustansir, son of 'Abd ar-Rahmān III and Murjan, was the second Umayyad caliph of Córdoba. Historians have left us with an unflattering physical portrait of him, transcribed by Lévi-Provençal as a fragile, freckled, red-haired man with large black eyes and a saggy body.⁶⁶

Despite this, most primary sources agree in extolling the breadth of his intellectual qualities. Excellently trained by the greatest preceptors of his day, who recognised early that he was gifted, al-Hakam is portrayed as a prominent political thinker, builder, and intellectual.⁶⁷ However, most of these sources vacillate about his homosexuality. That he did not produce a suitable heir before the age of forty-six has been ascribed either by some to his being more attracted to men or by others due to him being too absorbed in his books to care for sensual pleasures. The fact that his homosexuality is reported euphemistically has left historians with an ambiguous profile of this 'scholar caliph'. By the mid-tenth century, most existing Greek and Hellenic works had been translated into Arabic by a joint committee of Arab Muslims and Iberian Mozarab Christians, a committee that al-Hakam had inaugurated for this task. He enlarged and beautifully decorated Córdoba's mosque. By 965, al-Hakam II had built the largest castle in Europe. He was devoted to books and learning, and his Muslim library exceeded some 400,000 volumes. He even sent his agents to purchase 'first edition' books from the Muslim east, such as *kitāb al-Aghāni* (Book of Songs) by Abu al-Faraj al-Isfahāni.⁶⁸ He spent hours reading and annotating manuscripts of diverse forms of religious and secular learning, including astronomy, philosophy, and *dahrīyah* writings (rejecting notions of an after-life) by ibn Hazm.⁶⁹ His annotations were collected by ibn al-'Abbar in a chapter comprising *fawā'ida jammah fi anwā'a shattā* ('lots of benefits in a variety of ways').[70] Al-Hakam won the esteem of the Christian kings to the north, and they regularly solicited his arbitration in their own disputes.[71]

Lévi-Provençal and his editor Ribera note that al-Hakam's librarian was a eunuch. They consider the appointment of one of the palace slaves to such a position to be quite normal because, from the tenth century onwards, many Andalusian slaves were entrusted with jobs that up to that point had been reserved exclusively for the Arab nobility.[72] The Andalusian chronicles pointed out that the predilection of the caliph al-Hakam II for the love of boys (*hubb al-walad*) aroused some controversy. Some imply that he was homosexual, with ibn Hayyān not hesitating to attribute the late fatherhood of al-Hakam to this inclination. One of the justifications posited is that, by the time al-Hakam came to the throne upon the death of his father 'Abd al-Rahman III in 961, he was already an old man with no issue. His lack of interest in women was known and remarked upon by his contemporaries, notably 'Isa al-Rāzi, whose text ibn Hayyān preserved for us in the seventh volume of the *Muqtabis*. Lévi-Provençal notes a 'somewhat congenital tendency towards homosexuality' among Andalusians.[73] Moreover, the caliph's predilection for men was said to be so strong that he kept a male harem.

In his youth, al-Hakam's affections seem to have been entirely homosexual. But it was requisite for the new caliph to produce an heir. The impasse, we are told, was resolved by his taking a concubine who dressed in boy's clothes and was given the masculine name of Jaa'far.[74] The concubine, Subh, might have dressed as a *ghulam* (young man), adopting a short haircut and wearing trousers like *al-ghulamiyyāt*, to make herself more attractive to the caliph, knowing his inclination for males. However, it is also possible that she did this to gain better access to his male-dominated royal court and impose her only son Hisham as successor.[75]

Was al-Hakam's homosexuality a rumour or a fact?

There is undoubtedly some truth in the allusion that Muslim chronicler Ahmed al-Maqqarī, in his *Analectes II*, makes to the 'pederasty' (*hubb al-walad*) of al-Hakam II, before his accession to the throne.[76] According to Lévi-Provençal, the phrase '*kana mimman istahwāhu hubb al-walad wa afrata fihi*', as found in al-Maqqarī's book *nafh al-Tayyib*, is a strong reference to al-Hakam's homosexuality or preference for boys. But this phrase, *hubb al-walad*, is rendered by some Arabic historians as 'parental love', referring instead to his strong love for his son Hisham and his rush in proclaiming an inexperienced child as his successor when already prostrated by illness, thereby jeopardising dynastic continuity.[77] Some historians insist on the evidence that the term *walad* means 'son', used on many occasions in

Andalusian texts to refer to an Umayyad infant, and others refer to *walad* meaning the same as *ghulam*.[78] That it is preceded by *hubb* (love) and *afrata* (exaggerated) led scholars to infer that it is an overt reference to his homosexuality as the cause of his late paternity and his difficulty in ensuring a suitable successor. Lévi-Provençal notes that ibn Hayyān, in this phrase, does not hesitate to condemn al-Hakam's actions regarding his succession, accusing him of having been carried away excessively by his love for boys, giving him no time to prepare a reliable heir and leading him to make the fatal mistake of ruling out any other adult male relative as his designated heir. This was at the expense of one of his brothers or another member of the Umayyad lineage who could have performed the imamate 'without favouritism' (*bila muhābāt*).[79] A similar criticism based on this argument is also made by ibn al-Khaṭib. Likewise, Pascual de Gayangos y Arce notes that ibn Bassām, copying ibn Hayyān, records that al-Hakam II's excessive paternal love blurred his circumspection and pushed him to appoint his son Hisham, still a child, to be his successor in preference to any of his brothers or nephews who were highly skilled and more experienced in the management of the caliphate's affairs.[80]

That al-Hakam took a concubine only after his accession to the caliphate is used as a proof of his homosexual orientation. According to al-Maqqarī, in the second volume of his *al-hawliyāt*, there is some truth regarding al-Hakam's homosexuality before he became caliph. For al-Maqqarī, this only became evident after his advent when he became concerned about having a son likely to succeed him. This led to the belief, according to the same chronicler, that the vice of homosexuality, so common in Muslim Spain across all ages, was the reason for al-Hakam II's late paternity.[81] Al-Hakam's work contains verses expressing love and lust, the most famous of which is:

> To God I complain about the merits of the affluent / unfair to me, and not from my faith I kept my dwelling away from him and his rebuff heightened /I am on my old yearning as I used to. Had I known that my longing would be so intense / I would not have divulged nor would I have withdrawn.[82]

In this context, however, proof of homoerotic lust is regarded with considerable reluctance, particularly by Muslim historians. For us, the task lies in looking to source materials that might not provide a firm answer for the entire reality but might at the very least shed some light on the case of al-Hakam II, whose books were all burned publicly by al-Manṣūr ibn Abi 'Amir because they were considered heretical. Although homoerotic poetry, between the tenth and thirteenth centuries, particularly in the genre known as *mujūn* (obscene) poetry, attests to the homosexual orientation of its owners, it is difficult to give absolute credence to the question of al-Hakam's homosexuality in a passage such as the one quoted above.

Conclusion

The lives of both Mohammed al-Amin and al-Hakam al-Mustansir reflect their eras' stance on homosexuality. In many ways, these two caliphs typify how contemporary portrayals of their lives simultaneously illustrate the process by which history is 'altered by authorial perspective and the erasure of non-heteronormative space' within the Abbasid and Umayyad caliphates.[83]

Any examination of the wide-ranging accounts of these caliphs' lives reveals the historical biases of their time and those of our current time as well. Then, as now, some historians recognise al-Amin's homosexuality in different ways and through different lenses. Some have argued that anti-al-Amin chroniclers may have engaged in historical revisionism, referring to al-Amin as 'queer' or deviant to discredit him as a caliph. The same impasse applies to al-Hakam because his homosexuality remained a remarkably obscure subject, often referred to with euphemism, sanctimony, and even denial, especially in Arabic primary sources. Thanks to al-Tifashi's major treatises on eroticism, many progressive socio-cultural attitudes towards sexualities and alternative sexual practices, largely unknown or censored in contemporary Arab and Muslim societies, have been brought out into the light. His work also challenges conventional views of Islam as a repressive religion and develops instead the sex-positive dimension of Muslim spiritual and social life. All in all, there are still remarkable gaps in this area of social history. Homosexual love has not only been little studied in this context, with very little research undertaken regarding it during the period under examination here, but also enormous amounts of Arabic primary source material have been lost to us. On the other hand, Western records regarding homosexual activity range from details of slave relationships to encounters in the highest levels of royalty and nobility, stimulating further exploration to uncover the hidden lives of Muslim caliphs and their courts.[84] The ready elimination of homosexuality from past and contemporary narratives shows the ways in which certain truths are vulnerable to obliteration just as many Arabic historians erased queer spaces and reinvented the past to accommodate their respective contemporary presents.

Notes

1 Sami Awad, *Droit musulman et modernité: diagnostiques et remèdes* (Charleston, NC: CreateSpace Independent Publishing Platform, 2014), 80.
2 Ahmad al-Tifashi (1184–1253) was a Berber poet, writer and anthologist in Arabic. He compiled a twelve-chapter anthology of Arabic poetry and jokes

about erotic and sexual practices that featured both heterosexual and homoerotic entries with a partiality towards the latter.

3. Marc Daniel, 'Arab Civilization and Male Love', trans. Winston Leyland, in *Reclaiming Sodom*, ed. Jonathan Goldberg (New York: Routledge, 1994), 60.
4. Joseph Massad, *Desiring Arabs* (Chicago: University of Chicago Press, 2007), 59. In this book, Massad tends to extend Edward Said's study of 'Orientalism' by analysing the latter's impact on Arab intellectual production. It links Orientalism to definitions of sex and desire.
5. Jamal Jum'a, *Nuzhat al-Albāb fī ma la Yūjad fi Kitab* (London: Riad al-Rayyes Books, 1992), 35.
6. When speaking of the beloved, poets in most cases used the masculine gender. In classical Arabic, it is legitimate to use the masculine form of the word for beloved, such as *mahbub* or *habib*, and for conventional metaphors like the gazelle (*ghazāl, shadin, rim, zabiy, rasha*) and the moon (*badr* or *qamar*).
7. El-Rouayheb refers to Umar Basha, who wrote several Arabic monographs on such poetry, assuming that the poets were singing the praise of their beloved women and never realised that many of the poets he discussed were interested in boys. Khaled El-Rouayheb, *Before Homosexuality in the Arab-Islamic World, 1500–1800* (Chicago: University of Chicago Press, 2009).
8. Jamal Jum'a, *Nuzhat al-Albāb*, 35.
9. Louis Crompton, 'Male Love and Islamic Law in Arab Spain', in *Islamic Homosexualities: Culture, History, and Literature*, ed. Stephen O. Murray and Will Roscoe (New York: New York University Press, 1997), 151. See https://digitalcommons.unl.edu/englishfacpubs/61 (accessed 27 November 2023).
10. Sabine Schmidtke, 'Homoeroticism and Homosexuality in Islam', *Bulletin of the School of Oriental and African Studies*, 62.2 (1999): 260–266.
11. Muhammad ibn Hazm, *The Ring of the Dove: A Treatise on the Art and Practice of Arab Love*, trans. A.J. Arburry (London: Luzac Oriental, 1953), 258–259.
12. Crompton, 'Male Love and Islamic Law', 150.
13. Crompton, 'Male Love and Islamic Law', 258–259. Abu Bakr was the founder and first caliph of the *Rashidun* Caliphate (r. 632–634).
14. Crompton, 'Male Love and Islamic Law', 149.
15. Crompton, 'Male Love and Islamic Law', 148.
16. Ibn Hazm, *The Ring of the Dove*, 244.
17. Ibn Bajja Abu Bakr, *Rasa'il ibn Bajja al-ilāhiyyah*, ed. M. Fakhry (Beirut: Dar al-Jil, 1992), 2, 66. The philosopher Ibn Bajja is better known to Latin Europe as Avempace.
18. Jurji Zaydan, *Tarikh al-Tamaddun al-Islami*, 5 vols. (Cairo: Maktabat al-Hilal, 1906), Vol. 5: 130. Al-Nahda al-adabiyyah was a nineteenth-century movement inspired by contacts with the West and renewed interest in the great classical literature.
19. Cynthia Robinson, *In Praise of Song: The making of courtly culture in al-Andalus and Provence, 1005–1134 A.D.* (Leiden: Brill, 2002), 141. The term Majlis al-Uns refers to a private place or a wine party where guests are received and entertained.

20 John Boswell, *Christianity, Social Tolerance, and Homosexuality* (Chicago: University of Chicago Press, 1980), 196. For *al-ghulamiyyāt*, see Habib Zayat, 'al-mar'a al-ghulamiya fi al-Islam', *al-Mashriq* 50 (1956): 153–192.
21 Thomas Bauer, 'Male–Male love in Classical Arabic Poetry', in *The Cambridge History of Gay and Lesbian Literature*, ed. E.L. McCallum and Mikko Tuhkanen (Cambridge: Cambridge University Press, 2014), 107.
22 The boys were rewarded if they mastered an art, then they were dispatched to the elite's households to serve. Despite opposition from clerics, the practice of sodomy has survived in Islamic countries until only recent years, according to Murray and Roscoe in their work on Islamic homosexualities.
23 Gerald R. Hawting, ed., *Muslims, Mongols and Crusaders*, an anthology of articles published in the *Bulletin of the School of Oriental and African Studies* (London: Routledge Curzon, 2005), 204.
24 Fatimids flourished from the tenth to the twelfth centuries, were of Arab origin and traced their ancestry to Mohammad's daughter Fatima.
25 Cynthia Robinson, 'Love in the time of *Fitna*: "Courtliness" and the "Pamplona" Casket', in *Revisiting al-Andalus: Perspectives on the material culture of Islamic Iberia and beyond*, ed. Glaire D. Anderson and Mariam Rosser-Owen (Leiden: Brill, 2007), 99–115.
26 Khaled El-Rouayheb, *Before Homosexuality in the Arab-Islamic World, 1500–1800* (Chicago: University of Chicago Press, 2005), 30.
27 Sayf al-Dawla (Sword of the Dynasty) was the founder of the Emirate of Aleppo, encompassing most of northern Syria and parts of the western Arab peninsula.
28 Tayeb al-Hibri, *Re-interpreting Islamic Historiography* (Cambridge: Cambridge University Press, 1999), 1.
29 Gabrieli, Francesco, 'Al-Amine', in *The Encyclopedia of Islam, Volume I*, 2nd edn (Leiden: Brill, 1960), 437–438.
30 M. Rekaya, 'al-Ma'mun', in *The Encyclopedia of Islam, Volume I*, 2nd edn (1987), 437–438.
31 Nabia Abbot, *Two Queens of Baghdad: Mother and Wife of Harun al-Rashid* (Chicago: University of Chicago Press, 1946), 172.
32 Abbot, *Two Queens*, 181.
33 Abbot, *Two Queens*, 186.
34 Mas'udi, *Akhbar al-Zaman*, Volume VI (Cairo: Matba'at Abd al-Hamid Ahmad Hanafi, 1938), 323–324. Mas'udi (d. 956) was an Arab historian, geographer, and traveller.
35 Muhammad al-Tabari, *The History of al-Tabari*, Volume 31: *The War between Brothers: The Caliphate of Muhammad al-Amin A.D. 809–813/A.H. 193–198*, trans. Michael Fishbein (Albany, NY: New York State University Press, 1992), 950–951.
36 al-Tabari, *History*, 18. See also Reubin Levy, *A Baghdad Chronicle* (Cambridge: Cambridge University Press, 1929), 79. Records have also preserved a picture of this caliph prancing around in a merry-go-round on a wooden hobby-horse in the midst of a great crowd of singers and entertainers. He also indulged in

more extravagant and novel pleasures, be it at his several palaces or on his unique river barges that sailed the river Tigris on their mission of pleasures.

37 Stefanie Lee Martin, *The Role of Homosexuality in Classical Islam* (Knoxville, TN: University of Tennessee Press, 1997), 2.
38 al-Tabari, *History*, 950–951; Ibn Athir, *al-Kāmil fi al-Tarikh*, Volume VI, ed. Omar Abd As-salam Tadmouri (Beirut: Dar Sader, 2009), 205.
39 Abbott, *Two Queens*, 210–211.
40 Walther, Wiebke, *Women in Islam* (Princeton, NJ: Markus Wiener Publishing, 1993), 173.
41 Abbott, *Two Queens*, 211.
42 al-Suyuti Jalalu al-Din, *Tā'rikh al-Khulafa'* (Beirut: Dar al-Kutub al-'ilmiyah, 1996), 119.
43 Peter C. Scales, *The Fall of the Caliphate of Córdoba: Berbers and Andalusis in conflict* (Leiden: Brill, 1994), 48.
44 Scales, *The Fall of the Caliphate*, 59.
45 Scales, *The Fall of the Caliphate*, 60. Abu Nuwas was an Abbasid poet famous for the *khamriyyāt* – 'wine songs'; they represent the works of one of the Islamic world's most controversial poets. In the words of the poems' translator, Alex Rowell, Nuwas's rhapsodies on drinking, partying and fornicating with both sexes are 'as edgy and subversive today as they must have been at the time'; *Vintage Humour: The Islamic Wine Poetry of Abu Nuwas*, ed. and trans. Alex Rowell (London: C. Hurst, 2017), where 'I am a reprobate' is on p. 96.
46 Josef W. Meri, *Medieval Islamic Civilization: An Encyclopedia*, Vol. I (London: Routledge, 2006), 10; Ibn Athir, *al-Kamil*, 378.
47 Ibn Athir, *al-Kamil*, 164–165; al-Ka'bah is the building at the centre of Islam's holy masjid al-Haram in Mecca, Saudi Arabia.
48 Abbott, *Two Queens*, 212.
49 Abbott, *Two Queens*, 213.
50 al-Tabari, *History*, 797–803; Ibn Athir, *al-Kāmil*, 169.
51 Ibn Athir, *al-Kāmil*, 169–170.
52 Mas'udi, *Akhbār al-Zaman*, 421–422.
53 Hugh Kennedy, *The Early Abbasid Caliphate; A political history* (London: Routledge, 2016), 148.
54 al-Suyuti Jalalu al-Din, *Tā'rikh al-Khulafa'*, ed. Saleh Ibrahim, 2nd edn (Beirut: Mu'assasat al-Kutub al-Thaqafiyah, 1996), 120.
55 James E. Lindsay, *Daily Life in the Medieval Islamic World* (Westport, CT: Greenwood Press, 2005), 17.
56 al-Tabari, *History*, 212. Shanif and Kauthar, mentioned in the poem, were al-Amin's favourite eunuchs.
57 Boswell, *Christianity*, 196.
58 Louis Crompton, *Homosexuality and Civilization* (Harvard, MA: Harvard University Press, 2006), 43.
59 Abdelwahab Bouhdiba, *Sexuality in Islam* (London: Routledge & Kegan Paul, 1985), 131.
60 Daniel Eisenberg, 'Homosexuality', in *Encyclopedia of Medieval Iberia*, ed. Michael Gerli (New York: Routledge, 2003), 398–399.

61 Crompton, 'Male Love and Islamic Law', 151.
62 Arie Schippers, 'The Mujun Genre by Abu Nuwas and by Ibn Quzman: A comparison', in *The Rude, the Bad, and the Bawdy: Essays in honour of Professor Geert Jan Van Gelder*, ed. Adam Talib, Marlé Hammond, and Arie Schippers (Cambridge: Gibb Memorial Trust, 2014), 80–100.
63 Heather Ecker, *Caliphs and Kings: The art and influence of Islamic Spain* (Washington DC: The Hispanic Society of America and the Arthur M. Sackler Gallery, Smithsonian Institution, 2004), 200.
64 Crompton, 'Male Love and Islamic Law', 151.
65 Richard Alois Nykl, *Hispano-Arabic Poetry and its Relations with the Old Provencal Troubadours* (Baltimore, MD: J.H. Furst Company, 1946), 143.
66 Évariste Lévi-Provençal, *Muslim Spain until the fall of the Caliphate of Córdoba, 711–1031*, trans. Emilio Garcia Gomez (Madrid: Espasa-Calpe, 1957), 126. French edn: *Histoire de l'Espagne Musulmane, Volume II* (Paris: Maisonneuve Larose, 1999), 126–127.
67 Mohamed Ibn Harith al-Khichni, *Akhbār al-fuqaha'e wa al-muhadithin* (Beirut: Dar al-Kutub al-'Ilmiyyah, 1999), 19. See also 'Ayyād Al-Qadi, *Tarteeb al-madarik wa taqreeb al-masalik, Vol. I* (Beirut: Dar al-Kutub al-'Ilmiyyah, 2013), 94.
68 al-Hakam's castle at Gormaz was 446 metres long, 89 metres wide and 1,200 metres in perimeter. Situated close to the road that goes from Aranda de Duero to Medinaceli, it was sacked in the Berber siege of Córdoba in 1100.
69 Hanna Kassis, 'A glimpse of openness in medieval society. 'Al-Hakam II of Córdoba and his non-Muslim collaborators', in *The Man of Many Devices, Who Wandered Full Many Ways. Festschrift in Honor of János M. Bak*, ed. Balázs Nagy and Marcell Sebők (Budapest: Central European University Press, 1999), 160–166.
70 Muhammad Al-Murrakushi, *Kitab al-daylwa al-takmilah li kitab al-mawsul wa al-Silah, Volume I* (Tunis: Dar al-Gharb al-Islami, 2011), 290.
71 E. Michael Gerliand, ed., *Medieval Iberia: An Encyclopedia* (London: Routledge, 2003), 77.
72 Évariste Lévi-Provençal, *Muslim Spain until the fall of the Caliphate of Córdoba, 711–1031*, trans. Emilio Garcia Gomez (Madrid: Espasa-Calpe, 1957), 126.
73 Lévi-Provençal, *Muslim Spain*, 127.
74 Crompton, *Homosexuality and Civilization*, 167.
75 D. Fairchild Ruggles, 'Mothers of a Hybrid Dynasty: Race, genealogy and acculturation in al-Andalus', *Journal of Medieval and Early Modern Studies* 34 (2004): 173. For *al- ghulamiyyāt* see M.A. AI-Bakhit, L. Bazin and S.M. Cissoko et al., eds, *History of Humanity: From the Seventh to the Sixteenth Century, Volume IV* (Paris: UNESCO, 1994), 812.
76 al-Maqqari, *Analectes sur l'histoire et la littérature des Arabes d'Espagne*, Vol. II (Amsterdam: Oriental Press, 1967), 59.
77 Ruslan Wahab and Mardyawati Y, 'Term of Child in Analysis of Languages Various by the Quran', *Journal of Research and Multidisciplinary* 4.1 (2021): 393–400, at 398.

78 Semantically the word *ghulam* means a young man or a boy who has started puberty, in the age range 14–21 years, whose lust is burning and begins to peak. That is why in Arabic *al-Ghulmah* means lust (see al-Asfhani, t.th.; 376).
79 Alejandro García-Sanjuán, 'Islamic legality and political legitimacy in the Caliphate of Córdoba: the proclamation of Hisham II (360–66 / 971–76)', *Al-Qantara* 29.1 (2008): 45–77, at 70.
80 Ibn al-Khatib, *Tārīkh Isbāniyah al-Islāmīyah, aw, Kitāb A'māl al-a'lām fī man būyi'a qabla al-iḥtilām min mulūk al-Islām*, ed. Évariste Lévi-Provençal, new ed. (Cairo: Maktabat al-Thaqafah al-Diniyah, 2004); Ahmed ibn Mohammed al-Makhari, *The History of the Mohammedan Dynasties In Spain, Volume I*, trans. Pascual de Gayangos (London: Routledge Curzon, 2002), 157.
81 Lévi-Provençal, *Muslim Spain*, 447–448.
82 'Annan M. Abdallah, *Dawlat al-Islam fi al-Andalus, Volume I* (Cairo: Maktabat al-Khanj, 1997), 513.
83 Felipe Rojas and Peter E. Thompson, eds, *Queering the Medieval Mediterranean: Transcultural Sea of Sex, Gender, Identity and Culture* (Leiden: Brill, 2021), 63.
84 Rebecca Joubin, 'The Multifarious Lives of the Sixth Abbasid Caliph Mohammad al-Amin', *International Journal of Middle East Studies* 52 (2020): 643–663.

Bibliography

Primary sources

Al-Asfahani Abu al-Faraj. *Kitāb al-Aghāni, Volume I*. Beirut: Dar Sader Publishers, 2004.

Al-Asfhani, Al Raghib, *Mu'jam Mufradat Alfaz al-Qur'an*, Beirut: Daar al-Fikr, t.th.

Al-Maqri. *Analectes sur l'histoire et la littérature des Arabes d'Espagne, Volume II*. Leiden: Brill, 1855–1859.

Al-Mas'udi. *Akhbār al-Zamān, Volume VI*. Cairo: Maṭba'at'Abd al-Hamid Ahmad Hanafī, 1938.

Al-Murrakushi, Muhammad. *Kitab al-dayl wa al-takmilah li kitab al-mawsūl wa al-Silah, Volume I*. Tunis: Dar al-Gharb al-Islami, 2011.

Al-Qadi, 'Ayyad. *Tarteeb al-madārik wa taqreeb al-masālik, Volume I*. Beirut: Dar al-Kutub al-'Ilmiyyah, 2013.

Al-Rifai'I, Ahmed Farid. *'Asr al-Ma'mun, Volume I*. Cairo: Dar al-Kutub al-Misriyah, 1927.

Al-Suyuti Jalalu al-Din. *Tā'rikh al-Khulafa'*. Beirut: Dar al-Kutub al-'ilmiyah, 1996.

Al-Tabari. *The History of al-Tabari: Ta'rikh al-Rusul wa al-Mulūk: The War Between Brothers. Volume XXXI*, ed. Ehsan Yar-Shater and trans. Michael Fishbein. Albany: State University of New York Press, 1992.

Al-Tifashi Ahmed. *Nuzhat al-Albab fi ma la Yūjad fi Kitab*, ed. Jamal Jum'a. London: Riad al-Rayyes Books, 1982.

Al-Ya'qubi Ibn Wadih. *Mushākalat al-nas li-zamanihim*, ed. Matthew S. Gordon, Chase F. Robinson, Everett K. Rowson, and Michael Fishbein. Leiden: Brill, 2018.

Ibn al-Khatib. *Tārīkh Isbāniyah al-Islāmīyah, aw, Kitāb A'māl al-a'lām fī man būyi'a qabla al-iḥtilām min mulūk al-Islām*, ed. Évariste Lévi-Provençal. New edition. Cairo: Maktabat al-Thaqafah al-Diniyah, 2004.

Ibn Athir, Ali. *al-Kamil fi al-Tarikh*, ed. Omar Abd As-salam Tadmouri. Beirut: Dar al-Kitab al-'Arabi, 1997.

Ibn Athir, Ali, *al-Kāmil fi al-Tarikh,* ed. Omar Abd As-salam Tadmouri, Volume VI. Beirut: Dar Sader, 2009.

Ibn Bajja Abu Bakr. *Rasā'il ibn Bājja al-ilāhiyyah. Ibn Bajja's Metaphysical Essays*, ed. M. Fakhry. Beirut: Dar al-Jil, 1992.

Ibn Harith al-Khichni, Mohamed. *Akhbar al-fuqahā'e wa al-muhadithin*. Beirut: Dar al-Kutub al-'Ilmiyyah, 1999.

Ibn Hazm. *The Ring of the Dove: A treatise on the Art and Practice of Arab Love*, trans. A.J. Arburry. London: Luzac Oriental, 1953/1994.

Mas'udi, Akhbar al-Zaman, Volume VI (Cairo: Matba'at Abd al-Hamid Ahmad Hanafi, 1938).

Nuwas, Abu, *Vintage Humour: The Islamic Wine Poetry of Abu Nuwas*, ed. and trans. Alex Rowell (London: C. Hurst, 2017)

Secondary sources

Abbott, Nabia. *Two Queens of Baghdad: Mother and Wife of Harūn al-Rashid*. Chicago: University of Chicago Press, 1946.

Abdallah, 'Annan M. *Dawlat al-Islam fi al-Andalus, Volume I*. Cairo: Maktabat al-Khanj, 1997.

Al-Makhari, Ahmed ibn Mohammed. *The History of the Mohammedan Dynasties In Spain. Volume I*, trans. Pascual de Gayangos. London: Routledge Curzon, 2002.

Awad Aldeeb (Abu-Sahtieh), Sami. *Droit musulman et modernité: diagnostiques et remèdes*. Charleston: Createspace Amazon, 2014.

Bauer, Thomas. 'Male–Male love in Classical Arabic Poetry'. In *The Cambridge History of Gay and Lesbian Literature*, ed. E.L. McCallum and Mikko Tuhkanen, 107–123. Cambridge: Cambridge University Press, 2014.

Boswell, John. *Christianity, Social Tolerance and Homosexuality*. Chicago: University of Chicago Press, 1980.

Bouhdiba, Abdelwahab. *Sexuality in Islam*. London: Routledge & Kegan Paul, 1985.

Crompton, Louis. 'Male Love and Islamic Law in Arab Spain'. In *Islamic Homosexualities: Culture, History, and Literature*, ed. Stephen O. Murray and Will Roscoe, 142–157. New York: New York University Press, 1997.

Crompton, Louis. *Homosexuality and Civilization*. Cambridge, MA: Harvard University Press, 2006.

Daniel, Marc. 'Arab Civilization and Male Love', trans. Winston Leyland. In *Reclaiming Sodom*, ed. Jonathan Goldberg. New York: Routledge, 1994.

Ecker, Heather. *Caliphs and Kings: The art and influence of Islamic Spain*. Washington DC: The Hispanic Society of America and Arthur M. Sackler Gallery, Smithsonian Institution, 2004.

Eisenberg, Daniel. 'Homosexuality'. In *Encyclopedia of Medieval Iberia*, ed. Michael Gerli, 398–399. New York: Routledge, 2003.

El-Rouayheb, Khaled. *Before Homosexuality in the Arab-Islamic World, 1500–1800*. Chicago: University of Chicago Press, 2005.

Fairchild Ruggles, D. 'Mothers of a Hybrid dynasty: Race, Genealogy and Acculturation in al-Andalus'. *Journal of Medieval and Early Modern Studies* 34 (2004): 65–94.

Gabrieli, Francesco. 'Al-Amine'. In *The Encyclopedia of Islam, Volume I*. 2nd edn. Leiden: E.J. Brill, 1960.

Garcia-Sanjuan, Alejandro. 'Islamic legality and political legitimacy in the Caliphate of Cordoba: the proclamation of Hisham II (360–66 / 971–76)'. *Al-Qantara*, 29.1 (2008): 45–77.

Gerliand, E. Michael, ed. *Medieval Iberia: An Encyclopedia*. London: Routledge, 2003.

Hawting, Gerald R., ed. *Muslims, Mongols and Crusaders*, an anthology of articles published in the *Bulletin of the School of Oriental and African Studies*. London: Routledge Curzon, 2005.

Hibri, Tayeb al-. *Re-interpreting Islamic Historiography*. Cambridge: Cambridge University Press, 1999.

Joubin, Rebecca. 'The multifarious lives of the sixth Abbasid Caliph Mohammed al-Amin'. *International Journal of Middle East Studies*, 52 (2020): 643–663.

Jum'a, Jamal. *Nuzhat al-Albāb fi ma la Yujad fi Kitāb*. London: Riad al-Rayyes Books, 1992.

Kassis, Hanna. 'A glimpse of openness in medieval society: al-Hakam II of Cordoba and his non-Muslim collaborators'. In *The Man of Many Devices, Who Wandered Full Many Ways. Festschrift in Honor of János M. Bak*, ed. Balázs Nagy and Marcell Sebők, 160–166. Budapest: Central European University Press, 1999.

Kennedy, Hugh. *The Early Abbasid Caliphate: A political history*. London: Routledge, 2016.

Lévi-Provençal, Evariste. *Muslim Spain until the fall of the Caliphate of Córdoba 711–1031*, trans. Emilio Garcia Gomez. Madrid: Espasa-Calpe, 1957.

Levy, Reubin, *A Baghdad Chronicle* (Cambridge: Cambridge University Press, 1929).

Lindsay, James E. *Daily Life in Medieval Islamic World*. Westport, CT: Greenwood Press, 2005.

Martin, Stefanie L. *The Role of Homosexuality in Classical Islam*. Knoxville, TN: University of Tennessee Press, 1997.

Massad, Joseph. *Desiring Arabs*. Chicago: University of Chicago Press, 2007.

Meri, Josef W. *Medieval Islamic Civilization: An Encyclopedia, Volume I*. London: Routledge, 2006.

Nykl, Richard A. *Hispano-Arabic Poetry and its Relations with the Old Provencal Troubadours*. Baltimore, MD: J.H. Furst Company, 1946 (reprint Whitefish, MT: Literary Licensing, 2011).

Rekaya, Mohamed. 'al-Ma'mun'. In *The Encyclopedia of Islam, Volume I*. 2nd edn. Leiden: Brill, 1987.

Reubin, Levy. *A Baghdad Chronicle*. Cambridge: Cambridge University Press, 1929.

Robinson, Cynthia. *In Praise of Song: The making of courtly culture in al-Andalus and Provence, 1005–1134 A.D.* Leiden: Brill, 2002.

Robinson, Cynthia. 'Love in the time of *Fitna*: "Courtliness" and the "Pamplona Casket"'. In *Revisiting al-Andalus: Perspectives on the material culture of Islamic Iberia and beyond*, ed. Glaire D. Anderson and Mariam Rosser-Owen, 99–112. Leiden: Brill, 2007.

Rojas Felipe, and Peter E. Thompson, eds. *Queering the Medieval Mediterranean: Trans-cultural Sea of Sex, Gender, Identity and Culture*. Leiden: Brill, 2021.

Ruggles, D. Fairchild, 'Mothers of a Hybrid Dynasty: Race, genealogy and acculturation in al-Andalus', *Journal of Medieval and Early Modern Studies* 34 (2004).

Scales, Peter C. *The Fall of the Caliphate of Córdoba: Berbers and Andalusis in conflict*. Leiden: Brill, 1994.

Schippers, Arie. 'The Mujūn Genre by Abu Nuwas and by Ibn Quzman: a comparison'. In *The Rude, the Bad, and the Bawdy: Essays in honour of Professor Geert Jan Van Gelder*, ed. Adam Talib, Marlé Hammond, and Arie Schippers, 80–100. Cambridge: Gibb Memorial Trust, 2014.

Schmidtke, Sabine. 'Homoeroticism and Homosexuality in Islam: A review article'. *Bulletin of the School of Oriental and African Studies*, 62.2 (1999): 260–266.

Wahab, Ruslan, and Mardyawati Y. 'Term of Child in Analysis of Languages Various By The Quran'. *Journal of Research and Multidisciplinary*, 4.1 (2021): 393–400.

Walther, Wiebke. *Women in Islam*. Princeton, NJ: Markus Wiener Publishing, 1993.

Zayat, Habib. 'al-mar'a al-ghulamiyya fi al-Islam'. *al-Mashriq* 50 (1956): 153–192.

Zaydan, Jurji. *Tarikh al-Tamaddun al-Islami*. 5 vols. Cairo: Maktabat al- Hilal, 1901–1906.

8

The Tour de Nesle Affair: succession and sexuality in fourteenth-century France

Emily Lalande

[Marguerite] continually wept and cried, not for her trouble, but her sin, and particularly because, on account of what she had done, other noble women would be subjected to suspicion.

(Chronicle of Jean of St Victor)[1]

The marriages of Philip IV of France's four children, although initially arranged to strengthen the aged king's regime, brought severe consequences for the succession of the French throne and extinguished the Capetian dynasty, which had been lauded for its 'miracle' of a line of direct male descent from its founder, Hugh Capet, for over three centuries. Philip IV's only daughter, Isabella of France, married Edward II of England, while his three sons, Louis, Philip, and Charles married three Burgundian heiresses: Marguerite, heiress to the duchy of Burgundy, and Jeanne and Blanche, heiresses to the county of Burgundy. The cracks in these marital alliances manifested in 1314, when the king had both Marguerite and Blanche of Burgundy imprisoned for their alleged adulterous relationships with the Aunay brothers, a pair of knights serving in his court. He also arrested Jeanne of Burgundy for knowingly abetting her sisters-in-law in their adultery. These accusations of adultery, regardless of the likelihood of its actual occurrence, had far-reaching ramifications upon the French succession.

The perception of their disordered sexualities not only affected them but also their issue, which left the French succession vulnerable and disorganised. By the end of 1314, Philip IV had died, and his eldest son inherited the throne as Louis X. Louis's wife, Marguerite of Burgundy, died during her imprisonment, leaving him with only a daughter Jeanne to succeed to his throne. In 1329, Jeanne ascended the throne of Navarre as Jeanne II of Navarre in accordance with the decision made by the *Cortes* (general assembly) of Navarre in May 1328.[2] Upon her father Louis X's premature death in 1316, his brother had claimed the throne of France as Philip V and bypassed

Jeanne's claim entirely. Philip V had four daughters with his wife, Jeanne of Burgundy, but with his likewise early death, the throne once again passed to his brother rather than to any of his daughters. When the third royal son, Charles IV, died without surviving issue, the throne passed to a Valois cousin rather than to any of the previous kings' Capetian daughters – or indeed Isabella of France's son, Edward III of England. This brought an end to the Capetian dynasty's hegemony over the French throne and enabled the cadet Valois line to succeed to the kingdom.

This chapter presents a new perspective on how female sexuality was intertwined with the inability of female claimants to succeed to the French throne following the Tour de Nesle Affair. It does not seek to answer the question of guilt or innocence in the case of the Burgundian princesses, but rather seeks to demonstrate how their perceived guilt impacted their female line. A queen's, or prospective queen's, alleged adultery could have dire effects not only for herself, but for her issue. That said, there are several cases throughout western Europe of kings succeeding to the throne despite controversy surrounding their mothers. These include Henry VII's claim to the English throne resting on his descent from John of Gaunt's extramarital affair with the non-royal Katherine Swynford, and Anne of Austria's regency for her son, Louis XIV, marred by rumours of her close relationship to Cardinal Mazarin. Edward III of England, Isabella of France's son, ascended the English throne despite his mother's potential adultery with Roger Mortimer.[3] However, this was not the case for female heiresses whose mothers stood accused of sexual impropriety – with a single notable exception in Elizabeth I of England.

After the Tour de Nesle Affair, two other notable cases emerged in western Europe in which a woman's ability to succeed to the throne was affected by her mother's perceived or actual infidelity. The first, in fifteenth-century Castile, is that of the *infanta* Juana, known as Juana *la Beltraneja*, daughter of Enrique IV of Castile and his second wife Juana of Portugal. Enrique IV's opponents posited that Juana was borne from an adulterous relationship between Juana of Portugal and Enrique's court favourite Beltrán de la Cueva, hence her sobriquet *la Beltraneja*. This possibility culminated in the War of Castilian Succession after Enrique IV's death in 1474. His sister Isabella was proclaimed queen of Castile. She moved quickly to cement her sovereignty, sending Juana *la Beltraneja* to a convent, thus making her claim to the throne thereafter impossible to support. Juana's mother's other adulterous relationship with Pedro de Castilla y Fonseca, which resulted in two sons, only added to her notoriety and made her daughter's claim to the throne untenable. Like Jeanne II of Navarre, while Juana was never disinherited by her father, her mother's sexual impropriety made her claim to the throne of Castile unattainable.

The second case is that of Elizabeth Tudor, whose father Henry VIII accused her mother Anne Boleyn of adultery in 1536. After her mother's execution, the imperial ambassador Eustache Chapuys, writing to the Spanish Habsburg Cardinal Granvelle, reported that the Archbishop of Canterbury had declared Elizabeth illegitimate due to the lack of a 'valid' marriage between Henry and Anne Boleyn. Cramner based part of his argument upon Henry's earlier adulterous relationship with Anne's sister, Mary Boleyn.[4] Although Henry later tried to rehabilitate Elizabeth, the claims of illegitimacy due to her mother's alleged sexual misdeeds were resurrected under Mary I, who declared Henry VIII's marriage to Catherine of Aragon valid, and hence his illegitimate progeny with Anne Boleyn was unable to inherit.[5] Despite being declared illegitimate by the Second Succession Act of 1536, and subsequently returned to the line of succession by the somewhat controversial Third Succession Act of 1543–44,[6] when she came to the throne in 1558, Elizabeth was still technically illegitimate yet able to succeed to the throne.

While Elizabeth overcame the persistent stain surrounding her own birth, her reign remained prey to intermittent accusations of illegitimacy, exemplified by the tract *De origine ac progressu schismatis Anglicani* by the Catholic writer Nicholas Sander. He asserted that Elizabeth I was not only the progeny of one of Anne Boleyn's supposed adulterous unions (there were many to choose from: her brother George, Mark Smeaton, Henry Norris, Francis Weston, or William Brereton), but also that Anne Boleyn was herself Henry VIII's daughter through an earlier relationship with her mother, Elizabeth Boleyn.[7] Elizabeth I never moved to have her birth declared legitimate as her sister Mary had, choosing instead to emphasise her connection and resemblance to her Tudor ancestors as well as her strategic and effective self-fashioning as both the Virgin Queen and the mother of her people.

Though the disinheritance of these two women (and, in Elizabeth's case, subsequent succession) took place two centuries after the Tour de Nesle Affair, there was an enduring connection between female inheritance and a mother's sexual continence throughout the medieval and early modern periods. It is this continuity this chapter seeks to interrogate through a direct study of female succession – or the lack thereof – after the Tour de Nesle Affair, which culminated in the extinguishing of Capetian kingship in France and the rise of the Valois dynasty. As alluded to earlier, a royal woman's sexual impropriety not only resulted in shame and punishment for herself, but also had far-reaching effects capable of harming her issue and a ruling dynasty's ability to maintain its sovereignty.

There have been several studies of the Tour de Nesle Affair, especially as it relates to Philip IV and his sons, but these are limited largely to describing the lives of the women implicated in the affair and their supposed disordered sexualities. The affair appears most often as a footnote in studies of other

Capetian monarchs,[8] as well as in studies of the Salic Law and its influence upon successions in premodern France. However, both types of study disregard the specificity of female sexuality as essential to the fates of the Burgundian princesses and their daughters.[9] None focus on how the guilt (real or perceived) of the Burgundian women involved impacted the futures of their issue, nor yet that of other royal women in the kingdom of France.

By the same token, in narratives of their daughters and ancestors, the three Burgundian princesses also generally appear as footnotes. This chapter therefore situates the sexualities of these three women explicitly in the history of the French succession and monarchy, foregrounding the troubling assumptions of their sexualities. Moreover, the Tour de Nesle Affair and its consequences emphasise the impact that sexualities and, most cogently here, aberrant female sexualities had on the succession in premodern France.

Sources and female sexuality

For the purposes of this chapter, the genealogy of Philip IV's family and their spouses merits explanation. Philip IV, King of France, wed Jeanne I of Navarre, Queen of Navarre, in 1284, and so therefore their children were heirs to both the French and Navarrese thrones. Their four children were Louis of Navarre, who inherited Navarre when Jeanne died in 1305, and later became Louis X of France in 1314; Philip of Poitiers, who became Philip V of France in 1317; Charles of Artois, who became Charles IV of France in 1322; and Isabella of France, who became Queen of England in 1308. Louis of Navarre married Marguerite of Burgundy, daughter to the Duke of Burgundy, in 1305, and they had a single daughter, Jeanne, who would later become Jeanne II of Navarre. Philip of Poitiers married Jeanne of Burgundy, first daughter to the Count of Burgundy, in 1307, and they had four daughters: Jeanne, Marguerite, Isabella, and Blanche. Charles of Artois married Blanche of Burgundy, the second daughter of the Count of Burgundy, in 1307, and they had two children who did not survive infancy. Finally, Isabella of France married Edward II of England in 1308, and had four surviving children, including the future Edward III of England. The named personages in this genealogy make up the key figures in this chapter.

After an extended dispute between Philip IV and Pope Boniface VIII, and conflict with the French barons, including the merciless suppression of the Knights Templar, the Tour de Nesle Affair unfolded at the end of Philip's reign. Despite the controversies marring his reign, Philip IV managed to unify France under a more pragmatic administration and began to establish a national French identity.[10] By dint of his marriage to Jeanne I of Navarre, Philip IV perpetuated France's sovereignty over Navarre, Champagne, and

Brie, administering the Navarrese kingdom from Paris. Jeanne provided Philip with four children who survived into adulthood: Louis, Philip, Charles, and Isabella. After his mother's death, the eldest son Louis inherited the kingdom of Navarre, and later the French throne on the death of his father Philip.

In keeping with his own marital alliance, Philip IV sought to bring further territorial advantages to the French kingdom via his sons' marital partnerships. In particular, Philip concerned himself with both the wealthy county of Burgundy and the larger duchy of Burgundy. The heir to the county of Burgundy was the teenage Jeanne of Burgundy, and with her inheritance of the county of Burgundy came the potential for her (and her husband) to inherit the county of Artois through her mother, Mahaut of Artois.[11] Finding himself in dire financial circumstances, Jeanne's father, Othon IV, Count of Burgundy, pledged both his daughter's hand and the county of Burgundy to the king of France and to the benefit of the king's eldest son. Though Mahaut did later bear him a son, Othon did not change the arrangement with Philip IV.[12] Initially, Philip IV had promised Othon that Jeanne's hand would go to his eldest son Louis; however, after the birth of Othon's unexpected male heir who might inherit Burgundy and Artois, Jeanne married his second son, Philip.

Philip IV arranged instead for Louis to marry Marguerite, the granddaughter of Louis IX of France through her mother Agnes of France. The duchy of Burgundy presented an attractive alliance because it represented the most senior peerage in the kingdom of France and Marguerite's father pledged an immense dowry in money and lands to Philip. The last of Philip's sons, Charles was engaged to Jeanne of Burgundy's younger sister, Blanche, ratifying control over the county of Burgundy and achieving an even greater financial settlement for both Philip IV and Burgundy.[13] This final marriage was complicated by the fact that Blanche of Burgundy's mother, Mahaut of Artois, was Charles's godmother. This degree of alleged consanguinity would eventually be the reason for Charles to annul his marriage to Blanche following the Tour de Nesle Affair. Philip IV's daughter, Isabella, was married to the future Edward II of England in an arrangement created by Pope Boniface VIII in the hope of inspiring a durable peace between France and England.

With these four marriages nicely bedded down, Philip IV had created a network of alliances within and without France, achieving significant financial gain. However, these marriages came at a cost. Papal dispensations had to be issued for the marriages of Louis and Marguerite, and Philip and Jeanne, due to close degrees of consanguinity – both couples having common great-grandparents. Although Charles and Blanche were more closely related by blood than either of the other two couples, Philip IV did not request a papal dispensation for their match. These issues of consanguinity meant that all three of the royal sons' marriages were on shaky ground, leaving the women especially vulnerable to controversy.

This controversy was ignited in 1314 when rumours emerged that two of Philip IV's daughters-in-law, Marguerite and Blanche, had engaged in adultery with the knights Philip and Gautier of Aunay. The third daughter-in-law, Jeanne, stood accused of aiding and abetting the women in their adultery and hiding it from their respective husbands. This scandal became known as the Tour de Nesle Affair because the alleged adulterous liaisons took place in the Tour de Nesle in Paris. Philip had all three women and the accused adulterers arrested during Easter Week.[14] The Aunay brothers, sons to a vassal and supporter of the king's brother Charles of Valois, were brutally executed for treason in very short order. Pope Clement V died soon after these arrests, leaving the papal seat vacant for a year with no pope enthroned to grant the necessary annulments to Philip IV's sons, which would have left them free to remarry. None of the women were condemned to death as the Aunay brothers had been, remaining under arrest to await their fates.

At the end of 1314, Philip IV died, and with that event the status of the women's imprisonment shifted. Almost immediately after his father's death, his second son Philip, by then Philip of Poitiers, had his wife Jeanne of Burgundy freed and declared innocent by the *parlement* of Paris. At some point in 1315, Marguerite of Burgundy died in prison, either of illness or, as sordid rumours would have it, by strangulation.[15] She was technically queen consort of France at the time, her husband having become Louis X upon the death of his father Philip IV. Louis quickly married Clementia of Burgundy to secure a male heir. Blanche, the last of the imprisoned princesses, remained incarcerated in various chateaux, Charles only able to have their marriage annulled in 1322. Even after the annulment, Blanche was not freed from detention and died of illness in 1326.

Among the variety of sources pertaining to the Tour de Nesle Affair, none was written by anyone within the women's circles. Two household accounts, one of Philip of Poitiers and Jeanne of Burgundy, and the other of Isabella of France, reflect significant disruption within the courts of the two royal princesses as well as in Philip IV's during the spring of 1314.[16] Neither of these household accounts identifies the exact circumstances of this disruption, but two contemporary chronicles mention it. Both *Les Grands Chroniques de France*, a ten-volume history of the French kingdom compiled over two centuries, and *La Chronique métrique de Philippe le Bel*, a chronicle of Philip IV's reign, possibly written by Geoffrey of Paris, record the scandal and the fates of the implicated princesses. Tracy Adams discusses the major differences between these two accounts of the scandal. In *Les Grands*

Chroniques, the author effectively scapegoats the princesses for the conflicts at the end of Philip IV's reign, including in-fighting with his barons, while *La Chronique métrique* expresses doubt about the princesses' guilt, pointing instead to political motivations for their imprisonment.[17] That these contemporary chroniclers disagreed about the details of the Tour de Nesle Affair demonstrates the difficulty in determining the veracity of the accusations against the princesses.

Les Grands Chroniques de France were compiled by a series of authors commissioned by succeeding monarchs of France to write about their reign and their predecessors. For the period of Philip IV's rule, *Les Grands Chroniques* rely on Guillaume de Nangis's and Girard de Frachet's contemporary accounts but remove certain elements of them, including the recorded 1314 revolt by regional rebels against Philip IV's unpopular tax levies.[18] *Les Grands Chroniques* are a royalist account and therefore seek to glorify French monarchs, including both Philip IV and his male successors. In its account of the Tour de Nesle Affair, this glorification comes at the expense of the Burgundian princesses, blaming their disordered sexualities for the disastrous end to Philip IV's reign, and focusing upon the women as a major cause of the degradation of the Capetian dynasty.

On the other hand, *La Chronique métrique de Philippe le Bel* is not a blatantly partisan text. The authorship of *La Chronique métrique* has been called into question by Jean Dunbabin and Tracy Adams. Given its rhymed lines and satirical comment, both scholars suggest that it was written for popular consumption rather than for the court. As other works by Geoffrey of Paris were directed to French kings, this calls into question the claims to his authorship. Without royal sponsorship, the author or authors of *La Chronique métrique* had no reason to maintain the king's reputation or to blame the Burgundian princesses for the bungled French succession. It is *La Chronique métrique* and not *Les Grands Chroniques* that records Louis X's deathbed avowal that his issue with Marguerite of Burgundy, namely the future Jeanne II of Navarre, was legitimate.[19] This paternal insistence upon Jeanne's legitimacy might call into question claims of her mother's adultery. The striking differences between the two chronicles covering the Tour de Nesle Affair seem to indicate how the princesses' sexualities were used to scapegoat them, successfully or not, for the political unrest arising from the later stages of Philip IV's reign and those subsequently of his sons.

Regardless of the chronicles written after the affair, the French Crown treated two out of the three princesses as though they were guilty. Jeanne of Burgundy was the most fortunate of the three princesses in both her fate and the circumstances that ensured her safety. Not only did her marriage with her husband seem to be a love match, but Jeanne had political significance due to her inheritance of the county of Burgundy.[20] Moreover, she proved herself fertile by giving birth to four surviving daughters and later to a son, who barely survived a year. Neither Marguerite nor Blanche shared her good fortune. With a brother who inherited the duchy of Burgundy, Marguerite had no land claims independent of her husband. She gave birth to only one surviving child during her ten-year marriage to Philip's eldest son Louis: a daughter named Jeanne. Blanche was even more unlucky. She did not hold counties as her elder sister did, and she did not give birth to a single child who survived into adulthood. In effect, both Marguerite and Blanche were disposable in a manner that Jeanne was not, ultimately condemning them to their fates of imprisonment and early death.

Regardless of whether the princesses were guilty of adultery, their narrative of female infidelity proved powerful and enduring, especially with regard to the comportment of France's princesses and queens. Even Isabella of France, sister to the three princes discussed here, became implicated in the affair, accused of revealing the adultery to her father because she had spent time with him directly prior to the arrests; she was later herself accused of an adulterous affair with Roger Mortimer.[21] In narratives of the Tour de Nesle Affair, royal men retained their innocence while royal women carried the burden of scandal, regardless of their involvement, and however tangential that might have been. This points to the responsibility weighing on the shoulders of royal women to uphold the reputations of the royal family. Marguerite of Burgundy's alleged affair with one of the Aunay brothers brought her fidelity to Louis into question at the time of the birth of their daughter Jeanne. A mother's infidelity – or perceived infidelity – could have immense consequences for her offspring.

Inheritance and invalidation

At the time of the Tour de Nesle Affair in 1314, Philip IV was grandfather to Marguerite of Burgundy's daughter, Jeanne, as well as to Jeanne of Burgundy's four daughters and Isabella of France's son, Edward. He also had three relatively young sons, two of whom would go on to remarry after the deaths of their wives. However, within two decades of his death, the direct Capetian line was entirely extinguished and Philip's nephew instead inherited the French throne as the first Valois king, Philip VI. The Capetian line had been known as the 'Capetian miracle' due to an uninterrupted line, of more than three centuries, of direct male heirs from the reign of Hugh Capet who took the throne in 987.[22] Each Capetian king fathered a son who went on to inherit the throne, perpetuating this 'miracle' until Philip IV's heirless three sons, and the controversy of the Tour de Nesle Affair, ended the direct Capetian line.

Technically, two of Philip's three sons did have a male successor. Louis, who became Louis X upon his father's death, died in June 1316 leaving behind a pregnant second wife. The *parlement* of Paris and nobles of France held their breaths and rejoiced when Clementia of Hungary gave birth to a son the following November. Unfortunately, the boy (Jean I, later named Jean the Posthumous), died within six days of his birth.[23] In the months between Louis's death and Clementia's delivery, Philip of Poitiers acted as regent of France on behalf of the unborn child.[24] Philip himself had a son, another Philip, which bolstered his claim to the regency as he had essentially proved himself capable of siring male issue. Upon Jean the Posthumous's death, the question became: who would succeed? Louis X's daughter Jeanne or his brother Philip?

Born to Louis X and Marguerite of Burgundy in 1312, Jeanne's legitimacy was never brought into question publicly by either her father or her grandfather and was in fact reaffirmed by Louis X on his deathbed.[25] By the time her father became king of France, Jeanne was roughly two years old. At his death, she was about four years old, and heiress to the crowns of both France and Navarre. Unlike France, Navarre had a history of female rulers. Jeanne's own claim to Navarre came via the female line. Her grandmother, Jeanne I of Navarre, was the first queen regnant of the kingdom, and co-ruled it with Philip IV. In 1305, the crown had passed to Jeanne I's first-born child, Louis, instead of passing to her husband Philip. Louis subsequently ruled over Navarre for eleven years before his death brought the French Crown to rest on Jeanne's head – or it ought to have done. With at least one crown inherited from her father and his deathbed declaration of her legitimacy, as well as her direct descent from Louis IX through both of her parents, Jeanne had a powerful claim to the French throne.

Yet this claim ultimately failed. In 1315, Jeanne's uncle, Philip de Poitiers, became King Philip V of France and his wife Jeanne, the only rehabilitated victim of the Tour de Nesle Affair, became his queen. Though Philip was perfectly willing to act as regent for Louis X's son in his minority, there was no question of him doing the same for Jeanne, though there had originally been some negotiation concerning her position, had Clementia's child been a daughter.[26] Philip was crowned king in January 1317 and a month later he convened an assembly that declared that 'no woman could succeed to the French throne'.[27] However, this declaration had no basis in ratified French law at the time – and it did not gain immediate approval from all of the French peers with Jeanne's grandmother Agnes of France attempting to reinforce and negotiate her granddaughter's claim.

It is important here to acknowledge that, while there had never been a Capetian queen regnant of France, women still commanded and exerted royal and princely authority. Philip IV himself declared that his wife, Jeanne

I of Navarre, would be regent for their son Louis in the case of his premature death, and made his brother Charles of Valois swear to obey her under such circumstances.[28] Half a century beforehand, Louis IX's mother Blanche of Castile led his government in his youth and acted as his regent during his absence on crusade.[29] As mentioned earlier, Jeanne I of Navarre was also a queen in her own right, heiress not only to Navarre, but also to the appanages of Champagne and Brie.

Notwithstanding this, there was historical precedent for aberrant sexualities endangering the positions of French queens. The ninth-century Carolingian king Charles III attempted to divorce his wife Richardis of Swabia based on accusations of adultery, which she denied her entire life.[30] In 1148, rumours circulated involving Eleanor of Aquitaine and her alleged adultery against her husband, Louis VII of France, with her uncle, Raymond of Antioch.[31] Four years later, under the pretext of consanguinity, Louis VII divorced Eleanor, who had only provided him with female issue – much as the Burgundian princesses would almost two centuries later. Charles IV would use similar laws of consanguinity to have his marriage to Blanche of Burgundy annulled after the Tour de Nesle Affair. A century after Charles IV's annulment, another French queen was discarded due to her alleged defective sexuality. Louis XII repudiated Jeanne of France to marry Anne of Brittany, citing a lack of consummation of his first marriage due to Jeanne's 'imperfect, polluted and hexed in body, [which was] unfit for commerce with a man'.[32] Unlike the Burgundian princesses, Jeanne of France did not stand accused of adultery. Rather, her physical insufficiencies rendered her body 'unfit' for sex with a king. A queen's body, whether overtly sexual in cases of adultery or so 'imperfect' that the queen herself became asexual, could discredit her own authority and, in the case of the Tour de Nesle Affair, that of her daughters.

This deft and useful link between sexuality and authority allowed power to slide from Jeanne II's grasp and into that of her uncle. Although the assembly of February 1317 declared that no woman could succeed to the throne of France, there was no binding law commanding that this would be so. The impetus for this declaration regarding female inheritance came from Philip V, but was supported by many burghers, barons, and prelates. Naturally, the notable exception to this came from the duchy of Burgundy in the shape of Jeanne's grandmother, the formidable Agnes of France, daughter of the saint king Louis IX. This meant that Jeanne, unlike her uncle Philip V, was doubly descended from Saint Louis. In the face of such a strong claim to the throne, could her sex really matter so much?

Unfortunately for Jeanne, her sex was only one strike against her. She also had to contend with rumours surrounding her own legitimacy, regardless of her grandfather and her father's assertions. While Louis X had recognised

Jeanne as his legitimate daughter on his deathbed, he left no written affidavit or proof beyond this oral declaration.[33] This might not have been sufficient to call her legitimacy into doubt had her mother not been embroiled in an adultery scandal alleged to have begun prior to Jeanne's birth. In their confessions, the Aunay brothers said that their adultery had begun three years before their arrests, which would put the beginning of their relationships back to 1311, the year before Jeanne's birth.[34] Her father's deathbed reassertion that she was his daughter does indicate that at the very least there were rumours pertaining to her legitimacy, and that these rumours potentially placed her in an even more vulnerable position when confronted by the machinations of her uncle.

In a 1318 meeting between Philip V and Jeanne's maternal family to obtain their support of his kingship, Jeanne was forced to renounce her rights to the thrones of both France and Navarre – though this renunciation could not be ratified until she reached the age of twelve and ultimately never occurred.[35] Her rights to Champagne and Brie through her paternal line were maintained even after she gave up her rights to France and Navarre, and it was declared furthermore that she would inherit them if her uncle died without male issue.[36] Had there been strong evidence-based questions surrounding her parentage, it seems unlikely that she would have inherited the Navarrese crown. After all, her claims to Navarre, Champagne, and Brie all rested upon her paternal inheritance, from her grandmother Jeanne I of Navarre and through her father Louis X. Her parentage was not sufficiently doubted to jeopardise her ultimate succession in Navarre – despite the fact that Jeanne would not succeed to Navarre until she reached her majority and after the deaths of her two uncles. Although Jeanne was not declared illegitimate by the scandal of her mother's alleged adultery, she did not have sufficient standing to force her dynastic claims to the French throne.

Along with her sex and her mother's scandal, Jeanne's young age helped Philip V immensely in his claim to the French throne. She was approximately four years old when first her father, and then her infant half-brother, died with no one to support her claims except for the family of her disgraced mother. Her father's family were caught up in their own claims to the French throne and Louis X's youngest brother Charles would use the exact same pretext as his brother Philip to claim the throne when Philip died. Jeanne was too young to be considered for consummated marriage and therefore had no powerful in-laws to champion her, as Philip V had done with Mahaut of Artois and his consort Queen Jeanne's claim to the county of Burgundy. Nor was Jeanne of age to make any courtly allies as Philip had done.

Like his elder brother Louis X, Philip V did not enjoy a long reign over the French and Navarrese kingdoms. He died in 1322 after only five years on the throne, a victim of chronic ill health. Though he himself fathered a son soon after Louis X's death, the boy died in the first year of his reign. Philip left behind no male heirs, but rather four daughters: Jeanne, Marguerite, Isabelle, and Blanche. Much as Philip had, his younger brother Charles quickly ascended to the throne, completely ignoring the rights of Philip V's female heirs, the eldest of whom was about twelve years old.[37] Unlike Jeanne II, Philip V's daughters had a clearer path to the throne as there were no issues surrounding their legitimacy. In the end, however, they all experienced the same disappointment as their cousin. Much like Jeanne II, Philip V's daughters were still able to inherit substantial territories later in life, including both the counties of Burgundy and Artois, but their claims to the French throne remained unfulfilled.

Capets and crowns

During the complicated successions of Philip V and Charles IV, there was another potential female successor across the Channel, and Isabella of France, unlike Jeanne II or any of Philip V's daughters, was well into adulthood. There were no rumours of illegitimacy surrounding her birth, nor around the birth of her son, the future Edward III. She had a hypothetically powerful husband in the king of England but had her own set of domestic and international conflicts to contend with while her brothers ruled France in quick sequence. In 1326, Queen Isabella became embroiled in scandal, usurping the crown of England from her husband Edward II in favour of her young son, Edward III. Her regency in England lasted until 1330. In these circumstances, she largely avoided the inheritance question in France until her final brother died in 1328 and does not appear to have been involved in the claims of any of her nieces.

Like his elder brothers, Charles IV suffered from ill health and did not rule for long. As mentioned earlier, he failed to have his marriage to the incarcerated Blanche of Burgundy annulled until 1322. He then remarried twice, but still did not manage to produce a male heir. His third wife, Jeanne d'Evreux, had three daughters, one of whom, Jeanne, was born after Charles IV's death. As was the case for Clementia of Hungary, a regent was declared for the unborn child – in Clementia's case, for a son John I, who lived for less than a week. There was no fourth brother to inherit the throne after Charles IV. Philip of Valois, Charles's paternal cousin, was appointed regent. He was the son of Charles of Valois, himself the younger brother of Philip IV and one-time ally of the Aunay brothers. Jeanne d'Evreux's child was a daughter, and Philip of Valois maintained his position as ruler after her daughter Blanche's birth.[38] Unlike Jeanne II of Navarre, the infant's maternal family does not appear to have fought for the inheritance rights of Charles

IV's daughters. At this point, the nascent precedent of passing over female heirs had been established; first by Philip V passing over Jeanne and then by Charles IV passing over Philip's daughter, also called Jeanne.

The only closer male claimant to the throne of France was Edward III of England, who was already by this point King of England but subject to the regency of his mother Isabella and her probable lover Roger Mortimer. But what of Isabella's claim to the throne of France? Could she be passed over as easily as Jeanne II of Navarre or her cousins? Interestingly, Isabella's own regency for her son Edward III was complicated – and ultimately ended – by rumours surrounding her relationship with her ally, Roger Mortimer.[39] The perception of this relationship certainly influenced her popularity within the English court and with her own son, and in 1330, like the Aunay brothers, Mortimer was ultimately arrested and sentenced to a traitor's death.

In the spring of 1328, Philip VI held a meeting at St Germain-en-Laye with representatives from all the potential claimants to the French throne.[40] He solidified his sovereignty by offering Jeanne II and her husband, Philip d'Evreux (another prince of French royal blood), the territories of Longueville and Mortain, and the county of Angoulême, while taking Champagne and Brie for himself due to their proximity to Paris.[41] The daughters of Philip V and Charles IV received financial settlements, effectively bought out of their claims to the succession, and Philip VI also granted money to Jeanne II's maternal family for their support.[42] Finally, the *Cortes* of Navarre requested that Jeanne II claim the throne of Navarre, allowing her at least to secure her paternal birthright and forcing the French crown to relinquish its hold over Navarre.

Isabella of France's claim, however, existed in a different context from those of her nieces. Unlike the ignored princesses, she had her own powerbase, as did her son Edward. Philip VI and his nobles subsequently excluded them both from the French line of succession, based on a twofold explanation empowered by the earlier exclusion of Jeanne II and her cousins: the inability of a woman to inherit the French throne combined with the inability of a foreigner to inherit the French throne.[43] A *tous nobles*, a fifteenth-century genealogical chronicle of the French kings, emphasises the former point in its assertion that

> This Isabella, daughter of king Philip the Fair and wife to Edward of England, wanted to have France after the death of her brothers who, as would be seen afterwards, died without male heirs of their body. And there began a great debate, as no woman could succeed to the kingdom of France. And if a woman did succeed, Isabella would not have the right. Because her brothers each had a daughter who should succeed before her.[44]

As Edward's claim came down through his mother and he himself was born outside of France, unlike the French princesses, his claim was even less valid than theirs. This arbitrary and expedient ruling would be the pretext of Edward III later asserting his right to the French crown, engulfing both France and England into an intermittent war that endured for some 116 years, better known as the Hundred Years War.

Isabella's claim to the French throne did not suffer directly because of the Tour de Nesle Affair, like that of Jeanne of Navarre, but rather because of the legacy of female omission initiated by her brothers to disinherit their nieces. Despite this, Jeanne could be understood as the longest-surviving victim of the affair. Both her parents had died by the time she reached the age of five, after which her legitimacy fell into question, with subsequent kings of France ignoring her birth right. Her claim to the Navarrese throne, which did allow female inheritance, was usurped twice by both of her uncles, leading to the *Cortes* on their own initiative to demand that the crown fall to Jeanne. For all that she suffered because of the Tour de Nesle Affair and her mother's disgrace, her Book of Hours incorporated her mother's coat of arms and, during her reign in Navarre, Jeanne had her mother's tomb draped with a 'tapis vert' embellished with the arms of France, Navarre, Champagne, and Burgundy.[45] Her mother retained a central place in Jeanne's imagery and memory.

Between Philip IV and Philip VI, the ruling dynasty of France changed from the Capetians to the Valois. This change was due to the deliberate exclusion of any and all female claimants to the throne. There was a direct line of descent from Philip VI that would have allowed the Capetians to retain the throne; at the time of his death, he had four surviving children and half a dozen grandchildren. However, all his surviving grandchildren except for Edward III were female, which provided other princes of the blood and his own sons with excuses to ignore hereditary claims and forge their own paths to the French crown. This would have severe ramifications for the kingdom of France throughout the rest of the century and into the next, as both English and Navarrese kings began to enforce their own claims to the French throne and question the legitimacy of Philip VI's Valois line, effectively igniting and sustaining the Hundred Years War.

Conclusion

The Tour de Nesle Affair is an important episode in the history of medieval France, particularly as it contributed to the extinguishment of the Capetian line and the rise of the Valois dynasty, and triggered the Hundred Years

War. Moreover, it was a scandal that had dire familial and political consequences for at least the four women directly touched by it. Marguerite of Burgundy and Blanche of Burgundy both died in detention, either of health broken by the conditions in which they were kept, or perhaps murdered. Marguerite's daughter, Jeanne, lost her mother and her birthright because of the scandal. Jeanne of Burgundy was briefly imprisoned alongside her sister and sister-in-law before securing her freedom, only to watch her own daughters lose their claims to the French throne.

The life trajectories of these women have tended to be lost within the greater implications of the Tour de Nesle Affair and the notoriety of its attendant scandal. Little scholarly study has emerged surrounding the experiences of the accused princesses after their convictions save for Brown's seminal work on Blanche of Burgundy's relationship to her mother, Mahaut of Artois, and her imprisonment based upon an archival study of her land holdings and finances.[46] Unlike Blanche, Marguerite and Jeanne of Burgundy only lingered in prison for a short time. Jeanne was released at the request of her husband and declared innocent by the *parlement* during his brother's reign, while Marguerite died a year into her imprisonment. None of these women left behind any written traces of their marriages, children, or imprisonments and their voices can only be discerned faintly in the subjective scribblings of interested chroniclers of the French kingdom and Capetian dynasty.

The Tour de Nesle Affair, and specifically its demonstration of the dangers of divergent female sexuality, held the door open for the first outright exclusion of female heirs under the Capetian dynasty in France. Jeanne II of Navarre's claim to the throne was usurped by her uncle because 'women could not inherit', and her mother's conviction for adultery led to questions about her legitimacy that enabled that usurpation to pass relatively unhindered. Her mother's death in prison and her father's death two years later left her without parents to protect her or her claims, resulting in Philip V's rapid success in bypassing her entirely to claim the crown of France. Philip V's brother and successor, Charles IV, followed his lead in bypassing both Jeanne's claim and those of Philip's four daughters.

Not only did the Tour de Nesle Affair damage perceptions of French royal women, but it also directly contributed to the lack of male heirs after both Louis X and Charles IV. Louis and Marguerite only had a daughter to show for their ten years of marriage, and Louis had to wait for Marguerite's death before he could marry Clementia of Hungary. He died soon after his marriage, leaving a pregnant wife behind with no chance of subsequent male heirs. Charles IV waited almost a decade for the pope to annul his marriage to Blanche of Burgundy, and so was not able to have legitimate offspring who could inherit his holdings until after the annulment. Although Charles did his best to make up for the lost time, marrying twice during his reign, he could not sire a male heir. The imprisonments of both Marguerite of Burgundy and Blanche of Burgundy for their sexual impropriety therefore had a direct effect on the hitherto miraculous Capetian line of succession.

And what then of sexuality? Did sexual impropriety and women's ability to commit adultery inform whether or not a woman could ascend the French throne? The answer to that question is frustratingly oblique. Chronicles report that Philip V held an assembly to announce that women could not succeed to the throne of France, but no reason as to why is given and there is no direct chronicle account of the meeting. Female regency, such as that offered to Jeanne I of Navarre by Philip IV, continued unencumbered after the Tour de Nesle Affair. Women were never excluded from political roles in the kingdom of France; but significantly from the direct rulership of it. Regardless of a firm answer to the questions raised in this present discussion, women's sexual transgressions did appear to bear directly upon their daughters' succession rights as the case of the Tour de Nesle Affair would seem to demonstrate. At the very least, gossip about Jeanne II's parentage provided a pretext for chroniclers to posit why she did not and could not inherit the French throne. Her mother's imprisonment and subsequent death also robbed Jeanne of a powerful maternal ally and left her at the mercy of her paternal uncles upon her father's death.

The supposed 'dangerous sexualities' of the women implicated in the Tour de Nesle Affair caused significant harm in their wake. Their daughters and their sister-in-law, Isabella of France, suffered from the enduring consequences of the scandal, and Philip V resurrected the claim that a woman could not succeed to the throne of France to seize it for himself. Both Charles IV and Philip VI replicated his template to press their own claims. The Tour de Nesle Affair and its attendant fallout would seem to illustrate the far-reaching repercussions that disordered royal sexualities had on the French line of succession. In the following centuries, similar questions about legitimacy and sexual continence would erupt both in France and more widely in Europe but never again would a woman come as close to inheriting the French throne as had Jeanne II of Navarre – nor would she have it so definitively torn from her grasp.

Notes

1. Jean of Paris or St Victor, 'Excerpta e Memoriali historiarum, auctore Johanne Parisiensi, Sancti Victoris Parisiensis canonico regulari', *Recueil des Historiens des Gaulles et de la France*, 21.659.
2. Elena Woodacre, *The Queens Regnant of Navarre: Succession, politics, and partnership, 1274–1512* (New York: Palgrave Macmillan, 2013), 61.

3 Benz St John agrees that scholars are mostly unanimous in believing that Isabella and Roger Mortimer were lovers, but pointing out that Seymour Phillips has raised doubts that their relationship was anything more than political. Lisa Benz St John, *Three Medieval Queens: Queenship and the Crown in fourteenth-century England* (New York: Palgrave Macmillan, 2012), 4, 176, n.11, citing Seymour Phillips, *Edward II* (New Haven, CT: Yale University Press, 2010).
4 *Letters and Papers, Foreign and Domestic, Henry VIII, Volume 10, January–June 1536*, ed. James Gairdner (London: Her Majesty's Stationery Office, 1887), 380–381. *British History Online*, available at www.british-history.ac.uk/letters-papers-hen8/vol10 (accessed 22 November 2023).
5 Peter Lake, *Bad Queen Bess? Libels, secret histories, and the politics of publicity in the reign of Queen Elizabeth I* (Oxford: Oxford University Press, 2016), 269.
6 'The Third Act Of Succession', in *Select Documents of English Constitutional History*, ed. G.B. Adams and H.M. Stephens (New York: Macmillan), 264–267.
7 'The Third Act of Succession', 258–259.
8 Elizabeth A.R. Brown has written extensively on the scandal in the context of Philip IV's life, focusing on the familial ties that Philip attempted to build and then break after the scandal. Her research into the historiography of the affair also addresses the twelve-year imprisonment of one of the princesses, Blanche of Burgundy, and relates it back to the French court. The works of Joseph R. Strayer and Jean Favier form the basis of current historiography regarding Philip IV. Tracy Adams has looked at the scandal from a literary perspective, addressing how different chronicles speak about the scandal to alternately scapegoat and absolve the princesses of guilt to support the French kings. Elena Woodacre is an exception to the lack of studies about the Tour de Nesle Affair with regard to the princesses' issue, as her landmark study *The Queens Regnant of Navarre* discusses the scandal in the context of Jeanne II of Navarre's life. See the bibliography.
9 Andrew W. Lewis has written extensively about succession in the Capetian era, while Craig Taylor and Charles T. Wood have both written about female succession more generally throughout medieval France. Elie Barnavi focused on the language of the Salic Law in his work, specifying that the Salic Law was not implemented at the time of the Tour de Nesle affair but that the scandal formed a baseline for its future use in the fifteenth century. Derek Whaley also discussed the Tour de Nesle affair in *The Routledge History of Monarchy* in his chapter entitled 'From a Salic law to the Salic law', which describes how female exclusion became ratified into French law at the end of the medieval period. See the bibliography.
10 Joseph R. Strayer, *The Reign of Philip the Fair* (Princeton, NJ: Princeton University Press, 2019), 35.
11 E.A.R. Brown, 'Philip the Fair and His Family', *Medieval Prosopography* 32 (2017): 138.
12 Brown, 'Philip the Fair and His Family', 142.
13 Brown, 'Philip the Fair and His Family', 173.

14 *La Chronique métrique attribuée à Geffroy de Paris*, ed. Armel Diverrès (Strasbourg, 1956), 297–298.
15 E.A.R. Brown, 'Philip the Fair of France and His Family's Disgrace: The adultery scandal of 1314 revealed, recounted, reimagined, and redated', *Mediaevistik* 32.1 (2019): 76.
16 Brown, 'Philip the Fair: The adultery scandal', 77.
17 Tracy Adams, 'Between History and Fiction: Revisiting the Affaire de la Tour de Nesle', *Viator* 43.2 (2012): 168.
18 Adams, 'Between History and Fiction', 174.
19 Adams, 'Between History and Fiction', 181.
20 Adams, 'Between History and Fiction', 182.
21 Jules Michelet, *Oeuvres complètes*, ed. Gabriel Monod, 40 vols (Paris 1893–1898), 3:164.
22 S.L. Field and M.C. Gaposchkin, 'Questioning the Capetians, 1180–1328', *History Compass* 12.7 (2014): 567.
23 M.A. Norbye, 'Genealogies and dynastic awareness in the Hundred Years War. The evidence of *A tous nobles qui aiment beaux faits et bonnes histoires*', *Journal of Medieval History* 33.3 (2007): 312.
24 Norbye, 'Genealogies', 312.
25 *La Chronique métrique*, 236, lines 7711–7714.
26 E.A.R. Brown, 'The Ceremonial of Royal Succession in Capetian France: The double funeral of Louis X', *Traditio* 34 (1978): 258.
27 Woodacre, *Queens Regnant*, 54; translation by Elena Woodacre from the *Chronicon Girardi de Fracheto*, 47: 'Tunc etiam declarum fuit quod ad coronam regni Franciae mulier non succedat'.
28 Brown, 'The Ceremonial of Royal Succession in Capetian France', 236.
29 S.L. Field and M.C. Gaposchkin, 'Questioning the Capetians, 1180–1328', 572.
30 Peggy McCracken, *The Romance of Adultery: Queenship and sexual transgression in old French literature* (Pittsburgh: University of Pennsylvania Press, 1998), 11.
31 McCracken, *Romance*, 1.
32 Murielle Gaude-Ferragu, *Queenship in Medieval France, 1300–1500*, trans. Angela Krieger (New York: Palgrave Macmillan, 2016), 38.
33 Brown, 'The Ceremonial of Royal Succession in Capetian France', 235.
34 Brown, 'The Ceremonial of Royal Succession in Capetian France', 234.
35 Woodacre, *Queens Regnant*, 55.
36 Woodacre, *Queens Regnant*, 55.
37 Craig Taylor, 'The Salic Law, French Queenship, and the Defense of Women in the Late Middle Ages', *French Historical Studies*, 29.4 (2006), 550.
38 Elie Barnavi, 'Mythes et réalité historique: Le cas de la loi salique', *Histoire, Économie et Société*, 3.3 (1984): 331.
39 Chapter 4 in this volume, 'Isabella of France and Roger Mortimer: lovers or allies?' by Michael R. Evans, delves further into the subject.
40 Woodacre, *Queens Regnant*, 57.
41 Woodacre, *Queens Regnant*, 60.

42 Woodacre, *Queens Regnant*, 60.
43 Norbye, 'Genealogies and dynastic awareness in the Hundred Years War', 312.
44 Norbye, 'Genealogies and dynastic awareness in the Hundred Years War', 312; Bibliothèque Nationale de France, MS Français 5059, fol. 18v, trans. Emily Lalande. 'Ceste Ysabel fille du roy Philippe le bel et femme de Edouart d'Angleterre voulut avoir France apre's la mort de ses freres qui, comme sera cy après dit, morurent sans hoir masle de leurs corps. Et y mist grant debat, mais femme ne succede point au royaume de France. Et quant femme y eust succedé si n'y avoit elle nul droit. Car ses freres avoient chacun une fille qui eussent succedé avant elle'.
45 Marguerite Keane, 'Louis IX, Louis X, Louis of Navarre: Family ties and political ideology in the Hours of Juana of Navarre', *Visual Resources*, 20.2–3 (2004): 238; Woodacre, *Queens Regnant*, 59.
46 E.A.R. Brown, 'Blanche of Artois and Burgundy, Château-Gaillard, and the Baron de Joursanvault', in *Negotiating Community and Difference in Medieval Europe: Gender, power, patronage and the authority of religion in Latin Christendom*, ed. Scott Wells and Katherine Smith (Leiden: Brill, 2009), 223–248.

Bibliography

Primary sources

Jean of Paris (Jean of St Victor). 'Excerpta e Memoriali historiarum, auctore Johanne Parisiensi, Sancti Victoris Parisiensis canonico regulari'. In *Recueil des historiens des Gaules et de la France. Tome Vingt et unième*, ed. Joseph-Daniel Guigniaut and Natalis de Wailly, 630–668. Paris: Imprimerie Impériale, 1855.

La Chronique métrique attribuée à Geffroy de Paris, ed. Armel Diverrès. Strasbourg: Université de Strasbourg, 1956.

Les Grandes Chroniques de France, ed. Jules Viard. 10 volumes. Paris: Société de l'Histoire de France, 1920–1953.

Letters and Papers, Foreign and Domestic, Henry VIII, Volume 10, January–June 1536, ed. James Gairdner. London: Her Majesty's Stationery Office, 1887.

Michelet, Jules. *Oeuvres completes*, ed. Gabriel Mono. 40 vols. Paris: Calmann-Lévy, 1893–1898.

Select Documents of English Constitutional History, ed. G.B. Adams and H.M. Stephens. New York: Macmillan, 1914.

Secondary sources

Adams, Tracy. 'Between History and Fiction: Revisiting the Affaire de la Tour de Nesle'. *Viator* 43.2 (2012): 165–192.

Barnavi, Elie. 'Mythes et réalité historique: Le cas de la loi salique'. *Histoire, Économie et Société* 3.3 (1984): 323–337.

Benz St John, Lisa. *Three Medieval Queens: Queenship and the Crown in fourteenth-century England*. New York: Palgrave Macmillan, 2012.

Brown, Elizabeth A.R. 'The Ceremonial of Royal Succession in Capetian France: The double funeral of Louis X'. *Traditio* 34 (1978): 227–271.
Brown, Elizabeth A.R. 'The Political Repercussions of Family Ties in the Early Fourteenth Century: The marriage of Edward II of England and Isabelle of France'. *Speculum* 63.3 (1988): 573–595.
Brown, Elizabeth A.R. 'Blanche of Artois and Burgundy, Château-Gaillard, and the Baron de Joursanvault'. In *Negotiating Community and Difference in Medieval Europe: Gender, power, patronage and the authority of religion in Latin Christendom*, ed. Scott Wells and Katherine Smith, 223–248. Leiden: Brill, 2009.
Brown, Elizabeth A.R. 'Philip the Fair and His Family'. *Medieval Prosopography* 32 (2017): 125–185.
Brown, Elizabeth A.R. 'Philip the Fair of France and His Family's Disgrace: The adultery scandal of 1314 revealed, recounted, reimagined, and redated'. *Mediaevistik* 32.1 (2019): 71–103.
Favier, Jean. *Philippe le Bel*. Paris: Fayard, 1978.
Field, Sean L., and M. Cecilia Gaposchkin. 'Questioning the Capetians, 1180–1328'. *History Compass* 12.7 (2014): 567–585.
Gaude-Ferragu, Murielle. *Queenship in Medieval France, 1300–1500*. Trans. Angela Krieger. New York: Palgrave Macmillan, 2016.
Keane, Marguerite. 'Louis IX, Louis X, Louis of Navarre: Family ties and political ideology in the Hours of Juana of Navarre'. *Visual Resources* 20.2-3 (2004): 237–252.
Lake, Peter. *Bad Queen Bess? Libels, secret histories, and the politics of publicity in the reign of Queen Elizabeth I*. Oxford: Oxford University Press, 2016.
Lewis, Andrew W. *Royal Succession in Capetian France: Studies on familial order and the state*. Cambridge, MA: Harvard University Press, 1981.
McCracken, Peggy. *The Romance of Adultery: Queenship and sexual transgression in old French literature*. Pittsburgh: University of Pennsylvania Press, 1998.
Norbye, Marigold Anne. 'Genealogies and dynastic awareness in the Hundred Years War. The evidence of *A tous nobles qui aiment beaux faits et bonnes histoires*'. *Journal of Medieval History* 33.3 (2007): 297–319.
Strayer, Joseph R. *The Reign of Philip the Fair*. Princeton, NJ: Princeton University Press, 2019.
Taylor, Craig. 'The Salic Law, French Queenship, and the Defense of Women in the Late Middle Ages'. *French Historical Studies* 29.4 (2006): 543–564.
Whaley, Derek. 'From a Salic law to the Salic law'. In *The Routledge History of Monarchy*, ed. Elena Woodacre, Lucinda H.S. Dean, Chris Jones, Russell E. Martin, Zita Eva Rohr. Abingdon: Routledge, 2019.
Wood, Charles T. 'Queens, Queans, and Kingship: An inquiry into theories of royal legitimacy in late medieval England and France'. In *Order and Innovation in the Middle Ages: Essays in honour of Joseph R. Strayer*, ed. William Chester Jordan, Bruce McNab, and Teofilo F. Ruiz, 385–400. Princeton, NJ: Princeton University Press, 1976.
Woodacre, Elena. *The Queens Regnant of Navarre: Succession, politics, and partnership, 1274–1512*. New York: Palgrave Macmillan, 2013.

9

Chaste kings and unsuitable women: sex, interfaith relations, and sovereignty in the *Castigos* of Sancho IV of Castile

David Cantor-Echols

In numerous letters sent to a host of Spanish churchmen throughout the thirteenth century, successive popes bemoaned reports that the Jewish residents of dioceses across the Iberian Peninsula abjured the Fourth Lateran Council's 1215 decree (hereafter Canon 68) that Jews and Muslims 'of either sex, and in all Christian lands, and at all times, shall easily be distinguishable from the rest of the population by the quality of their clothes'.[1] According to these papal missives, the danger inherent in Jews' refusal to wear specific garments, or in some cases an identifying badge, was the same one first identified at Fourth Lateran: the resulting inability to distinguish between Christians and non-Christians could produce 'such confusion that no differences are noticeable. Thus, it sometimes happens that, by mistake, Christians have intercourse with Jewish or Saracen women, and Jews and Saracens with Christian women'.[2] A representative letter, sent by Innocent IV to the bishop of Córdoba on 13 April 1250, cites the Council's decree and expresses concern that the Jews of the diocese 'do not observe this statute, and as a result they may dare to indulge in the sin of forbidden intercourse under the veil of error', thus necessitating that the statute be all the more 'firmly observed'.[3] In the decades following Fourth Lateran, strikingly similar directives were sent by the papacy not only to Spanish bishops (of Toledo, Burgos, and Tarragona) but also to sees in France, Germany, Hungary, and elsewhere. The wide geographic distribution of these letters' recipients, as well as the letters' frequency and similarity both to one another and to Canon 68, would seem to lend credence to R.I. Moore's contention that 'Lateran IV laid down a machinery of persecution for Western Christendom'.[4]

The present chapter is not concerned with debating when or whether Christian Europe 'became a persecuting society', nor is it concerned with measuring Fourth Lateran's supposedly singular influence on the identification and subjugation of religious minorities. This study does not focus on the ultimate phenomenon of religious persecution, whether as a putative goal or an incidental side effect of statutes like Fourth Lateran's Canon 68. Rather, it interrogates the ways such legislation specifically warned against and sought to regulate sexual intercourse between Christians and non-Christians. Nowhere were the boundaries between these groups more consequentially transgressed than in matters of sex, which is 'why medieval Christian anxieties ... about the integrity of the self were so often expressed in sexual terms'.[5] As will be argued here, the particular type of regulation set forth in Canon 68, repeated and expanded in various forms and contexts throughout the thirteenth century, reflected Christian elites' sustained anxieties about their own authorities to govern complex societies whose internal and external boundaries were permeable and unfixed. Since 'powers are attributed to any structure of ideas, and ... rules of avoidance make a visible public recognition of its boundaries',[6] we can see in medieval Christian prohibitions on sex with religious minorities an effort to identify threats to ruling authority and thereby reinforce that authority's claims to power.

The following analysis focuses on a conspicuously royalist rather than papal example of these elite Christian worries over interfaith sex and political authority, Sancho IV of Castile's *Castigos* ('admonitions'), a mirror for princes comprising fifty chapters of moral lessons written for the king's son and heir apparent. As I shall argue, Sancho's *Castigos* (c.1292) articulated a vision of the Christian socio-political order which was inextricably rooted in questions of sex, and which viewed the sexual activities of the sovereign as holding profound implications for the spiritual and political integrity of the body politic. In seeking to ground politics in sex and, more specifically, by warning against the dangers of royal intercourse with Jewish and Muslim women, Sancho participated in the same policing of the boundaries between Christian and 'other' undertaken by Canon 68. But beyond this, he directed heightened scrutiny towards royal sexual contact with non-Christians, locating in the potential for this behaviour a firm limit to Christian authority over diverse and rapidly changing societies such as Castile's. If Fourth Lateran had endeavoured to visually cordon off Jews and Muslims, Sancho sought with his *Castigos* to make visible and unambiguous the chastity and sexual discretion of the king, which he depicted as intrinsic to royal self-mastery and sound Christian governance.

Sancho IV (r. 1284–1295) ascended to the Castilian throne in the wake of the storied yet tumultuous reign of his father, Alfonso X 'The Learned' (r. 1252–1284), whose ambitious intellectual projects and designs on the Holy Roman imperial title elicited sustained criticisms from the Castilian clergy and high nobility. Sancho had played no small part in the unrest that marked the final decade of his father's rule, and the prince led the baronial rebellion against Alfonso, which culminated in the formal censure of the king at the April 1282 meeting of the Castilian *Cortes* (parliament) at

Valladolid. Among the charges levelled against Alfonso were perjury, abrogation of the law, and mental incapacity. These accusations built upon the complaints of fiscal mismanagement brought against Alfonso by the Castilian clergy three years before, and it was with the support of the barons, the towns and cities, and the Church that Sancho wrested the fiscal, judicial, and military prerogatives of the royal office from his father, leaving Alfonso X with only his crown and title.[7] As David Nirenberg has shown, displeasure with Alfonso's expansive administration and increasing delegation of royal authority reverberated into Sancho's reign, and a rejection of the alleged Judaising fiscality that characterised 'The Learned' king's tenure can be seen to animate the *Castigos* themselves.[8] Taking as his consort the prominent noblewoman María de Molina, Sancho presided as king over a realignment of the interests of the Castilian Crown with those of the high nobility.[9] It is with the context of Sancho's alliance with Castile's grandees in mind that we might begin to grasp the close attention paid in the *Castigos* to the careful maintenance of clear sexual boundaries in a society underpinned by the ideal of chivalry. We will examine first what the text prescribes for intra-Christian sexual conduct before analysing its prohibitions on sex with non-Christians.

Chapter VI of the *Castigos* asserts that 'chivalry of noblemen was created ... so that they would have shame', a virtue which in turn: instils 'the fear of God and gives knowledge of Him'; 'diverts bad deeds and shows the way to doing good ones'; and 'makes a man know his lineage and have shame for his line and for himself and for those who will come after him'.[10] Shame, then, is seen to be a guiding moral virtue within the chivalric order Sancho outlines, and given the king's position atop this hierarchy, so much the more is his own sense of shame a matter of grave political consequence. Sancho instructs his son,

> A king's shame is like a white mantle without a stain. A king who loses his sense of shame ... is like a leper who has lost his lips and his nose to leprosy. If a king has a sense of shame, he will not go astray with the wife of his vassal, and he will feel shame for the sake of the husband who lives with and depends upon him. For example, consider how much evil befell Spain because of what the king Don Rodrigo did with La Cava, the daughter of Count Julian. There are plenty of recent examples of lustful kings as well.[11]

We will return in due course to another of these 'recent examples' of destructive royal sexuality. First, chivalry here can be taken not merely as a shared code of conduct but as a means of structuring elite social relations, with shame being seen to act as a foundational and indispensable regulating virtue. What is more, a king's vassal is not only his lieutenant and dependant, but he is a full-fledged member of the royal household. Therefore, a king's lack of shame in fornicating with his vassal's wife (or daughter, in the case of Rodrigo and La Cava) has the potential to upset the entire social order to the point of the king's personal disfigurement and the destruction of his realm.

As Sancho informs his son, Rodrigo's lack of shame, along with its disastrous aftermath, was hardly an isolated example of lustful kingship gone horribly wrong. But it was the sole case that Sancho saw fit to discuss in more than one passage of the *Castigos*, and thus it merits additional attention here. In medieval Castilian historiography, the rape of La Cava functions as something like the original sin of Spanish kingship, a grievous sexual crime committed by a Christian ruler with devastating consequences, both immediate and transhistorical. In brief, the North African nobleman Julian is supposed to have sent his daughter to be educated at the court of his lord, Rodrigo, the last Visigothic king of Spain. Rodrigo raped the girl, thereby betraying his vassal, who then retaliated by conspiring with the leaders of the Berber armies which would soon cross the Strait of Gibraltar, toppling Rodrigo and ending his line, ushering in the Peninsula's conversion to Islam.[12]

While the particulars can be seen to vary across chronicles, the general sequence of events just described provided crucial coordinates for generations of Iberian Christian historians, who began grappling with the spiritual and political aftermath of the Muslim conquest almost as soon as it had been completed. Although earlier Arabic and Latin sources attest to the existence of Count Julian, Sancho's passing mention of Julian and La Cava is among the earliest records of these figures in the Castilian vernacular tradition, and very likely is the first to name the count's daughter as such.[13] Sancho does not identify Julian as a Christian, but he marshals this exemplum to illustrate the importance of shame in maintaining the ideal Christian royal–noble bond. Moreover, the prologue to the *Castigos*, which opens with a treatment of the Biblical story of Adam and Eve, draws on the legendary story of Rodrigo and Julian both to historicise the composition of the text and to ground it in a specific moral framework. 'I made [this book]', Sancho writes, 'in the year [1292] that, with the help of God, I won Tarifa from the Moors, who had held it in their power for more than six hundred years, ever since the king Don Rodrigo lost it because of the evil and abominable treason of the bad Count Julian'.[14] In the immediate context of the prologue, the rape of La Cava goes unmentioned, even if the intended readership was perhaps assumed to be aware of the legend through other means.[15] The prologue to the *Castigos* seeks primarily to capitalise on the redemptive glory of Sancho's victory at Tarifa, which the reader is to interpret as having reversed centuries of political humiliation and wayward religious belief. But even if the text refers to Julian's betrayal of Rodrigo as a commonly known historical event, it is only upon reading the subsequent characterisation of the count's actions as direct consequences of Rodrigo's 'shameless' sexual behaviour that the Muslim conquest of Iberia is revealed as a punishment for deviant royal sexuality.

Just as Sancho's capture of Tarifa from Muslim control was supposed to have reversed Rodrigo's sexual misdeeds, so also were other 'recent examples of lustful kings' to be viewed on a wide historical continuum, where their significance could be made legible by comparison with earlier cases. In addition to that of Rodrigo and La Cava, Sancho urges his son to consider the example of 'so wise a man' as Solomon, who questioned his law and faith by flirting with paganism under the influence of 'women of other beliefs'. The ramifications of Solomon's dalliances, Sancho notes, were not felt by the wise king himself but by his descendants.[16] Ranging widely across an array of literary and historical touchstones, Sancho places this Biblical exemplum in direct conversation with a relatively recent and now well-known Castilian one which receives its first (but hardly its last) textual treatment in the *Castigos*: the story of Alfonso VIII of Castile and the Jewess of Toledo.

The fascination down the ages with this tale of forbidden Christian-Jewish love has received ample treatment elsewhere, such that we need not rehearse its reception here.[17] The details and moral-political implications of the exemplum as presented by Sancho follow closely on his discussion of Solomon's relations with gentile women and are rendered in much the same mode as the legend of Rodrigo and La Cava. But here, Sancho removes all doubt as to whether the paramour in question was of the same faith, and the identification of Alfonso VIII's lover as a Jewish woman is all the more significant, as it marks the transgression not of an internal chivalric boundary (lord/vassal) but of an external, spiritual one (Christian/other). Sancho instructs his heir, addressing him as 'fijo' twice in short succession,

> Likewise carefully consider, my son, and be chastened, my son, by what happened to the king Don Alfonso of Castile, who won the battle of Úbeda [Las Navas de Tolosa, 1212]. Because of the seven years that he lived a wicked life with a Jewess of Toledo, God dealt him a great injury and punishment at the battle of Alarcos [1195], in which he was defeated and fled, and then he and everyone in his kingdom were miserable. The most fortunate were those who died [at Alarcos]. And because the king [only] later confessed to God, [He] killed his sons, and his grandson, the king Don Fernando [III], the son of his daughter, [later] took charge of the kingdom. [Alfonso] repented for committing such a bad sin ... for which he made amends by founding the convent of Las Huelgas de Burgos ... And God then gave him good fortune against the Moors in the battle of Úbeda. But even though he was fortunate in that battle, it would have been much better if he had not been first defeated at the Battle of Alarcos, in which misfortune he fell because of his sin. It is written in the histories of old that God punishes the subjects for the sins that kings (who

are the leaders of others) commit. And so as to give kings greater punishment, God makes an example of those who are around them ... and in this way God doubles [kings'] grief.[18]

The *Castigos*' discussion of how the defeat at Alarcos had disrupted the Castilian succession was likely more than a little personal for Sancho, the second son of Alfonso X, whose uprising against 'The Learned' king had been precipitated in part by his successional dispute with his late older brother's orphaned sons, whom Alfonso had indicated should succeed him before Sancho.[19] While disruption of Alfonso VIII's dynastic line (from which Sancho himself descended) had not ultimately resulted in catastrophe for the kings of Castile, it was nevertheless as a direct consequence of Alfonso's prolonged affair with a woman of another faith that he had handed a Muslim army a signal victory. The ignominy of Alfonso's defeat was not to be as crushing or as permanent a condition for Iberian Christians as Rodrigo's had been, but Sancho took pains to impress upon his son the larger dangers that sex with non-Christian women still entailed for king and subjects alike.

In the socio-political universe of Sancho's *Castigos*, the unwanted potential for sexual mixing with Jews and Muslims lurks not in the problem of these minorities' invisibility in Christian society, a spectre raised by the Fourth Lateran's Canon 68 and conjured repeatedly in subsequent papal correspondence. Beyond this, the *Castigos* express no concern for the sexual behaviour of ordinary Christians, Jews, and Muslims as an independent variable in the social and political affairs of Castile. Rather, the *Castigos* focus primarily on the sexual comportment of the king and the example he sets for his subjects (discussed further below). In this respect, while Sancho's text would appear to stand in stark contrast to the ambitious regimes of identification and surveillance outlined by Canon 68 or by the seventh part of Alfonso X's law code, *Siete Partidas*, the *Castigos* in fact invert the guiding logic of these statutes by making the king, not Jews or Muslims, more conspicuous in society. Despite this important distinction, however, the *Castigos*' discussion of the threatening attributes inherent in non-Christian women evinces a taxonomising impulse that bears some resemblance to the one informing Canon 68's direction that Jews and Muslims should wear distinguishing dress. We turn now to a discussion of Sancho's classification of Jewish and Muslim women, assessing these passages of the *Castigos* in light of the earlier regulations devised by the Fourth Lateran Council and Alfonso X.

In contrast to the concerned descriptions of rampant interfaith mixing found in Canon 68 and elsewhere, the *Castigos* offer no judgment on the interfaith sexual tendencies of Jews and Muslims living under Christian rule. Indeed, the lone Jew or Muslim explicitly identified in the text, the

Jewess of Toledo, quite possibly never existed. In the *Castigos*, then, the sexual habits of Jews and Muslims find their importance as a category of political thought only when Jewish or Muslim women become the objects of royal desire. The sexual habits of the king are the text's primary concern, and its prohibitions on sex with non-Christian women are articulated as part of a wider admonition to avoid 'sins of fornication' with a variety of 'unsuitable women' including women religious, married women, and virgins.[20] Each of these female archetypes would have been instantly recognisable to any medieval reader, but Sancho is careful to mark out as alien the 'Jewess' and the 'Moorish woman'.[21] At the same time, he defines these 'unsuitable' types of women relative to a normative Christian identity. Drawing on polemical discourses common throughout thirteenth-century Europe, Sancho highlights the catalysing role played by Jewish women at the inception of Christian history while he presents Muslim women as vessels for a dangerous system of muddled unbelief threatening Christendom in the present. With these characterisations, Sancho seizes the kingly prerogative to instruct and traces in the potential for sex with non-Christian women a boundary which his son would cross at his own peril and that of the kingdom. In this way, rather than distinguishing Jewish and Muslim communities in society through the deployment of badges or specified garments, Sancho identifies the direst threats to Christendom by way of discursively constructing them in idealised feminine forms located at prescribed distances from the person of the king. It is the duty of the king, the *Castigos* argue, to maintain that distance as an example for others.[22]

Following an opening excursus on the nobility of virginity (discussed below), Chapter XXI of the *Castigos* implores its princely readership to 'never desire to sin or have much interaction with a Jewess or with a Moorish woman, because the Jewess is a woman of another law, which is hostile to yours, and the Moorish woman is a woman of other beliefs that insist on the destruction and dishonour of your own'. The king then tells his heir of 'the sin that exists in both', sketching on one hand a familiar Christian narrative of the Jews' betrayal and mockery of Christ on the Cross, and on the other hand characterising Islam as both a wilful distortion of Christianity and a religion with no intrinsic beliefs.[23] The opposition of Judaism's 'hostile' ignorance and denial of Christian truth to Islam's 'destructive' antagonism towards Christianity does not preclude Sancho's treatment of sex with Jewish and Muslim women as a single type of deviant behaviour to be avoided. But he dedicates considerable space to explaining the negative characteristics of both faiths as embodied by their female adherents.

Addressing Judaism first, Sancho instructs his son that 'the Jewess is of the lineage of those who killed your Lord Jesus Christ … [and who] said very loudly: 'Crucify him! Crucify him! May his blood be spilled before us and our children!'[24] In addition to the part they are alleged to have played in the Crucifixion – denying Christ, offering him vinegar to drink, adorning him with the crown of thorns, and piercing his right side with the lance – the Jewess and her coreligionists 'continue to deny him today'.[25] And since the prince is born of a Christian lineage while the Jewess descends from those who spilled Christ's blood, Sancho admonishes his son that he 'should not yearn for any union' with Jews.[26]

> Moreover, they deny that He is the one who brought them out of captivity in Egypt, where they languished under Pharaoh. And they deny that he is the Messiah, the one for whom they waited, and in so doing they deny all of the holy prophesies of the prophets and patriarchs.[27]

Owing to this history, Sancho enjoins his heir to 'flee from' and not 'take pleasure in' or 'bring your face close to that of a Jewess in friendship'.[28]

In Sancho's telling, the Jews harbour a clear enmity towards Christian theology, but they are also seen to have played an undeniable role first in the life of Christ and the Crucifixion and second in offering, through their continued ignorance and denial of the faith, living witness to Christianity's inherent truth. Thus, the Jews' uncomfortable but longstanding proximity (theological and physical) to Christians, and their antagonistic yet closely situated 'lineage', made 'approaching the Jewess' face in friendship' a distinct possibility in a multifaith Christian society like late medieval Castile, as the example of Alfonso VIII made clear. The *Castigos*' harsh denunciation of the Jews notwithstanding, Sancho expressed anew a longstanding royal ambivalence towards the close ties linking Crown and Jewry.[29]

Drafting his monumental law code some decades earlier, Alfonso X claimed in *Partida* VII that the Jews 'still celebrate Good Friday ... by way of contempt; stealing children and fastening them to crosses, and making images of wax and crucifying them, when they cannot obtain children'. But, in spite of these alleged simulations of the Passion, Alfonso notes, 'the great Christian sovereigns have always permitted [the Jews] to live among them ... because ... it was constantly in the minds of men that they were descended from those who crucified Our Lord Jesus Christ'.[30] Both to make this deep history of Christian-Jewish animosity and interdependence visible in contemporary society, and to enforce a boundary between these groups, *Partida* VII commands, in the spirit of Fourth Lateran's Canon 68, that 'all Jews male and female living in our dominions shall bear some distinguishing mark upon their heads so that people may plainly recognise a Jew, or a Jewess'. Jews found to be in violation would be fined or publicly lashed if they were unable to pay.[31] Although *Partida* VII indicates severe punishments for both Muslim and Jewish men who have sex with Christian women,[32] the requirement that Jews – but not Muslims – be visibly marked out is not explicitly couched with respect to the threat of sexual mixing, nor is attention given to the sexual activities of Muslim or Jewish women. In this way, Alfonso's legislation can be seen to both follow and diverge from Canon 68, and it also marked a reversal of the policy of his father, Fernando III.

According to a letter of Honorius III sent to the archbishop of Toledo on 20 March 1219, Fernando had asked the pope to grant Castile's Jews dispensation from having to wear an identifying sign on grounds that they were so upset by Canon 68's requirement that they had begun to emigrate to Muslim lands, depriving the king of crucial 'revenue which in large measure derives from these same Jews'.[33] Jewish communities may have endured in Europe at the pleasure of Christian kings, but the fiscal ties binding this marked-out group to the royal office engendered a symbiotic relationship which in turn, as Sara Lipton has shown, yielded unwanted cultural associations and political accusations that posed significant challenges to royal authority.[34] Sancho's *Castigos* thus responded strenuously to the notion of royal Judeophilia in Castile. The text reinvigorated the prohibition on interfaith sex by centring the sexual judgement of the king and simultaneously conceptualising the Jews' hermeneutical role in Christian society in a manner similar to *Partida* VII's characterisation.

If Sancho's discussion of the theological reasons for avoiding sex with Jewish women still allows for Judaism's pivotal role in the formation of Christian religion and identity, his approach to Islam is altogether more hostile, and he denies the Prophet Muhammad and his followers any part in shaping the Christian historical narrative or in helping constitute the contemporary Christian social order. Sancho eschews the etymological approach to categorising Islam modelled in *Partida* VII, which explains that '*Surracenus*, in Latin, means Moor, in Castilian', tracing the term's root to Sarah and Hagar in the Old Testament and discussing (albeit somewhat inaccurately) the differences in belief among Muslim sects.[35] When it comes to Islam, the *Castigos* offer none of the scholarly nuance on display in 'The Learned' king's *Partida* VII, and instead operates solely in a polemical mode, borrowing tropes from what John V. Tolan has described as an antihagiographical Christian tradition of depicting the life of Muhammad.[36] What is more, the *Castigos* take a much more overtly misogynistic and even dehumanising tack in its description of the Moorish woman than it does with the Jewess.[37]

Whereas the *Castigos*' idealised Jewess enjoys a lineage, history, and humanity of her own, however inimical they might be to Sancho's, the king instructs his son that he 'should not wish to count the Moorish woman as a woman at all, but rather count her as a beast, because she lacks any law whatsoever'. In addition to dehumanising the Moorish woman in this way, the *Castigos* portray the Islam she practises as a perverted, upside-down

Christianity whose adherents prize 'those things which our law holds as sins, but which for them are salvation; and that which we hold as salvation, they view as sin'. Gratification of the flesh is a guiding principle of Islam, Sancho contends, and Muslims pursue this goal as a means to spiritual fulfilment in direct contravention of both the Old and New Testaments. While the Jewess is seen to belong to a misguided people who accept the Old Testament but reject or fail to understand the Christian interpretation of it, Muslims are depicted as rejecting Scripture outright, pursuing only their carnal desires.[38] This emphasis on the libidinal nature of Muslims was a common feature of thirteenth-century anti-Muslim polemics penned by Spanish Christians, and Sancho along with his probable collaborators on the *Castigos* might have engaged with some of those very works.[39] Sancho concludes his discussion of the dangers posed by the Moorish woman by maintaining that 'the Moor is nothing more than a dog and the Moorish woman is nothing more than a bitch. And he who sins with a Moorish woman through his own will is as one who sins with a bitch or with a beast, since she has no law or belief'.[40] The text's sustained emphasis on both the animal qualities and sexual appetites of Muslim women and men – Jewish men go unmentioned in the *Castigos* – serves to heighten all the more the magnitude of transgressing the boundary between Christianity and Islam.

Despite the specific features of their respective forms of anti-Christianity, Judaism and Islam are presented as twin threats by Sancho, who locates in the sovereign's risk of sexual contact with women of either faith certain ruin. Rather than seeking, as *Partida* VII had done, to assert royal authority by regulating minorities' commercial enterprise, religious observance, involvement in secular administration, and intimate contact with ordinary Christians – which for Alfonso X included intercourse but also cohabitation and sharing meals[41] – Sancho's *Castigos* identify sex as the interreligious fault line of primary consequence, offering no discussion of these other forms of interfaith contact. The potential for sex to blur the hard boundaries between Christian and non-Christian provided the impetus for Sancho's decision to develop the sexual discretion of the king as a guiding political virtue. To conclude our analysis, we turn to a discussion of the role that royal chastity plays in Sancho's vision for a society where the sexual comportment of the king needed to be visible and beyond reproach if boundaries with non-Christians were to be properly maintained.

As Purificación Martínez has argued, Sancho's *Castigos* promote a model for kingship which also functions as a performance of ideal masculinity within a homosocial political system where bonds of socio-political relation were overtly gendered.[42] Within that system, Sancho states in the text's prologue, 'all men are obliged to instruct, rule, and supervise their children ... [so that they] set an example of good living for others – and this pertains even more to kings and princes, who have to govern kingdoms and peoples'.[43] But while we have already encountered the ways in which the *Castigos* provide negative examples of libidinous kingship's undesirable ramifications, the reader is offered no corresponding positive examples of chaste kings. Instead, the notion of the sovereign as a role model for his children and subjects is rendered throughout the *Castigos* in more figurative, strikingly visual language. The king's good example is compared to a gleaming emerald – a stone whose meaning Sancho links to the Castilian word for 'polished', or 'fastidious' – a focal point to which the entire kingdom turns its attention for guidance.[44] And though the undergirding shame of chivalry is compared to an immaculate white cloak, as discussed above, Sancho offers a vivid contrast to that plain raiment in his description of royal sexuality. Having offered an encomium to the ideal of virginity in the same chapter of the *Castigos* which warns against sex with Jewish and Muslim women and which relates the example of Alfonso VIII and the Jewess, Sancho asserts, 'Virginity and chastity in the king ... [are] like a mantle adorned in gold on which there is not a single stain'.[45]

So draped in fine fabrics of pure white and shimmering gold, his chaste example shining like a precious stone, the king was to be the most conspicuous member of a society where boundaries of faith were not always as obvious as Christian authorities would have liked. And while interrogating the homosocial political environment in which the *Castigos* were composed can help us understand the text's careful attention to cultivating a model for masculine self-control, it is only by taking into account the wider anxieties the text shares with Canon 68 and *Partida* VII that we fully understand its focus on interfaith sex and the chastity of the king.

As Thomas F. Glick and Oriol Pi-Sunyer urged scholars of medieval Iberia to consider more than half a century ago, cultural contact begets both cultural change and reactions to it, and we can see in the ways a group structures its internal and external interactions an attempt to fix boundaries which were in flux.[46] The normative character of certain types of medieval evidence, namely legal sources like *Partida* VII and ecclesiastical decrees like Canon 68, should encourage scholars to interpret the efforts mounted by the intelligences behind these sources as attempts to account for cultural contact by asserting the boundaries of a wider community and their authority over it.[47] Sancho's *Castigos* present just such a case, and we ought to view the 'mirror for princes' genre it exemplifies as a normative literary form which assimilated ideas about kingship from other sources (chronicles, poetry, theology, philosophy) while offering its circumscribed royal readership lessons on governance rendered in a prescriptive mode which did not always acknowledge the changing socio-political circumstances to which it responded.[48] The *Castigos* echoed Canon 68 and *Partida* VII's acute sense of the potential for illicit sex between Christians and non-Christians as well as the harm such unwanted contact could produce. Indeed, as we have seen, Sancho's entire conception of Spanish history hinged upon an understanding of the dire consequences of sex between Christians and non-Christians. Crucially, the specific interfaith mixing that Sancho warned against was not that of ordinary Christian, Muslim, and Jewish subjects in Castile, but rather centred on royal indiscretion with religious minorities. Whereas the earlier texts examined here sought to police interfaith contact at the 'bottom' of society, the *Castigos* took a 'top-down' approach to the same problem. This difference in focus, with attention given to royal sexuality rather than the behaviour of common people, nevertheless arose from a similar impulse to assert ruling authority. But in theorising royal authority anew in terms of abstention from interfaith sex, Sancho sought to stabilise shifting boundaries of faith and royal authority in his own person instead of in the body politic.

Notes

1 Solomon Grayzel, *The Church and the Jews in the XIIIth Century: A study of their relations during the years 1198–1254, based on the papal letters and the conciliar decrees of the period* (Philadelphia: Dropsie College for Hebrew and Cognate Learning, 1933), 309: 'statuimus, ut tales utriusque sexus in omni Christianorum provincia, et omni tempore qualitate habitus publice ab aliis populis distinguantur'. All translations of the Council's canons are my own.

2 Grayzel, *Church and the Jews*, 309: 'sed in quibusdam sic quedan inolevit confusio, ut nulla differentia discernatur. Unde contingit interdum quod per errorem Christiani, Judeorum, seu Saracenorum, et Judei seu Saraceni Christianorum mulieribus commisceantur'.

3 Grayzel, *Church and the Jews*, 283: 'Licet in sacro generali concilio provida fuerit deliberatione statutum ut Judei a Christianis habitu distinguantur ... Judei tamen in Corduensis civitate et diocese commorantes statutum hujusmodi, sicut accepimus, non observant, propter quod damnate commixtionis excessus sub erroris potest velamento presumi. [...] Volentes igitur statutum ipsum firmiter observari, Fraternitati tue per apostolica scripta mandamus quatinus si est ita, Judeos ipsos ad deferendum signum quo a Christianis qualitate habitus distinguantur'.

4 R.I. Moore, *The Formation of a Persecuting Society: Authority and deviance in western Europe, 950–1250*, 2nd edn (Oxford: Blackwell, 2007), 10.

5 David Nirenberg, 'Conversion, Sex, and Segregation: Jews and Christians in medieval Spain', *American Historical Review* 107.4 (2002): 1073.

6 Mary Douglas, *Mary Douglas: Collected Works. Vol. II: Purity and Danger: An analysis of concepts of pollution and taboo*, 2nd edn (London: Routledge, 2003), 160.

7 A considerable body of scholarship has treated the complex circumstances surrounding the near-deposition of Alfonso X. For a concise overview, see Joseph F. O'Callaghan, *The Learned King: The reign of Alfonso X of Castile* (Philadelphia: University of Pennsylvania Press, 1993), 252–269. On the specific complaints of the Castilian Church with respect to Alfonso's fiscal policies, see Peter Linehan, 'The Spanish Church Revisited: The episcopal *gravamina* of 1279', in *Authority and Power*, ed. Brian Tierney and Peter Linehan (Cambridge: Cambridge University Press, 1980), 127–147.

8 David Nirenberg, 'Deviant Politics and Jewish Love: Alfonso VIII and the Jewess of Toledo', *Jewish History* 21 (2007): 15–41.

9 Peter Linehan, *History and the Historians of Medieval Spain* (Oxford: Clarendon Press, 1993), 463–505. Linehan provides a useful summary of the disputed union of Sancho and María de Molina (on grounds of consanguinity) and the ultimate dispensation granted by the papacy.

10 Hugo O. Bizzarri, ed., *Castigos del rey don Sancho IV* (Frankfurt and Madrid: Vervuert and Iberoamericana, 2001), 105. I rely throughout this chapter on Bizzarri's authoritative critical edition of Sancho's *Castigos*. All translations of the original Castilian text are my own. 'La vergüença raygada en el coraçon del omne bueno e de la buena muger guarda el temor de Dios e dal conosçençia contra Él. La vergüença desuía los malos fechos e da carrera por que se fagan los buenos. La vergüença faze conosçer a omne el linaje onde viene e que tome vergüença de su linaje e de sí mesmo e de los que han de venir dél ... Por eso fue fecha la cauallería de los fijosdalgo, por que ouiesen vergüença'.

11 Bizzarri, *Castigos*, 106. 'Tal es la vergüença en el rey commo el panno blanco en que non ha manzilla ninguna. E tal es el rey quando pierde vergüença ... commo el gafo que por gafedat ha perdido los beços e las narizes. E si el rey ouiere vergüença en sí, non errará con la muger de su vasallo, e vergüença aurá de su marido que biue con él e de sí mesmo. *Verbi graçia* para mientes quánto mal vyno en Espanna por lo que fizo el rey don Rodrigo con la Caba, fija del conde don Jullán. E désto podríamos traer aquí otros nueuos enxemplos de reyes luxuriosos'.

12 Roger J.H. Collins, *The Arab Conquest of Spain: 710–797* (Oxford: Blackwell, 1989), 32, 35–36. See also Nicola Clarke, *The Muslim Conquest of Iberia: Medieval Arabic narratives* (London: Routledge, 2012), 108–111.

13 On the appearances of these figures in early Castilian chronicles, see Geraldine Hazbun, *Narratives of the Islamic Conquest from Medieval Spain* (New York: Palgrave Macmillan, 2015), 1–2. Regarding the extensive literary reception of La Cava throughout the Middle Ages and beyond, see Elizabeth Drayson, *The King and The Whore: King Roderick and La Cava* (New York: Palgrave Macmillan, 2007).

14 Bizzarri, *Castigos*, 74. 'E fízelo en el anno que con ayuda de Dios gané a Tarifa de los moros, cuya era que auía más de seysçientos annos que la tenía en su poder, desque la perdió el rey don Rodrigo, que fue el postrimero rey de los godos por la maldat e trayçión abominable del malo del conde don Jullián'.

15 Geraldine Hazbun discusses the treatment of the rape of La Cava in Alfonso X's *Estoria de Espanna*, which dates to the final years of the king's reign and possibly could have served as one of the sources for Sancho's discussion of this episode in the *Castigos*. See Hazbun, *Narratives*, 18.
16 Bizzarri, *Castigos*, 205. 'El rey Salamón, que fue tan sabio omne, mugeres de otra creençia le tiraron de la su ley e le fiçieron que dexase el Dios de Dauid, su padre, e a desonrra del tenplo que fiziera él a Dios fiziese otros tenplos de las dehesas e de los dioses de los gentiles, por la qual cosa Dios houo grand sanna contra él. E commo quier que lo non acalonnase en el galardón lo que prometiera a Dauid, su padre, colonnolo en Robohán, su fijo, con Gerobohán, su seruiente'.
17 David Nirenberg synthesises several of these treatments by way of resituating the legend within its immediate political-theological context: the perennial charge of Judeophilia levelled against Spanish kings who employed Jewish tax farmers and delegated their expanding monarchical authorities to influential favourites, whose unique bond to the royal office was often critiqued in terms of supposed Jewishness. See Nirenberg, 'Deviant Politics', 15–18.
18 Bizzarri, *Castigos*, 205–206. 'Otrosí, para mientes, mío fijo, e toma ende, mío fijo, castigo de lo que contesçió al rey don Alfonso de Castilla, el que vençió la batalla de Húbeda. Por siete annos que viscó mala vida con vna judía de Toledo, diole Dios grand llaga e grand majamiento en la batalla de Alarcos en que fue vençido e fuyó e fue mal andante él e todos los de su regno. E los que y mejor andança ouieron fueron aquellos que y morieron. E por que el rey se conosçió después a Dios e demás matol los fijos varones e houo el regno, el rey don Fernando, su nieto, fijo de su fija e se repintió de tan mal pecado commo éste que auía fecho por el qual pecado por emienda fizo después el Monesterio de las Huelgas de Burgos ... E Dios diole después buena andança contra los moros en la batalla de Húbeda. E commo quier que y buen andança houo, muy mejor la ouiera si la desauentura de la batalla de Alarcos non le ouiera contesçido primero en la qual desauentura él cayó por el su pecado. Escripto es en las estorias antiguas que por los pecados que fazen los reyes da Dios majamiento en los pueblos, que por que ellos son cabeças de los otros. Y por dar Dios a los reyes mayor majamiento, fase escarmiento en aquellos que son so ellos ... en esta manera se fase el pesar doblado'.
19 Teofilo F. Ruiz, *Spain's Centuries of Crisis: 1300–1474* (Oxford: Blackwell, 2007), 53–61.
20 Bizzarri, *Castigos*, 189. 'Mío fijo, por amor de Dios te ruego que te castigues e te guardes de non fazer pesar a Dios en pecados de fornicios. E entre todo lo ál te guarda sennalada mente de non pecar con muger de orden nin con muger casada nin muger virgen nin judía nin con mora, que son mugeres de otra ley e de otra creençia'. In light of the space available here, I will treat only what the *Castigos* have to say about sex with Jewish and Muslim women. For an analysis of medieval Castilian exempla regarding the other archetypal categories of women mentioned by Sancho, see María Eugenia Lacarra, 'Representaciones de mujeres en la literatura española de la Edad Media (escrita en castellano)', in

Breve historia feminista de la literatura española (en lengua castellana), Volume II, ed. Iris M. Zavala (Barcelona: Anthropos, 1995), 21–68.

21 *Moro/a* ('Moor') is typically used to refer to Muslims in medieval Castilian sources, both polemical and otherwise. I will translate the term as 'Moor/ Moorish woman' to preserve the original meaning as best as possible.

22 Sancho's *Castigos* was hardly unique or original in underscoring chastity as a desirable, even exemplary, royal virtue. Roughly two decades earlier, Geoffrey of Beaulieu's *Life of St. Louis*, to name an influential example, spoke approvingly of its titular subject's abstention 'from carnal relations' with his own wife during prescribed times of the year. Louis was so abstemious that, 'if ... during these days of abstinence ... he should feel an inordinate movement of the flesh, he would rise from the bed and stride about the room until his rebellious body had calmed down'. The *Life*'s description of Louis' extreme chastity as well as its praise of his other self-abnegating habits, such as donning a hair shirt, would later be held up as models of saintly kingship in Boniface VIII's 1297 bull *Gloria Laus*, which canonised the French king. See L.F. Field, M.C. Gaposchkin, and S.L. Field, eds, *The Sanctity of Louis IX* (Ithaca, NY: Cornell University Press, 2013), 79, 169.

23 Bizzarri, *Castigos*, 201–204. 'Otrosí, mío fijo, commo te desuso ya dixe, guárdate non quieras pecar nin auer grand afazimiento con judía nin con mora, ca la judía es mujer de otra ley contraria de la tuya, e la mora es mujer de otra creençia de porfía a desfazimiento e a desonrra de la tuya. E quiero te yo agora decir cómmo cae el pecado en cada vna déllas'.

24 Bizzarri, *Castigos*, 201. 'E pues menbrarte deue commo los judíos dixeron a grandes bozes: "¡Cruçificadle! ¡Cruçificadle! e la su sangre sea derramada e esparcida sobre nós e sobre nuestros fijos."'

25 Bizzarri, *Castigos*, 202. 'E menbrarte deue de cómmo la generaçión de que la judía viene negaron a Ihesu Christo que non era su rey e lo niegan oy día ... E cómmo tomarás tú, mío fijo, sabor en la judía que es de ley e de generaçión de aquellos que fezieron desabor a Nuestro Sennor Ihuesu Christo e dandol a beuer venagre e fiel buelta de so vno, e quel metieron por las sus manos e por los sus pies clauos con que le plegaron en la cruz, e le pusieron la corona de espinas en la cabeça por escarrnio diciendo que Él era su rey, e que le dieron la lançada por el costado derecho, por la qual lançada fue abierto el su costado'.

26 Bizzarri, *Castigos*, 201–202. 'Pues que tú has nombre christiano, que quiere dezir fijo de christiano, non deues querer ayuntamiento con aquellos que esperesçieron la sangre de Ihesu Christo, tu Sennor'.

27 Bizzarri, *Castigos*, 202. 'Otrosí, de cómmo niegan que non es él ... que los sacó de tierra de Egipto del catiuerio en que yazían en poder del rey faraón. Otrosí, niegan que Ihesu Christo non es Mesías, el que ellos esperauan, mas que avn ha de venir, e por esta entençión corronpen todas las profeçías e las santas escripturas que dixeron los profetas e los patriarcas'.

28 Bizzarri, *Castigos*, 201–202. 'Otrosí, non deues en afazimiento llegar el tu rostro a la cara de la judía, que es de aquella generaçión de los que escupieron a Ihesu Christo, tu Sennor, en la faz, e que le dieron en ella muchas palmadas ... Por

ende, non ha razón de tomar omne sabor en el logar ó non ay sabor ninguno nin ay razón por que lo deua y auer. E quien se menbrase de todas estas cosas todos los sabores oluidaríe e fuyríe délla'.

29 Nirenberg, 'Deviant Politics', 27–33.
30 Samuel Parsons Scott, trans., *Las Siete Partidas, Volume 5: Underworlds: The dead, the criminal, and the marginalized (Partidas VI and VII)*, ed. Robert I. Burns (Philadelphia: University of Pennsylvania Press, 2001), 1433. For reasons of space, I quote from Parsons Scott's definitive English translation of the *Partidas*, which was probably drafted in stages from the 1250s into the 1270s as part of Alfonso X's bid to become Holy Roman Emperor. Whether the code enjoyed active legal force prior to its formal promulgation in 1348 is the subject of scholarly debate. See Ruiz, *Spain's Centuries of Crisis*, 117.
31 Parsons Scott, *Siete Partidas*, 1437.
32 Parsons Scott, *Siete Partidas*, 1436, 1441–42.
33 Grayzel, *Church and the Jews*, 150. 'Ex parte karrissimi in Christo filii nostril Fernandi illustris regis Castelle … fuit propositam coram nobis quod Judei existentes in regno Castelle, adeo graviter ferunt quod de signis ferendis ab ipsis statutum fuit in concilio generali ut nonnulli eorum potius eligant ad Mauros confugere quam signa hujusmodi bajulare … ex quibus ipsi regi, cujus proventus in Judeis ipsis pro magna parte consistunt'.
34 Sara Lipton, 'Isaac and the Antichrist in the Archives', *Past & Present* 232 (2016): 3–44. The polemical conflation that Lipton traces, of Jewishness, fiscality, and royal administration in thirteenth-century England, bears striking similarities to the contemporaneous criticisms brought against Castilian kings.
35 Parsons Scott, *Siete Partidas*, 1438.
36 John V. Tolan, *Sons of Ishmael: Muslims through European eyes in the Middle Ages* (Gainesville, FL: University of Florida Press, 2008), 1–18.
37 Purificación Martínez, '"Ca así commo yo soy tu padre": Género, masculinidad y poder en *Castigos del rey don Sancho IV*', *La Corónica: A Journal of Medieval Hispanic Languages, Literatures, and Cultures* 44.2 (2016): 124, 129.
38 Bizzarri, *Castigos*, 202–205. 'Otrosy, mío fijo, non quieras contar la mora por muger, mas cuéntala por bestia, ca non ha ley ninguna. Que Mahomad, el su maestro, que les dio aquella mala creençia en que ellos están por tal de meter más la gente en aquella mala creençia, todas aquellas cosas que la nuestra ley da por pecado e por mal vso es a ellos por saluaçión; e las que nos damos por saluaçión es a ellos por pecado. E los moros non han otra creençia sinon aquel que más puede soltar la su carrne a los sabores del mundo, aquel tienen por más saluo. E esto es contra el Viejo Testamento e contra el Nueuo que fizo Ihesu Christo'.
39 Tolan, *Sons of Ishmael*, 135, 146.
40 Bizzarri, *Castigos*, 205. 'El moro non es sinon perro e la mora non es sinon commo vna perra. E quien peca con mora por conplir su voluntad es tanto commo si pecase con perra o con bestia, pues que ley non ha nin creençia'.
41 Parsons Scott, *Siete Partidas*, 1436.
42 Martínez, 'Género, masculinidad y poder', 122.

43 Bizzarri, *Castigos*, 73. 'Todo omne es obligado de castigar, regir e aministrar sus fijos ... [para que puedan] dar enxenplo de bien beuir a los otros – e esto pertenesçe mayor mente a los reyes e príncipes que han de gouernar reynos e gentes'.

44 Bizzarri, *Castigos*, 142–143. 'E así commo estas piedras preçiosas han nombre esmeraldas, que quiere dezir cosa esmerada, assí el rey deue ser esmerado entre todos los otros en buena creençia e en buenas costumbres, ca a enxenplo del rey se torrnan todos los otros'.

45 Bizzarri, *Castigos*, 200, 276. 'Tal es la viginidat e la castidat en el rey ... commo el panno todo cubierto de oro en que non ha manzilla ninguna'.

46 Thomas F. Glick and Oriol Pi-Sunyer, 'Acculturation as an Explanatory Concept in Spanish History', *Comparative Studies in Society and History* 11.2 (1969): 136–154. Incorporating then-novel approaches from cultural anthropology, this influential study argued that the topic of medieval Iberian interfaith relations 'lends itself ideally to the study of acculturation', but that Hispanists had been 'partial to static interpretations of culture'. Glick and Pi-Sunyer closed the article by lamenting that 'studies which describe mechanisms of cultural change are infinitesimal, and Spanish medieval studies are in need of greater precision in sorting out the varieties of [interfaith] contact situations and processes of acculturation'. In the decades since, the discipline has risen to their challenge with alacrity.

47 Janina M. Safran, *Defining Boundaries in Al-Andalus: Muslims, Christians, and Jews in Islamic Iberia* (Ithaca, NY: Cornell University Press, 2013), 17–18.

48 Cary J. Nederman, 'The Mirror Crack'd: The *Speculum Principum* as political and social criticism in the late Middle Ages', *European Legacy* 3.3 (1998): 18–38.

Bibliography

Primary sources

Bizzarri, Hugo O., ed. *Castigos del rey don Sancho IV*. Frankfurt and Madrid: Vervuert and Iberoamericana, 2001.

Grayzel, Solomon. *The Church and the Jews in the XIIIth Century: A study of their relations during the years 1198–1254, based on the papal letters and the conciliar decrees of the period*. Philadelphia: Dropsie College for Hebrew and Cognate Learning, 1933.

Scott, Samuel Parsons, trans. *Las Siete Partidas, Volume 5: Underworlds: The dead, the criminal, and the marginalized (Partidas VI and VII)*, ed. Robert I. Burns. Philadelphia: University of Pennsylvania Press, 2001.

Secondary sources

Clarke, Nicola. *The Muslim Conquest of Iberia: Medieval Arabic narratives*. London: Routledge, 2012.

Collins, Roger J.H. *The Arab Conquest of Spain: 710–797*. Oxford: Blackwell, 1989.
Douglas, Mary. *Mary Douglas: Collected Works. Vol. II: Purity and Danger: An analysis of concepts of pollution and taboo*. 2nd edn. London: Routledge, 2003.
Drayson, Elizabeth. *The King and The Whore: King Roderick and La Cava*. New York: Palgrave Macmillan, 2007.
Field, Larry F., M. Cecilia Gaposchkin, and Sean L. Field, eds. *The Sanctity of Louis IX: Early Lives of Saint Louis by Geoffrey of Beaulieu and William of Chartres*. Ithaca, NY: Cornell University Press, 2013.
Glick, Thomas F. and Oriol Pi-Sunyer. 'Acculturation as an Explanatory Concept in Spanish History'. *Comparative Studies in Society and History* 11.2 (1969): 136–154.
Hazbun, Geraldine. *Narratives of the Islamic Conquest from Medieval Spain*. New York: Palgrave Macmillan, 2015.
Lacarra, María Eugenia. 'Representaciones de mujeres en la literatura española de la Edad Media (escrita en castellano)'. In *Breve historia feminista de la literatura española (en lengua castellana). Volume II*, ed. Iris M. Zavala, 21–68. Barcelona: Anthropos, 1995.
Linehan, Peter. 'The Spanish Church Revisited: The episcopal *gravamina* of 1279'. In *Authority and Power: Studies on medieval law and government presented to Walter Ullmann on his seventieth birthday*, ed. Brian Tierney and Peter Linehan, 127–147. Cambridge: Cambridge University Press, 1980.
Linehan, Peter. *History and the Historians of Medieval Spain*. Oxford: Clarendon Press, 1993.
Lipton, Sara. 'Isaac and the Antichrist in the Archives'. *Past & Present* 232 (2016): 3–44.
Martínez, Purificación. '"Ca así commo yo soy tu padre": Género, masculinidad y poder en *Castigos del rey don Sancho IV*'. *La Corónica: A Journal of Medieval Hispanic Languages, Literatures, and Cultures* 44.2 (2016): 111–137.
Moore, R.I. *The Formation of a Persecuting Society: Authority and deviance in western Europe, 950–1250*. 2nd edn. Oxford: Blackwell, 2007.
Nederman, Cary J. 'The Mirror Crack'd: The *speculum principum* as political and social criticism in the late Middle Ages'. *The European Legacy* 3.3 (1998): 18–38.
Nirenberg, David. 'Conversion, Sex, and Segregation: Jews and Christians in Medieval Spain'. *The American Historical Review* 107.4 (2002): 1065–1093.
Nirenberg, David. 'Deviant Politics and Jewish Love: Alfonso VIII and the Jewess of Toledo'. *Jewish History* 21 (2007): 15–41.
O'Callaghan, Joseph F. *The Learned King: The reign of Alfonso X of Castile*. Philadelphia: University of Pennsylvania Press, 1993.
Ruiz, Teofilo F. *Spain's Centuries of Crisis: 1300–1474*. Oxford: Blackwell, 2007.
Safran, Janina M. *Defining Boundaries in Al-Andalus: Muslims, Christians, and Jews in Islamic Iberia*. Ithaca, NY: Cornell University Press, 2013.
Tolan, John V. *Sons of Ishmael: Muslims through European eyes in the Middle Ages*. Gainesville: University of Florida Press, 2008.

10

Sine communi favore: the intersection of power, perception, and sexual morality in the careers of Piers Gaveston and the 'royal favourites' of fourteenth-century England

Audrey Covert

In this chapter, I focus on a combination of legal and chronicle sources to investigate the intersection of gender and sexual morality via an examination of the career of Piers Gaveston and his relationship with Edward II. The chapter contextualises Gaveston within a comparison of other contemporary 'royal favourites', in particular Alice Perrers, and her relationship with Edward III. The careers and reputations of these favourites are defined by their relationships with their respective royals, and their sexual involvement – or, perhaps more importantly, the perception and discussion of their sexual involvement – in these relationships had impact, both contemporarily and in historical scholarship. In the case of Piers Gaveston, contemporary accusations of sexual immorality were used as a tool to undermine his position and to frame understandings of the events of his life. This chapter utilises the term 'royal favourites' as it encapsulates most clearly the position of both Alice and Piers, as well as other similarly placed contemporaries, without reducing or minimising the complex intricacies of their social, political, and economic ties and positions. Beyond comparing these particular relationships, this chapter examines the terminology used to describe these 'royal favourites' and argues that there is a double standard of proof required to define these relationships, particularly when it comes to suggesting that a sexual element was involved.

Beyond the transgressive nature of the acts themselves, societal issues with same-sex sexual relationships stemmed from pervasive concerns over gender-norms, particularly masculinity. Much academic and popular attention has been paid to the debate surrounding the nature of the relationship between Edward II and Piers Gaveston, with convincing arguments both in support of and refuting a sexual element.[1] While this continues to be a compelling area of research and discussion, it seems that this is, and will continue to be, one of the many frustrating questions that will never be completely resolved. The contemporary accounts which highlight Edward's 'excessive love' for Gaveston, and Edward's singlemindedness to ensure Gaveston remained at his side, despite it always being a poor political decision, leave no doubt that the relationship was incredibly close and defining for both men.[2] This enduring love held by Edward was mirrored in the chronicles, which highlighted his desire for revenge, and his joy, for instance, at the later execution of the Earl of Lancaster, on whose land Gaveston had been executed, noting specifically that this execution of Lancaster was seen as retaliation for the death of Gaveston, even a decade later.[3]

While the contemporary chroniclers make no direct mention of a sexual relationship between the two men, the commentary certainly highlights the uniqueness, and impropriety, of their relationship. The *Vita Edwardi Secundi* compares the relationship between Edward and Gaveston to that of the biblical Jonathan and David and to the classical Achilles and Patroclus – each of which have been at times analysed within the frameworks of platonic brotherhoods, homosociality, homoeroticism and homosexuality – but goes on to say that while these relationships stayed within the bounds of what is 'usual', the relationship between Edward and Gaveston crossed these bounds, and goes so far as to name Gaveston a *'maleficus'* for bewitching Edward.[4] The *Vita* describes the relationship as: 'Certainly I do not remember having heard that one man so loved another. Jonathan cherished David, Achilles loved Patroclus; but we do not read that they went beyond what was usual'.[5]

The divergent trajectories of the careers of Piers Gaveston and Alice Perrers result from two important differences: gender and social position. Even accounting for their differences, the issues society had with each remain remarkably similar: each was able to leverage their relationship for huge amounts of wealth and influence, upsetting those who were passed over in their favour. Piers Gaveston was the son of a continental knight and Alice Perrers was likely the daughter of a goldsmith. Both Gaveston and Perrers remained attached only informally to their respective Edwards, with – or possibly without – sexual elements, but their 'official' socio-political positions were very different. The depictions of Alice Perrers in the contemporary *St Albans Chronicle* of Thomas Walsingham maintain an image of a greedy villain, particularly in the deathbed scene of Edward III, where she is described as removing the rings from the king's fingers as he lay dying.[6] When it came to being perceived as having transgressed gender boundaries and norms, the societal concern with Perrers was that she held too much power and influence; the traditional opinion regarding Gaveston was that his relationship with Edward II crossed the bounds of an appropriate male relationship. Systematic comparison of the lives and careers of these royal favourites creates a space for the nuanced exploration of the intersection of gender, power, and sexual morality by isolating, as much as is possible, and then examining the different factors which may have affected the trajectories of their careers.

Late medieval chroniclers were openly disturbed by the close nature of the relationship between Edward and Gaveston: the *Chronicon de Lanercost* describes their relationship as questionable 'on account of the undue intimacy which lord Edward the younger had adopted toward him [Gaveston]'.[7] The fascination with their relationship is mirrored in later depictions, such as Christopher Marlowe's *Edward II*, which places the relationship between Edward and Gaveston at the centre of the drama, rather than other sociopolitical explanations for the events of the period, reinforcing and reflecting the lasting negative reputations of these men.[8] These depictions are also mirrored in the modern scholarship, with recent re-examinations sparking debate between historians.[9] However, a closer examination of the chronicle sources suggests that the resounding hatred of Gaveston by his contemporaries was sparked by a combination of jealousy over his rise in wealth and power and, reportedly, disdain for his arrogance regarding his elevated status.

Neither the fourteenth-century contemporaries of Piers Gaveston nor historians since have been particularly kind to him, and he is often pointed to by the medieval chroniclers as a scapegoat for the political and social unrest of Edward II's reign. Without doubt, Gaveston's presence in England and at Edward's side caused lengthy debate and overt disdain from their contemporaries, but it is worth attempting to ascertain which pieces of Gaveston's biography, in particular, caused so much disdain.

Piers Gaveston was the son of a Gascon knight, Arnaud de Gabaston, who was in service to Edward I from the 1270s.[10] Edward twice used Arnaud as a hostage, the second time in France from 1294 until 1296, when he escaped to England. Piers likely first arrived in England in the late 1290s with his father and served Edward I as well, accompanying Edward's forces to Flanders in 1297. In 1300, he was transferred to the household of the future Edward II, forming the relationship which would define his life and career.[11]

For the first few years, Gaveston's position in the prince's household did not raise any concerns. By 1305, however, Gaveston's close proximity to the prince began to prove problematic when tensions arose between the prince and his father, leading Edward I to dismiss a portion of the prince's household, including Gaveston. By October, the rift between king and prince had been closed and Prince Edward had returned to court with his entire retinue. In May 1306, Prince Edward was knighted in preparation for leading the English forces in Scotland, fighting there having resumed after the murder of John Comyn by Robert Bruce in February. During the ceremonies, Prince Edward knighted several of his companions, including Gaveston. In reference to the events of 1311, but providing an appropriate depiction of the events of 1306–1307, the *Vita Edwardi Secundi* states that Edward II had two priorities: the first, to defeat Robert Bruce in Scotland, and the second, to keep Piers Gaveston at his side, against the wishes of the barons.[12]

Parliament rolls from 15 November 1306 list Gaveston among twenty-two men who were to have their land and wealth seized after leaving the king's service in Scotland to go abroad to compete in a tournament.[13] In January 1307, all the deserters were pardoned, with a single exception – Piers Gaveston. The following month, Edward I ordered Gaveston to be exiled to Gascony until recalled; both the prince and Gaveston were made to swear that they would not contravene these orders.[14] J.S. Hamilton suggests that the choice to single out Gaveston was made due to concerns over the close relationship between Gaveston and the prince, noting that these concerns likely stemmed from the excessive financial generosity the prince showed to Gaveston, rather than concern over a sexual relationship, but stating that 'at least in the case of Gaveston, there is no question that the king and his favourite were lovers'.[15] In other words, the issue was not so much Gaveston's actions in Scotland – as is made clear by the pardons of the other deserters – but rather the prince's actions at home. The prince's pleas for Gaveston's return during his first removal in 1305 had made clear how much he cared for Gaveston and his continued presence. Consequently, Gaveston's exile in 1307 might be viewed as a proxy punishment for Prince Edward. In his *Historia Anglicana*, Thomas Walsingham reports that on his deathbed Edward I cautioned his son not to recall Gaveston '*sine communi favore*', recognising *in extremis* the potential danger the anger of the barons held for his heir.[16]

After the death of Edward I, Edward II recalled Gaveston to England, gifting him the earldom of Cornwall and marrying Piers to his own niece, the daughter of Gilbert de Clare.[17] This was done without the approval or support of the English barons and marks the early beginnings of conflict between Edward and his nobility. The *Anonimalle Chronicle* discusses these events, stating that 'This king dishonoured the good people of his land and honoured its enemies, such as flatterers, false counsellors and wrongdoers, who gave him advice contrary to his royal estate and the common (profit) of the land, and he held them very dear'.[18]

This episode is commented upon widely in the contemporary accounts and highlights the common thread of this chapter: a royal favourite who is seen to have been given status – socio-political, economic, or both – beyond what was considered proper. Two elements of Piers' status are emphasised in the complaints – his foreign birth and his low status. As noted earlier, the *Anonimalle Chronicle* refers to Piers as the opposite of 'the good people of [Edward's] land' and as England's enemy.[19] Unlike Alice Perrers, whose anonymity allowed her to build a career without the baggage of family, Piers's continental origins only further aggravated his enemies at court but did not provide a safety net should he need to leave, as his father and brother had also travelled to England. Several chronicles refer to Gaveston as '*alienigena*', in reference to his Gascon origins.[20] Focusing on Gaveston's 'foreignness' is an interesting choice given that that there were certainly others in Edward's court who had similar backgrounds; and, as a Gascon, he was by birth a subject of the English crown.[21] This accusation of foreignness is important because it applies to Gaveston alone, without implicating Edward, and therefore might have been chosen deliberately as a point of focus by Gaveston's enemies to demonise his presence at court. In the introduction to their edition of the *Anonimalle Chronicle*, Childs and Taylor suggest that one of the reasons the later crisis over Edward's favouritism of Hugh Despenser, whom the *Vita Edwardi Secundi* describes as 'even less deserving than Piers', was different from the response to Gaveston was due to Despenser's Englishness and familial nobility.[22]

Edward's choice to gift Gaveston with the earldom of Cornwall was particularly galling to their contemporaries. Recognising the importance of Piers' status in Edward's court was one of the first significant actions taken by Edward upon succeeding to his father's crown. Its placement as the opening event in many of the contemporary chronicles recognises both this chronology and its importance.[23] In the introduction to her translation of the *Vita Edwardi Secundi*, Wendy Childs suggests that the author of the *Vita* began writing sometime between 1310 and 1313, and that the writing of the *Vita* was 'no doubt prompted by the drama of the exile or the murder of Gaveston', going on to note that the first section of the text, which covers the years 1307–1311, centres almost entirely upon Gaveston.[24] The earldom had previously been held by Edmund, 2nd Earl of Cornwall, grandson of King John. Earlier, this title had been revived in the 1070s for the half-brother of William the Conqueror, in the 1140s for the illegitimate son of Henry I, and in the 1220s for Edmund's father, Richard, second son of King John. For Edward II to add Sir Piers Gaveston to that list was offensive to the other English magnates. According to the *Vita*, Edward went as far as to insist that Gaveston be addressed exclusively by his new title, rather than his name, due to his 'unswerving love for him'.[25] In addition to gifting Gaveston with the earldom, Edward also married Gaveston to his niece Margaret de Clare, daughter of Edward's sister Joan and her husband, Gilbert de Clare, Earl of Gloucester. The *Vita* notes that the marriage was designed to protect Gaveston in his new position: that 'this marriage tie did indeed strengthen his position considerably; for it greatly increased the goodwill of his friends and restrained the hatred of the baronage'.[26] This effort clearly failed, creating more hostility towards Gaveston rather than protecting him from it.[27]

After 1307, Gaveston was twice more exiled, both times in an attempt by Edward to stem the tide of burgeoning hatred towards Gaveston over his increasing social and financial status and political control. When Edward travelled to France for his own wedding in late 1307, Gaveston was appointed regent during his absence, to the utter disgust of several chroniclers.[28] Edward's return to England with his bride, the princess Isabella of France, did not diminish his relationship with Gaveston at all. Trokelowe in the *Annales* reports that when Edward landed at Dover, a group of magnates were there to meet him and 'having run to Piers among them; giving him kisses and repeated embraces, he was adored with a singular familiarity. Which special familiarity, already known to the magnates, furnished fuel to their jealousy'.[29] The condemnation of the chroniclers was echoed in reports of Edward's coronation in February 1308, in which Gaveston immediately preceded Edward in the procession, bearing the cross of St Edward, the reaction to which is described in the *Annales Paulini* as 'for which the people and the clergy were not undeservedly indignant'.[30] This episode, in particular, serves to highlight not only Gaveston's socio-political rise, but also the physical proximity he maintained to Edward. Edward's actions during Gaveston's periods of exile display the intense desire of the king to always keep Gaveston physically close. The *Vita Edwardi Secundi* suggests that in Gaveston's presence Edward would not speak to or address any other person, further insulting and angering the other nobles in his court.[31] The *Annales Paulini* also report the indignation of Queen Isabella's uncles, who had travelled with her to England for the coronation, in 'seeing that the king spent more time at [Piers'] couch than the queen's'.[32] The *Historia Anglicana* similarly reports the distress of Isabella over Edward's actions and relationship, her reports to her father, Philip IV of France, and his complaints, in turn, to his contacts in England.[33]

In April 1308, the barons, led by the Earl of Lincoln, demanded Gaveston's exile and the confiscation of his estates. Edward held out, before consenting in May to prevent the outbreak of civil war. Edward appointed Gaveston his lieutenant in Ireland, transforming the disgrace of exile into a political honour. The *Vita Edwardi Secundi* suggests that it was Gaveston's arrogance, above all else, that was the root of the hatred of the barons, quoting a contemporary verse: 'His arrogance was, then, intolerable to the barons and the main cause of both the hatred and the rancour. For it is commonly said, "You may be rich and wise and handsome, / But insolence could be your ruin"'.[34] Before Gaveston had even left for Ireland, Edward was working to find support among the barons to recall him. By the end of June 1309,

Gaveston had returned to England and been reinstated as the Earl of Cornwall, with the support of a few key English magnates.[35]

In 1311, Edward was presented with a list of forty-one regulations known as the Ordinances which had been drafted by the Ordainers, a body of twenty-one magnates elected by their peers, whose goal was to eradicate abuses and reform the royal government.[36] Gaveston's presence was directly addressed in ordinance twenty, which opens by stating 'that Piers Gaveston has led the lord king astray, advised the lord king badly, and persuaded him deceitfully and in many ways to do wrong'.[37] It was a personal attack upon him and his position, and is also demonstrative of how he was seen as a symbol of the corruption of the system. The list of charges is long and includes the return from his first exile without 'common assent' and that those who did approve his return did so on condition of good behaviour, which he has not followed.

There is an interesting parallel in the conception of Gaveston's punishment to that which applied to Alice Perrers, favourite of Edward III, in the Good Parliament of 1376: While the 1376 ordinance calls out Perrers' abuses and orders her not to repeat them, the punishment of forfeiture and exile is not carried out unless and until she returns to her previous ways. Both are presented as warnings against future bad behaviour, rather than as immediate punishment for past behaviour.[38] That said, Gaveston clearly had not changed his ways, and his punishment was determined to be permanent exile from England and all English possessions. Edward fought against the implementation of the Ordinances from the outset. However, Gaveston was briefly exiled again in October, possibly to Flanders, but returned to England by early January 1312 at the latest. Gaveston's return, along with the other disagreements between the king and his barons, led to the outbreak of hostilities in England in early 1312. Gaveston was left at Scarborough to defend against a baronial siege in May. His forces were unable to hold out against the siege, and he agreed to terms on 19 May, and was taken prisoner and held by the Earl of Pembroke. While in Pembroke's custody, Gaveston was seized by the Earl of Warwick, who assembled a body of magnates to confer and condemn Gaveston, before executing him on 19 June 1312.[39]

The *Vita Edwardi Secundi* employs a classical reference to Achilles when discussing Edward's desire for revenge against those who had executed Gaveston, and invokes the stories of Samson and Solomon when recounting the death of Lancaster.[40] Interestingly, there is one exception to this depiction in the chronicles: Walsingham seems to suggest that the birth of Edward's son, shortly after Gaveston's death, caused Edward's love for Gaveston and anger over his death to fade, and henceforth he was more agreeable to his barons: 'from that day, by God's order, the love of his son grew, and the memory of [Piers] faded in his heart; the king yielded more easily to the will of his nobles than before'.⁴¹ No other chronicle makes this claim, instead suggesting that Edward's anger and desire for revenge was unabated until the execution of Lancaster in 1321. After Gaveston's death, the *Vita* returns to this comparison with David and Jonathan, stating 'love is depicted which is said to have surpassed the love of women'.⁴²

This chapter assumes that some form of deep emotional, and likely physical, relationship existed between the two men, and that the lack of direct accusations stems from the need to protect Edward as the king, one still without an heir at the time of Piers' death, or from fear of retaliation from those still loyal to the king.⁴³ Contemporary terms for the relationship between Piers Gaveston and Edward II vary, but all imply, to varying degrees, a significant closeness between them. The *Annales Londonienses* describe Piers as he 'who was his partner in his youth' and Walsingham's *Historia Anglicana* describes him as he 'whom the king embraced more specially and regarded more intimately'.⁴⁴ Depending upon which side of the debate surrounding the sexual nature of the relationship they fall, modern historians will alternately refer to Edward and Gaveston as 'lovers', 'companions', 'sworn brothers' or, often, 'favourite'. Sexualised or not, none of these terms undermine Gaveston's position in relation to Edward or in their relationship. On the contrary, most terms seemingly place them on an equal footing, despite their relative social positions.⁴⁵

Discussions of whether the relationship between Edward and Gaveston was sexual or not are an excellent example of the double standard of proof required to suggest a sexual element in same-gender relationships as compared to different-gender ones. While no definitive proof that Edward and Gaveston did have a sexual relationship has ever been found, there is also no definitive proof that they did not have one either. However, the default assumption for two men is generally to assume a platonic relationship, whereas a similar relationship between a man and woman would be assumed to be sexual. In this particular case, the relationship of Alice Perrers and Edward III produced acknowledged children, suggesting beyond (reasonable) doubt the existence of a sexual relationship. Relationships with female 'favourites' that do not produce any children are still assumed by default to have been sexual, while those with male 'favourites' are generally assumed not to have been. One clear example of this is the series of female partners of King David II of Scotland – Margaret Drummond, Agnes Dunbar, and Katherine Mortimer – none of whom had any children by him, but all of whom were treated as his sexual partners.⁴⁶

Alice Perrers and Katherine Swynford, the eventual third wife of John of Gaunt, are often referred to as 'mistresses'. In particular, Swynford's later position as John's wife is often listed second to her earlier, and longer, extra-marital relationship. The lack of a widely used gender-neutral or male-oriented term that mirrors the usage of 'mistress' in modern English scholarly work displays (or at least sustains) a disregard for recognition of relationships of this type. By utilising the broader, gender-neutral 'favourites', this chapter advocates for a more nuanced examination of the sexual and social relationships surrounding those in power, and of the power structures surrounding these relationships.

In the case of Alice Perrers, her career is an example of transgressing the traditional female gender norms of the period through her political and financial dealings. Laura Tompkins' work examines Alice using degendered language to analyse her socio-political position, placing Alice as 'one of the leading members of a small group of royal favourites... [who] in the first half of the 1370s contributed to a growing political crisis', and one who 'controlled the person, policy, and patronage of the rapidly ageing and ineffectual king in the final years of his reign', suggesting that her position in Edward's court was more than just the recipient of excessively generous favouritism.[47] While Alice might not be able to hold titles herself, she was certainly able to influence who else might receive them. In contrast, the case of Piers Gaveston is not necessarily an example of Gaveston transgressing gendered norms, but rather of Edward doing so, by choosing a man as a favourite and a partner. While the choice of a male favourite was not novel, it remained a dangerous choice politically due to the direct competition it put Gaveston in with other magnates. Gaveston's gender meant that he could be gifted titles and defined political power as compared to Alice's less defined power, accessed primarily through patronage and influence with the king. While Alice had the opportunity to benefit or harm her male contemporaries at court, Gaveston's rise in status and title was an insult and a tangible loss to his contemporaries. Edward II's status prevented direct accusations against him, leaving Gaveston as the most convenient scapegoat for concerns over their relationship and his rise in status, as well as Edward's rulership and masculinity.

There is little known conclusively about Alice Perrers' life before she entered into the service of Queen Phillipa of England, wife of Edward III, likely sometime in the early 1360s. Given her exponential rise to wealth and power in the late 1360s and 1370s, and her subsequent fall, trials, and court cases, it is not surprising that a significant amount of academic work has been dedicated to attempting to trace her origins and early years. Mark Ormrod and Laura Tompkins have each written a series of papers and chapters in recent decades which examine various pieces of her career and previous theories of her origins to create a convincing, if still uncertain, picture of her personal history.[48] Alice herself was silent on the particularities of her natal family, mentioning only her children with Edward III in her will.[49]

Historians have had difficulty in identifying both Alice's natal family and the identity of her first husband, though diligent work by Ormrod and Tompkins has filled many of these gaps. Ormrod notes that:

> Alice had brought no family baggage with her to her position as a royal mistress, and, in the period between the death of [her first husband] Janyn Perrers and the publication of her [second] marriage to William Windsor, she played very consciously the role of *femme sole*, undertaking extensive property and financial dealings in her own name and right.[50]

Alice never formally acknowledged any family other than her children with Edward – her intent was to be the king's favourite and only the king's favourite. For a time, her intent clearly worked as Alice was able to amass significant amounts of land and wealth and wield tangible social power through her influence and patronage. Like Piers Gaveston in 1311, the ferocity of the attacks against Alice during the Good Parliament stemmed from the anxieties of a patriarchal system needing to reassert control over an individual who had stepped too far outside their prescribed social position. While her lack of 'family baggage' may have been one of the reasons Alice was so successful at amassing the wealth and property she did, it is also likely the reason she struggled so much to hold onto it. Her societal position was quite precarious – as shown by the ease with which the parliament was able to strip her of her accumulated land and wealth – having no powerful family backing to support her in maintaining or regaining it. The sheer scope of the vitriol found both in contemporary accounts of Alice and in written history into the modern era is astounding for a woman with such a modest background, especially when compared with her contemporaries, such as Katherine Swynford.[51] While Alice was seen as the seducer of the pious Edward III, John of Gaunt was well known for his extra-marital relationships and his illegitimate children – one chronicler described him as a *magnus fornicator* – and so Katherine can more easily be depicted as the seduced, rather than as a seductress.[52]

In fourteenth-century England, Piers Gaveston likely seemed a more obvious threat to the status of others in high positions of power than Alice Perrers would have been, though Perrers was also able to realise power at a significant level. The parallels of the careers of and commentary on Gaveston and Perrers, in particular, are striking given how different one might expect the situations of a man and woman in these circumstances to be. Using a degendered lens to examine Gaveston and Perrers' careers, the downfall of each comes from the excessive financial and socio-political power they derived from the relationships with their respective Edwards.[53] Each was given a large amount of land and wealth, and each was able to develop significant social power through influence and patronage and, in the case of Gaveston, political position. With two particularly important exceptions – namely, the regency in 1308 and the Irish lieutenancy in 1308–1309 – Gaveston never sought nor held significant political office, and his primary assertion of power was through influence and patronage, but the opportunity to wield so-called 'hard power' would have undoubtedly been available to him had he chosen to pursue it.[54]

The significant difference between these two cases comes in the nature of their downfall – Alice was dispossessed of the majority of her wealth and land whereas Gaveston was captured and executed through unsanctioned military action. Each had potential power through their relationships and wealth, but Alice was only able to realise this power while she maintained these elements – she had influence over the king, and through both his and her own patronage networks, but did not hold official political power. This 'soft power' enabled Alice to effectively gather and manage the resources she needed to support and sustain herself, and her lack of official position may have even allowed her access to resources and networks that official structures could not access.[55] However, this method of power was also much harder to define and maintain; once Edward III died, her power was no longer protected and she was unable to sustain it.[56]

By way of contrast, Gaveston's execution highlights the inability of magnates to restrain the power he had attained, and likely their concern that he would continue to grow it and utilise it further – particularly after having been named regent. In the introduction to his study of Piers Gaveston, Hamilton notes that 'patronage is at the center not only of baronial animosity to Gaveston, it is at the center of – indeed, one might say it is the dynamic, driving force behind, the entire reign of Edward II'.[57] Arguably, the same might be said for the reign of Edward III, or at least for the final years of his reign. The difference in attitude towards Alice and Gaveston could stem from one of several sources. Most obviously, the death of Edward III left Alice unprotected in a way Piers was not in 1312. Edward II had shown he would not be prevented from keeping Gaveston close by him, and from showering him with land and titles. Gaveston's death may have been seen as the only way to eliminate his power and influence. Had Edward III survived or Edward II predeceased Gaveston, the narrative around these favourites might have been very different.

A striking parallel found in the career stories of each of these 'royal favourites' is that their stories are defined by their relationships with their 'royal'. Just as Alice was the 'seductress' of the pious Edward III, and Katherine was the one 'seduced' by John of Gaunt, Piers Gaveston's career appears to be defined by Edward II's actions, not by his own. The enduring reputation of Alice Perrers found in the chronicles is predominantly sourced from Thomas of Walsingham, the St Albans chronicler whose *Chronica maiora* is a key text for the study of fourteenth- and early fifteenth-century English history. Such charges have been repeated by subsequent historians and commentators in the centuries since the appearance of Walsingham's *Chronica*.

The chronicles certainly suggest that Gaveston's personality – in particular, his arrogance – did not endear him to his contemporaries, but the true hatred over Gaveston stemmed from the titles, wealth, and power provided to him via his relationship with Edward. The enduring characterisations of Gaveston may stem not from contemporary depictions of him, but rather from his association with Edward, and from later depictions of Edward, particularly in the years between Gaveston's death and his own. The *Vita Edwardi Secundi*, in an entry from 1313, laments the lost possibilities of Edward's reign up to that point, placing the blame on Gaveston's shoulders: 'All hope vanished when he became king of England. Piers Gaveston led the king astray, threw the country into confusion, consumed its treasure, was exiled three times, and then, returning, lost his head'; the 'Gesta Edwardi de Carnavan' similarly accuses Gaveston's presence of causing 'the hearts of great men [to be] torn to pieces by their lord king'.[58]

Childs suggests that, of all the figures of this period, the most significant reassessment of character by modern scholars has been for Piers Gaveston: increasingly, his military actions and successes have been noted, while the specifics of his relationship with Edward have been continually reinterpreted and the relevance of these specifics questioned.[59] Comparison of the career and relationship of Gaveston to his contemporary 'favourites' suggests that existence of a sexual relationship between him and Edward II was not the primary concern; the implication of such a relationship – contextualised within medieval understandings of gender and sexual morality – was a socio-political tool that could be used by Gaveston's enemies to attempt to undermine his power and by contemporary chroniclers to frame the events of the period. Contemporary concerns about Gaveston himself stemmed primarily from his origins and his extreme rise to wealth and influence during the early years of Edward's reign, and the perceived threat he posed to the power of the other magnates of England.

Notes

1 For more on the two arguments to this debate, see J.S. Hamilton, *Piers Gaveston: Earl of Cornwall, 1307–1312* (Detroit: Wayne State University Press, 1988), 15–17, 109–112; Pierre Chaplais, *Piers Gaveston: Edward II's Adoptive Brother* (Oxford:

Clarendon Press, 1994), 109–114; Michael Prestwich, *The Three Edwards: War and State in England, 1272–1377* (London: Weidenfeld & Nicolson, 1980), 80; *The Anonimalle Chronicle 1307–1334: From Brotherton Collection MS 29*, trans. Wendy R. Childs and John Taylor (Leeds: Yorkshire Historical Society, 1991), 30; Tison Pugh, '"For to be sworne bretheren til deye": Satirizing queer brotherhood in the Chaucerian corpus', *Chaucer Review* 43.3 (2009): 289–290.

2 'Annales Paulini, 1307–1340', in *Chronicles of the Reigns of Edward I and Edward II*, ed. Stubbs, 2 vols (London: Longman, 1882–1883), 1:259. 'Rex vocavit Petrum, prae amore nimio, fratrem suum'. *Anonimalle Chronicle*, ed. Childs and Taylor, 80–82. 'Cesti roi aima cherement de coer ascuns gentz qi son piere sovent foith li defendi la compaignbnie de eux, come une sire Peres de Gavastoun qi fust par le bone roi son pere exile, et par les bons pers de la terre'.

3 *Anonimalle Chronicle*, ed. Childs and Taylor, 108. 'et par my cel decapitacion sire Pieres de Gavastoun avant nome qi le roi milt [*sic*] ama'.

4 *Vita Edwardi Secundi: The Life of Edward the Second*, trans. Wendy R. Childs (Oxford: Clarendon Press, 2005), 28. 'Modem autem dileccionis rex noster habere non potuit, et propter eum sui oblitus esse dicerertur, et ob hoc Petrus malificus putaretur esse'. For more on its use of biblical and classical references, see *Vita*, ed. Childs, xxiv–xxxi; Pugh, 'Satirizing', 282–310; M.S. Morales and G.L. Mariscal, 'The Relationship between Achilles and Patroclus according to Chariton of Aphrodisias', *Classical Quarterly* 53.1 (2009): 292–295; Andreas Krass, 'Over his dead body: Male friendship in Homer's *Iliad* and Wolfgang Peterson's *Troy* (2004)', in *Ancient Worlds in Film and Television*, ed. A.-B. Renger and J. Solomon (Leiden: Brill, 2013), 151–173.

5 *Vita*, ed. Childs, 28–29. 'Sane non mimini me audisse unum alterum ita dilexisse'.

6 Walsingham, *The St Albans Chronicle: The Chronica maiora of Thomas Walsingham*, ed. J. Taylor, W.R. Childs, and L. Watkiss, 2 vols (Oxford: Clarendon Press, 2003), 1:118–121. 'Huiuscemodi occasionibus et illa surripuit regi quiquid eradere de minibus eius posset'.

7 *Chronicon de Lanercost*, ed. Joseph Stevenson (Edinburgh: Impressum Edinburgi, 1839), 210: 'propter hoc quamdam familiaritatem indebitam quam dominus Edwardus junior concepterat erga eum'. My translation.

8 David Stymeist, 'Status, Sodomy and the Theater in Marlowe's *Edward II*', *SEL* 44.2 (2004): 236–238; Goran Stanivukovic and Adrian Goodwin, 'Gaveston in Ireland: Christopher Marlowe's *Edward II* and the casting of queer brotherhood', *Textual Practice* 31.2 (2017): 379–380; Alan Bray, 'Homosexuality and the Signs of Male Friendship in Elizabethan England', in *Queering the Renaissance*, ed. Jonathan Goldberg (Durham, NC: Duke University Press, 1994), 48–53; for later examples, see: Peter Horne, 'The Besotted King and his Adonis: Representations of Edward II and Gaveston in Late Nineteenth-Century England', *History Workshop Journal* 47 (1997): 30–48; Michael G. Cornelius, 'Reconfiguring a Man's "Place": Space, Sexuality and Piers Gaveston in Henry Sewell Stokes' *Restormel*', *Pennsylvania Literary Journal*, 2.2 (2010): 91–116; Sid Ray, 'Hunks,

History, Homophobia: Masculinity politics in *Braveheart* and *Edward II*', *Film & History: An Interdisciplinary Journal of Film and Television Studies*, 29.3–4 (1999): 22–31.
9 Hamilton, *Piers Gaveston*, 16–17, 109; Chaplais, *Piers Gaveston*, 6–22.
10 Thomas Walsingham, *Thomae Walsingham: Quondam Monachi S. Albani, Historia Anglicana*, ed. H.T. Riley, 2 vols (London: Longman, Green, Longman, Roberts and Green, 1863–1864), 1:120; *Vita*, ed. Childs, 26.
11 Hamilton, *Piers Gaveston*, 22–24, 29–30.
12 *Vita*, ed. Childs, 26. 'Verum occupatus rex circa duo, unum circa expungnacionem Roberti de Brutz, in quo remissus agebat, pro eo quod maior pars baronum Anglie ad istud negocium non ferebat auxilium ... erat circa retencionem Peteri de Gauestone, ad cuius expulsionem et exilium omnes fere barones Anglie unanimiter laborabant'. ('It is true that the king was occupied with two things: one the defeat of Robert the Bruce, in which he acted negligently, on account of the fact that the greater part of the barons did not provide aid to this cause ... [the second] about retaining Piers Gaveston, for whose expulsion and exile almost all the barons of England were endeavoring unanimously'.) My translation.
13 *The Parliament Rolls of Medieval England. Edward I*, ed. C. Given-Wilson, P. Brand, S. Phillips, M. Ormrod, G. Martin, A. Curry and R. Horrox (Woodbridge: Boydell, 2005), roll 16, column b.
14 *Polychronicon Ranulphi Higden Monachi Cestrensis*, ed. J.R. Lumby, 9 vols (London: Longman & Co.; Trübner & Co., 1865–1886), 8:295.
15 Hamilton, *Piers Gaveston*, 16–17.
16 Walsingham, *Thomae ... Historia Anglicana*, 1:115: 'without common favour'. My translation.
17 'Annales Londonienses', in *Chronicles*, ed. W.Stubbs, 2 vols (London: Longman, 1882–1883), 1:151; 'Annales Paulini', 1:257–258; *Polychronicon*, ed. Lumby, 8:297; 'Gesta Edwardi de Carnavan', in *Chronicles*, ed. Stubbs, vol. II, part II (London: Longman & Co.; Trübner & Co., 1882–1883), 2:28; 'Vita et Mors Edwardi Secundi Regis Angliae', ed. William Stubbs, vol. II, part IV (London: Longman & Co.; Trubner & Co., 1883), 2:297; *Vita*, ed. Childs, 4.
18 *Anonimalle Chronicle*, ed. Childs and Taylor, 82. 'Cesti roi dehonura les bones gentz de sa terre et honura les enemis, come flatours, mauconseilers eet meffesours, qi li conseillerent encounter sa coroune et encontre commun (profit) de la terre et les tint assetz chier'.
19 *Anonimalle Chronicle*, ed. Childs and Taylor, 82.
20 Walsingham, *Thomae ... Historia Anglicana*, 1:120. 'Iste Petrus filius fuerat cujusdam generosi, sed alienigenae de Wasconia. *Vita*, ed. Childs, 4. 'quia Petrus alienigena erat a Vaesconia oriundus'. 'Gesta Edwardi de Carnavan', ed. Stubbs, 2:32.
21 Hamilton, *Piers Gaveston*, 110.
22 *Anonimalle Chronicle*, ed. Childs and Taylor, 31; *Vita*, ed. Childs, 52.
23 'Annales Londonienses', ed. Stubbs, 151; 'Gesta Edwardi de Carnavan', ed. Stubbs, 28; *Vita*, ed. Childs, 4–5; 'Vita et Mors', ed. Stubbs, 297.
24 *Vita*, ed. Childs, xxii–iii, xxxix.

25 *Vita*, ed. Childs, 8. 'Rex autem continuum amorem erga eum habebat, in tantum ut exiret a curia regis preceptum publicum ne quis eum nominee proprio uocaret, uidelicet dominum Petrum de Gauestone, set comitem Cornubie nominaret'.
26 *Vita*, ed. Childs, 6. 'Sane hec copulacio matrimonialis partem eius non modicum uallebat; fauorem namque amicoreum sibi uehementer augebat et odium baronem refrenabat'.
27 *Vita*, ed. Childs, 4, 26. 'Maior tamen pars baronum terre non consensit ... proprter inuidiam'.
28 *Vita*, ed. Childs, 8. 'Regnum autem in manu Petri in custodia deputatur, Mira res, qui nuper ab Anglia exul erat et eiectus, eiusdem terre ian factus est gubernator et custus'.
29 Trokelowe, *Annales*, trans. H.R. Thomas (London: Longman, Green, Reader and Dyer, 1866), 65; Hamilton, *Piers Gaveston*, 47 (Hamilton's translation): 'Inter quos Petrum occurrentem, datis osculis et ingeminatis amplexibus, familiaritate venerabatur ingulari. Quae familiaritas specialis, a magnatibus praeconcepta, invidiae fomitem ministravit'.
30 *Annales Paulini*, 1:261. 'Ex quo non immerito indignati sunt populus atque clerus'. My translation.
31 *Vita*, ed. Childs, 28; Chaplais, *Piers Gaveston*, 69; Hamilton, *Piers Gaveston*, 75: Reportedly, Gaveston further angered the other earls by choosing insulting nicknames for them, including calling the Earl of Warwick 'the Black Dog', naming the Earl of Lincoln 'burst-belly' and the Earl of Pembroke 'Joseph the Jew'.
32 *Annales Paulini*, 1:262; see also '*Vita et Mors*', ed. Stubbs, 2:297: 'cernentes quod rex plus exerceret Petri triclinium quam reginae'. My translation.
33 Walsingham, *Thomas ... Historia Anglicana*, 125: 'Regi Franciae, patri suo, lacrymabiliter, quereretur se honore debito destitutam. Ob quam causam, Rex Franciae cunctos Anglicos, sibi notos, pro talium abusionum tolertantia durius increpavit' / 'She tearfully complained to the King of France, her father, that she had been deprived of her due honor. For this reason, the King of France rebuked all the English known to him more severely for tolerating such abuses'. My translation.
34 *Vita*, ed. Childs, 28–29: 'Erat igitur baronibus fastus eius intollerabilis et prima causa odii simul et rancoris. Nam uulgariter dicitur, "Si tibi copia, si sapienicia, formaque detur, /Sola superbia destruit omnia si comitetur".' See also *Vita*, ed. Childs, 6–8.
35 Hamilton, *Piers Gaveston*, 72–74.
36 'Annales Londonienses', 15315–15316; Hamilton, *Piers Gaveston*, 79.
37 *Vita*, ed. Childs, 34–35: 'quod Petrus de Gauestone dominum regem male duxit, domino regi male consuluit, et ipsum ad male faciendum deceptorie et multiformiter induxit'. See also Michael Prestwich, ed., 'A New Version of the Ordinances of 1311', *Historical Research* 57 (2007), n. xxix.
38 *Parliament Rolls, Edward II*, 1376 April, 2.329–345; Thomas Walsingham, *Gesta Abbatum Monasterii Sancti Albani*, trans. H.T. Riley, 3 vols (London: Longman, Green & Co., 1869), 3:230–232.

39 *Vita*, ed. Childs, 42–51; '*Vita et Mors*', ed. Stubbs, 298.
40 *Vita*, ed. Childs, 178, 214.
41 Walsingham, *Thomae … Historia Anglicana*, 1:135, 1.164: 'Ab illo die, Deo disponente, crevit amor filii, et evanuit in ejus corde Petri memoria; … et Rex voluntati suorum procerum facilius solito condescendit'. My translation. At the later death of Lancaster in 1321, Walsingham attributes Edward's decision to single out Lancaster to his poor actions in the rebellion that preceded his capture, rather than to his anger at the execution of Gaveston as other chroniclers do.
42 *Vita*, ed. Childs, 52–53: 'quem dicitur super amorem mulierum dilexisse'.
43 Prestwich notes that even those veiled accusations seen in the chronicles were not published until after Edward II's death in 1327: Prestwich, *The Three Edwards*, 80.
44 '*Annales Londonienses*', 1:151; Walsingham, *Thomae … Historia Anglicana*, 1:121: 'qui fuit consors ejus in adolescentia sua'. My translation. *Chronicon de Lanercost*, ed. Stevenson, 210: 'quem … Rex in amplexus specialius admittebat, et familiarius respiciebat'. My translation. Hamilton, who asserts unequivocally that the relationship between Edward and Gaveston was sexual, notes that the objections to this relationship in the chronicles 'make reference to Edward's inappropriate behavior in loving Piers *too much*, not in loving him', and suggests this might reflect a tacit acceptance of a sexual relationship between them: Hamilton, *Gaveston*, 110. This may be failing to take into account the platonic usage of the word 'love', and that 'loving too much' could reflect crossing the line from platonic to sexual love.
45 Hamilton, *Gaveston*, 15–17, 109–112; Chaplais, *Gaveston*, 109–114.
46 Bruce Webster, 'David II', *Oxford Dictionary of National Biography*, last modified 6 January 2011, available at https://doi.org/10.1093/ref:odnb/3726 (accessed 25 November 2023): scholars generally assume David to have been infertile, as despite two marriages and several known mistresses (several of whom had children from other relationships), he had no known issue, legitimate or not; Mark Ormrod, 'Who Was Alice Perrers?' *Chaucer Review* 40.3 (2006): 225, 229n.27; Walter Bower, *Scotichronicon*, ed. Watt, 9 vols (Aberdeen: Aberdeen University Press, 1987), 7:321; 'Quam pre ceteris mulieribus [Katerine Mortimer] rex pretulit in amore; propter quam nimium reg[-ina] fuit neclecta et complexa concubine'. ('How much the king preferred this other woman [Katherine Mortimer] in love; on account of which the queen was neglected and surrounded with concubines'.) My translation.
47 Laura Tompkins, 'Edward III's Gold-Digging Mistress: Alice Perrers', in *Women and Economic Power in Premodern Royal Courts*, ed. C. Sarti (York: Arc Humanities Press, 2020), 60; Laura Tompkins, 'Alice Perrers and the Goldsmiths' Mistery: New evidence', *English Historical Review* 130.547 (2015): 1361.
48 See: Ormrod, 'Who Was Alice Perrers?', 219–229; Mark Ormrod, 'Alice Perrers and John Salisbury', *English Historical Review*, 123.501 (2008): 379–393; Mark Ormrod, 'The Trials of Alice Perrers', *Speculum* 83.2 (2008): 366–396; Tompkins, 'Alice Perrers', 1361–1391; Tompkins, 'Edward III's Gold-Digging Mistress', 59–71.

49 Tompkins, 'Alice Perrers', 1361–1362.

50 Ormrod, 'The Trials', 369.

51 Alice's most prolific medieval critic and commentator in general was by far Thomas Walsingham: see Walsingham, *Chronica Maiora*, trans. Preest, 25–26, 28, 32–33, 47; Walsingham, *Gesta Abbatum*, 227, 229, 230, 231, 233–238, 249, 255–256, 379; Walsingham, *St Albans Chronicle*, 1: 42–46, 50, 56–58, 62, 100, 112, 118–120, 168–170, 974–976, 986, 990. For modern scholarship examples, see Vincent, *Lives of Twelve Bad Women* (London: T.F. Unwin, 1897); Bickley, *King's Favourites* (London: Methuen, 1910); Tout, *The History of England from the Ascension of Henry III to the Death of Edward III (1216–1377)* (London: Longmans, Green, 1905); MacFarlane, *The Nobility of Later Medieval England* (Oxford: Clarendon, 1973).

52 C.Given-Wilson and A.Curteis, *The Royal Bastards of Medieval England* (London: Routledge, 1984), 147.

53 In her chapter subtitled 'Beyond Binaries of Gender', Theresa Earenfight examines how power could manifest differently in different periods of a life and attempts to de-gender power and associated concepts to better understand the relational nature of power and how it could be exercised, in particular by women: Theresa Earenfight, 'A Lifetime of Power: Beyond Binaries of Gender', in *Medieval Elite Women and the Exercise of Power, 1100–1400*, ed. H.J. Tanner (Basingstoke: Palgrave Macmillan, 2019), 271–293.

54 Hamilton, *Piers Gaveston*, 111: Hamilton notes that this is in contrast to Edward's later favourite, Hugh Despenser the younger, and that the actions and personalities of the two are at times conflated in the chronicles; Prestwich, *The Three Edwards*, 85.

55 The 2018 collection edited by Susan Broomhall, *Women and Power at the French Court, 1483–1563* (Amsterdam: Amsterdam University Press, 2018) examines the particulars of the different avenues of power available to women in early modern France – the observations and conclusions within are useful to this earlier period as well. From this collection, see in particular Susan Broomhall, 'In the Orbit of the King: Women, power, and authority at the French court, 1483–1563', 9–40; Aubrée David-Chapy, 'The Political, Symbolic, and Courtly Power of Anne de France and Louise de Savoie: From the genesis to the glory of female regency', 43–64; Jonathan A. Reid, 'Imagination and Influence: The creative powers of Marguerite de Navarre at work at court and in the world', 263–286; and David Potter, 'The Life and After-Life of a Royal Mistress: Anne de Pisseleu, Duchess of Étampes', 309–334.

56 Broomhall, 'In the Orbit of the King', 24, 31.

57 Hamilton, *Piers Gaveston*, 15.

58 *Vita*, ed. Childs, 68–69. 'Tota spes euanuit dum factus est rex Anglie. Petrus de Gauestone regem duxit in deuium, terram turbauit, consumptsit thesaurum, tribus uicibus exilium subiit, et postea rediens caput perdidit'. '*Gesta Edwardi de Carnavan*', ed. Stubbs, 2:33: 'a domino suo rege corda magnatum distrahebant'. My translation of '*Gesta*'.

59 *Vita*, ed. Childs, xxxv.

Bibliography

Primary sources

'Annales Londonienses'. In *Chronicles of the Reigns of Edward I and Edward II*, ed. William Stubbs. 2 vols. London: Longman & Co.; Trübner & Co., 1882–1883.

'Annales Paulini, 1307–1340'. In *Chronicles of the Reigns of Edward I and Edward II*, ed. William Stubbs. 2 vols. London: Longman & Co.; Trübner & Co., 1882–1883.

The Anonimalle Chronicle 1307–1334: From Brotherton Collection MS 29, ed. Wendy R. Childs and John Taylor. Leeds: Yorkshire Historical Society, 1991.

Bower, Walter, *Scotichronicon*. 9 vols, ed. D.E.R. Watt. Aberdeen: Aberdeen University Press, 1987.

Chronicles of the Reigns of Edward I and Edward II, ed. William Stubbs. 2 vols. London: Longman & Co.; Trübner & Co., 1882–1883.

Chronicon de Lanercost, ed. Joseph Stevenson. Edinburgh: Impressum Edinburgi, 1839.

The Parliament Rolls of Medieval England, ed. Chris Given-Wilson, Paul Brand, Seymour Phillips, Mark Ormrod, Geoffrey Martin, Anne Curry, and Rosemary Horrox. Woodbridge: Boydell, 2005, available at www.sd-editions.com./PROME/home.html (accessed 25 November 2023).

Polychronicon Ranulphi Higden Monachi Cestrensis, ed. Joseph Rawson Lumby. 9 vols. London: Longman & Co.; Trübner & Co., 1865–1886.

Trokelowe, Johannis de. *Annales*, ed. Henry Riley Thomas. London: Longman, Green, Reader and Dyer, 1866.

Vita Edwardi Secundi: The Life of Edward the Second. Trans. Wendy R. Childs. Oxford: Clarendon Press, 2005.

'Vita et Mors Edwardi Secundi Regis Angliae'. In *Chronicles of the Reigns of Edward I and Edward II*, ed. William Stubbs. 2 vols. London: Longman & Co.; Trübner & Co., 1882–1883, vol. II, part IV.

Walsingham, Thomas, *The Chronica Maiora of Thomas Walsingham, 1376–1422*. Trans. David Preest. Woodbridge: Boydell Press, 2005.

Walsingham, Thomas. *Gesta Abbatum Monasterii Sancti Albani*, ed. Henry Thomas Riley. London: Longman, Green and Co., 1869.

Walsingham, Thomas. *The St Albans Chronicle: The Chronica maiora of Thomas Walsingham*, ed. John Taylor, Wendy R. Childs, and Leslie Watkiss. 2 vols. Oxford: Clarendon Press, 2003.

Walsingham, Thomas. *Thomae Walsingham: Quondam Monachi S. Albani, Historia Anglicana*, ed. Henry Thomas Riley. 2 vols. London: Longman, Green, Longman, Roberts and Green, 1863–1864.

Secondary sources

Bickley, Francis, *King's Favourites*. London: Methuen, 1910.

Bray, Alan, 'Homosexuality and the Signs of Male Friendship in Elizabethan England'. In *Queering the Renaissance*, ed. Jonathan Goldberg, 40–61. Durham, NC: Duke University Press, 1994.

Broomhall, Susan, ed. *Women and Power at the French Court, 1483–1563*. Amsterdam: University of Amsterdam Press, 2018.

Chaplais, Pierre. *Piers Gaveston: Edward II's Adoptive Brother*. Oxford: Clarendon Press, 1994.

Cornelius, Michael G. 'Reconfiguring a Man's "Place": Space, Sexuality and Piers Gaveston in Henry Sewell Stokes' *Restormel*'. *Pennsylvania Literary Journal* 2.2 (2010): 91–116.

Earenfight, Theresa. 'A Lifetime of Power: Beyond Binaries of Gender'. In *Medieval Elite Women and the Exercise of Power, 1100–1400: Moving Beyond the Exceptionalism Debate*, ed. Heather J. Tanner, 271–293. Basingstoke: Palgrave Macmillan, 2019.

Given-Wilson, Chris, and Alice Curteis. *The Royal Bastards of Medieval England*. London: Routledge, 1984.

Hamilton, J.S. *Piers Gaveston: Earl of Cornwall, 1307–1312*. Detroit: Wayne State University Press, 1988.

Horne, Peter. 'The Besotted King and his Adonis: Representations of Edward II and Gaveston in Late Nineteenth-Century England'. *History Workshop Journal* 47 (1997): 30–48.

Krass, Andreas. 'Over his dead body: Male friendship in Homer's *Iliad* and Wolfgang Peterson's *Troy* (2004)'. In *Ancient Worlds in Film and Television*, ed. Almut-Barbara Renger and Jon Solomon, 151–173. Leiden: Brill, 2013.

MacFarlane, K.B. *The Nobility of Later Medieval England: The Ford Lectures for 1953 and Related Studies*. Oxford: Clarendon, 1973.

Morales, Manuel Sanz and Gabriel Luna Mariscal. 'The Relationship between Achilles and Patroclus according to Chariton of Aphrodisias'. *The Classical Quarterly* 53.1 (2009): 292–295.

Ormrod, Mark. 'Who Was Alice Perrers?' *The Chaucer Review* 40.3 (2006): 219–229.

Ormrod, Mark. 'Alice Perrers and John Salisbury'. *The English Historical Review* 123.501 (2008): 379–393.

Ormrod, Mark. 'The Trials of Alice Perrers'. *Speculum* 83.2 (2008): 366–396.

Prestwich, Michael, ed. 'A New Version of the Ordinances of 1311'. *Historical Research* 57 (2007): 189–203.

Prestwich, Michael. *The Three Edwards: War and State in England, 1272–1377*. London: Weidenfeld & Nicolson, 1980.

Pugh, Tison. '"For to be sworne brethren til deye": Satirizing Queer Brotherhood in the Chaucerian corpus'. *The Chaucer Review* 43.3 (2009): 282–310.

Ray, Sid. 'Hunks, History, Homophobia: Masculinity politics in *Braveheart* and *Edward II*'. *Film & History: An Interdisciplinary Journal of Film and Television Studies* 29.3–4 (1999): 22–31.

Stanivukovic, Goran, and Adrian Goodwin. 'Gaveston in Ireland: Christopher Marlowe's *Edward II* and the casting of queer brotherhood'. *Textual Practice* 31.2 (2017): 379–397.

Stymeist, David. 'Status, Sodomy and the Theater in Marlowe's *Edward II*. *Studies in English Literature, 1500–1900* 44.2 (2004): 233–253.

Tompkins, Laura. 'Alice Perrers and the Goldsmiths' Mistery: New Evidence Concerning the Identity of the Mistress of Edward III'. *The English Historical Review* 130.547 (2015): 1361–1391.

Tompkins, Laura. 'Edward III's Gold-Digging Mistress: Alice Perrers, gender, and financial power at the English royal court, 1360–1377'. In *Women and Economic Power in Premodern Royal Courts*, ed. Cathleen Sarti, 59–71. York: Arc Humanities Press, 2020.

Tout, T.F. *The History of England from the Ascension of Henry III to the Death of Edward III (1216–1377)*. London: Longmans, Green, 1905.

Vincent, Arthur, *Lives of Twelve Bad Women: Illustrations and reviews of feminine turpitude set forth by impartial hands*. London: T.F. Unwin, 1897.

Webster, Bruce. 'David II'. *Oxford Dictionary of National Biography*, last modified 6 January 2011, available at https://doi.org/10.1093/ref:odnb/3726 (accessed 25 November 2023).

Index

Abbasid dynasty 173–177, 179, 180, 185, 188n.45
Abu Nuwas, Arabic poet 179, 188n.45
adultery 12, 51, 55, 66n.44, 71–75, 77–79, 89, 91–98, 160, 190, 195, 196, 199–201, 203–204, 208–209
Ælfgifu, queen-consort of King Eadwig 12, 50–59, 63
Æthelgifu, mother-in-law of King Eadwig 51–53, 56–57, 59
Æthelweard, historian; nobleman 53
al-Amin, Abbasid caliph 174, 176, 178–180, 185
al-ghazal, amatory poem or ode 179, 186n.6
al-Hakam, Abbasid caliph 6, 174, 181–185
al-Ma'mun, Abbasid caliph 177, 179–180
Alexandria 38
Alfonso I, king of Portugal 75–76
Alfonso X, king of Castile 215–216, 219, 221, 223, 226n.7, 227n.15, 229n.30
Annales Londonienses 239
Annales Paulini 91, 237
Anonimalle Chronicle (1307–1334) 235–236
Arthurian Romance 97, 141n.67

B, hagiographer 49–50, 55–58, 62
binaries 3, 7, 8, 106, 166n.4

Blanche of Burgundy 196, 197, 205, 208, 209, 210n.8
Boswell, John E. 1–2, 181
Braveheart, film (1995) 96, 244–5n.8, 250
Bridlington Chronicle 92
Brut Chronicle, also known as the *Prose Brut* 92, 94
Byrhtferth of Ramsey, hagiographer; historian 55, 57, 58
Byzantium 11, 30, 33, 35, 37

calenge/chalengen 55
Capet, house of, Capetian dynasty 13, 194–196, 200–202, 207–209, 210n.9
Caracalla, Roman emperor 30–31, 34, 38
Castigos (admonitions) 214–231
categorisation 6, 7, 8, 34
Charles IV, king of France 89, 195, 197, 203, 205–206, 208–209
Charles VII, king of France 96
chastity/chaste ideals 9, 11, 106, 110, 115, 134n.11, 181, 215, 223, 224, 228n.22
criticism 5, 12, 14, 90, 93, 120, 133–134n.7, 134n.9, 137n.31, 178, 184, 215, 229n.34
Chronicon de Lanercost 234
Clinton, Hillary 95
consanguinity 5, 51, 54–55, 59, 62–63, 161, 198–199, 203, 226n.9

consortium coniugali 3
Constantinople 31, 33, 34, 37–38
cross-dressing 154
Cueva, Beltrán de la 96, 105, 116, 138n.36
Cynesige, bishop of Lichfield 49, 52, 53, 58, 62, 63

desire 6, 8, 123, 154–159, 161, 162, 165, 186n.4, 220, 233, 238, 239
Despenser, Hugh the younger 89, 92, 236, 248n.54

Eadmer of Canterbury, hagiographer 50–54, 56–58, 60–61, 63
Eadwig, king of England 49–70
Edward I, king of England 234–235
Edward II, king of England 89–104
Edward III, king of England 89, 91, 94–96, 195, 197, 205–207, 233, 238–241
Edward of Westminster, son of Henry VI of England and Margaret of Anjou 96
Eleanor of Aquitaine 5, 72, 74, 77, 78, 94, 96, 98, 203
Elisabeth de Vermandois, consort of Philip, count of Alsace 75–78
Enrique IV, king of Castile 105, 118, 138n.36, 195
eunuchs 37, 176–180, 183
Eve 3, 4, 35, 120, 123, 125, 130, 217
execution 196, 233, 239, 242, 247n.41

female agency 71, 79
female inheritance 153, 154, 160, 196, 203, 207
female sexuality 7, 35, 123, 133n.5, 195, 197, 208
Flanders 75–79, 234, 238
Foucault, Michel 1–2, 33
Fourth Lateran Council 214, 219
Froissart, Jean 92

Gabaston, Arnaud de, father of Piers Gaveston 234
Gaimar, Geffrei, historian 51
Garden of Eden 4, 106, 120, 125, 130, 140n.56

Gaveston, Piers
  nature of his relationship with Edward II 234–243
gender 3–8, 13, 14, 15, 33, 34, 43n.42, 43n.43, 93, 106, 115, 118, 128, 132n.6, 223, 233, 239, 240, 241, 243, 248n.53
Geoffrey, count of Anjou 5, 74, 96
Gervase of Canterbury 94
Gesta Edwardi de Carnavan 245n.17, 20, 23, 248n.59
Gesta regum 57, 60, 61
Good Parliament, the (1376) 238, 241
ghulam 174–176, 183, 184
ghulamiya 187n.20
ghulamiyya 187n.20, 189n.75
ghulamiyyāt 175, 183
Golden Legend, the 110
gossip 5, 18n.17, 71, 75, 76, 78, 79, 178, 209

Harun al-Rachid, Abbasid caliph, father of al-Amin 178–179
Heldris of Cornwall 153–157, 159, 161–163, 165
Henry II, king of England 72–74, 76–79
Henry the Young King, titular king of England, duke of Normandy, count of Anjou and Maine 78
Henry VI, king of England 96–97, 195
Henry of Huntingdon, historian 50
heteronormativity 154
heterosexuality 33
Historia Anglicana of Thomas Walsingham 235, 237, 239
Historia Augusta 30, 35–36
homosexuality 2, 5, 33, 34, 173, 174, 177, 178, 180–185, 233
homosociality 4, 233
Hundred Years War 96, 207

Ibn Hazm, Andalusian Muslim polymath 175, 182
identity 1, 6, 12, 13, 15, 30, 53, 56, 106, 120, 133n.5, 133–4n.5, 156, 163–164, 197, 220, 22, 241
Immaculate Conception 116, 118, 125, 138n.41, 141n.60

Isabel I, queen-regnant of Castile 5, 105–149
Isabella of France, queen-consort of England 11, 12, 89–104, 194, 197, 201, 237
Isabeau of Bavaria, queen-consort of France 5, 9, 19n.31, 96
illegitimacy 134, 196, 205

James of Avesnes 75
Jeanne of Burgundy 195, 197, 198, 199, 208
Jeanne II of Navarre 195, 197, 200, 205, 206, 208, 209, 210n.8
Jewess of Toledo (Rahel la Fermosa), supposed lover of Alfonso VIII, king of Castile 208, 218, 220–224
John of Gaunt, duke of Lancaster 239, 241, 242
John of Worcester, historian 50, 54
jongleurs 156, 157, 164
Jezebel 50, 63n.3, 90, 97
Joanna of Portugal, queen-consort of Castile 96
Juana, *infanta* of Castile, *la Beltraneja*, daughter of Enrique IV of Castile 195
Juana of Portugal 195
Julia Domna, Roman empress 30–36, 38, 41
Justinian, Roman emperor 31, 32, 34, 38

Katherine Swynford, duchess-consort of Lancaster, third wife of John of Gaunt 195, 239, 241

Lanercost Chronicler 92, 94, 95
Late Antiquity 12, 29, 32, 34, 39, 40
le Baker, Geoffrey, English chronicler 90, 92, 93, 97
le Bel, Jean, Liégeois chronicler 92, 94, 96
legitimacy 10, 11, 13, 14, 59, 96, 105, 106, 200, 202–205, 207, 208, 209
Lincoln, bishop of 91
Louis VII, king of France 6, 9, 71, 94, 203

Louis X, king of France 94, 197, 199, 200, 202–205, 208

Machiavelli, Niccolò 3
male love and male lovers 13, 120, 173, 180–182
Margaret of Anjou, queen-consort of England 96, 98
Marlowe, Christopher 234
Marguerite/Margaret of Burgundy 96, 195, 197, 199, 200, 200–202, 208–209
Margaret de Clare 236
marriage 8–10, 13, 44n.50, 58, 60, 63, 74, 76, 77, 94, 96, 110, 115, 125, 128, 134n.11, 136n.11, 136n.21, 137n.24, 137n.27, 157, 158, 194, 196–201, 203–205, 208, 236, 241
Melusine 12, 125, 127–130, 142n.75, 143
Mirror of Conscience, the 123, 125
Mortimer, Roger, earl of March 11, 12, 89, 90–95, 97–98, 195, 201, 206
Mujūn, Arab erotic poetry, celebration of male love 184
Murimuth, Adam 91, 92

Nottingham Castle 91

Osbern of Canterbury, hagiographer 50, 53, 54, 57, 60, 61
Ordinances (of 1311) 238
Orleton, Adam, bishop of Hereford 97, 98
Oxford 95

Perrers, Alice 233, 234, 238–242
Philip IV, king of France 13, 194–202, 205, 207, 209, 210n.8, 237
Philip V, king of France 194, 195, 197, 202–206, 208, 209
Philip of Alsace, count of Flanders 75–79 83n.37
Portugal 12, 73, 74, 75, 76, 81n.15, 83n.28, 106
Procopius of Caesarea, historiographer 31, 32, 34–38, 41n.12

queenship 90, 115, 132n.4
queer, queerness 1, 6–7, 13, 174, 185

Ralph Diceto, archdeacon of Middlesex, dean of St Paul's Cathedral 75, 76
Raymond, prince of Antioch 5, 94
reputation 5, 8, 11, 12, 33, 61, 72, 79, 90, 91, 128, 159, 200
revenge 157, 164, 233, 238, 239
Richard II, king of England 9, 97
Richard of Devizes 94
Rochester, bishop of 94
Rodrigo (Visigoth king) 94, 133n.5, 216–219, 226n.11
Roger of Howden, English chronicler 75, 76
Roman Empire 29, 30, 38, 39
royal favourites 10, 14, 226, 232, 240, 242
royal succession 96
rumour 11, 14, 18n.17, 58, 60, 72–76, 78, 92, 94, 95, 98, 195, 199, 203–206

Salic Law 197, 210n.9
Sancho IV, king of Castile 14, 215
scandal 2, 5, 7, 9, 11, 12, 50–59, 62, 63, 72, 74, 75, 76, 78, 79, 106, 107, 133n.5, 178, 199, 201, 204, 208, 210n.8
sexual activity 3, 5, 14, 72, 185
sexual morality 30, 43n.7, 55, 232, 233, 243
sexualities 1–8, 10–15, 33–35, 174, 185, 194, 197, 200, 203
Siete Partidas 219
slander 12, 29, 33, 105–106, 116, 132n.4, 133n.5
St Albans Abbey 90
St Albans Chronicle 219, 233, 242
St Catharine of Alexandria 110, 113–115

St Dunstan, archbishop of Canterbury 50, 51, 54, 58, 60, 61
St Frideswide's Abbey, Oxford 95, 97
St Oda, archbishop of Canterbury 49, 52, 53, 54, 56–59, 62, 63
Scalacronica 91, 92, 94
sovereignty 3, 5, 10, 11, 13, 14, 15, 106, 195, 196, 197, 198, 206
Strickland sisters 89

Theodora I, Roman/Byzantine empress 31, 35
Theresa, princess of Portugal 76–77
Thomas Walsingham 233, 235
Tour de Nesle Affair 96, 97, 194–209, 210n.8–9
transvestism 160
Trokelowe Annales 237
Trokelowe, John 90

Umayyad, first Muslim dynasty 6, 133n.5, 173, 175, 182, 184, 185

Vermandois 76, 79
Victor, [Sextus] Aurelius, historiographer 30, 33, 34–38
Virgin Mary 5, 9, 106, 115, 118, 120, 123, 125, 128
Vita Edwardi Secundi 91, 233, 235, 236, 237, 238, 243

Wallace, William 96
Walter de Fontaines 75, 83n.33
Walter Map 12, 72–79, 83n.33, 96
Wars of the Roses 10, 96
William of Malmesbury, hagiographer; historian 50, 60

Zenobia, Queen of Palmyra and Roman usurper 29, 35–36, 45n.58
Zubaida, first wife of Harun al-Rashid, mother of al-Amin 177, 178

EU authorised representative for GPSR:
Easy Access System Europe, Mustamäe tee 50,
10621 Tallinn, Estonia
gpsr.requests@easproject.com

www.ingramcontent.com/pod-product-compliance
Lightning Source LLC
Chambersburg PA
CBHW052058300426
44117CB00013B/2183